SLAVERY AND THE JEWS OF MEDIEVAL EGYPT

Slavery and the Jews of Medieval Egypt

A HISTORY

CRAIG PERRY

PRINCETON UNIVERSITY PRESS
PRINCETON & OXFORD

Published by Princeton University Press
41 William Street, Princeton, New Jersey 08540
99 Banbury Road, Oxford OX2 6JX

press.princeton.edu

GPSR Authorized Representative: Easy Access System Europe - Mustamäe tee 50, 10621 Tallinn, Estonia, gpsr.requests@easproject.com

ISBN 9780691263571
ISBN (e-book) 9780691274270

Library of Congress Control Number: 2025936728

British Library Cataloging-in-Publication Data is available

Editorial: Fred Appel and Tara Dugan
Production Editorial: Sara Lerner
Jacket Design: Katie Osborne
Production: Erin Suydam
Publicity: William Pagdatoon
Copyeditor: Leah Caldwell
Jacket Credit: © Veneranda Biblioteca Ambrosiana /
Icas94 / Mondadori Portfolio / Bridgeman Images

This book has been composed in Minion 3

Printed in the United States of America

10 9 8 7 6 5 4 3 2 1

FSC
www.fsc.org
MIX
Paper | Supporting responsible forestry
FSC® C008955

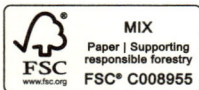

For Elana

CONTENTS

LIST OF FIGURES

NOTES ON THE TEXT

THIS BOOK is based largely on documents from the Cairo *geniza*. Photographs of most documents are available through the Friedberg Genizah Project (FGP, https://fjms.genizah.org) under their shelf marks. Documents are cited in the notes according to abbreviated shelf marks, but full shelf marks are provided in the index of *geniza* texts cited. Arabic and Judeo-Arabic (a variety of Middle Arabic in Hebrew script) are transliterated according to the guidelines provided by the *International Journal of Middle Eastern Studies*, except that the initial *hamza* is not indicated and the definite article *al-* is not elided. Hebrew and Aramaic are transliterated according to the convention of the *Association of Jewish Studies Review*, except that *tet* is rendered as ṭ, *tsadi* as ṣ, *qof* (*kuf*) as *q*, and the final *he* without a mappiq is not indicated except for words commonly spelled in English as such (e.g., *Torah*, *Mishneh Torah*). I do not force correct scribal misspellings or grammar in my transliterations unless indicated, and then only when the misspelling or other error changes the intended meaning of the text. Judeo-Arabic spelling does not always conform to the rules of classical Arabic, though it is generally transliterated as such.[1]

Jewish men mentioned in *geniza* documents had Hebrew and Arabic names. For Hebrew names that have common English forms, I have used them (Nathan for Natan, Solomon for Shelomo, etc.). I retain the Arabic equivalents (Sulaymān for Solomon, Mūsā for Moses, etc.) to make clear when the original text uses the Arabic instead of the Hebrew. Women usually only had Arabic names. People, men especially, are also called by honorifics, nicknames, and other identifiers indicating a place of their residence or origins (al-Baghdādī, from Baghdad; *al-tājir*, "the trader"). In Hebrew and Arabic names, people are identified by their personal names followed by their fathers, and sometimes grandfathers. These genealogies are indicated by "b" (*bar*, *ben*, *ibn*, or *bin*) for "son of" and "bt." (*bat*, *ibnat*, or *bint*) for "daughter of." I use the English names and spellings without diacritics for most locations (Fustat and not Fūsṭāṭ, Cairo and not al-Qāhira, Jerusalem and not Yerushalayim or al-Quds).

Enslaved people generally only bear personal names (*isms*) like Success (Tawfīq), Blessed (Mubāraka), and so on. I use the Arabic names and indicate its English translation the first time it is mentioned in the text, unless its meaning is ambiguous. The original and translated names of enslaved and freed people are provided in appendixes 1 and 2.

Readers should familiarize themselves with this book's short glossary, which provides a list of the most common Arabic, Hebrew, and Aramaic terms for "slave" that are found in *geniza* texts. I often leave the most common of these terms untranslated for the benefit of specialists who are interested in the semantics of medieval slavery. As is common in slavery studies, I often prefer "enslaved person/man/woman/child" instead of "slave" in my writing for a few reasons. Enslaved people were not permanent "slaves." Many were freeborn people who lost their freedom through violence. Others eventually gained their freedom. Moreover, enslaved people were also mothers, fathers, sons, daughters, skilled laborers, intimate familiars, and so on. Thus, the use of "enslaved people" is meant to emphasize that slave status was only one, often temporary, facet of their identities.[2] When I translate the writing of a slave owner, I use the term "slave" because slave owners did not share this critique. They meant to write "slave."

Translations are my own unless otherwise indicated. Some of my translation choices depart from the English translations preferred by others. For example, I render *bar Yisra'el* and *bat Yisra'el* (son and daughter of Israel) as "Jew."

In translations, I use the following conventions:

- [Square brackets] indicate that there is a lacuna in the manuscript or that the writing is illegible. Words inside square brackets thus indicate a suggested reconstruction of the text. Ellipses with no brackets indicate my omission of words within the quoted text.
- I use (parentheses) in translations when I add my own clarifying words, or when I am spelling out an abbreviation. For example, *geniza* writers would commonly write the abbreviation R'E (*nun-ayin* in Hebrew script) for (whose) r(est) is in E(den) after the name of a deceased person (similar to how RIP is used).

I give years according to the Common Era (CE)—though *geniza* documents most commonly use the Seleucid calendar—and sometimes the anno mundi or Islamic *hijrī* calendars.[3] The coins mentioned are usually gold dinars or silver dirhams. Exchange rates varied depending on the quality of the coinage and the era, but 1 dinar usually equaled around 40 dirhams. The pioneering *geniza* scholar S. D. Goitein suggests that 2 dinars was enough to sustain a middle-class family for a month.[4]

ACKNOWLEDGMENTS

IN RESEARCHING and writing this book, I have received generous support from several institutions. Between 2014 and 2017, I was a principal co-collaborator on the Documents and Institutions in the Medieval Middle East project (DIMME) that was funded by a Collaborative Research Grant from the National Endowment for the Humanities and directed by Professor Marina Rustow. Rustow and the NEH grant supported me as a postdoctoral researcher in the history department at Johns Hopkins University and then in the Department of Near Eastern Studies at Princeton University. The NEH support was crucial in supporting my early career in the years between completing my PhD and beginning my first faculty position. In spring 2016 I was a Dorset Visiting Fellow at the Oxford University Centre for Hebrew and Judaic Studies, where I was part of the research seminar "Israel in Egypt, Egypt in Israel" directed by professors Miriam Frenkel, Sarah Pearce, and Alison Salvesen. Between 2016 and 19, I was a faculty member in the Department of Judaic Studies at the University of Cincinnati. I am grateful for the support from my department, the College of Arts and Sciences, the University Research Council, and the Taft Research Center. In 2019 I joined the faculty in the College of Arts and Sciences at Emory University. I give thanks to the college, the Department of Middle Eastern and South Asian Studies, the Tam Institute for Jewish Studies, the Judith Evans London Director's Fund, the Scholarly Works and Publishing Fund in the Center for Faculty Development and Excellence, the Fox Center for Humanistic Inquiry's Major Works Review Grant, and the Islamic Civilizations Studies Graduate Program in the Laney Graduate School for their support of my research and this book's publication. In spring 2025, I completed the final editing for the book while at the American Academy in Rome, where I was the Andrew W. Mellon Family Foundation Rome Prize winner in Medieval Studies.

This book has benefited greatly from my collaboration with the NEH-funded DIMME research group, with whom I read and workshopped scholarly editions and translations of several *geniza* documents that I use as evidence in the book.

I thank Tamer El-Leithy, Eve Krakowski, Marina Rustow, and Naïm Vanthieghem. Throughout my research for this project, I have also taken delight and benefited from reading sources in Arabic and Judeo-Arabic with Amir Ashur, Pratima Gopalakrishnan, Roxani Margariti, Rachel Richman, Devin Stewart, Moshe Yagur, and Oded Zinger. Ofra Yeglin has also generously consulted with me about some of my translations of Hebrew texts. Hossein Samei consulted with my interpretation of some Persian materials. Of course, any and all errors in this book are mine alone.

The relatively small subfield of documentary *geniza* studies continues to support collegial collaboration. My research has benefited from discoveries generously shared with me by Ashur, Alan Elbaum, Brendan Goldman, Krakowski, Margariti, Rustow, Yusuf Umrethwala, Yagur, Zinger, and the other scholars acknowledged here and in the book's notes. Moreover, the teams behind the Friedberg Genizah Project and the Princeton Geniza Project, two field-changing digital resources, have been an indispensable part of my research since the very beginning. It was my coursework with David Eltis in graduate school that convinced me to become a scholar of slavery. I remain forever grateful for his invitation to join the editorial team for *The Cambridge World History of Slavery: Volume 2, AD 500–AD 1420*. The experience of working with the other co-editors and volume contributors was a privilege and one that has shaped how I wrote this book.

Additionally, I have benefited from much feedback on chapter drafts as given by colleagues and students over the last decade. I workshopped an early version of chapter 6 with the History Department Research Seminar at the University of Cincinnati and the Works in Progress group at the Annual Meeting of the Association for Jewish Studies, run at that time by Rena Lauer and Jessica Marglin. At Emory, Devin Stewart has organized writing groups with whom I workshopped earlier versions of chapters 2, 3, 5, 6, and 7. Thanks to my colleagues who have provided valuable feedback in this venue, including Petra Creamer, Courtney Freer, Geoffrey Levin, Harshita Kamath, Scott Kugle, Roxani Margariti, as well as Cheryl Crowley and the participants in the Asian and Middle Eastern Studies Seminar. It was a particular pleasure to workshop the introduction with the students in my fall 2022 seminar "Readings in Judeo-Arabic," as well as to read together some of the original sources upon which this book is based. Thanks to Leah Bader, Wittika Chaplet, Anwesha Das, Lex Davis, Mert Ozbay, and Sasha Rivers. Thanks are also due to Michelle Armstrong-Partida, who read earlier drafts of my introduction as well as chapters 4 and 5; to Rachel Schine for her feedback on chapter, 5, and the conclusion; to Pratima

Gopalakrishnan for reading versions of chapters 4, 5, and 6; to Moshe Yagur for reading chapters 7 and 8; to Yagur and Zinger for reviewing appendixes 1 and 2; and to my colleagues at the American Academy in Rome for workshopping my conclusion (especially to Caroline Goodson and Carol Harrison, who read it twice). I give special thanks to Matthew Gordon, Krakowski, Eltis, and the two anonymous reviewers for Princeton University Press who read and commented on the entire manuscript before I completed my final revisions. There is not space here to acknowledge the people and institutions who have hosted me via Zoom or in-person to present aspects of this research and to engage in lively and generative discussions about it. I am grateful for all of those opportunities.

As this book moved toward and into press, several people helped me pull it all together. Thanks to Sasha Rivers for compiling the initial bibliography and to Aaron Tyutyunik for revising it after revisions. Ulrike Guthrie provided developmental editing for the whole manuscript. Ælfwine Mischler compiled the general index. I'm grateful to Fred Appel at Princeton University Press for publishing this book and to Emma Wagh, Sara Lerner, Leah Caldwell, and Tara Dugan for assisting in this process.

Last but not least, I want to thank my family for their support and patience, both as I have worked on this book and throughout my various personal and professional journeys.

ABBREVIATIONS

AIU	Alliance Israélite Universelle (Paris)
ALAD	Khan, *Arabic Legal and Administrative Documents*
AR	Arabic
AS	Additional Series
BL	British Library
BODL	Bodleian Library
BT	Babylonian Talmud
CUL	Cambridge University Library
DK	David Kaufmann Collection
EI2	*Encyclopaedia of Islam*, Second Edition
EI3	*Encylopaedia of Islam*, Third Edition
EJIW	*Encyclopedia of Jews in the Islamic World*
ENA	Elkan Nathan Adler Collection
F	Freer Collection
FGP	The Friedberg Genizah Project
HEB	Hebrew
HEID	Heidelberg University
IOM	St. Petersburg: Russian Academy of Sciences, Institute of Oriental Manuscripts
JRL	John Rylands Library
L-G	Lewis-Gibson Collection
M	*Mishnah*
MISC	Miscellaneous
MOSSERI	Jacques Mosseri Collection
MS	Goitein, *A Mediterranean Society*
MT	Moses Maimonides, *Mishneh Torah*
NLI	National Library of Israel
NS	New Series
OR	Oriental

PER	Papyrus Sammlung Erzherzog Rainer
PGP	The Princeton Geniza Project
RNL	National Library of Russia
T-S	Taylor-Schechter Genizah Collection
YT	Jerusalem Talmud

GLOSSARY

ʿAbd—Arabic for male "slave" but rarely used in practice with this literal meaning. *ʿAbd* is a common component of men's Arabic names in which the term has a pious connotation. For example, ʿAbd al-Raḥmān is "servant of the Merciful (God)."

Amta—*Geniza* writers use this Aramaic term for "slave girl" when legal conventions demanded it, as in deeds of manumission, and also analogously to *jāriya*, *waṣīfa*, and *shifḥa* (see below).

ʿAtīq, fem. *ʿatīqa*—A gendered Arabic term for a freed person.

ʿEved—The Hebrew term for male "slave" and cognate with the Arabic *ʿabd*. *ʿEved* is uncommon in documentary *geniza* texts as a reference to an enslaved man. The term is more commonly used in Jewish legal sources, as in Moses Maimonides's the *Mishneh Torah*.

Ghulām (pl. *ghilmān*)—In *geniza* sources, the Arabic term *ghulām* usually indicates an enslaved man who served as a factotum for merchants, communal leaders, and other officials. The term can also indicate an enslaved (or freed) soldier.

Jāriya (pl. *jawārī*, sometimes *jawāri* in Judeo-Arabic *geniza* texts)—The most common Arabic term used for "slave girl" in the *geniza* documents and in the medieval Arabic sources that are contemporaneous with them. When juxtaposed with the term *waṣīfa* (see below), *jāriya* may emphasize a more common type of enslaved maid in comparison to an enslaved personal attendant (*waṣīfa*).

Jins (pl. *ajnās*)—An Arabic term (cognate with the Latin *gens*) that I translate as "type" but that may also connote what is commonly called ethnicity, race, stock, species, etc.

Maʿtūq, fem. *maʿtūqa*—Another gendered Arabic term for a freed person.

Mawlā—This Arabic term is used both to denote the patron (former slave owner) and the client (freedman) linked in a patronage relationship. In Islamic law, the patronage relationship (*walāʾ*) was a formal one. Jews and their former slaves sometimes used this language, though it was not a recognized legal institution in Jewish law.

Meshuḥrar, fem. *meshuḥreret*—The gendered Hebrew term for a freed person.

Shifḥa (pl. *shifḥot*)—The most common Hebrew term used by *geniza* writers to denote a "slave girl." Used interchangeably with *jāriya* and *waṣīfa* (see above).

Umm walad, umm al-walad—Arabic for "mother of (the) child." *Umm walad* is a legal category in Islamic law. When an enslaved woman gave birth to her Muslim owner's child, that child was born a free Muslim. In most schools of Islamic law, the *umm walad* gained her freedom upon the death of that owner, and she could not be sold by him after the birth of their child (or its conception in some traditions).

Waṣīf, fem. *waṣīfa*—The second-most common Arabic term used for "slave girl" in the *geniza* documents. When juxtaposed with *jāriya, waṣīfa* may indicate a "higher class" of enslaved woman whose primary role was closer to personal attendant than a maid who performed drudge work.

SLAVERY AND THE JEWS OF MEDIEVAL EGYPT

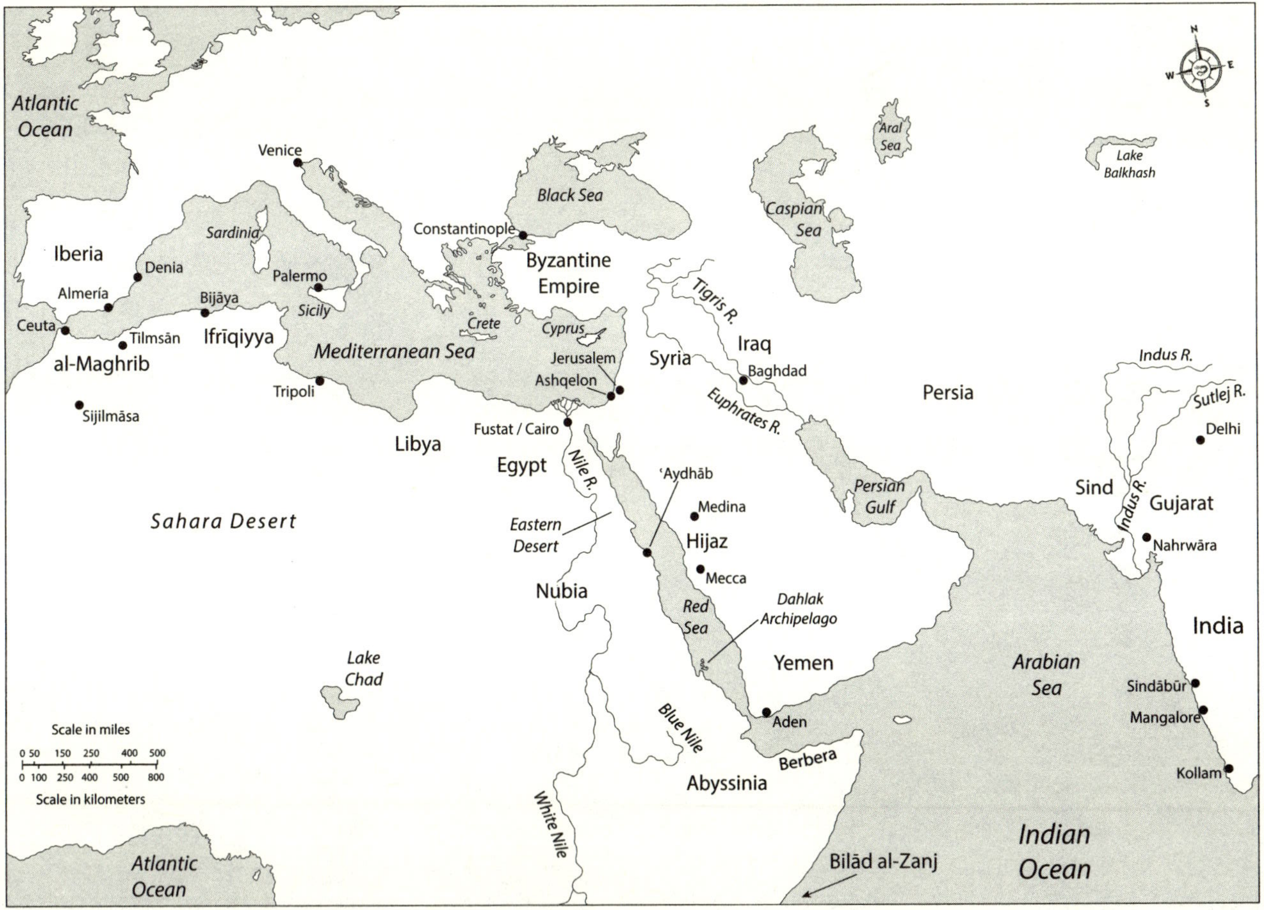

MAP 1. From Iberia to India, ca. 1000–1250. Map created by John Wyatt Greenlee of Surprised Eel Mapping.

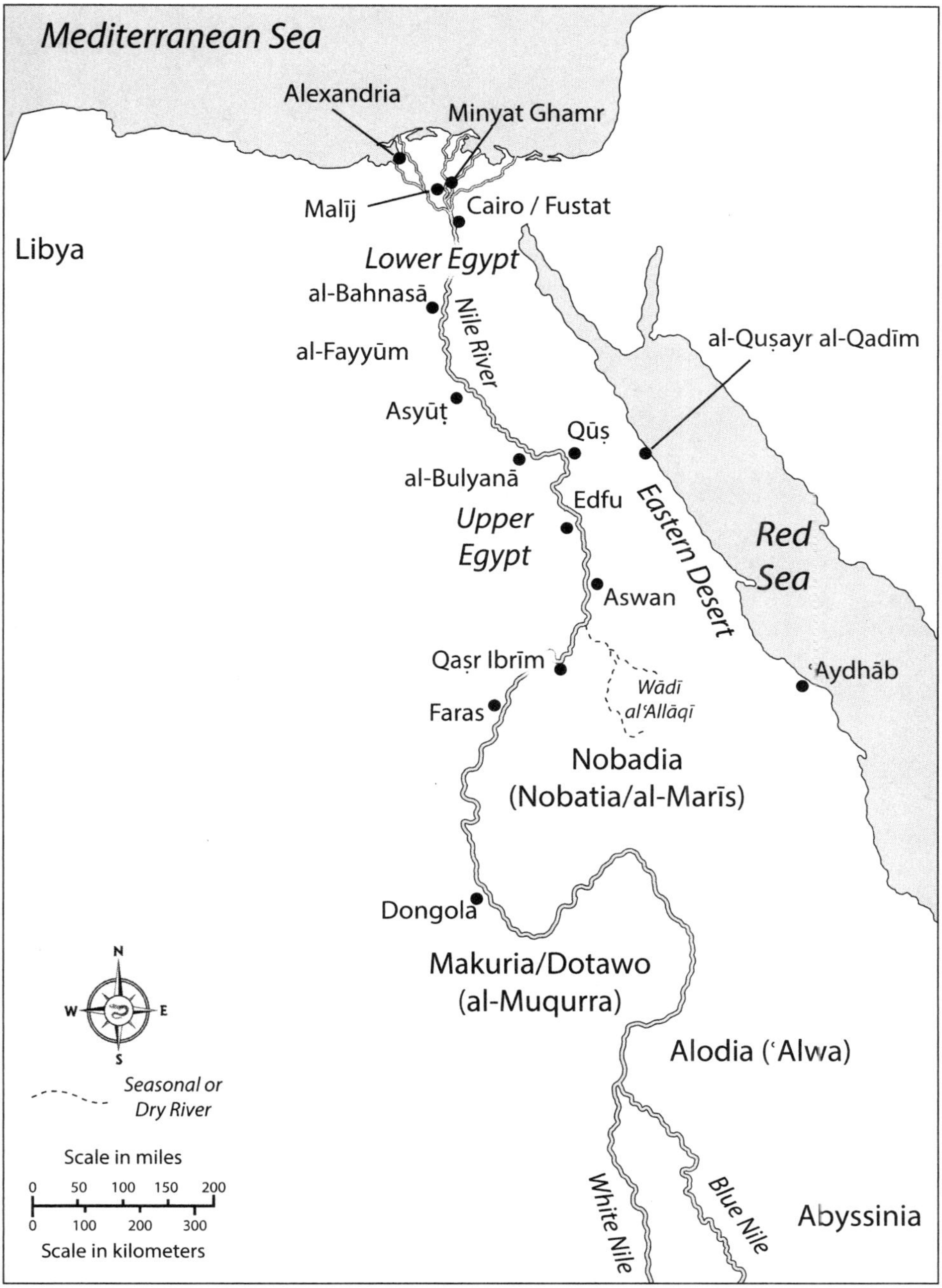

MAP 2. Egypt and Northeast Africa, ca. 1000–1250. Map created by John Wyatt Greenlee of Surprised Eel Mapping.

Introduction

IN DECEMBER OF 1144, a group of Jewish merchants and travelers gathered in the Red Sea port of ʿAydhāb (maps 1 and 2) to record and sign a deposition about a heated conflict between two of their associates (figure 0.1).[1] One of them, another Jewish merchant called Ibn Jamāhir, had gone to the local chief of police (*wālī*), a Muslim official, and beseeched him to punish Ṣāfī (Pure), a *ghulām* (enslaved man), for slander. Ṣāfī was known to the Jewish community in ʿAydhāb because he served as a factotum for the head of a rabbinic academy in Fustat (Old Cairo).[2] While the chief of police summoned Ṣāfī, Ibn Jamāhir recruited some of his Muslim colleagues to serve as witnesses on his behalf. They testified that Ṣāfī had slandered and demeaned Ibn Jamāhir with unspeakable profanity. Ṣāfī responded indignantly: "You had a *jāriya* (a slave girl) and got her pregnant. When she bore you a son, you banished her along with [your] s[on] to Berbera," on the Somali coast.[3] Ibn Jamāhir was unrelenting in his demand that Ṣāfī be punished. The chief of police ordered that Ṣāfī be flogged in front of the Jewish merchants in the town before he was thrown into jail.

Of all the stories I have encountered in researching and writing this history of slavery and the slave trade, it is the case of Ibn Jamāhir's "banished" *jāriya*, her son, and the *ghulām* Ṣāfī to which I have returned the most often. Like the majority of enslaved people whose histories are told in this book, she and her child appear and disappear from the written record in a flash. Two handwritten lines contain the twenty-odd words (thirteen in the Judeo-Arabic) that attest to the life of this mother and child.[4] Still, their history foregrounds many of the themes that animate this book, themes that cut across the scales of historical inquiry from the global to the local and from the history of urban society to the microhistories of individual lives.

Slavery was ubiquitous in the medieval Middle East, yet we know surprisingly little about its practice in everyday life. The narrative and prescriptive sources,

FIGURE 0.1. A court deposition from the Red Sea port of ʿAydhāb, ca. 1144. T-S 12.582. Paper. 16.5 × 25 cm. Reproduced by kind permission of the Syndics of Cambridge University Library.

like chronicles, belles lettres, and legal writings, that have long been the bedrock of medieval Middle Eastern studies tend to privilege elite settings. These types of sources thus tend to highlight the lives of refined courtesans and the concubine-mothers of the caliphs rather than the more common experiences of the enslaved people bound to urban households and to traveling merchants like Ibn Jamāhir. Alongside traditional narrative and legal sources, this book brings evidence to bear from a large corpus of everyday documentary records such as letters, bills of sale, marriage documents, and court testimonies. Jews produced and preserved most of the documents studied in this book, not because they were the largest or most important group of slave owners. Rather, it was because the custodians of one Egyptian synagogue had enough storage for disused papers that they were never compelled to dispose of nearly a millennium's worth of worn-out books and documents.[5]

While these records were preserved by Cairo's Jewish community, they tell us a great deal about Egyptian society more broadly. This was a world in which Jews transacted with Christian associates and appeared before Muslim courts to defend their rights as slave owners. Merchant and family letters demonstrate the workings of the transregional slave trade that trafficked men, women, and children across the Mediterranean, northeast Africa, and the Indian Ocean. Once in Egypt, enslaved people were thrown into a churning local slave trade through which they could be sold and resold many times over the course of their lives. Finally, it is through the everyday writings of the slave-owning classes that this book learns about the personhood of the enslaved individuals who did not produce their own written records.

This book centers Jewish men and women as slave owners for a few reasons. First, despite being a minority, Egyptian Jews preserved the largest cache of surviving documentary evidence for the topics of slavery and the slave trade in the world between the late tenth and mid-thirteenth centuries. Second, the history of slavery opens up a revealing window into the formation of medieval Jewish culture and its place in the larger Islamic Middle East. The very presence of enslaved people in Jewish households engendered this culture and sparked debates about the boundaries of the community and the nature of Jewish power in an Islamic society where Jews were simultaneously privileged and subordinated. Lastly, many enslaved people gained their freedom, became Jews, and remained in the Jewish community as the mothers and fathers of Jewish children.

Other enslaved people, for various reasons, were consigned to historical oblivion.[6] The banished *jāriya* and her son fall into the latter category. Though we cannot trace their history beyond the court deposition in ʿAydhāb, this book tells the history of people like them and how their lives in slavery were conditioned by factors ranging from geopolitics and famine to the contingencies of everyday life and individual choices. This book is my argument for how global medieval scholarship can integrate subaltern subjects to historicize more fully the medieval societies to which they belonged.

A Brief History of Slavery in the Medieval Middle East

Slavery and slave trading were present in pre-Islamic Arabia and across the vast territories that Muslim forces would conquer during the seventh and eighth centuries.[7] These conquests meant both the periodic intensification of enslavement through capture and the gradual incorporation of slavery laws and customs from the conquered societies across what scholar Bernard Freamon calls the "Afro-Irano-Semitic" complex.[8] During this expansion, the demographic centers of Jewish life were also encompassed by an Islamic imperium that stretched from Iberia across North Africa to Iraq and Iran. Jewish travelers and traders took part in economic and social networks that stretched to Yemen, India, and as far as Java and China.[9] Slavery, along with other forms of coerced labor and unfreedom, was part of life in these places.[10] Enslaved people were one of many commodities whose forcible trafficking loosely knit together a near-hemispheric constellation of medieval societies. It is a fair generalization to state that most peoples in the Middle Ages belonged to groups that were at one time or another both vulnerable to enslavement *and* owners of slaves.[11]

Urban households were a primary site of slavery across the late antique and medieval Middle East. Not only did enslaved people perform the work necessary for the daily and seasonal routines of family life,[12] they were also pressed into other kinds of labor based on their household's demographics and economic activities, labor such as wet-nursing and child-rearing, running errands, working in an artisan's shop or apothecary, tending to animals and plants, and so on.[13] As you will read below, Egyptian Jews had a term for this kind of slavery, and I assume that they shared this sense with their Muslim and Christian counterparts. They called it slavery *lil-khidma*, which translates to "slavery for personal service."[14] Sex and childbearing were other kinds of labor that enslaved women were forced to perform routinely. Slave-owning men also used enslaved men and boys for sex, though direct evidence of this exploitation is scant.[15]

In comparison to plantation slavery in the early modern Atlantic, gang labor in agriculture appears to have been much less common in the medieval Middle East. There are two notable exceptions to this pattern in Egypt and Iraq.[16] In the

Eastern Desert between the Nile River and Red Sea coast, Arab entrepreneurs from Egypt used enslaved labor to extract precious metals and minerals from the mines there. In eighth- and ninth-century Iraq, enslaved laborers from northeast and east Africa, often referred to as the *Zanj*, worked to convert territory in the country's south into arable land. The *Zanj* are generally well known in Islamic history and the world history of slavery because they participated in a series of revolts against the ʿAbbasid caliphate, whose seat was in Baghdad. Scholars surmise that the caliphate abandoned the intensive use of enslaved gang labor after the last of these revolts to prevent a recurrence of these events.[17]

While enslaved gang labor was not the norm in medieval Muslim societies, the caliphates did rely substantially on other forms of slavery for their political survival. The first of these developments was what the historians Majied Robinson and Elizabeth Urban call the "the rise of the concubine-born caliph."[18] As these scholars show, in the late Umayyad and early ʿAbbasid era, rulers increasingly used enslaved women as childbearing concubines as a strategy for solidifying dynastic loyalties and power. In Islamic law, the children born to free Muslim men and enslaved women were free Muslims. Thus, their offspring could rise to become caliphs (and caliph-imams in Twelver and Ismaʿīlī Shiʿism).[19]

The second development was military slavery. In the ninth century, ʿAbbasid caliphs began to purchase enslaved Turks and Central Asians to use as soldiers for protection amid intradynastic political strife. The caliphate's preference for Turks and Central Asian soldiers has been attributed to their skill in horsemanship and archery.[20] For centuries to come, many Near Eastern armies enlisted enslaved and freed soldiers. By the eleventh century, armies from Iberia and North Africa to Afghanistan and northern India had also adopted the practice.[21]

Eunuchs were also commonly found in service of the palace and army of Muslim societies as they were in the Sassanian and Byzantine realms.[22] Islamic law prohibited the mutilation required to "manufacture" eunuchs, but it was legal to import castrated boys from outside the *dār al-Islām* (territories under Islamic political control). Within the palace, eunuchs were gatekeepers and attendants. Since they could not produce children by the caliph's wives and concubines, eunuchs served and guarded the harem. In the Fatimid and later ʿAbbasid era, eunuchs were entrusted with sacred knowledge and duties as the keepers of the Fatimid Imāms' religious texts and as guardians of the tomb of the Prophet Muḥammad in Medina.[23]

Another specialized kind of slavery was the elite female courtesan (*qayna*, pl. *qiyān*).[24] At least from the Umayyad era forward, a class of highly trained enslaved women appears in courtly settings as singers, musicians, dancers, and objects of male desire.[25] In ʿAbbasid Baghdad there was a competitive market for the purchase of the most sought-after women, some of whom eventually attained their freedom and even came to buy and command their own retinues of enslaved maids and attendants. Medieval authors composed biographies of many courtesans, and their images were painted on valuable ceramics of the era and in illustrated manuscripts; they even adorn the ceiling of the Cappella Palatina in Palermo, Sicily, where they were possibly painted by craftsmen from Fatimid Egypt.[26]

While slavery *lil-khidma* was common across the medieval Middle East and North Africa, scholarly attention has long focused on the histories of the soldiers, eunuchs, courtesans, and concubine-mothers who were central to the political and cultural life of the caliphates. As a general rule, though not an absolute one, authors of the narrative and literary sources that tell these histories were not concerned with the experiences of enslaved people bound to more common households.[27] In contrast, this book draws on the abundant evidence for slavery *lil-khidma* found in documentary sources, since these records were created and kept by the classes of people who frequently purchased enslaved people for personal service.

The Cairo *Geniza* and the History of Slavery

The brief mention of Ibn Jamāhir's banished *jāriya* and her child survived the centuries because someone eventually discarded a written deposition in the *geniza* of the Ben Ezra synagogue in the bustling city of Fustat, today one of greater Cairo's many layers. The Ben Ezra *geniza*, today called "the Cairo Geniza," is one of many *genizot*, but it is distinguished by its size, density, and age, with its approximately four hundred thousand manuscript pages and fragments, a great proportion of which date back to between the eleventh and thirteenth centuries.[28]

Today, the Cairo *geniza* is divided among university and other collections worldwide. Approximately 10 to 15 percent of the *geniza* are documentary sources, such as marriage records, letters, wills, and various court records, not to mention bills of sale for enslaved people and their deeds of manumission.[29] These *geniza* documents are written primarily in Judeo-Arabic, a variety of the Arabic language written in the Hebrew script and used by Jews for centuries as a language of communication and cultural production from Iberia to India. Writers, mainly scribes and educated men, also used Hebrew and Aramaic. They tended to switch between these languages for any number of reasons, whether rhetorical or technical.[30] Jews also acquired, reused, and eventually discarded Arabic-script materials in the *geniza*.[31]

These *geniza* documents are distinct from other kinds of historical evidence for a few reasons. First, because of its density and coherence, the Cairo *geniza* attests to a large but interconnected cast of characters in any given generation, such that one can trace many connections among individuals—including slave owners and the enslaved.[32] Second, the *geniza*'s proximity to imperial Cairo (founded in 969 CE), the capital of the Fatimid caliphate (969–1171) and the Ayyubid sultanate (1171–1250), makes it an unusually rich source for the study of the interregional slave trade. The state, along with the city's merchant and professional classes, purchased slaves, whom they imported from regions including Nubia, India, and Byzantium. Significantly, the bureaucracies, courts, and mercantile networks that orchestrated this trade created a substantial paper trail. Finally, the religious diversity of Fustat meant that the *geniza*, although it was housed in a Jewish religious institution, preserved documents drawn up not just by and for Jews, but also by and for Muslims and Christians—an opportunity that allows historians to tell the story of the larger Egyptian society.

There are major challenges involved in rendering *geniza* documents legible as historical sources, for the *geniza* chamber was not an organized archive. Rather, it held heaps of haphazardly discarded materials that are often fragmentary because of physical deterioration and human handling. For example, records that had reached the end of their initial and ephemeral usefulness were frequently reused and torn apart and used for scrap paper. When antiquities collectors began to empty the *geniza* in the nineteenth century, parts of a once whole document were sometimes separated inadvertently into different crates. Some fragments have since been reunited by enterprising researchers, and more recently with the help of image recognition software.[33] Even whole and relatively legible documents may lack information like names, dates, and so on. Writers also took much for granted that outsiders, and modern readers, want to know. When merchants wrote to each other, for example, they tended to refer to previous correspondence to which researchers are often not privy.

The responses to these challenges involve generations of scholarship and, increasingly, collaborative efforts made more common by digital tools, like the Friedberg Genizah Project (FGP) and the Princeton Geniza Project (PGP). Similar developments are present among scholars who study the thousands of Arabic-script documents that were preserved in Egypt and beyond, namely in the Arabic Papyrological Database (APD). Fortunately for this book, *geniza* scholars have thus far identified the largest and contextually densest corpus of slavery-related documents for the Middle East between the eleventh and thirteenth centuries.[34] My study of *geniza* documents alongside contemporaneous writings by Muslim and Christian authors convinces me that these materials together yield rare and groundbreaking insights into the history of slavery and the slave trade in Jewish communities and Islamic societies for this period.

Geniza sources and their subjects tell a fuller story when they are read in tandem with other contemporaneous writings in Hebrew and Arabic, as well as with published translations of materials in other languages such as Persian and Sanskrit. For example, family and merchant letters from the *geniza* suggest how individuals organized the trafficking of individuals across distances great and small. As the historian Jessica Goldberg argues, *geniza* merchant letters were ephemeral tools meant to convey useful information for immediate concerns and not to be enduring, public texts.[35] This ephemeral nature means that authors provide useful and up-to-date information about the shipping news, or they express a sudden need to purchase an enslaved person with disarming frankness and without a concern for posterity. Merchants' activities also required them to interact with a variety of ancillary characters, including ship captains, slave brokers, tax collectors, market inspectors, and others who did the quotidian work of the slave trade. Of these actors the documents provide rare snapshots, but often without further context about who these people were or what their exact roles were. For this background, other kinds of writings, such as slave-buying guides and market-inspector (*ḥisba*) manuals illuminate the larger world that lurks, as it were, in the epistolary shadows. Travel writing is also complementary, as these authors sought to produce writings that would interest curious readers and be preserved for posterity. They are apt, then, to focus on aspects of the slave trade that merchant letter-writers were not apt to include (as you will see in the works of Nāṣir-i Khusraw and Benjamin b. Jonah of Tudela).

This book draws on Jewish rabbinic works that were written in the same times and places as the *geniza* documents studied in this book. Among them, the responsa of Moses Maimonides (d. 1204) and his son Abraham Maimonides (d. 1237), himself a jurist and philosopher, provide us with some of the most detailed and coherent narratives about disputes over slavery in the Jewish community. Responsa (Heb. *teshuva*, pl. *teshuvot*; Ar. *fatwā*, pl. *fatāwā*) are sets of questions sent to legal authorities and those authorities' replies. Some of the responsa I study are preserved in the *geniza* and are directly addressed to Abraham Maimonides or signed in his own hand.[36] As I discuss in chapter 5, scholars debate the value of responsa for social history. Readers will notice, especially in parts two and three of the book, that there is a striking verisimilitude between some responsa queries and specific cases described in documentary *geniza* sources. Both kinds of sources, for instance, report how women appeared before Muslim judges, who interrogated their personal histories to determine whether they were lawfully enslaved.[37] The interplay between responsa and documentary records permits the greater contextualization of both as historical sources.

Another work essential to this history is Moses Maimonides's legal code, the *Mishneh Torah*, which he completed in Egypt around 1178. The *Mishneh Torah* is one of the greatest and most enduring products of medieval rabbinic culture.[38] In fourteen books, Maimonides sought to compile all the Oral Law in one text so that a person would need no other source besides it and the Written Law (i.e., the Torah). Though it was not his intention, the *Mishneh Torah* also serves as a kind of archive for the social history of medieval slavery.[39] I juxtapose the laws of slavery found in the *Mishneh Torah* with his own responsa and evidence from *geniza* documents to illuminate how Egyptian Jews tried, and sometimes failed, to regulate slavery in the Jewish community. In some cases, Maimonides's condemnation of Jewish men's sexual use of enslaved women echoes in the criticism that Jewish communal officials leveled against men who purchased them for sex. In other cases I mine incidental, everyday details that he uses to explain and clarify his rulings. These details sometimes point to histories that are otherwise invisible to us.[40]

Geniza *Scholarship on the Slave Trade*

This book builds upon generations of trailblazing scholarship.[41] S. D. Goitein remains the chief architect of historical *geniza* studies, and it was he who first brought the case of Ibn Jamāhir, Ṣāfī, and the banished mother and son to light. In his six-volume magnum opus, *A Mediterranean Society*, he presents a panoramic view of the Jewish community and Egyptian society between the late tenth and mid-thirteenth centuries. One chapter in volume 1, "Slaves and Slave Girls," remains a standard reference in writings on slavery in the medieval Middle East.[42] In his copious endnotes and personal research archive, Goitein identified hundreds of *geniza* documents that pertained to slavery, only some of which he discusses in his published works.[43]

Goitein viewed his work on slavery, as he did *Mediterranean Society* as a whole, to be a provisional sketch upon which future scholars would expand.[44] And indeed, from the early 1970s to the present, *geniza* scholars have continued to study slavery in the Jewish households and communities of medieval Egypt as part and parcel of their inquiries into larger topics of marriage, gender, law, and the mercantile economy. Mordechai Friedman and Amir Ashur have shown how Jewish men's use of enslaved women shaped written marriage agreements, as free brides and their families sought to protect their own status against the real and perceived threat of men's use of sexual slavery.[45] Miriam Frenkel, Eve Krakowski, and Oded Zinger have generated new approaches that use gender as a lens through which to view and analyze the dynamics of household and communal politics in which enslaved people figured.[46] The histories of enslaved people themselves have received less attention—with some notable exceptions.

My motivation to research and write this book was further stoked when I read Amitav Ghosh's genre-crossing book *In an Antique Land* alongside his academic research and the foundational works of Goitein and Friedman.[47] Ghosh's work is pioneering in how he sought to narrate the life of an enslaved person who is documented, albeit tersely, in *geniza* sources. More recently, Moshe Yagur has analyzed the lives of enslaved and freed individuals in his broader studies of religious conversion.[48] Mark R. Cohen's study of poverty and the poor also illuminates the margins of the Egyptian Jewish community where some enslaved and freed people found themselves among the many people accepting donations of bread flour and clothing.[49] Histories by Roxani Margariti, Jessica Goldberg, and Phillip Lieberman (see also Ackerman-Lieberman) provide a crucial framework for how I study the world of *geniza* merchants and their letters, personal networks, and business dealings.[50] Marina Rustow's analysis of politics and power struggles in the Jewish community, and their connection to Islamic rule, inform how I portray Jewish debates about slave ownership and the interface between Jews and Islamic rule in this book.[51]

In their landmark publications, Goitein, Moshe Gil, Friedman, and Frenkel stress that there is no *geniza* evidence that Jews participated in the "wholesale" slave trade, meaning that Jews did not traffic in large numbers of human beings for profit.[52] Indeed, my research confirms that there is no evidence that Jews trafficked enslaved people in large numbers for profit to, or within, Egypt between the eleventh and thirteenth centuries.[53] This does not mean that Jews did not ever trade in slaves for profit during the Middle Ages. Evidence suggests they may have had some role in wholesale slave trading in ninth-century Iraq and the thirteenth-century Crown of Aragon, for example.[54]

Before I explain how an outsized focus on the question of wholesale slave trading has distracted scholars from a larger and more complex history, I want to note why this preoccupation exists. In the Middle Ages, the topos of the Jewish slave trader (and manufacturer of eunuchs), along with fear of Jewish domination of non-Jews, was a durable and potent element of religious polemics, narrative writings, and legal statutes.[55] As Michael Toch argues, modern historians misinterpret some of this evidence, and ignore other data, such that their writings overstate the extent of Jewish slave-trading and economic "monopoly" in medieval Europe.[56] Polemics that draw on myths of Jewish domination of the slave trade persist, and they are one ingredient that fuels contemporary antisemitism.[57] Contemporary antisemitism, in the words of Eric Ward, is "the theoretical core" of White Nationalist ideologies that have animated deadly violence against Jews, Blacks, Asians, immigrants, and others in recent years.[58] For all those reasons, it has been and remains necessary to critique ahistorical myths that stoke racism and violence.[59] The myth that Jews *dominated* the slave trade is one such example.

Perhaps this fraught history and state of affairs help explain why *geniza* scholarship on the slave trade never moved beyond the question of how centrally Jews were involved in it as wholesalers between roughly 1000 and 1250. Yet, for this period, the *geniza* holds one of the world's densest corpora of documentary materials that illustrates how the slave trade operated within one of the era's preeminent political, economic, and cultural centers—Cairo. Without careful consideration of this evidence, largely produced and preserved by Jews, I argue below that historians have sometimes misinterpreted key evidence, overlooked certain modes of slave trading, and thus failed to apprehend how a historically dynamic and multimodal slave trade operated.[60] My arguments rely both on comprehensive use of the available evidence and on an interrogation of the assumptions that scholars have made in their search for the wholesale slave trade.[61]

Scholarly preoccupation with the elusive quarry of the wholesale trade is analogous to another bias in medieval scholarship that favors long-distance trade in luxury goods over the more voluminous regional trade in staple commodities.[62] Collectively, using a corpus of more than four hundred *geniza* documents, I argue that the most active and voluminous slave trade was within local and regional Egyptian markets. Moreover, wholesale trading in large numbers of enslaved people by nonstate actors was not common in the period between roughly 1000 and 1250 CE; there is no evidence that a wholesale slave trade was a regular or reliable way that enslaved people were trafficked to and within Egypt.

To integrate Jewish slave owners into this history, I ask you, reader, to hold two opposing ideas in your mind and consider that they are both accurate, if incomplete, assessments of Jewish history. Medieval Jews were nearly everywhere a subordinated group, frequently as a recognized communal body and sometimes as individual subjects of medieval polities. Medieval Jews also had privileges by virtue of their very subordinated position, as the "servants of the court (*servi camerae*)" and as protected subjects (*dhimmīs*) within the caliphates.[63] Moreover, these privileges permitted Jews access to power through their vertical alliances with sovereign rulers in both Christian and Muslim contexts.[64] You will read examples of this in the chapters that follow for Islamic Egypt.

Jewish slave-owning was a very particular kind of power.[65] It was extremely rare, for instance, for a Jewish man to possess the military powers reserved for Muslim men in the state apparatus, like Ismāʿīl b. al-Naghrīla (d. 1056, more popularly known as Samuel ha-Nagid) in eleventh-century Granada.[66] Yet it was not uncommon for Jewish men and women to possess and legally dominate other human beings as slave owners. As a form of domination, slavery was both intimate and violent. Sex, eating, child-rearing, childbirth, physical violence, illness, and deathbed declarations—these are the domains in which owners and enslaved people are asymmetrically entangled. This intimacy evoked visceral reactions from everyone involved, including from Muslims who sometimes observed Jewish slave-owning with resentment and scorn, just as they condemned and suspected the Muslims who handled the nasty business of the slave trade.[67]

Slavery illustrates how Jewish subordination and Jewish power were two sides of the same structural coin. The very letter of Jewish subordination empowered Jews as slave owners, even as it constrained their slave owning in specific ways. For example, Jews in Islamic societies could not own Muslims. Slave purchases by Jews and Christians could become a sign of social disorder for rulers like the volatile and enigmatic Fatimid caliph al-Ḥākim, who forbade slave traders from selling enslaved people to Jews and Christians at the beginning of the eleventh century.[68]

Scholarship on Slavery in the Islamic Middle East and Beyond

Once we recognize that "wholesale" trading was only one mode of this trade, and that Jewish sources and subjects shed light on other common modes of slave trading, this book's contribution to scholarship on the history of slavery becomes more clear. Part 1 complements recent scholarship on the slave trade to medieval Egypt by Hannah Barker and Jelle Bruning, whose studies focus respectively on the chronological periods after and before this book's focus.[69] My approach emphasizes that the local resale market was, in fact, the most voluminous one, even though most of the enslaved people who were continually resold within Egypt had been imported from outside of Islamic territory. Chapter 2, on the import trade, argues that it comprised different strands—diplomatic, state-sponsored, and mercantile—that operated variously and should thus be interpreted differently when historians extrapolate from the evidence. Barker's findings show that there was indeed wholesale slave trade to Egypt during the Mamluk sultanate (1250–1517), though Bruning's study of documentary evidence from ʿAbbasid-era Egypt has more in common with what we find in the *geniza* documents during the Fatimid and Ayyubid periods (969–1250).

The focus on different modes of slave trading brings into clearer relief how both the demand and supply for enslaved people were driven by various strategic interests and not only by power imbalances between polities and people.[70] The Egyptian state sought enslaved people for its army, and it purchased many others for use in the palace and state apparatus, not to mention as sex slaves and child-bearers. Egyptian merchants, artisans, and others purchased enslaved people for household labor, sex, and to aid their own professional work. Moreover, regional powers from Christian Nubia and the Ḥadāriba Beja in northeast Africa, to dynasties in Yemen and Goa, nurtured political economies that relied on the control and taxation of luxury goods, travel, and trade, including of enslaved people.[71] These political economies sometimes complemented the rule of empires, but they could also oppose them, as it sometimes behooved rulers to refuse to send enslaved people to Islamic rulers when their relations broke down.[72]

The argument that slavery and slave trading were strategies used to various ends shows up across the history of the medieval Middle East. As mentioned previously, the late Umayyad and ʿAbbasid caliphates' use of enslaved concubines as reproductive "vessels" for dynastic rule was born out of political exigencies.[73] Parts 2 and 3 of the book illustrate how, in society more broadly, slave owners and enslaved people both acted strategically, and in relation to one another, to exercise what scholars have come to call "interagency."[74] Interagency emphasizes that historical subjects do not act as autonomous agents independent of others, but always interdependently and in relation to other actors. Or, as Vinciane Despret states, "There is no agency that is not interagency."[75] The laws and culture of slavery conditioned how the interagency of slave owners and enslaved people was entangled, but these factors alone did not determine their "scopes of action."[76] Individuals in both groups had identities grounded in their relations with people outside of the "master-slave" dyad, though the chances for enslaved people to form these ties were relatively attenuated.

Though I do not often use the term "interagency" in this book's core chapters, it is a framework that underlies their key arguments. Part 2 of the book analyzes how the agency of male and female slave-owners relied on, and was conditioned by, enslaved labor. Free women used enslaved women and girls not only to alleviate their own labor, but also to protect and project feminine honor and prestige, as Krakowski has illustrated.[77] Male owners also used slavery, and competed with each other over its control, in ways that engendered masculinity, a process that I came to understand better through my engagement with the work of medieval Europeanists including Ruth Karras, Debra Blumenthal, and Michelle Armstrong-Partida.[78]

As a way of thinking, interagency also nurtures an interpretive stance that acknowledges that the slave owner's attempt to exercise power provokes a response from those she seeks to control.[79] Though enslaved people did not leave behind their own first-person writings, this book is rife with examples of how their actions were the impetuses for the creation of written works that describe their lives despite the intention of the slave-owning classes who primarily wielded such written instruments as tools of control. The logic of source creation and survival also cuts in the other direction, as an impediment to knowledge about enslaved individuals. Specifically, the everyday violence of slavery is largely absent from documentary sources because it was only written about when the violence against an enslaved person had consequences for a slave owner. Most violence that was suffered and absorbed by enslaved people, from beatings to rape, never generated a record.

The turn to the concept of interagency also reckons with what historian Walter Johnson has called "the master trope" of "agency," which critiques the tendency of social historians to conflate too strictly "agency" with "resistance" to slavery.[80] Such an approach flattens the humanity of enslaved and freed people, who made their way in the world sometimes by using the terms of slavery to their advantage and by choosing, strategically, from among the mostly horrible choices that were allowed them. Chapters 7 and 8 illustrate how so.

In pushing against the limits of what is possible to know about the lives of enslaved individuals, I wrote parts of chapters 4 and 7 in engagement with archaeologists of slavery who confront the "invisibility" of slavery in the material record of the medieval Islamic world and Europe, where the material culture of slavery and the slave trade largely resembles the material culture of society and trade as a whole.[81] As the archaeologist Paul J. Lane puts it, we can learn a lot about slavery from not only "confirming the presence of enslaved people" in material culture, but also by "understanding the wider implications of the fact of their presence."[82] The book's focus on the implications of enslaved people's presence is part of my larger argument for the value and potential of social history, and histories of everyday life, in global medieval studies.

Connected, global histories often center elite actors, luxury commodities, and intellectual currents, in part because these are the contents that the surviving narrative and literary sources tend to privilege. Alongside these histories, we ought to also recognize that proto-global connections also involved the violence of enslavement, human trafficking, and forced servitude.[83] Moreover, as the book's conclusion will argue, memories of these individuals and the history they represent linger in contemporary Middle Eastern societies.

How to Read this Book

At its heart, this book is a work of detection and integration. Like many historians, I frequently confront the reality of writing about people who did not create their own records, and I encounter the limits, ambiguities, and silence of the historical archives that, as the product of the slave-owning classes, were never meant to be the basis of a social and cultural history of slavery, let alone enslaved lives. Where possible, I overcome these obstacles using different methods. In other instances, I dwell in the ambiguity of the sources and ruminate about interpretive possibilities without resolving what must remain unknown.[84] In both cases, I try to be deliberate, transparent, and cautious in prodding at the limits of what the written texts themselves can tell us and when I suggest what the plausible outcomes of a given, ambiguous scenario were based on what we know from larger assemblages of evidence. I want to show readers, and not just tell them, how it is possible to write the social history of medieval subalterns. This mode of storytelling explains why some parts of the book are almost forensic in their approach to specific pieces of often fragmentary evidence: the method is an invitation to readers to participate actively in the construction of this history.

This book is also the product of two additional abiding scholarly commitments, both related to different kinds of integration. The first is the integration of Jewish and world histories, or Jewish sources and subjects, into narratives of premodern global history, especially in medieval Islamic contexts. Overall, I argue that Jewish slave-owning mainly reflects the practices of slavery in the larger Islamic society, of which Christians were also a major slave-owning group. At other points, specific aspects of Jewish slave-owning, and the lives of the enslaved people bound to Jewish households, are strongly inflected by Jewish law and culture. The book's narrative thus shifts its focus among Jews, Muslims, and sometimes Christians. It also foregrounds the interplay among these slaving cultures and highlights points of convergence and divergence.

The second form of integration is between the parts and whole. In this case, the parts are the three different scales across which this book proceeds, from the macro level of the interregional slave trade to Egypt, to a focus on slavery *lil-khidma* in the Egyptian Jewish community, and, finally, on to the biographies of the women, children, and men whose enslavement, trafficking, and presences (and absences) animate the whole book. Because the book tells the history of slavery from these different vantage points, parts one and two may raise questions for readers that are not immediately answered. You will read, for instance, in part 1 of the book about the slavery laws and the slave trade but not immediately about the experiences of the enslaved people who were the victims of human trafficking. It is in part 3, and chapter 7 specifically, that you read about how a six-year-old Indian girl would have experienced the multimonth passage from western India to Cairo. In this chapter, one also sees how sales were crucial moments when enslaved people could assert themselves to scuttle a planned transaction or to force their owners to make an unwanted one.

The parts of the book successively build up the historical world in which the lives of enslaved people and enslavers were entangled, and what readers learn in parts 1 and 2 of the book provides context for part 3 and the book's conclusion. Part 1 begins with a chapter that provides an overview of the Islamic and Jewish laws of slavery. The interplay between these two systems is also crucial. Chapter 1 argues that medieval Jews in Egypt lacked an effective framework for sexual slavery in contrast to Islamic law. This failure to regulate sex slavery led to a host of unintended consequences that are further explored in parts 2 and 3 of the book. Enslaved people also understood the interplay between Islamic and Jewish law, and they sometimes used the subordinated position of their Jewish owners within Islamic law to protect themselves.

Chapter 2 studies the hemispheric slave trade to Egypt, and the intercity trade within it. The chapter demonstrates that the slave trade to Egypt was multimodal and argues that these modes must be parsed to historicize the overall trade. Each of these different modes, the diplomatic, state, and mercantile trades, operated for different purposes and reflect distinct patterns. The mercantile mode was, in this era, decentralized, and scholars searching for the wholesale trade largely overlooked it or dismissed it as relatively insignificant. I argue that it was likely a primary way that enslaved people were trafficked over time outside of temporary "pulses" in the supply of slaves caused by epochal warfare and famine.[85]

By thus separating the various strands of the slave trade, chapter 2 argues for a new approach to the study of the medieval slave trade in the Middle East and beyond. I use these findings to argue that scholars have misinterpreted certain evidence for the medieval slave trade. A prime example of such a misapprehension is that of the *baqṭ*, which refers to a diplomatic agreement between Islamic Egypt and the Christian Nubian kingdom of Makouria and Nobatia in the seventh century.[86] By the eleventh century, the *baqṭ* did not exist except as a historical precedent, though diplomatic gifts (*hadiyyas*) that resembled the earlier *baqṭ* were an important part of geopolitical relations between Egypt, Nubia, and other polities, for which the *geniza* also furnishes new evidence. Finally, this chapter analyzes the forces and historical contingencies that coerced free people into slavery in the African lands just beyond the Egyptian frontier.

Chapter 3 argues that the center of gravity of the Egyptian slave trade was local, not transregional. Many enslaved people experienced upheaval throughout their forced servitude as they were sold and resold several times. Formal sales were only one method by which Jews transferred enslaved property. Wedding dowries, gifts, and bequests were primary methods that owners used to transfer enslaved people as both laborers and intergenerational wealth. Such documents of dowries and gifts, along with a large corpus of bills of sale for enslaved people, illustrate how Egyptian Jews fashioned a usable Jewish slavery law that allowed them to transact and protect their property rights in the larger Islamic legal environment.

This chapter also demonstrates the contingencies and ambiguities of medieval racialization. All non-Muslim people outside of Islamic territories could legally be enslaved. But Jewish sources reveal how Egyptian Jews coded black-skinned people as "slaves" in their informal writings, even though "Black"[87] was not yet used as one of the many long-standing ethnic categories that scribes were instructed to note in bills of sale, such as Nubian, Indian, and Abyssinian.

As the introduction to part 2, chapter 4 begins the book's focus on the physical, economic, and social locations of slavery in medieval Egypt, particularly in Fustat and Cairo. We have precious little direct evidence about what slavery *lil-khidma* entailed in the medieval Middle East, not to mention how enslaved people experienced it. Chapter 4 addresses this challenge by illustrating how enslaved laborers would have moved through the domestic and urban spaces about which we do know. It reads, for example, archaeological and textual evidence of water retrieval and food preparation alongside medieval cookbooks in which enslaved women are credited with recipes to visualize how enslaved people fit into medieval urban society.

Chapter 4 also analyzes the professions of the slave-owning classes documented in the *geniza*. It classifies the main professional groups as medical workers (apothecaries and doctors), artisans, communal leaders, and merchants. These professional clusters highlight, respectively, the different socioeconomic roles that enslaved people were forced to play as specialized laborers, as symbols of piety and prestige, and as sex slaves. Merchants are by far the largest single slave-owning group, a fact I attribute largely to these men's desire for sex with enslaved women. Many *geniza* merchants were mobile, and their stints in locations from North Africa to India could last for several years. Within a larger sexual economy that included polygyny, prostitution, and other extramarital sex, Jewish men had the least risk and the most control as slave owners.

Chapter 5 continues the study of sexual slavery by examining how Jewish men practiced sexual slavery even though it was not sanctioned by Jewish law. This chapter studies the rhetoric and behavior both of the jurists and leaders who discouraged sexual slavery and the men who defied their efforts. There were a host of unintended consequences. Some slave-owning men abandoned their free wives and children when they took an enslaved woman for sex. The enslaved women themselves lacked the protections that Islamic law gave to the childbearing enslaved women who belonged to Muslim men.

Another consequence was masculine competition over the regulation of slavery within the Jewish community. Some men performed a masculinity of dominance and asserted their prerogative as enslavers in the face of Jewish leaders who largely lacked the coercive tools to enforce their rulings. Other men cultivated a masculinity of piety that they performed by freeing enslaved women and then supporting their integration into the local community as freed, marriageable Jews. *Geniza* evidence also shows that some enslavers performed according to both masculine ideals. Enslaved and freed men also asserted their masculinity, as this chapter and part 3 of the book will illustrate.

Chapter 6 shines a spotlight on the free women who owned enslaved people and who made up one-quarter of the slave-owning classes. Beyond relief from household labor, free women also purchased and inherited enslaved girls because slave ownership was a feminine status marker and a form of social capital. Still, free women had to defend their rights as slave owners against the encroachments of their husbands and other male relatives, a fact that illustrates how Jewish women were doubly subordinated as *dhimmīs* and due to their gender in a patriarchal society. When Jewish courts were unable or unwilling to do so, women could sue Jewish men in Muslim courts. In this way, women's slave-owning provides further insight into how masculinity was shaped by Jewish men's subordination to Muslim men, the latter of whom had more privilege and power in Islamic society.

Part 3 of the book contains the individual histories and collective biography of the more than two hundred enslaved and freed people documented in the *geniza* corpus. Chapter 7 focuses on the lives of enslaved people, and it begins by showing that it is possible to trace the life trajectories of some enslaved individuals despite the ambiguity created by naming practices in which enslaved people are not identified beyond their personal names. The chapter follows the life course of enslaved people from their births and childhoods, when slave owners seem to have viewed children as young as five or six as minimally competent for active servitude. The vast majority of the enslaved person's life course was an undifferentiated (by slave owners at least) passage from the age of "sexual maturity" (*bulūgh*) through either their manumission, their death with slave status, or their exit from the written archive.

Chapter 7 also focuses on the strategies that enslaved people used to exert what little power they could, along a continuum of resistance and accommodation, to protect themselves and to build their lives. In some cases, enslaved people practiced a kind of urban marronage in the "underworld" of medieval Cairo. Others used the terms of slavery and *dhimmī* law for their own purposes by converting to Islam and thus forcing their Jewish owners to sell them. Other people used their knowledge of the law to avoid an unwanted sale or to press their owners to provide the daily maintenance that slavery law required. In rare cases, enslaved people created their own families through marriage to each other.

Chapter 8 studies the freed men and women who chose to remain a part of the Jewish community. Some of them married Jews and had children. Others continue to appear in *geniza* documents because they continued the work they had done for their owners and within the same social and economic networks. The ways that freed people charted their life-paths largely resemble how freeborn Jews did so. The dowries of some freedwomen contained the kind of clothing and furnishings that free women received in their dowries. Freed men and women owned property, and others invested capital in business ventures and traded in imported goods.

The history of manumission, in Jewish law, is also a history of religious conversion as former slaves moved from the liminal category of slavery to become "full" Jews with their emancipation. Chapter 8 further analyzes how the Jewish laws of slavery, manumission, and conversion worked to erase the personal histories of freed people. By the second and third generations, the descendants of freed people were not identified as such. And the onetime presence of their forebearers, whether Nubian, Indian, and so on, was effectively muted. The multiethnic diasporas that formed through the violence of the slave trade, as seen in part 1 of the book, were partly absorbed into Arab-Islamic society and its Jewish communities and their histories as enslaved people eventually erased.[88]

The book's conclusion focuses on how the three parts of the book work together to tell the two stories at the heart of the book. The first is the integration of Jewish and medieval world history through the lens of slavery. As in its Muslim and Christian counterparts, slavery was a constituent part of medieval Jewish culture in one of its most storied settings. Roughly one of every four enslaved people in the Egyptian Jewish community became a freed Jew and remained a part of the community in different capacities. Though Jewish history has a vocabulary for Sephardic Jews from Iberia, Ashkenazi Jews from central Europe, and Maghribi Jews from North Africa, the structures of law and religion conspire such that the passage of formerly enslaved Nubian, Indian, and other Jews has yet to be fully accounted for. The largest of these coerced diasporas was Nubian, and the conclusion ends by considering how a Jewish history of slavery figures into the stories that Nubians in modern Egypt tell themselves about the painful memories of slavery and how its legacy resonates in the present.

PART I

Slavery Law and the Slave Trade

1

Jewish Slave-Owning in an Islamic Society

As subjects of the Fatimids and the Ayyubids, all Jews were subordinated *and* protected by Islamic law. Muslim rulers also recognized Jewish law and communal institutions. The arrangement was the same for the much more numerous Coptic Christians of Egypt, who were similarly classified as an *ahl al-dhimma* (a protected people). These *dhimmīs*, as they are collectively called, were embedded in a system of legal pluralism in which many, perhaps most, of their affairs were conducted and adjudicated according to their own religious traditions (*dīn* in the Arabic sources). Protected groups also had access to Islamic legal forums through Muslim judges (*qāḍīs*) and petitions to state tribunals for the redress of grievances (*maẓālim*).[1] It was natural and necessary, therefore, that Egyptian Jews had knowledge of Islamic law and that many of them interacted with Islamic institutions.

Enslaved people were forced participants in this society. This coercion, however, did not prevent them categorically from taking actions to shape their own life paths despite their greatly limited options. As part 3 of the book illustrates, enslaved people also understood fundamental aspects of both Jewish and Islamic law, and they put this knowledge to use. For these reasons, this chapter presents a short overview of Islamic and Jewish slavery laws, as well the interplay between these two traditions. These overviews are not comprehensive. Instead, the focus is on the topics that provide the most essential context for the history told in later chapters.

Islamic Slavery Law: A Short Overview

A useful point of departure for Islamic slavery law are the four normative concepts that the scholar Kurt Franz identifies in early Muslim sources, the Quran and *ḥadīth* in particular: enslaved people are considered "human beings, and not mere chattels"; slavery is a legal status, not an inherent one, and this makes manumission possible; enslaved people and their owners belong to households and have personal relations with each other; and slave owners are encouraged to be kind and "to opt for manumission."[2] While Muslims did not adopt the Aristotelian point of view that servility was innate in some human beings, they did accept that God ordained the temporary enslavement of prisoners of war and unprotected groups outside of the Islamic imperium.[3] One of slavery's paradoxes is that its occasional amelioration through law and culture both allowed for limited social mobility on the part of unfree people *and* supported the perpetual entrenchment of the institution in society.

Of great importance for the history of the slave trade to and within medieval Egypt were Islamic laws that governed who could be legally enslaved. These laws were both territorial and based on personal status. They were territorial in the sense that all Muslims and *dhimmīs* within the caliphates were protected from enslavement inside of the Islamic imperium. Outside of Islamic territories, personal status was of great consequence. All Muslims were theoretically protected from enslavement by other Muslims everywhere.[4] *Dhimmī* groups were not protected from enslavement outside of *dār al-Islām*; slave traders could enslave them and import them for sale in Islamic territories. You will read in this book, for example, about Nubian Christians who were enslaved beyond Egypt's frontier and trafficked into the caliphate where Muslims, Jews, and other Christians purchased them. Another critical dynamic that surfaces in part 3 of the book is the conversion of enslaved people to Islam. Such a conversion would, by law, compel a *dhimmī* owner to sell the new convert to a Muslim buyer. The enslaved person did not gain their freedom as a result of conversion, as Muslims could lawfully own someone who converted to Islam after their enslavement.

Some types of enslaved people gained limited rights and protections once inside of Islamic territory according to their gender. Boys and men, for example, were not supposed to be castrated within the *dār al-Islām* or in the Byzantine empire. For this reason, the eunuchs who served the emperors, caliphs, and sultans were first violently mutilated in locations that spanned Afro-Eurasia: Spain, France, Bohemia, the Caspian, Armenia, Upper Egypt (at or across the Islamic frontier), Sudan, Ethiopia, India, Central Asia, and China. The geography of castration evolved as territories became Christianized or Islamized and the gelding of boys was outlawed in one place and moved to another. Christian and Muslim elites continued to import eunuchs from across the medieval Mediterranean and beyond.[5]

For enslaved girls and women, the most effective protection granted them was by virtue of patrilineal descent and the law of the *umm walad* (or *umm al-walad*), which translates to "mother of (the) child."[6] Law permitted Muslim men the sexual use of the enslaved women whom they purchased. If an enslaved woman bore her owner's children, they were born free Muslims and legitimate heirs. The enslaved mother also gained two rights. Her owner could not sell her, and she became a freed person upon his death. The *umm walad*'s protections were not perfect. Slave-owning men could deny paternity, for example.[7] Still, this law, coupled with patrilineal descent, profoundly shaped the culture of slavery, and sexual slavery, for all.

In practice, many enslaved people also exercised limited rights in daily life. They had freedom of movement so that they could complete the errands and various kinds of labor asked of them. One class of enslaved men, the *ghilmān* (sg. *ghulām*), traveled long distances as factotums for officials and merchants. They participated in their owners' economic and social networks and drew an allowance for expenses. Historical evidence demonstrates that enslaved people could control their own capital, though not all schools of Islamic law recognized this right.[8] A major theme of parts 2 and 3 of this book is the mobility of enslaved people in Cairo and other urban settings.

For enslaved people themselves, mobility also provided chances for them to acquire knowledge and to form their own social associations outside of the surveillance of the households to which they were bound. In rare cases, enslaved people married each other and had children, who were born with slave status in contrast to the offspring of free Muslim men by their concubines.[9] Islamic law sought to protect familial ties, especially those between mothers and children. There is documentary evidence that families of enslaved parents and children were sold together in medieval Egypt, though this does not mean that families were never broken up through the slave trade.[10]

Enslaved people could attain freedom through different forms of manumission.[11] Manumission is encouraged in Islamic scriptures as an act of piety and expiation of wrongdoing. *'Itq* (*'ataqa, i'tāq*) was manumission by the owner's volition and was, in theory, irrevocable.[12] Owners could also arrange for their enslaved property to become free upon their death in a form of manumission called *tadbīr*.[13] In these forms of manumission, the enslaved children of a manumitted woman would also gain their freedom. A third form of manumission in Islamic law is *kitāba* (also *kitāb* and *mukātaba*).[14] In this arrangement, enslaved people acquired a contract to purchase their freedom (often in installments) from their owner and became free once they had completed the payments.[15]

In Islamic law and society, manumission did not sever the ties between freed people and their former owners but rather created a new bond of dependency (*walāʾ al-ʿitq*) between patron (*mawlā*) and client (also called *mawlā*).[16] This patron-client bond can be understood as a type of kinship tie. The former owner and patron provided the new freedman primarily with social capital and, in some cases, economic aid. The patron gained the right to inherit from his freed client's estate. Patronage relationships between former owner and freed person mattered not only because they shaped these ties after manumission, but also because they sometimes colored how owners and enslaved people related to each other in slavery. Owner and enslaved person were to each other a potential kind of future kin. As we will see in later chapters, though Jewish law had no comparable law of patronage between freed people and their former owners, this Islamic practice still exerted influence on how individual Jewish slave owners acted.[17] Before considering such cultural interplay, a short description of Jewish slavery laws is in order.

Jewish Slavery Law: A Short Overview

As a subordinated group in Islamic Egypt, Egyptian Jews had much of their slavery law settled for them according to the broad strokes outlined above. For some aspects of this law, the Talmudic precept that "the law of the kingdom (in which Jews were subjects) is the law (for the Jews, too)" applied.[18] Jews followed Islamic law in that they did not own enslaved Muslims,[19] and the people who they did purchase belonged to groups whose enslavement the state sanctioned.

Still, in the realm of quotidian life, household slavery fell into the category of affairs that Muslim authorities allowed all *dhimmīs* to regulate according to their own laws. Jews were free to transact with each other, and with Egyptian Christians. Jewish law held that enslaved people, both male and female, should follow the same religious commandments as those expected of free Jewish women, though this practice is not mentioned in *geniza* documents.[20] For transactions between Jewish buyers and sellers, scribes composed multilingual (Judeo-Arabic, Aramaic, and Hebrew) bills of sale that used legal formularies drawn from Jewish precedents.[21] Jews also freed enslaved people by drawing up and delivering writs of manumission according to Jewish law.[22] These documents had legal standing in Islamic courts.

Disputes over slave ownership did erupt from time to time, and individual slave owners were accused of flouting the law and exceeding the boundaries of acceptable behavior. When Jewish leaders sought to mediate such conflicts or bring offending slave owners to heel, they confronted the limits of their power. As *dhimmīs*, Jewish leaders did not have coercive tools such as corporal punishment and imprisonment at their disposal. Jewish leadership's inability to enforce Jewish slavery law will prove to be consequential in later chapters.

Canaanite Slavery and Religious Conversion

Medieval Jewish jurists recognized two categories of slavery law, those applying to the "Hebrew slave (*'eved 'ivri*)" and the "Canaanite slave (*'eved kena'ani*)."[23] Hebrew slavery functioned like indentured servitude of cultural "insiders." This slavery was temporary, and the Hebrew slave had many specified rights.[24] Canaanite slavery is best understood as the enslavement of enemy "outsiders," whom the biblical Israelites captured as prisoners of war.[25] Canaanite slavery was permanent and hereditary unless an owner chose to free a slave.[26] Here the principle of matrilineal decent in Jewish law is a critical factor. Jewishness passed through the mother, not the father. Thus any Jewish man's child born to an enslaved woman was born with slave status and as a non-Jew.

The categories of the Hebrew and Canaanite slave would both remain salient in discussions of Jewish law, but the category of Hebrew slave became obsolete in practice centuries before the period of this study, as did other biblical laws of slavery.[27] For example, the practice of freeing slaves during the sabbatical and Jubilee years, if it ever was practiced regularly, was not a feature of Jewish life in the Middle Ages.[28] Jewish slavery law in medieval Egypt were the laws of "foreign," or "Canaanite" slavery. The language in the bills of sale that slave owners kept as proof of their ownership reflects that this kind of slavery was perpetual and that manumission was the owner's (and their heirs' after them) sole prerogative. While the Jewish laws of Canaanite slavery are clear in regard to its perpetuity and inheritability, the medieval laws for the religious conversion of Canaanite slaves to Judaism injected ambiguity into their status within the Jewish community at large. These laws considered the enslaved people owned by Jews to occupy a liminal category that cannot easily be mapped onto any biblical ideal.[29]

Enslaved people's legal and religious liminality is evident in the medieval Jewish laws of conversion. When Jewish parties purchased slaves, the purchase effected a partial religious conversion of the enslaved person to Judaism. The enslaved were no longer classified as one of the non-Jewish "nations (*goyyim*)," but neither were they considered fully Jewish.[30] When the owner freed the enslaved person with a writ of manumission (*geṭ shiḥrur, sheṭar ḥerut*), the formerly enslaved person then gained the full status of Jew.[31] In the words of the one such writ (figure 8.1), "I am freeing you; now you are free; now you belong to yourself; you are permitted to join the community of Israel, to adopt a new name in

Israel, and to do what you like as do all free persons."[32] As the final chapter of this book illustrates, some enslaved people did indeed adopt a new name and remained in the Egyptian community as Jewish wives and mothers and as Jewish husbands and fathers. Other freed people disappear from the historical record after their manumission.

Sexual Slavery and Jewish Law

Islamic and Jewish slavery laws depart most significantly on the subject of free men's sexual exploitation of enslaved people. This book argues that Egyptian Jewish jurists and community leaders lacked a clear and enforceable approach to Jewish men's use of sex slaves. Slave owners, their families, and laity expressed confusion over what the law was and how it should be implemented. A few legal factors loom large. First, there was confusion over Jewish law and sex with enslaved people, in part because Jewish tradition contained precedents for its practice. Egyptian jurists and rabbinic leaders, however, rejected these precedents. Second, Islamic law both permitted sexual slavery and, through its laws of patrilineal descent, recognized the children born to enslaved women and Muslim men as freeborn Muslims. As further specified above, the enslaved mother (*umm walad*) also gained some rights. The role of patrilineal descent in Islamic slavery law casts into starker relief how matrilineal descent in Jewish law created huge challenges in a society where women were disproportionately exploited as slaves and in no small measure due to men's desire and demand for enslaved sex workers. The first of these factors, jurists' rejection of Jewish precedents for sexual slavery, requires further explanation.

In their prolific writings, the Iraqi geonim (sg. gaon), the leaders of the venerable rabbinic academies (yeshivas) there, discussed Jewish men's sex with enslaved women in the centuries before the *geniza* documents and the writings of Moses Maimonides began to shed further light on the Egyptian context. A paradigmatic example that jurists used to think through this issue was the case of Bustanay and Azādwār. The legend goes that, after the Muslim conquest of Sassanid Persia, the caliph ʿUmar b. al-Khaṭṭāb (d. 644) gave the enslaved concubine named Azādwār to the first Jewish exilarch of the Islamic period, Bustanay b. Kafnay (ca. 618–70). Bustanay took Azādwār as a second wife, and she bore three of his sons. Bustanay also had two elder sons by his first wife, who was a Jewish woman. When Bustanay died, the elder sons born to his Jewish wife challenged the legitimacy of the concubine Azādwār's children by arguing that Azādwār had never converted to Judaism. The elder sons insisted that her children be considered foreign slaves who could not legally inherit from Bustanay's estate.[33]

The multivocal nature of Jewish law about sex with enslaved women is evident in how later Iraqi jurists weighed in on this case of Bustanay, Azādwār, and their children. Natronai b. Hilai (ca. 857–65 as gaon of the rabbinic academy in Sura) declared that Azādwār's children should be considered legitimate heirs by invoking a principle found in the Babylonian Talmud: "One does not have illicit sexual relations when one can do it legally."[34] As the scholar B. Z. Wacholder explains, "The legal fiction behind this ruling was that, there being no evidence to the contrary, it should be assumed that the master freed his slave before he had sexual intercourse with her."[35] A later gaon, Aaron (943–60 as gaon), issued a minority opinion that had even more far-reaching implications: any sexual act between a captive woman and her master proved that he had emancipated her.[36] Later geonim did not adopt Aaron's opinion, but they continued to field legal queries that probed the very question. A query sent to the gaon Natronai b. Hilai explains:

> Many people in our places buy attractive slave women, claiming that they buy them for household service (*'avdut*), but we suspect that they buy them for another purpose (i.e., for sex). Is it proper to leave them under suspicion? If someone says, "I have manumitted my slave and she is like my concubine (*pilegesh*)," should we accept what he says? Or should we investigate the case and oblige him to show the bill of manumission and to bring evidence that he has married her properly? Should the court investigate all that, or should it leave the case and presume that all men are trustworthy, so that whoever is suspect will remain suspect and whoever is trustworthy will remain so?[37]

The dilemma articulated here, and variations on its themes, were persistent and widespread. On the one hand, there is a sense that the suspected behavior is improper and that such an investigation is warranted. On the other hand, the query reflects both a reluctance to question the suspect men and even uncertainty about what exactly the law requires.

The opinions of Jewish jurists in the Islamic West also evince the multiplicity of legal approaches to questions about sex, slavery, and the offspring of enslaved women. Isaac b. Jacob al-Fāsī (d. 1103, often called "the Rif"), who lived both in the Maghrib and al-Andalus, produced a code of Jewish law that included laws about sex with slaves and that his successors referred to in their later legal writings.[38] In one of these later works, the author cites al-Fāsī as the source for a gaonic opinion that the son of a Jewish man by his slave woman should be considered his legal son and not a foreign slave.[39]

Though these legal discussions originated outside of Egypt, Egyptian Jews were familiar with their themes. For example, Jews in Egypt copied, read, and deposited worn-out texts about Bustanay and Azādwār in the *geniza*.[40] Jurists read the works of geonim including Natronai b. Hilai and cited them in their own writings.[41] Jews who migrated to Egypt brought with them knowledge and experience of diverse Jewish legal cultures, not to mention of other Muslim and Christian societies. Moses Maimonides is a case in point. He spent the first third of his life in al-Andalus, where he received his early education from his father, Maimon b. Joseph. Maimon had been the student of Joseph b. Migash, who had himself studied with the aforementioned al-Fāsī.[42]

The legal writings of Moses Maimonides serve as their own kind of archive for the legal and social history of slavery. In the *Mishneh Torah*, Moses states clearly that enslaved people are not supposed to be used for sex.[43] It is critical, however, to understand one of the reasons why:

> If a Jew has sexual intercourse with a foreign slave—whether or not she is his slave—the child born as a result is a foreigner for any purpose, and can be bought, sold, and used as a slave. . . . [44] (It is permissible) to sell (the foreign slave's) sons and daughters, as it is said, "From among them you will buy, and from their families that are with you, which they begat in your land (Lev. 25:45)." Every one of them is like a foreign slave for any purpose.[45]

In law and everyday life, the opposition to Jewish men's sex with slaves was mainly expressed by raising concerns about the status of children. They would be born as Canaanite slaves.[46] It bears emphasis that the rape of enslaved women was not forbidden because they had rights to control and protect their own bodies.[47] Indeed, Maimonides explains that Jewish women should not own males over the age of nine because "if she purchases male slaves," he explains, "she also legally acquires the slaves' bodies, just as (slave-owning) men do."[48]

Another dimension of Maimonides's prohibition of sexual slavery is his subtle recognition that Jews no longer had sovereign power and, therefore, they could not lawfully acquire enslaved women for sex as war captives. This reasoning is evident when we compare how Maimonides rejects two precedents in Jewish tradition that resemble sexual slavery even if biblical and rabbinic writers did not use this exact vocabulary to discuss them. The first rejected category was the *pilegesh*. *Pilegesh* is often translated as "concubine" or "slave-wife," though its use in the Hebrew Bible suggests that its meaning varied with context.[49] In the *Mishneh Torah*'s "Laws of Kings and Wars," Maimonides writes that only a Jewish sovereign could take "wives (*nashim*) and concubines (*pilagshim*)" captured during warfare.[50]

Maimonides also emphasized that a second precedent, the law of the "beautiful (captive) woman (*eshet yefat to'ar*)" was only valid during a time of war waged by a Jewish sovereign.[51] The law lays bare the brutality of war for captured women. Specifically, a Jewish king's soldier was justified in raping a captive woman as one of the spoils of war if he planned "to take her into his home" and marry her after a waiting period.[52] During this time, the captive woman was supposed to decide whether or not she was willing to join the Israelite community through a ritual immersion. A later chapter in this book analyzes a legal query that Maimonides received in which the writer asked him if this law of the "beautiful captive woman" could be applicable in the case of a Jewish man in Egypt who was suspected of using an enslaved Christian woman as his concubine.[53] In rejecting this proposal, Maimonides explains that "[the law of the 'beautiful captive'] is promulgated in the Holy Law (Torah) . . . because it was a time of (Israelite) conquest (*fī ḥāl al-futūḥ*)."[54] What connects, then, Maimonides's rejection of these two precedents is that there was no sovereign Jewish state whose rule would have legitimated Jews' lawful use of captive women for sex.

In the absence of a sanctioned form of sexual slavery and a solution to the problem of illegitimate children born to slave women, the preferred solution was ostensibly straightforward. If a Jewish man wanted to have sex with his slave woman he needed first to free her and then to marry her. In theory the order of events was crucial. Manumission should precede any sex between a man and his slave. The slave owner could not, in other words, decide later to free his slave after he had had sex with her. Instead, he was supposed to sell her to someone else and "distance himself from her."[55]

Despite the law, as chapters 4 and 5 make clear, Jewish men of certain socioeconomic classes frequently purchased women and used them for sex. In the "Laws of Inheritance," Maimonides introduces a scenario that illustrates these tensions between law and social practice:

> (If) a man had a slave woman, had a son from her, and he behaved toward him as one treats (his) sons. Or he said, "He is my son and his mother is a freedwoman" (i.e., he manumitted her). If the man is a scholar or a trustworthy man who is exacting in his strict observance of the commandments, then the son shall inherit from him. Nevertheless, the son is not allowed to marry a Jewish woman until he produces proof that his mother was emancipated and (only) afterwards gave birth, since she was previously presumed to be a slave woman. (But) if (the father) is a commoner, and needless to say, if he was among those who act freely in this way (i.e., he was not exacting in his strict observance), then (the son) is presumed to be a slave for all purposes. The brothers (the father's legitimate sons) may sell him. . . .[56]

Thus the *Mishneh Torah* itself reflects a complex social reality and the challenges that it presented to jurists and the laypeople that turned to them for guidance. The dynamics at work in these situations demand that we consider the interplay between Jewish and Islamic law and culture in Egyptian society.

The Interplay of Islamic and Jewish Slavery Law and Culture

With regard to Jewish men's use of enslaved women for sex, two dynamics show how the interplay between Islamic and Jewish law and culture played out in society. First, even though Jewish jurists, as *dhimmis*, were empowered to regulate much of Jewish personal law, they could not wield the coercive tools reserved for Muslim authorities that might have given them a stronger hand in compelling Jewish men to comply with those laws.[57] Even if they had such tools, it is not a given that they would have been able to stop this particular practice.

Second, Jews lived in an Islamic society where sex with enslaved child-bearing women was lawful and culturally accepted.[58] To some Jewish men, the prerogative to use sex slaves lawfully within the framework of Jewish law was alluring, and not only because they desired sex. They also wanted their progeny to be recognized unambiguously as free Jews who could eventually marry other Jews and enjoy good social standing in the Jewish community at large. Moreover, they were aware that precedents for licit sexual slavery existed in Jewish traditions. Eve Krakowski's research shows that this tension, between the appeal of Islamic law and culture on the one hand, and Egyptian Jews' abiding commitment to the details of Jewish law on the other, was common in the larger sphere of marriage and family law.[59] Jewish slave-owning further manifests these dynamics.

These tensions gave rise to ambiguities and ambivalence that Jewish leaders struggled to navigate. Some slave-owning men engaged in subterfuge and outright lying to conceal the nature of their slave owning because they knew that their actions went against Jewish law. Additionally, jurists did not want to put themselves in the position of policing the classes of men who were most likely to own slaves, not least because their prospects for forcing the outcomes they wanted were dim. Some of these men were also well placed socially; they donated money to synagogues, rabbinic academies, and other charitable causes.[60] Others were belligerent and litigious. There were reasons to tread lightly around both groups.[61]

Sexual slavery among Egyptian Christians shows that these dynamics were not limited solely to the Jewish community. In the eleventh century, the patriarchs of the Coptic Church in Egypt sought to combat concubinage among their clergy and wider membership.[62] The 62nd Coptic patriarch, Abrām b. Zurʿa (975–78), fought against its practice, especially among church archons, using the tool of excommunication. Some men targeted by the patriarch's campaign reacted in the extreme. One such Coptic official responded to Abrām's order of excommunication not by relinquishing his concubines, but by poisoning the patriarch.[63]

In that same era, Anbā Sawīrus, a metropolitan (regional head) of the Coptic Church, lamented to his Egyptian colleagues from his post in Abyssinia that "concubinage and polygyny were rampant" in the royal court there. Though Sawīrus persuaded the Abyssinian king and other men to reduce the number of women that they took, the king refused to dismiss one of his wives and their children. To avoid a kerfuffle, Sawīrus said that he eventually "made room for (the king) and turned a blind eye" to that remaining issue.[64] In the eleventh and twelfth centuries, an era contemporaneous with this book's focus, the Coptic patriarchs continued to issue canons that reiterated a ban on concubinage.[65] Further, church law did not recognize the children born to Coptic men and their concubines. As the historian Tamer el-Leithy notes, the church's "tireless regulation of concubinage" reflected the "tension between a pervasive social practice and its resolute legal prohibition."[66]

In addition to sexual slavery, the larger Islamic context shaped other aspects of Jewish slave-owning. Within the pluralistic framework of Islamic law and empire, Jewish courts and scribes developed documentary practices that were valid in both legal systems. Jews transacted with each other in Jewish courts, and they retained multilingual records (Judeo-Arabic, Aramaic, and Hebrew) that were all written in Hebrew script. Some kinds of documents, writs of manumission especially, were composed mostly in Aramaic and more strictly according to specific Jewish legal requirements and formularies.[67] The analysis of a full bill of sale in chapter 3 will show that these documents incorporated Jewish formularies such as those written in the Babylonian Talmud and the Iraqi gaon Hai b. Sherira's (d. 1038) book of Jewish legal formularies alongside Arab-Islamic legal terms related to specifics like warranties, taxes, and payment terms.

Jews preferred to conduct their slavery business in Jewish courts, with two main exceptions. First, when Jews and Christians bought enslaved people from each other, they chose to complete transactions in Muslim courts and they received bills of sale in Arabic script.[68] This protected both parties since Islamic law recognized and protected the rights of all *dhimmīs* as slave owners.[69] Second, Jews sued each other in Muslim courts, or threatened to do so, when there was a dispute over a sale or another matter that could not be resolved in Jewish courts or through other kinds of mediation.[70] A different, extreme appeal to

Muslim authority is evident in this book's opening pages that describe how the Jewish merchant Ibn Jamāhir pressed the Muslim chief of police to apprehend and flog the enslaved man, Ṣāfī, who belonged to another Jewish elite. In parts 2 and 3 of the book there are more examples of how Jews, and enslaved people, used Jewish and Islamic courts for different reasons.

As you read this history, it helps to remember that *dhimmī* laws could simultaneously protect Jews, empower them as slave owners, and reinforce their subordination vis-à-vis Egyptian Muslims. For much of the book, it may seem as if *dhimmī* laws did not impinge much on the daily lives of Jews and their slaves. In other moments, however, the *dhimmī* law jumps to the fore of the action. In a rare occurrence for the period, the Fatimid caliph al-Ḥākim (r. 996–1021) forbade Jews and Christians from entering the slave market in Cairo, among a host of other restrictions meant to emphasize the subordination of these *dhimmī* groups to Muslims.[71] As it happened, al-Ḥākim's successor the caliph al-Ẓāhir (r. 1021–36), lifted these restrictions and even acquired an enslaved woman from a Jewish courtier.[72]

There was always the latent threat that Jewish slave-owning could attract unwanted, and potentially punitive, attention from Muslim authorities. *Dhimmī* slave-owning could be construed as an affront to the social order because it manifested the dominance of non-Muslims, albeit over other non-Muslims. This dynamic is evident in chapter 7, which shows how enslaved people could use the *dhimmī* status of their owners strategically to protect themselves from harm, and sometimes in collaboration with Muslims. Still, when Jews did appear before Muslim judges for slavery-related matters, it was more often than not at the initiative of a Jewish party. The great majority of the time, Jews could expect Islamic law to protect their rights as slave owners.

This chapter fits into the book in two main ways. First, it uses the topic of slavery law in Islam and Judaism to illustrate one of the most durable themes in premodern Jewish history. That is, Jewish status was powerfully conditioned by the acceptance of a subordinated legal and social status for legal protection. This legal protection often entailed rights and privileges, some of which allowed Jews to exercise power over other subordinated and marginalized groups in any given society.[73] Slavery is a case in point.

Second, the overview of Islamic and Jewish slavery laws, as well as the interplay between them, provides essential context for all subsequent parts of the book. These legal regimes are a primary factor that shaped the geography and geopolitics of the interregional slave trade to Egypt. These same laws also explain the patterns of Jewish slave-owning evident in chapter 3 on local, everyday human trafficking. The interplay of Jewish and Islamic slavery law is evident in the gendered dimensions of slave owning that are central to part 2 of the book, as well as to understanding how Jewish men and women competed with each other over their rights as slave owners and the "proper" way to wield domination over enslaved people, especially in regards to sexual slavery. Finally, part 3 of the book illustrates how enslaved people were, despite their lawful subjugation, knowledgeable subjects who sometimes used these same legal regimes to protect themselves and to build their own attachments and lives in and out of slavery's dark shadow.

2

Parsing the Slave Trade to Egypt

THE HISTORY OF SLAVERY is intertwined with the rise of the Fatimid caliphate in Egypt. It was the freedman and army general Jawhar b. ʿAbdallāh who led an army composed of enslaved and freed soldiers to victory, first in the Maghrib (western North Africa), and then to the very conquest of Egypt in 969 from the Ikhshīdid dynasty (935–69), who governed for the ʿAbbasid caliphate.[1] Jawhar laid the foundations both of a new city, Cairo, that would serve as the Fatimids' new imperial capital,[2] as well as of the mosque of al-Azhar, which remains a center of Islamic learning and worship to this day. As the Fatimids relocated their seat of government from Ifrīqiyya (roughly modern-day Tunisia) to Egypt, the caliphs continued to bolster their fighting forces with enslaved troops from across Africa and Central Asia.[3] For most of its first century in Egypt, the Fatimid caliphate remained ascendant. It controlled territory from Ifrīqiyya and Sicily in the west to Syria and the Ḥijāz (western Arabia) in the east, again with the help of enslaved and freed forces.

One barometer of Fatimid ascendancy was the arrival of diplomatic embassies and prestige gifts from other sovereigns and vassals. The Zīrid rulers, who came to govern Ifrīqiyya as Fatimid vassals, sent gifts that included enslaved women, Slavic boys, and Black eunuchs to the caliphs al-Ḥākim (r. 996–1021) and al-Ẓāhir (r. 1021–36).[4] It is not incidental that al-Ẓāhir reciprocated and upped the ante, as was appropriate for a caliph vis-à-vis his amirs, by sending his vassals highly trained (meaning more valuable and prestigious) enslaved women and dancers as well as eunuchs. Al-Ẓāhir's son and successor al-Mustanṣir (r. 1036–94) received gifts of enslaved people from rulers in Yemen and the kingdom of Dāniyya (Denia) in al-Andalus (Islamic Iberia).[5] During al-Ẓāḥir's reign and with the aid of his aunt, the princess Sitt al-Mulk, the Fatimids began to repair diplomatic relations with the Byzantine empire. These relations had suffered during the reign of al-Ḥākim, who had ordered his forces to destroy the Church of the

Holy Sepulchre in Jerusalem in 1009. Treaties and diplomatic exchanges during al-Mustanṣir's rule were part of this rapprochement. In 1046, the Byzantine emperor Constantine IX Monomachos (r. 1042–55) sent to Egypt, along with a wealth of gold and other treasures, two hundred Muslim prisoners of war who had been held in captivity and who might otherwise have been used or sold as slaves. Seven years later, a Byzantine ruler[6] sent a gift to al-Mustanṣir that included enslaved Turkish boys and girls. For his part, al-Mustanṣir provided a Fatimid naval escort to safeguard Byzantine treasures that Constantine sent via Egypt for use in the reconstruction of the Holy Sepulchre.[7]

Gifts of enslaved people as part of regional and international diplomacy comprise the most conspicuous type of slave trading to eleventh-century Egypt found in historical sources. Despite its rich description relative to other kinds of slave trading, diplomatic gifts were only one mode of a multistranded slave trade that states, merchants, and everyday subjects used to traffic people to and within medieval Egypt. The Fatimid caliphate in Egypt supported a slave trade for its own purposes, particularly to acquire soldiers for its army. These state-sponsored trades were of less relevance to the majority of slave buyers, though the enslaved men and women who were initially bound to state elites did occasionally appear on the local resale market.[8] Most Egyptians during this era relied on a decentralized slave trade that was embedded as one part of a more regular long-distance trade in commodities and luxury goods. While this decentralized trade was the most important method that everyday subjects used to purchase enslaved people from outside of Egypt, this mode of buying was itself far less common than the local resale market, which is the subject of chapter 3.

In this chapter, I suggest that understanding the slave trade into Egypt requires us to examine each of these different strands or modes of slave trading that operated for distinct purposes and according to different conventions. Diplomatic slave-trading was an important part of geopolitical relations, but it was not perennial or reliable. Rather, diplomatic gifts occurred when political relations were being established, renewed, and reaffirmed. They were thus the exception rather than the rule as far as the overall slave trade is concerned.

Separating the trade into its different strands gives us a better understanding of how historical contingencies caused the geography and intensity of the slave trade to fluctuate over time. The workings of the slave trade also alert us to how states, nonruling elites, and the middling classes used slavery strategically.[9] The focus on the slave trade as a contingent set of strategies leads us to confront not just the demand for enslaved labor, but also the strategies of the polities that variously supplied slaves, facilitated a transit trade including slaves as cargo, permitted the slave raiding of outsiders, and sometimes resisted the delivery of slaves to expectant states and other buyers.[10]

Diplomatic Slavery

The Fatimid court chronicler al-Musabbiḥī (d. 1030) recorded the arrival of a diplomatic gift to Cairo in mid-June of the year 1024. During this month, "a gift (*hadiyya*) from the land of Nubia arrived, which included male slaves, female slaves, ebony wood, elephants, giraffes, and other things."[11] This specific *hadiyya* fits into a longer history of diplomacy conducted partly through reciprocal exchanges of goods and enslaved people between Islamic Egypt and the kingdoms of Nubia. The origins[12] of this exchange date to the middle of the seventh century, when the Muslim conquerors of Egypt, led by the third caliph ʿUthmān (r. 644–55), made an agreement with the Nubians on their southern border to cease hostilities. Though Muslim forces continued to expand westward across North Africa, and elsewhere across Eurasia, the Nubian forces repelled their initial raids. Later Muslim chroniclers reported that Nubian archers were so deadly that they could place their arrows in the pupils of their enemies' eyes.[13] Whether for that or some other reason, the first Muslim governor of Egypt sought a treaty with the Nubians.[14]

This specific diplomatic agreement came to be known as the *baqṭ*, from the Greek word for pact.[15] While no written version of this treaty survives, an eighth-century letter from the governor of Egypt to the Nubians indicates that both parties kept written records about the agreement and its modifications, at least through this period.[16] Scholars have reconstructed the terms of the seventh-century agreement from later writings, as is often necessary for the earliest history of the nascent Islamic empire. Nubia agreed to supply Muslim rulers with a number of enslaved people. In return, the Muslims would send wheat, cereals, and valuable textiles equal in value to that of the enslaved people delivered by the Nubians. The history of the *baqṭ*, both in the Middle Ages and in modern scholarship, is crucial because historians have often cited it as a main indicator of how the slave trade to Egypt functioned between the seventh and fourteenth centuries.[17]

Indeed, the *baqṭ* and diplomatic gifts like it are an important part of the story. But they aren't *the* story. The earliest written evidence for the *baqṭ* suggests that the terms of the agreement, as well as its fulfillment, were a source of frustration for one eighth-century Muslim governor of ʿAbbasid Egypt, Mūsā b. Kaʿb. In 758 Mūsā wrote a letter and sent it to the king of Nubia and Muqurra, who resided at this time in the city of Dongola, which was located on the east bank of the Nile

River in modern-day Sudan. In the letter, Mūsā forthrightly reminds the king that they had an agreement, which the Muslims had fulfilled. But, he continues, "you do not hand over to us what you owe of the *baqṭ* . . . and you do not return our slaves who run away to you."[18] Almost a century later, the Nubian ruler Zacharias II (ca. 822–40?)[19] rebuffed the demands of an envoy from Baghdad to send the ʿAbbasids gifts of enslaved people. His reasoning: "It is true that it is our duty to give tribute annually . . . but it was the duty of the king of the Arabs to send us tribute. . . . Now in as much as they have cut off [their tribute], we have also cut off [ours]."[20] Together this evidence shows that the *baqṭ* could not have been a sustained source of enslaved people for the ruling classes and other buyers in Egypt. Historian Jelle Bruning's research on the slave trade to ʿAbbasid Egypt supports this conclusion, as does the evidence from the Fatimid period.[21]

The medieval Egyptian historian al-Maqrīzī's (d. 1442) description of the *baqṭ* has in part led modern scholars to wrong conclusions about the durability of this seventh-century agreement. Al-Maqrīzī, who lived after Nubia had been conquered by the Mamluks, writes, erroneously, that the *baqṭ* was not a reciprocal exchange and that the Nubians had no claim to gifts from the Muslims.[22] The pre-Fatimid historian al-Masʿūdī (d. 956) reports that when the *baqṭ* exchange took place in 943, the 365 enslaved people included were designated for the state treasury (*bayt al-māl*) alone. An additional number of enslaved people, beyond the number included in the *baqṭ*, were designated for rulers and their officials in Aswan.[23] Even though some of these enslaved people were resold within Egypt for profit or for individual owners' prerogatives, it strains credulity to think that these sales were sufficient to satisfy the demand of the larger Egyptian market. Further, al-Maqrīzī appears to have revived the very term *baqṭ*, while al-Musabbiḥī, potentially an eyewitness to the arrival of gifts from Nubia in the eleventh century, only uses the word *hadiyya* (gift). This word choice matters because it suggests that, while gifts including enslaved people show up across time, the ways in which historical subjects understood these gifts were mutable and historically contingent.

Al-Musabbiḥī was a confidant of the Fatimid caliphs and was thus well positioned to record the caliphate's view of events in these years. Several months earlier, before the *hadiyya* from Nubia mentioned above, in August 1023, al-Musabbiḥī describes the arrival of another diplomatic mission. Significantly, this gift was not from the Nubians, but from the ruler of Muḥdatha, a settlement near Aswan, a man named Ibn Mukārim Abū Yazīd.[24] Ibn Mukārim was what we might call a petty ruler, or a vassal, for the Fatimids. He ruled over an Arab clan, the Rabīʿa, whose fortunes were connected in part to the gold and emerald

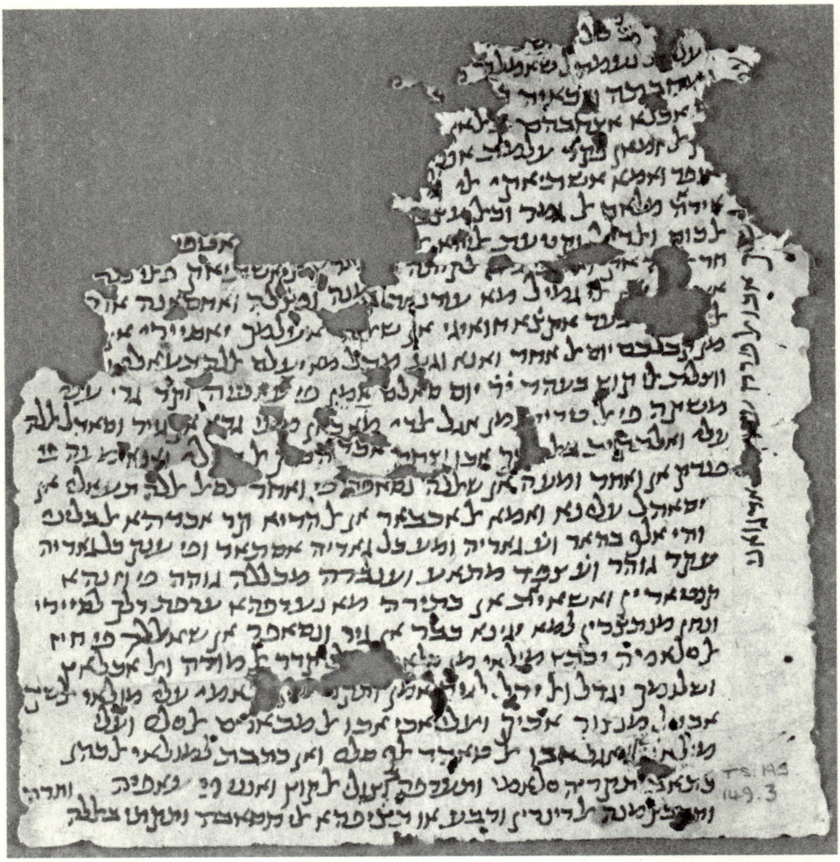

FIGURE 2.1. A merchant's letter describes the seizure of a diplomatic gift (*hadiyya*) that was meant for the Fatimid caliph in Cairo, ca. 1060s. T-S AS 149.3. Paper. 13.5 × 14.5 cm. Reproduced by kind permission of the Syndics of Cambridge University Library.

mining in the Red Sea hills of southern Egypt, an enterprise which itself was known to use enslaved labor.[25] His father had served the prior Fatimid caliph, al-Ḥākim (r. 996–1021), who bestowed on him the honorary title "Treasure of the State (*kanz al-dawla*)" for his leadership in suppressing a major rebellion in Upper Egypt almost two decades earlier. Al-Musabbiḥī again uses the term *hadiyya* to describe both Ibn Mukārim's gift of 1023 and the Nubian gift of 1024.

Al-Musabbiḥī's use of the term *hadiyya* helps us make sense of a *geniza* letter of which only about one-half survives (figure 2.1). It describes what we might today call a major international incident. The letter's author, probably a merchant, wrote to his associates in Fustat after he had arrived in the city of Qūṣ on the Nile. Qūṣ was a major point of transit for people, goods, and information along the routes between Cairo, the Red Sea port of ʿAydhāb, and to points beyond, including Yemen and India.[26] As merchant letter-writers frequently did, he relayed information relevant to the safety of trade and travel across these connected regions. "As for the news (*akhbār*)," he writes, "al-Bulyanī has seized the *hadiyya* (gift)." The writer details its important contents: "It contained 1,000 sacks of goods (*bahār*); seventy *jāriya*; each slave girl with a eunuch (*ustādh*) and a jeweled necklace around her neck; 70 trunks of textiles; an amber chain studded with jewels weighing two-hundred pounds; and many other things of which I have no knowledge."[27]

Though the letter itself does not mention who sent this *hadiyya*, a later historical source suggests the answer. The Yemeni author Idrīs ʿImād al-Dīn (d. 1468) wrote *ʿUyūn al-akhbār* (*Flowing Springs of History*) on the basis of sources that Fatimid rulers had sent to Yemen before the final collapse of the caliphate in 1171.[28] In it, Idrīs describes the bold seizure of a *hadiyya* sent by the ruler of Yemen ʿAlī b. Muḥammad al-Ṣulayḥī (d. 1066 or 1080?)[29] to the Fatimid caliph al-Mustanṣir. The control of this *hadiyya* became a pawn in a protracted civil war (*fitna*) between the Turkish and Black African factions of the Fatimid army that erupted in 1062 when the Turkish contingent attacked African forces, whom they perceived as rivals for higher pay and political influence. Turkish troops received the gift in Aswan and oversaw its loading onto ships for the journey down the Nile to Cairo. But a group of Black infantrymen intercepted the convoy of treasures, enslaved people, and diplomats. The Black troops then escorted the convoy to the city of Asyūṭ, about 450 kilometers north of Aswan. Al-Bulyanī, who is mentioned in the *geniza* letter, is probably either a reference to the leader of the African infantrymen who commandeered the *hadiyya* or of another armed group that was associated with the settlement of al-Bulyanā, located between Aswan and Asyūṭ.[30] The African troops brought the gift to Cairo, where Turkish forces attacked and defeated them.

The specific fate of the enslaved women and eunuchs is not reported, though it seems they were delivered to al-Mustanṣir along with the other treasures.[31] In 1069 al-Mustanṣir was compelled to sell valuable gifts from the Fatimid treasury to pay his soldiers during the latter stages of this same civil war. The leader of the insurgent Turkish faction, Ibn Ḥamdān, continued to defy al-Mustanṣir and fled Cairo for Alexandria. Before al-Mustanṣir's forces killed him for his insurrectionist ways, Ibn Ḥamdān had sent his own *hadiyya* to the Byzantine emperor Romanos IV Diogenes in 1071. Emperor Romanos reciprocated and sent gifts to Ibn Ḥamdān.[32]

The evidence for the diplomatic slave trade to eleventh-century Egypt supports two main conclusions. First, and mainly, that diplomatic slave trading was primarily a form of politics. Such gift exchanges were not perennial, or even regular. Exchanges of enslaved people, and luxury gifts more generally, reflect specific historical circumstances in which diplomatic relationships were being created, revived, or maintained. Polities withheld such gifts when relations deteriorated.[33] There was a proliferation of diplomatic slave-trading with Egypt in the eleventh-century because it was a time of geopolitical realignment. The configuration of power in the Islamic imperium was in flux as the Fatimids were ascendant in Egypt and the Levant while the ʿAbbasid caliphate, centered in Iraq, experienced political fragmentation. Sovereigns and vassals sent gifts to the Fatimid caliphate as part of their own political strategies. Diplomatic slave-trading to Fatimid Egypt largely disappears from the sources after the 1060s, the time at which this caliphate experienced internal strife and territorial loss. The intensification of military confrontations between Islamic polities and European Crusader forces in the late eleventh century further upended the earlier conditions that had encouraged diplomatic slave-trading through gifts, though exchanges of prisoners were a part of wartime diplomacy.[34]

The second conclusion about the diplomatic slave trade to Egypt is that scholars writing about the *baqṭ* should use this term with more historical specificity. For the *baqṭ* is a specific example of a more general practice that predated and outlived the specific agreement made between Islamic Egypt and the Nubian kingdom in the seventh century. In both narrative and documentary sources (e.g., in a Fatimid chronicle and a merchant letter from the eleventh century), writers describe all diplomatic gifts containing enslaved people as *hadiyyas*.[35] The salient point is that the use of *baqṭ* to describe all gifts from Nubia to Egypt is an anachronism that flattens historical dynamism and, in some cases, retroactively imposes a revisionist view onto centuries of contingent interactions.[36] It follows that historians should not use the notion of the *baqṭ*, or evidence of diplomatic slave-trading more generally, to extrapolate a census of the slave trade forward in time.[37] The value of the evidence for this trade lies in what it tells us about specific historical moments and about how diplomatic strategies impinged upon the lives of people who were enslaved and trafficked accordingly.

The State-Sponsored Slave Trade

Another major strand of the Fatimid-era slave trade to Egypt was the state-driven trafficking of men for use in the army.[38] Military slavery, encompassing the use of both enslaved and freed men, was an ongoing feature of the medieval Islamic world. It was the ʿAbbasid caliphate that first used this strategy from the ninth century onward, as its rulers and their challengers sought to marshal powerful and loyal fighting forces.[39] In Baghdad and, briefly, in Samarra, the troops were primarily Turkish and brought from Central Asian lands. Islamic polities from North Africa to North India later adopted the strategic use of unfree fighting forces from different regions outside of the *dār al-Islām*. In Ifrīqiyya, the Aghlabids imported African fighting men via trans-Saharan trade. In Ṭūlūnid and Ikhshīdid Egypt, the governors used men from across Africa in their infantry. When the Fatimids conquered Ifrīqiyya, and then Egypt, they continued to use and acquire these forces.[40]

Evidence for the state-sponsored slave trade to Fatimid and Ayyubid Egypt lies primarily in descriptions of the armies' demographics and hardly at all in discussions of how they were trafficked to and within Egypt. The descriptions show that the Fatimid army was multiethnic and that it comprised a mix of enslaved, freed, and free soldiers.[41] While medieval chroniclers enumerate the size of armies in specific times and places, it is frequently difficult to evaluate the accuracy of these reports. In his eleventh-century travelogue, Nāṣir-i Khusraw (d. ca. 1072–78) claims that a Fatimid military procession (ca. 1050) included 20,000 Kitāmī (also Kutāmī, from the Maghrib) and 15,000 Bāṭālī cavalrymen from North Africa; 20,000 Maṣmūdī men (from modern-day Morocco); 10,000 "Easterners (Turks and Persians)"; 50,000 Ḥijāzī Bedouin cavalrymen; 30,000 eunuch-cavalry (both Black and white, called *ustādhs*); 30,000 *Zanj* (East African) saber-wielding men; 10,000 "palace men" of various origins; and 30,000 "purchased slaves"—for an improbably high total of 215,000 troops.[42] We come closer to a more plausible number in a report attributed to al-Qāḍī al-Fāḍil (d. 1200), an official who served both Fatimid and Ayyubid rulers. He states that the registry of the Fatimid army bureau included 40,000 cavalrymen and 30,000 infantrymen toward the end of this caliphate's reign.[43] These various forces themselves comprised both free and unfree men. Al-Maqrīzī's discussion of a ninth-century Egyptian army provides a rough sense of possible proportions in his description of a force made up of 24,000 Turks, 40,000 Blacks, and 7,000 free, salaried soldiers[44]—one implication of this latter juxtaposition being that the Turks and Blacks were mostly enslaved and freed men.

We need to take these numbers with a grain of salt. Two scholars of premodern Islam have suggested a rule of thumb: "Numbers below 1,000 should be divided by 10, those over 1,000 by 100."[45] This chapter's focus, like the book's, is not on achieving a census of the medieval slave trade. Instead, its concern is with what medieval authors sought to convey in reporting the numbers as they did. Both the proportions of different groups present, and how specific groups enter the narrative sources when they do, suggest a particular history. What is most important to note is that it was the state that had the resources to purchase, import, then maintain large numbers of soldiers who were essential to their dynasties' survival in times of war and civil strife. An episode from the second half of the ninth century underscores this point. The 'Abbasid caliphate assigned a former Turkish slave-soldier, Aḥmad b. Ṭūlūn (d. 884), to be governor of Egypt. Initially, the 'Abbasids limited Ibn Ṭūlūn's access to financial resources so he could not acquire an army so large that it would permit him to become independent from the Iraqi center, at this time the city of Samarra. However, a rebellion against the 'Abbasids in Palestine compelled the caliphate to grant funds to Ibn Ṭūlūn so he could field an army and help suppress this revolt. These resources, along with increased tax revenues that Ibn Ṭūlūn exacted in Egypt, allowed him to purchase his own troops, who were said to be people from the realms of Byzantium (*Rūm*) and "the Blacks."[46]

In the centuries that followed, successive ruling dynasties in Egypt would periodically mount intensive efforts to purchase and import soldiers. As Nāṣir-i Khusraw's parade description suggests, one such period of intensive recruitment and trafficking was the first half of the eleventh century. During the reign of al-Ḥākim (996–1021), African troops became a larger part of the Fatimid army. The succeeding caliphs, al-Ẓāhir and al-Mustanṣir, continued to purchase African troops who were deployed throughout Lower and Upper Egypt, whom the chronicler Ibn Muyassar (d. 1200) calls interchangeably "the purchased slaves," "the Black slaves," "the slaves," or "the Blacks."[47] The intensification of this state-sponsored slave trade for the purpose of soldiers coincided with the rise of al-Ẓāhir's Black concubine, Raṣad, who became the mother of the next caliph, al-Mustanṣir. The Jewish courtier who gave Raṣad to al-Ẓāhir converted to Islam and became a minister for Raṣad when she was the dowager, since al-Mustanṣir was too young to rule immediately after his father's death.[48] The written sources observe this with some antipathy, as Black troops were often pitted, in fact and rhetorically, against other army factions organized by ethnic loyalties, the Turks in particular.[49] Thus the exigencies of dynastic rule often point us to the contingent history of the medieval slave trade and suggest how the volume of this trade could be scaled up under specific circumstances to traffic larger numbers of people than the more regular and decentralized trade could carry.[50] The sudden influx of, in this case, enslaved Black soldiers during the suspected shadow reign of a freed Black woman is important context for the discussion in the next chapter of how "Black" and "slave" became conflated in Egyptian writing of this era.

State resources matter because the logistics of trafficking large numbers of people were complicated and expensive. Though there are no surviving descriptions of the logistics of trafficking troops to Egypt in the period between 1000 and 1250, we can glean some insights from Idrīs's description of how Turkish forces supervised the loading onto ships in Aswan of the 140 enslaved people, textiles, and other valuables that the Ṣulayḥids sent to Fatimid Cairo from the Yemen. It took the soldiers thirty days to organize a convoy of ships and to dispatch it down the Nile.[51] This enterprise entailed hiring ship captains and crews, as well as the expenses of housing and feeding the enslaved cargo. This anecdote speaks to the overall complexity and cost of moving large groups of unfree people across large distances.

Gwyn Campbell and Marek Jankowiak have both considered these logistical challenges in greater detail.[52] Campbell, in his study of the maritime slave trade out of East Africa, emphasizes the challenges of "space, sanitation, and provisions" aboard ships that were among the factors that mitigated against using ships packed with enslaved people across the Indian Ocean. Jankowiak, who focused on the overland trade in Eurasia, also emphasizes the costs, risks, and instability of an overland trade that specialized in moving enslaved people *en masse*.

What were some of those risks? Well, ships sank. Raiders attacked caravans. Diseases spread in close quarters and as people encountered new contagions to which they had no acquired immunity. In the case of shipwrecks close enough to shore and in the Nile, inanimate commodities could be recovered by specialized salvage divers—but that was costly, too.[53] But the human cargo—the people—often drowned.[54] Thus another cost of the slave trade was the potentially devastating loss of capital that accompanied the death of human "cargo." As a conservative estimate, the 140 enslaved people reportedly trafficked to Egypt by the Ṣulayḥids could have sold on the open market for between 2,800 and 5,600 dinars. Before the advent of insurance for slave-trading ventures,[55] few private traders would have been able to sustain such a loss on their own or in the kinds of partnerships they used to mitigate personal risk.[56] When a Muslim merchant in eleventh-century Ifrīqiyya went bankrupt, he owed a combined sum of 4,000 dinars. The implications of such a huge debt were such that the local ruler intervened to manage repayments to creditors, some of whom were forced to absorb significant losses.[57]

Sovereigns and their ministers were some of the few parties who could marshal such resources to begin with and who could absorb any such losses. Even if we assume that the chroniclers are overstating the numbers of troops in the army and we minimize their figures accordingly, we are still left with a scale of slave trading that far exceeds the volume of people that traders trafficked when the state's interests and resources were not in play.

This mode of slave trading is better documented in the Ayyubid period and especially for the subsequent Mamluk sultanate. Hannah Barker shows that sultans were proactive about seizing opportunities to acquire large numbers of slaves when there was a pulse in the supply of enslaved people due to events and contingencies in the regions that they exploited for martial labor. For example, when the Ayyubid sultan al-Ṣāliḥ Najm al-Dīn Ayyūb (r. 1240–49) learned that the Mongol conquest of Russia had led to a spike in the availability of enslaved people, he sent merchants to purchase them "in great quantity."[58] This instance demonstrates how a state could pour massive resources into securing enslaved people for its strategic interests. Most merchants who staked their own capital—even those who worked in partnerships to mitigate risk—did not have the resources to specialize in the long-distance trafficking of large numbers of enslaved people. Egyptian merchants did, however, participate in the slave trade on a much smaller scale.

Mercantile Trade Within Egypt and Beyond

The periodic rhythms of the diplomatic and state-sponsored trades were complemented by a third mode of decentralized slave trading organized through the protean economic and social networks that made much of medieval travel, communication, and trade possible. In contrast to the larger numbers of enslaved people trafficked by states, this mercantile mode of slave trading appears to us as a trickle in which slave buyers organized the trafficking of small numbers of people, frequently single individuals, as one part of a mixed cargo that included other luxury and staple items. Documentary evidence for how slave imports operated is sparse for the period between 1000 to 1250. The little information that survives suggests that the specialist slave traders (*al-nakhkhāsūn*, sg. *al-nakhkhās*) were stationary importers and not merchants who managed the physical trafficking of large groups over long distances.[59]

The earliest datable cluster of *geniza* letters that shows mercantile slave trading dates to the 1040s through the 1060s.[60] The cluster is a group of five letters sent between the members of a well-documented merchant group of which Nahray b. Nissim (d. ca. 1098) was the most prominent member.[61] Not only do Nahray's own letters and accounts provide great insight into the eleventh-century mercantile economy at large, but other letters sent to him show that Egyptian Jews did not prefer or frequent the standing, urban slave markets that are mentioned in Arabic sources from this same era.[62] Instead, prospective buyers turned to their family networks, business associates, and well-placed communal figures for help finding a "suitable slave," a locution whose meaning was flexible based on the prospective buyers' desires. In other cases, it was a family member, usually a husband or father, who sought to purchase a slave for his wife or daughter.

The merchant and widower Mardūkh b. Mūsā lived in Alexandria with his children when he wrote to Nahray, then in Fustat, in 1047 for help in purchasing an enslaved girl to work in his household after he had been unable to find an acceptable person for sale among his Jewish associates in Alexandria. Mardūkh's letter reveals that he had previously asked Nahray a question about avoiding an oath that he was under pressure to take for an unspecified reason. If Nahray did not think there was a way out of the oath, then Mardūkh asks: "Please, my master, secure a slave-girl (*jāriya*) for me who is suitable for personal service (*lil-khidma*) from among those who are reliable, and who people testify is chaste. . . . If such a thing is possible, tell me in your letter what her price is."[63] Mardūkh's linkage of the oath and the purchase of a "chaste" slave girl is conspicuous, and we do not know the precise details behind it. One plausible explanation is that Mardūkh had earlier come under suspicion for having sex with an enslaved woman in his household, which was not permitted in Jewish law. Jewish men in Egypt who did have sex with their enslaved servants could be told to sell them or risk excommunication from the community.[64] When Mardūkh complains in this letter that there is no one at his home to "bring me a cup of water, and I am in utmost need of someone to serve me," he may well be lamenting his recent loss of an enslaved laborer and not just making an allusion to his widower status.[65] It seems unlikely that there were no enslaved people available to purchase in Alexandria, and more likely that Mardūkh sought to minimize any controversy over his purchase of a new slave locally by enlisting the aid of one of Jewish Egypt's most respected and well-connected merchant elites.

Later eleventh-century correspondence sent to Nahray shows how he and his associates managed the sales of one or two individuals within Egypt.[66] In two letters, Nahray's cousin and business associate, Nathan b. Nahray, asks where he should send a *jāriya*.[67] Nathan was also concerned about the logistics of paying customs duties for her: How much will the taxes cost? Will I pay it at the town gate? Will I sell her immediately upon arrival? Or will I need to keep her with me and pay for her maintenance?[68] It appears that Nathan planned to bring the enslaved woman with him from Fustat down the Nile to the town of Malīj, where Nahray was at the time. There are no further letters between Nathan and Nahray that discuss how the trafficking of this *jāriya* was completed. However, a letter some months later to Nahray from another of his merchant associates, Yeshuʿa b. Ishmael in Alexandria, discusses the sale of another *jāriya*.[69] Yeshuʿa confirms Nahray's view that this was "a good sale" and expresses relief that they obtained a price exceeding 16 dinars (possibly what they had paid for her, or the lowest price they were willing to accept). He then reports how much money Nahray needed to collect, from whom, and in what currency. Ten dinars were to come from their associate Ezra, and the remainder of the unspecified price from the unnamed buyer. Toward the end of the letter, Yeshuʿa suggests that Nahray direct Ezra to use some of the proceeds of this sale, it appears, to settle other debts or to purchase specific goods.

Whether these letters to Nahray represent a single sale or two different ones, their overall significance is similar. Here Nahray, Nathan, Yeshuʿa, and Ezra worked together to sell an enslaved person as part of their larger business activities and for a profit. The discussion of this woman's sale is mixed in with instructions and information about other commodities like pitch, lacquer, wheat, natron (a mineral salt with various uses), oils, and so forth. The Nahray correspondence corroborates the patterns evident in the Jewish merchant letters discussed above, between Egypt, Yemen, and India nearly a century later. First, there is no evidence that Jewish merchants specialized in the slave trade or even made it a significant part of their commercial businesses. Second, as in Nahray's activities, the mercantile mode of medieval human trafficking was usually embedded in local and interregional trade writ large as part of a mixed cargo.

Families and individuals, even those who were not involved in mercantile work, used letters to arrange human trafficking. Decades after Mardūkh the Alexandrian's request, a woman approaching her third trimester of pregnancy wrote to her uncle, a deputy overseer in the town of al-Bahnasā south of Cairo.[70] She asks him to buy her a five- or six-year-old "Black" girl from an importer who specialized in the sale of enslaved people and animals (*al-jālib*) and adds that she had heard there were many enslaved people available for purchase in the town.[71] Enslaved children as young as two years old were not uncommon in Egyptian *geniza* households.[72] Perhaps this mother-to-be could not find a child to purchase locally, or she was unhappy with the children whom she could purchase. It is more likely that she trusted her uncle to find her a young child for purchase in al-Bahnasā, where rumor had it that there many newly enslaved and imported people to be bought.

Merchant and family letters preserved in the Cairo *geniza* illustrate how prospective slave owners turned to their family and professional networks to arrange the trafficking of individuals to Fustat from afar, and between distant cities and villages within Egypt. In the fall of 1140, Khalaf b. Isaac in Aden wrote to his associate Ḥalfon ha-Levi b. Nethaniel in Egypt.[73] These two men were active in the Indian Ocean trade that flowed through this Yemeni port city, and they corresponded regularly about transactions and other business matters. In this letter, Khalaf tells Ḥalfon about strife in the city caused by fighting between rival factions. He reports on expenses and gives instructions for what kinds of textiles to purchase on his behalf, as merchants routinely did for one another. He also reports that some of their associates had drowned in a shipwreck, in which a shipment of corals was lost. During the Jewish festival of Sukkot, Khalaf adds, a ship arrived from "the land of the *Zanj*," northeast or east Africa, carrying newly enslaved people (*raqīq*).[74] Khalaf regrets that he was not able to purchase a male servant (*waṣīf*) for Ḥalfon.[75] In this same era (1137–47), another Jewish merchant, Maḥrūz b. Jacob in Aden, wrote to Sulaymān b. Abū Zikrī Kohen in Egypt before his return to India. Maḥrūz writes that he was glad to have learned that "the slave (*al-ʿabd*)" had reached Sulaymān in "complete safety."[76] In 1148, Sulaymān would again write to his father in Yemen with news about upheaval in the family's hometown of Sijilmāsa in Morocco. At one point he interjects, "Father, a small request. Because we have no slave girl (*jāriya*), might your associate—God willing—have one?" before turning abruptly to other business.[77]

When one considers the expenses and dangers of travel, not to mention the time it took, it might seem odd that Egyptian slave owners took the expense and risk of importing someone from India or East Africa when there was a bustling resale market within Egypt. So, why did they do it? Many buyers preferred imported slaves because it lent further prestige and exoticism to their possession. One trader who had recently departed Kollam (Quilon) in India for travel westward, wrote to his family in Fustat: "I have bought for Sitt [a]l-Ḥusn a slave girl (*jāriya*) who is six years of age, pearl bracelets, [. . .], clothing, and red silk."[78] He explained that he would give the young girl to someone who was returning to Egypt with a merchant convoy called "the Kārim."[79] The place of this six-year-old child in this slave owner's imaginary is also reflected in the names that buyers like him chose for her and others like her: Incense, Musk, Gazelle, Ruby, Gold, Pearl, and Turquoise.[80] Buyers of course hoped for their living adornments to be doubly useful as both laborers and status symbols. Slave owners who could afford the added expenses and risks of importing a young child from such distances likely also saw an additional benefit: the child's age, along with the language barrier, would have made her seem easier to control and mold. As for the experience of this child during her long, coerced journey, and her life prospects in bondage, these topics I explore further in chapter 7.

Once in Egypt, the Nile River was a corridor for regional and intercity human trafficking. Thus, an enslaved person would be passed to yet another set of handlers. A set of instructions for such human trafficking within Egypt is preserved in a partly destroyed letter.[81] The preserved text shows that the writer asked an associate to deliver a separate letter to "Abraham (Ibrāhīm) the slave trader (*al-nakhkhās*)" so that he would purchase an enslaved servant (*waṣīfa*) for a man nicknamed "the Diadem (*al-Nezer*)."[82] The author continues:

> Take her and deposit her with someone convenient until you go down[83] (the Nile). Deliver her and accompany her yourself. However much it costs for her provisions, renting her space on a ship, or otherwise—I will pay you. If there is a remainder from her price [. . .] I will pay it from what you owe [. . .] with you and deposit [. . .] Joseph, my associate.[84]

It is unclear whether this *waṣīfa* was meant to be the Diadem's personal slave, or whether his role was to receive her and to facilitate her further transport or resale.

This ambiguity underscores an important fact. The mercantile slave trade was decentralized and flexible, and it also involved the cooperation of specialist slave traders and a host of other men, whose participation in a slave transaction was only one facet of the services they provided to their known associates when needed. The Diadem's associate not only appointed the recipient to use a professional slave trader (*al-nakhkhās*) to purchase a slave, but also to "take her," "deposit her with someone," then "deliver her and accompany her." The *nakhkhās* (slave trader) tasked with buying a girl for the *Diadem* should have, according to the prescriptive advice of one twelfth-century market inspector (*muḥtasib*), kept a notebook in which he recorded the names of the buyer and seller, the name of the enslaved person sold, and her religious identity.[85] Her religion should have been noted to ensure that non-Muslims were not purchasing Muslims, and also to verify that the person to be sold had not been unlawfully enslaved.[86] As the next chapter illustrates, the scribes (possibly including the Diadem) who handled all manner of business from marriage documents to real estate deeds also kept notebooks in which they recorded slave sales.

Geniza evidence shows that most transactions among Jewish and Christian buyers did not involve agents or brokers unless there were extenuating circumstances. In the case of slave sales, it's likely that the owner appointed an agent because the owner could not, or did not want to, travel to conduct a sale in person. In one case, an unnamed author complains in a letter (or petition) to a judge that he has brought an enslaved woman to Fustat to sell. His plans, however, did not go as expected. He then wrote to ask the judge (*al-dayyan*) to take the woman from a third party and give her to yet another man, whom the writer "heard is a broker (*dallāl*)." The broker would then arrange her sale and be paid a commission.[87]

Fatimid-era Jewish merchants were not the only people who organized the trafficking of enslaved individuals using their personal networks. An ʿAbbasid-era letter (ca. late eighth/early ninth century) found in Edfu, Egypt, shows that there, too, someone wrote a letter on behalf of a woman who sought to purchase a "Black" woman or girl from a slave dealer. The recipient is told that another associate was informed of the plan and already had the gold for the purchase.[88] The author of a Mamluk-era letter found in the Red Sea port of al-Qusayr informs the recipient that an associate named ʿAbd al-Raḥman had been deputized to sell a *jāriya*. He continues with an order: "If the slave girl, whose sale has been certified, has arrived at your place, dispatch her to us immediately! You [already] know the legal procedures of [her] guardianship."[89]

These merchant letters illustrate a durable phenomenon that Jankowiak calls "capillary trade networks." These capillary connections complemented the earlier stages of slaving in which larger numbers of people were first enslaved and then transported to regional nodes known to have active markets.[90] Only Khalaf b. Isaac's letter from twelfth-century Aden directly references an earlier stage of the slave trade in which people were captured or purchased outside of the *dār al-Islām* and then imported into it, in this case "newly imported slaves (*raqīq*)" from "the lands of the *Zanj*."[91] The pregnant woman's request that her uncle in al-Bahnasā purchase an enslaved child for her implies the presence of a specialized importer within Egypt, whom she calls a *jālib* (an importer of animals and enslaved people).[92] We do not know, however, if specialized importers accumulated enslaved people for sale in large groups, whether they acquired them one or two at a time from a variety of different sources, or through both methods.[93] It is rare to find specific information about how individuals were coerced into slavery in the first place, but the *geniza* provides a glimpse that complements the descriptions of slave raiding found in medieval narrative writings.

Methods of Enslavement

Not surprisingly, enslavers used violence to force free people into slavery. In world-historical terms, it was warfare that most commonly led to enslavement. Victorious warriors could choose capture and enslavement in lieu of the mass murder of their surviving enemies and their foes' dependents. The victors would take some people as war booty. Others could be sold or ransomed to generate further profits. In periods of large-scale conquest, massive numbers of enslaved people flooded the slave markets, as they sometimes did during the Islamic expansion of the seventh and eighth centuries, the military campaigns of the Ghaznavids into eleventh-century South Asia, and during the Mongol conquests in the thirteenth and fourteenth centuries.[94] Maḥmūd of Ghaznī (r. 998–1030) launched a military campaign into the Indian subcontinent. Chroniclers report that his conquests generated such great numbers of newly enslaved captives that the prices for them plummeted.[95]

In Egypt, the capture of prisoners in warfare was not the primary way that the Fatimids, Ayyubids, and their subjects acquired enslaved people for the greater Egyptian market. Instead, most Egyptian buyers ultimately relied on the predation of professional raiders and kidnappers who operated at and beyond Egypt's African frontiers.[96] The Eastern Desert was particularly known as a region that slavers exploited. This region, about the size of Minnesota, lies between the Nile River, the Gulf of Suez, and the Red Sea. From antiquity through the Fatimid period and beyond, the Eastern Desert was a site of continuous habitation, pastoralism, farming, trade, and the transit of people and goods. Mining for gold and other minerals was an important source of wealth in the Eastern Desert, which was part of a larger geologic formation rich in such resources, the Arabian-Nubian Shield. This was especially the case in the eighth and ninth centuries, when there was a veritable gold rush to the desert on the part of Egyptians. The operators of these mines acquired enslaved people and put them to work extracting these precious goods. This desert is part of the Nile's fluvial plain and is crisscrossed with seasonally flowing wadis. The available groundwater was enough to support durable and significant human settlement, which slave raiders exploited for their own gains.[97]

Travel writers from the Fatimid era report that slavers organized raids to capture people in the Nubian and Eastern deserts for trafficking north to Egypt. Nāṣir-i Khusraw described the tactics that raiders used to capture people in "the province of Nubia" south of Aswan: "Traders go there taking beads, combs, and trinkets and bring back slaves to Egypt, where the slaves are either Nubian or Greek."[98] As Nāṣir traveled toward the Hijāz (western Arabia), he passed through the Red Sea port of ʿAydhāb. There he wrote about the Bajawi (Beja) people who lived in the mountains outside of the city: "This nation, the Bajawis, who live in this desert, are not a bad people and do not steal or make raids but tend their flocks. Muslims and others, however, kidnap their children and take them to sell in the cities of Islam."[99]

More than a century later, the Jewish traveler Benjamin of Tudela wrote his report about Egypt in 1170 at the very end of the Fatimid era, when the future Ayyubid sultan Ṣalāḥ al-Dīn (Saladin, 1138–93) was on the verge of consolidating his power in Cairo.[100] Reading Benjamin's description of slave raiding alongside the information provided in Nāṣir's writings is productive:

> When the people of Aswan go raiding in their land, they carry with them bread, grain, raisins, and figs. They throw this toward (these people), who come to get it. (In this way), they obtain many prisoners and sell them in Egypt and all the surrounding kingdoms.[101]

The use of treats as bait to lure unsuspecting people into traps for their enslavement, along with enslavement by opportunistic kidnapping, are topoi in literature that predate Nāṣir and Benjamin's writings.[102] The idea that people could be entrapped with treats clearly reflects racist ideas. The reality is that people were captured violently, and the demographics of the enslaved population in Egypt show the result of this activity in Egypt's African hinterlands. This racial thinking and its consequences I analyze in the next chapter.

The *geniza* preserves rare documentary evidence of this activity. A letter sent by two men to an associate in Cairo describes the unusual case of a *waṣīfa* who appeared before a Muslim judge. Apparently, she had once told others that she was a Muslim when she was kidnapped and enslaved in ʿAydhāb when she went to a water well. When pressed by the judge, the woman claimed to be Jewish and stated that she had nothing to do with Muslims. Her identity, and the reasons for the discrepancy between her statements, remain unknown to us.[103] Nevertheless, her reported speech is rare, concrete evidence of the persistent and ugly reality that lay behind literary topoi of enslavement by kidnapping.[104]

Who were the people that led these raids and kidnappings and then sold their captives into slavery? A key to identifying these slavers lies in the human geography and political economy of Nubian territories and the Eastern Desert, two regions that partly overlapped east of the Nile. This was a geographically contiguous zone of different polities competing for similar resources, such as gold, minerals, exotic animals, and humans for enslavement. The control of these resources was part of what gave the rulers here political legitimacy and power.[105] The Bajawi, or Beja, people whom Nāṣir mentions were among these groups and, crucially for this history, they included different kin groups who were sometimes at odds with each other and who variously occupied the

Eastern Desert between Egypt and Ethiopia. The fortunes of different Beja tribes and the other groups in Beja territories demonstrate that they were both enslavers *and* enslaved.[106]

For most of its medieval history, the land of Nubia was not united as a single kingdom. Rather, there were three kingdoms: Nobadia in the north, Makuria to its south, and Alwa below it. Nobadia and Makuria appear to have united sometime between the latter sixth and early eighth centuries. The political relationship between Makuria and Alwa fluctuated over time through hostilities and periods of peace. In the eleventh century, as the Fatimids and Nubians sought to establish diplomatic ties, the ruling families of Makuria and Alwa made an alliance solidified through marriage. The result was the first unified Nubian state from Nobadia to Alwa in over seven hundred years.

The Nubian name for this supra-regional kingdom is Dotawo. Dotawo maintained relatively peaceful relations with Fatimid Egypt, though it was not without its own internal strife and crises of political succession. Dotawo-Egypt relations changed markedly after the Ayyubid takeover of Egypt in 1171, when Saladin and his successors launched attacks into northern Nubia. Over the next century, Nubian rulers remained independent of Egypt and even launched attacks against the sultans there. Non-Nubian sources from this period depict a Nubian kingdom in increasing political turmoil. In contrast, Nubian documentary sources give the impression that social and economic life continued much as before, despite conflicts with foreign powers like Egypt.[107]

The reports of a late-tenth-century Fatimid envoy to Nubia, Ibn Sulaym al-Aswānī illuminates these disparate fortunes.[108] Ibn Sulaym presented a report to the Fatimid caliph al-ʿAzīz (r. 975–96), the product of his fact-finding mission to these lands. Not only had Ibn Sulaym read what prior Arabic writings had to say about his subject, he also consulted state documents from Egypt and Nubia and is even said to have met the Nubian kings of Makuria and Alwa. Beyond these sources, he gained intelligence from the courtiers and ordinary folk whom he met during his travels.

In his reports, Ibn Sulaym emphasizes the role that slavery and enslavement played in the regions' politics. Ibn Sulaym observes that the governor of Nubian al-Marīs in the north, close to Islamic territory, "receives all and answers all by giving slaves."[109] Farther south there was a garrison at Upper Maqs and another Nubian governor whose army was known to "raid urban and suburban populations" secretly.[110] This governor kept a tight control on hard currency to facilitate trade with Muslims to their north. In his and his subjects' trade with their southern neighbors, there was a barter economy that used "slaves, cattle, camels, iron, and grain."[111] Farther south still, the king of Nubian Alwa was said to enslave his own subjects arbitrarily. Ibn Sulaym viewed this as severe and oppressive conduct that the king's subjects were too afraid to contest.[112] Ibn Sulaym reports other instances about the enslaved—though he does not indicate of which Nubian polity they were subjects. Among the concubines of one late-ninth-century group, there were so many enslaved Nubian women that they acquired a reputation for being particularly cheap to buy.[113]

Recently deciphered Nubian sources found in Qaṣr Ibrīm show that the use of slaves in the barter economy continued at least into the twelfth and late thirteenth centuries. In November 1191, a Nubian woman sold the land and house she had inherited from her mother to another woman for "one male camel named 'Nubian,' 1 ornamental precious stone, 1 silver ring . . . and 1 slave."[114] In a land sale concluded during the reign of King David (r. 1268?–72 or 1275/76), a Nubian cleric (*eparch*) purchased a plot for the price of "eleven slaves and ten gold"[115] from one party and "eleven slaves, 8 gold, and [. . .] dirhams" from another.

Like the Nubians, the tribes of the Beja confederation and their subgroups were also agents, and sometimes targets, of the slave trade. Enslaved people were one major aspect of the Beja's wealth. Beja groups raided villages and towns and enslaved the inhabitants, including in Upper Egypt.[116] Their rulers exchanged enslaved people and rewarded their allies with them. Also like the Nubians, the Beja had diplomatic ties with the ʿAbbasid caliphs in Baghdad. Ibn Sulaym reports that the ʿAbbasid caliph al-Mutawakkil even made a *baqṭ* agreement with the Beja to establish peace following deadly raiding and fighting between Beja and the Muslims.[117] One Beja group, the Ḥadāriba, forged ties with the powerful Arab Rabīʿa group in Aswan, the same people who later sent enslaved people to the Fatimid caliphs as a gift.[118] Together, the Ḥadāriba and the Rabīʿa played central roles in the ninth-century Arab-Egyptian gold rush in the Eastern Desert. In their effort to control the mines, the Beja groups sometimes killed miners. They also provided enslaved labor for the mines, whom operators equipped with lanterns and ropes to descend below ground.[119]

The Beja's role in the slave trade would ostensibly seem to undermine Nāṣir-i Khusraw's description of this group as victims of slave raids by Muslims. Nāṣir's account is corroborated, however, by another roughly contemporaneous source written by the Iraqi Christian physician Ibn Buṭlān (d. 1066), who also visited Egypt in the eleventh century.[120] Drawing on earlier writings and, he explains, his own observations, Ibn Buṭlān wrote a treatise to advise slave buyers on how to select the right type of slave and to avoid being defrauded in the market. His guide brims with racial stereotypes about different types of people, types that I explore more fully in the next chapter. About the Beja, he bracingly writes:

> They are golden in color, with beautiful faces, smooth bodies, and tender flesh. If, as slave girls for pleasure, they are imported while they are still young, they are saved from mutilation, for they are circumcised and all the flesh from the upper part of their pudenda is incised with a razor until the bone appears. . . . Bravery and thievery are innate and ingrained in them; they cannot therefore be trusted with money and are unsuitable for use as treasurer or custodian.[121]

Another key to understanding the dynamics of enslavement in the Eastern Desert is recognizing that the Beja were a confederation of tribes whose relative power to enslave, and to protect their own members, differed. The Ḥadāriba, for example, enslaved others, but they are nowhere associated with slave status in the *geniza* corpus or, to my knowledge, in other Arabic documents. Moreover, there is not a single enslaved woman (or man) referred to as a Beja person. The *geniza* does show, however, that a different Beja subgroup was bound to households in Egypt. In 1190, the woman Saʿāda was purchased by a merchant in Cairo, and her ethnicity is identified as *Bāziyya*.[122] Just over a quarter-century later, the sale account of another unnamed woman describes her as *Bāziyya*; her sale is tersely recorded in a scribe's notebook among other transactions for real estate and the payment of debts.[123]

The *Bāziyya* (*Bāzī*) ethnicity is not a well-known one, and thus this people's presence in medieval Egypt as enslaved people has long gone unnoticed. Ibn Sulaym's writings provide the key to their identification. In his description of the Nubian country of Alwa, he tersely observes that "the race, called Bāza, from whose land come the birds [k]nown as the pigeons of Bāzīn," live in "the extremity" of the Beja lands.[124] Once again the juxtaposition of the documentary *geniza* with narrative sources enables us to understand both kinds of evidence more fully. In this specific case the sources illustrate why the Beja were known as both predator and prey in the Eastern Desert slave trade.

Famine and Enslavement

Another form of coercion that could lead to the enslavement of previously free people was hunger.[125] In Fatimid and Ayyubid Egypt, there were periodic famines precipitated by below-normal levels of the Nile's annual flooding and watering of agricultural lands. In his writings on the Fatimid era, al-Maqrīzī relates that parents in Upper Egypt (*al-Ṣaʿīd*) were forced to sell their children into slavery "for the cheapest prices" during one famine. He explains that "[s]ome of them were enslaved to people in Cairo. And some of them—too many to count—were transported to Syria, where they were sold to the corners of the earth as a captive is sold." He concludes laconically: "The slave girls were used for sex by their owners."[126]

The polymath ʿAbd al-Laṭīf al-Baghdādī (d. 1231) provides another chilling account of a famine between 1200 and 1202. When in consecutive years the Nile failed to flood, a multiyear famine followed. Al-Baghdādī reports graphically on the drought, the rising food prices, and large-scale emigration, and even provides horrific accounts of cannibalism driven by extreme hunger.[127] He bemoans that the famine led parents and others "who had no fear of God" to sell young girls and boys for cheap. "I myself was offered a pair of adolescent girls for a single dinar,"[128] he adds. Later, a mother asked him to purchase her daughter. When al-Baghdādī refused and explained to her that such an act was contrary to Islam, the mother pleaded in desperation that he take her as a gift. He observed that many of the newly enslaved people were trafficked to Iraq and "deepest Khurāsān."[129]

The reports of child sale by al-Maqrīzī and al-Baghdādī pose an interpretive challenge.[130] Were such practices underreported during "normal" times because they contravened Islamic law and morality, and because they happened illegally and outside of the institutions that produced paper trails? Or do these authors include these awful reports to emphasize just how terrible conditions became during times of famine?[131] The evidence does not allow us to answer these questions. I surmise that raiding and kidnapping were perennial sources of newly enslaved people in Egypt, though severe famine could lead to an increase in the number of children and others available for sale.

Durable generalizations about the slave trade in the Middle Ages must account not only for the demand and purchase of enslaved people, but also for the conditions that supported their initial enslavement and trafficking. This chapter's focus on the Nubian and Beja polities, and to a lesser extent on intermittent famines, has centered the role of structural factors and historical contingencies in large-scale enslavement that then fed the capillary networks that states and merchants used to traffic people to Egypt.

As with the Beja groups in the Eastern Desert, the plurality of Nubian polities and their intermittent rivalries went through cycles of competition and cooperation, as well as cycles of state formation and fragmentation. Competing polities and internal rivals viewed each other's members and subjects as legitimate targets for enslavement. In the wars and raids that took place across this vast and variegated geopolitical space, the aggressors violently enslaved their foes and, opportunistically, any vulnerable men, women, and children who lacked sufficient protection. Enslaved people served their captors in numerous ways: as laborers in mines and likely in domestic and agricultural settings, as exchangeable goods in transactions, as sex slaves, and as prestige gifts used in diplomacy and internal patronage networks. This history demonstrates that the slave trade to Islamic Egypt, and beyond to Syria and Iraq, is not a story of a stronger, more organized Arab-Muslim state extracting enslaved people from a less powerful, or disorganized, neighbor.

This chapter has argued that histories of the medieval slave trade in the Middle East must account for its fluctuating intensity and geography. Different modes of slave trading—diplomatic, state-sponsored, and mercantile—reflect different strategies and interests. This chapter has shown, for example, that the Egyptian-Nubian *baqṭ* was one specific instance of the more general category of diplomatic slave-trading. Diplomatic slave-trading is conspicuous in the narrative sources because chroniclers recorded these gifts as examples of imperial politics. Yet such diplomatic relations were subject to change and contingency. As historical evidence, these instances resist interpretations that would take the discrete shipment of, say, 140 enslaved women and eunuchs in a *hadiyya* from the Ṣulayḥids in the 1060s and then extrapolate that figure on an annual basis for any number of years.

This chapter has also illustrated how merchants and individuals who bought slaves used their business and personal networks to purchase and traffic enslaved people in small numbers. When we recognize the persistence of this decentralized mode of slave trading, it demands that we reevaluate how historians have interpreted some evidence. Among specialists, a well-known passage in the ninth-century work of the ʿAbbasid postmaster Ibn Khurradādhbih (d. 913) serves as a cautionary tale. He writes:

> Itinerary/itineraries of the Jewish merchants (known as) Rādhāniyya. . . . From the West they import eunuchs (*khadam*), young slaves of both sexes (*jawārī* and *ghilmān*), silk brocade (*dībāj*), beaver fur (*julūd al-khazz*), [pelts of] the sable (*sammūr*) and [other] furs, as well as swords.[132]

What did the slave trading of these so-called Rādhānite merchants look like? Did they traffic in large numbers of people, as did the Ṣulayḥid embassy that sent 140 enslaved people to Egypt? Or did they include small numbers of enslaved people among their larger, more diverse cargo of luxury goods, as did the Jewish and Muslim merchants discussed in this chapter?

Scholars have long interpreted Ibn Khurradādhbih's writing as evidence of a far-flung and voluminous trade in enslaved people. Instead, I argue that scholars have made Ibn Khurradādhbih's brief statement do more work than is reasonable in the historiography of the slave trade.[133] The Rādhānites more likely trafficked in small numbers of enslaved people, unless they were sponsored by state rulers. They may have bought and sold them for their own personal use during their journeys. They may have accepted small consignments of enslaved people on behalf of their associates in any number of ports of call. These scenarios are consistent with Ibn Khurradādhbih's description of their activity. More recent scholarship has begun to flesh out a larger context for the transregional medieval slave trade that shows how a multiplicity of state and merchant actors acted in specific settings.[134]

Scholarship on the Rādhānites also reflects the allure that the long-distance luxury trade has held for scholars, even though the heart of the medieval economies was often local and based on staple commodities. Likewise, despite the focus in narrative sources on long-distance diplomatic exchange and slave raiding beyond the frontiers of *dār al-Islām*, the most important site of human trafficking in medieval Egypt was local. Children born with slave status were bought and sold repeatedly during their lifetimes. Enslaved people who were imported into Egypt also changed hands frequently. Formal sales were only one part of this bustling local market. As property, enslaved people could also be bequeathed, gifted, and included in wedding dowries. This local human trafficking is the subject of the next chapter.

3

Everyday Human Trafficking and the Racialization of Slavery

ENSLAVED PEOPLE in medieval Egypt could be bought and sold repeatedly over the course of their lives, from early childhood and throughout their adult years. The partial life history of one enslaved girl illustrates the various contingencies that fueled the churn of the local slave market. What we know of her history is related in a legal query to Abraham Maimonides, where she is unnamed. For reasons that will become clear in chapter 7, I will call her Yaṣe'a.[1]

Yaṣe'a first appears as the *jāriya* of a Jewish woman called Leah.[2] Leah sold Yaṣe'a to a Christian buyer to pay off a debt to her former slave, whom she had freed, after the freedman gave her a loan during a crisis, probably the famine of 1201–2.[3] An associate of Leah's purchased Yaṣe'a from the Christian owner and then returned her to Leah.[4] Leah fell ill, died, and bequeathed Yaṣe'a jointly to her two daughters. Leah's debt to her freedman had still not been paid. Her daughters sold Yaṣe'a to him so they could pay their mother's debt. When the freedman decided to travel, he then sold Yaṣe'a to another Jewish man, called Reuben. Reuben then married one of Leah's daughters, and Yaṣe'a remained with them for three years until the other daughter claimed that she in fact retained ownership of a half share of Yaṣe'a. By this time, the freedman had died and Reuben could not find witnesses to refute his sister-in-law's claim to part-ownership of Yaṣe'a in Alexandria. A judge thus ruled that he and his sister-in-law must share Yaṣe'a's labor by alternating possession month by month. This arrangement only lasted a short while before Reuben and his sister-in-law were compelled to sell her to a Muslim buyer.[5] At this point, Yaṣe'a passes out of the historical record as far as we know. Her partial history is preserved only as one aspect of a longer prelude to a legal question that emerged about how Reuben and his sister-in-law should split the proceeds from Yaṣe'a's sale.

Within a period of four years or so, Yaṣe'a was bought, sold, and bequeathed at least eight times to at least seven different owners.[6] What is uncommon about her case is that we have a historical source that provides a continuous narrative for a portion of her life, in comparison to the usual fragmentary evidence that permits only a snapshot or two of an individual's trajectory into and through enslavement. What is common about Yaṣe'a's case is that she experienced multiple sales and thus multiple forced relocations to different households. Her transfer to new owners as part of an inheritance bequest also speaks to a less discussed mode of human trafficking that happened through legal mechanisms including wills, gifts, and wedding dowries. The whims of specific owners, and historical contingencies out of their control, also shaped Yaṣe'a's experience in slavery, as these factors influenced when she was sold and to whom.

While the previous chapter separated out the different strands or modes that people used to traffic others across long distances to and within Egypt, this chapter argues that the local slave resale market was the most active part of the overall slave trade. Local sales generated a large paper trail in bills of sale, scribal notebooks, inheritance deeds, and more. The evidence in these records illustrates how scribes and jurists fashioned a working Jewish slavery law that served slave owners within the larger framework of Islamic legal pluralism.[7] The paper trail from the local trade further shows how the interplay between specialized agents—brokers, scribes, judges, and merchants—and social networks that linked Egyptian Jews facilitated this market. Finally, the writings of these diverse actors reveal the demographics of Egypt's enslaved population and how the slave-owning classes used ethnicity, religion, and skin color to classify some people as lawfully enslaveable in contrast to the caliphs' and sultans' protected subjects.

Documentary Evidence and the Local Resale Market

The local resale market operated alongside, and overlapped with, the modes of slave trading that trafficked people into Egypt from outside of the *dār al-Islām*. The people who were forcibly imported to Egypt as part of diplomatic exchanges and state-sponsored slave trading could be resold by state officials and thus could find themselves with new owners in a completely different social domain. Outside of the imperial domain, buyers with the necessary connections could also purchase people through the capillary networks of the far-reaching mercantile trade. Far more often, however, buyers and sellers turned to the market in their own locale to buy a person who had already been trafficked to Egypt, or who had been born in Egypt with slave status, and who had thus been bound to an owner for varying lengths of time. In some cases, slave owners traveled to Egypt with their personal slaves, and they would sell them for any number of reasons. Finally, there were many people, classified as *muwallads*, who were born in Egypt to enslaved parents and thus had slave status.[8] From their childhood forward, these girls and boys were also subject to the vicissitudes of the local market.

Documentary evidence for the local resale market is relatively abundant in comparison to the smaller group of letters that illustrates the workings of the long-distance and intercity trade. Of the nearly 170 *geniza* documents that pertain to the slave trade in some way, most of them show that Egyptian Jews bought, sold, and otherwise acquired enslaved people in Fustat[9] from other Jews, including family members and other associates. Bills of sale make up 36 percent of this subcorpus followed by 23 percent for letters and then 10 percent for inheritance records. The remaining 31 percent is a miscellany of legal documents, accounts, dowries, and other fragments that resist easy classification.

Bills of Sale

The main documentary evidence for slave owning in Fatimid and Ayyubid Egypt comes from bills of sale that were preserved in the *geniza*. The overwhelming majority of these records were drawn up in Jewish courts, though some are written in Arabic script and follow Islamic legal conventions.[10] Jewish slave buyers wanted bills of sale as evidence to protect them from fraud and ensure them a clear title to their human property. Buyers wanted language in the bill of sale that confirmed they had paid in full, and that the seller had accepted their money. Sellers wanted to limit the conditions under which a buyer could return an enslaved person whom they thought had an undisclosed "defect" (Ar. *ʿayb*, pl. *ʿuyūb*). Both buyer and seller wanted scribes to compose bills of sale that had validity in both Jewish and Islamic courts. The scribes who drafted these documents drew from an array of Jewish and Islamic precedents and models to write bills of sale.

Sixty-two *geniza* bills of sale survive in varying states of legibility. Some are whole and nearly pristine, while others only survive as fragments due to tears and large holes in the paper. Thus, the information that we can glean from them varies across the corpus. The bills of sale that we can securely date proliferate from the 1080s onward and are predominantly from the twelfth century, with a small number from the first half of the thirteenth century.[11] *Geniza* bills of sale are multilingual legal instruments written in Judeo-Arabic, Aramaic, and Hebrew; Arabic-script bills of sale use only Arabic. Scribes employ a repertoire of technical language and formulaic phrases, and they report the speech of the transacting parties and their witnesses (never the speech of enslaved people).[12] In some cases, the scribes who drew up bills of sale copied verbatim from manuals of legal formularies, or from texts of the Babylonian Talmud.[13]

As discrete examples, no single bill of sale is completely typical or representative in all of its aspects. The example below (figure 3.1) has elements that are typically present in most bills of sale. It records the sale of the Nubian woman named Ḥidhq (Dexterity) in Cairo by two brothers to their sister, who were all children of Moses ha-Kohen, a Fatimid state official known also by the honorific "Splendor of the Dynasty (*sanī al-dawla*)."[14]

Ḥidhq's Sale, Cairo, January 10, 1105.

(Line 1) (This is) testimony that was given before us, we the undersigned witne[ss]es to thi[s] bill of sal[e] (2–4) on Tuesday, the 15th of (the Hebrew month of) Ṭeveṭ in the year one-thousand four-hundred and sixteen (January 10, 1105 CE) according to our customary method of counting,[15] in the city of Cairo, near Ṣoʿan Miṣrayim (Fustat),[16] situated on the Nile River: (4–5) Present among us were Abū Saʿd Khalaf and A[bū] al-Faḍl Yūsuf, the two sons of Moses ha-Kohen, the one known as the Splendor of the Dynasty. (5–7) They said to [us, "T]ake our testimony and make a symbolic purchase (*qinyan*)[17] with us effective immediately. Write and sign (a document) for me [*sic*] with all the languages of [claim]s and deliver it to our sister Zayn, called Sitt al-Dār. (7–9) Through (our own) free will we acknowledge before you that we received and took from her into our possession 20 dinars of gold specie of excellent weight. (9–12) For these (dinars) we sold her our Nubian slave girl called Ḥidhq, who is in our joint possession—in a complete, decided, irredeemable, proper, and enduring sale—given to and accepted by Zayn, our sister, and (given) to her heirs after her from this day forward in perpetuity. (13–14) We have no claim to this slave girl whatsoever, not even for a penny or more." (14–15) This Zayn took complete ownership of this slave girl and made a complete symbolic purchase. (15–17) This Zayn will rule over this slave girl who was sold to her (and may) acquire, transfer, bequeath, possess, sell, pledge, make use of her, set her free, and give her as a gift to anyone that comes forward. (17–18) No one may protest (her right of ownership), nor the right of her heirs after her from this day forward in perpetuity. (18–25) We take responsibility for this sale—we, Ḥalfon (Hebrew equivalent of Khalaf), Joseph, and our heirs after us—so that if anyone makes a claim and appeals to this Zayn or her heirs after us, we will pay, indemnify, release, acquit,

FIGURE 3.1. A bill of sale for the enslaved Nubian woman Ḥidhq, 1105. T-S 16.188. Paper. 17.5×31 cm. Reproduced by kind permission of the Syndics of Cambridge University Library.

clear, and deliver this sale and guarantee. We placed her (the slave girl) in the possession of this Zayn and her heirs after her in perpetuity. For this is not like a nonbinding promise, nor a fill-in-the-blank form,[18] but rather has the weight of all documents that (are legally valid) in court. All secret dispositions and conditions are nullified. This slave girl Ḥidhq is lawfully enslaved, exempt and cut off from free status (or manumission), from accusations, and from the claims of the king and queen.[19] No person has their mark[20] upon her. She is clear from all blemishes, from all boils that may emerge, and from old sores. (25–27) We (the witnesses) performed a symbolic purchase with Ḥalfon and Joseph, the sons of Moses ha-Kohen, Splendor of the Dynasty, for Zayn their sister according to all that was written and detailed above with an item suitable for doing so. (27–28) We write, sign, and give (this testimony) as a title of right and proof from this day forward. (28) Proper and confirmed. (28–29) Ṣedaqa ha-Levi the Cantor son of Solomon (whose) r(est) (is in) E(den) Aaron ha-Kohen son of Namir (whose) r(est) (is in) E(den). (30–31) Before us testified both of these two witnesses: Lord Ṣedaqa ha-Levi the elder son of Solomon (whose) r(est) (is in) E(den) and Lord Aaron ha-Kohen son of Namir (whose) r(est) (is in) E(den) (validated by) Abraham son of Nathan, head of the court of all Israel, (may the) m(emory of the) r(ighteous be) f(or a blessing).

Bills of Sale and Jewish Slavery Law in an Islamic Society[21]

The opening statement is written in Aramaic and in the voice of the witnesses: "(This is) testimony that was given before us, we the undersigned witne[ss]es to thi[s] bill of sal[e] . . ." Bills of sale invariably state the date of the transaction and the locality where the sale takes place. For *geniza* records, this is usually Fustat, and sometimes Cairo.[22] Scribes do not generally state whether the transaction took place in a particular building or setting, but they were probably completed at a regular Jewish court (Heb. *bet din*). A single exception to this practice suggests the rule. When the physician Yequtiel b. Moses sold the boy Fayrūz (Turquoise) to his uncle Judah b. El'azar, the bill of sale notes that the transaction was completed in Yequtiel's house, where he was confined with illness.[23] The date of sale is usually given using the Hebrew month with the year given according to the Seleucid calendar.[24]

Bills of sale provide a primary basis for the registers of known slave owners and enslaved people found in this book's appendixes. Scribes provided the names of sellers and buyers in some detail, at least by giving personal names, in this case Khalaf, Joseph, and Zayn, as well as the names of fathers, here Moses ha-Kohen for all parties. Egyptian Jews had both Arabic and Hebrew names, as is reflected in how the two brothers are identified in Ḥidhq's sale.[25] The scribe identifies the brothers by their Arabic names Abū al-Fadl Yūsuf and Abū Sa'd Khalaf, and later by the Hebrew equivalents Joseph and Ḥalfon.[26] Their sister, the buyer, is called only by her Arabic personal name Zayn and nickname Sitt al-Dār (lit. Lady of the House). In some bills of sale, professional titles are given, such as so-and-so the merchant, or the perfumer.

Prices are given most often in gold dinars, but sometimes in other currencies such as silver dirhams.[27] Here the scribe states that the gold was of "excellent weight" to emphasize the quality of the specie (it was not adulterated) and likely to indicate that it had been precisely weighed. Money was not always handed over on the spot, or all at once. Sellers could have the price credited to an account, and buyers sometimes paid in installments.[28] The price that Zayn paid for Ḥidhq is typical for this period. In *geniza* bills of sale, the average price of an enslaved person was 20 dinars. The lowest price recorded price is 10 1/4 ; the highest is 40 1/24.[29] To give this some context, Goitein estimates that 2 dinars was the cost of monthly upkeep for a lower-middle-class family in Fustat. A donkey often sold for around 2 dinars and a camel for 5.[30] The prices that buyers paid for enslaved people remained largely stable between the late eleventh and mid-thirteenth centuries. Perhaps more consequentially for slave owners, enslaved people also appear to have maintained their monetary value when they were resold. This meant that owners could hold enslaved people as wealth that they could pass down through inheritance or sell in a moment of need or even economic opportunity.

Though descriptions of enslaved people in *geniza* bills of sale are terse, in aggregate they suggest the demographic makeup of this population in the Jewish households of Cairo. The gender of the enslaved person is invariably indicated by the Judeo-Arabic, Hebrew, Aramaic, and Arabic terms used to describe their type. The numeric age of the person for sale is not given in bills of sale, but the scribe may note when he or she is prepubescent (Ar. *dūn al-bulūgh*), or when an enslaved child is sold along with her mother.[31] Bills of sale do not use the most common words for "slave" (Ar. *ʿabd*; Heb. *ʿeved*). Instead, writers used a range of vocabulary that was ambiguous. They identified women and girls using the Arabic *jāriya* or *waṣīfa*, with the Hebrew *shifḥa*, or the Aramaic *amta*. *Geniza* bills of sale called men and boys by the Arabic *ghulām* or *waṣīf*. In other kinds of writings, these terms do not invariably denote someone with the legal status of "slave." The most common term used for female slaves, *jāriya*, is sometimes used to refer to a free girl or someone's wife.[32] Likewise, *ghulām* could denote a free boy.[33] In bills of sale, however, each of these terms denotes a kind of "slave" in the sense of a legally unfree person.

Scribes' avoidance of the words *ʿabd* and *ʿeved* was a nod to pious traditions that exhorted slave owners to be gentler toward their human property in their speech and actions. The Arabic *'abd* and one of its plural forms, *'ibād*, were also used to denote people as "slaves of God," or "worshippers." A saying (*ḥadīth*) attributed to the Prophet Muḥammad encourages slave owners to address their slaves in "softer" terms: "None of you should say 'my slave,' 'my slave-woman' (*'abdī, amatī*), but he should say 'my lad' and 'my lass' and 'my boy' (*fatāya wa-fatātī wa-ghulāmī*)."[34] In the "Laws of Slavery," Moses Maimonides concludes the chapter by exhorting slave owners "not to embarrass a slave by our deeds or words, for the Written Law prescribes that they perform service, not that they be humiliated."[35] Despite such "linguistic mitigation," there is no ambiguity about how the same terms commodify the human being.

Scribes routinely identified enslaved people by their personal name (*ism*), type (*jins*), and occasionally by other factors such as distinguishing physical features. Ḥidhq is an Arabic word that means dexterity and also connotes cleverness and skillfulness.[36] In a bill of sale, the inclusion of the enslaved person's name is part of her description for the purposes of identification and commodification.[37] Ḥidhq was also how other people in the neighborhood would have known her. As we see in chapters 4 and 7, enslaved people were mobile agents that moved through the city. Sometimes they chose to flee and to take refuge in other parts of the city. Thus, enslaved people's names could be used to help identify and apprehend them.

Names are usually stated along with the person's *jins*, an Arabic term used to denote a person's ethnicity or origin. Ḥidhq is called a Nubian, which is the most common *jins* found in *geniza* bills of sale and in the Arabic-script ones found in other contemporaneous documents (figure 3.2). Nubian is followed in frequency by *muwallad* (born with slave status). We also find Indian, *Bāzī* (the Beja subgroup), Kushite, Abyssinian, and *Rūmī*.[38] Though enslaved people are sometimes called "Black," or described as such, scribes do not use "Black" as a stand-alone *jins* in bills of sale.[39] Physical descriptions appear only when there is something out of the ordinary, or when the enslaved person's physical body has a perceived "defect" or noteworthy condition. So, for example, we learn that the woman 'Ushshāq (Sitt al-'Ushshāq, Best of all Lovers) was pregnant when one woman sold her to another; the Abyssinian boy Muqbil (Fortunate) had tattoos; a "carob-colored" Christian woman had pox scars on her back.[40]

Scribes inserted coercion and validity clauses, along with warranties, into bills of sale to safeguard sellers and buyers since either party could challenge the transaction later. Coercion clauses could be more elaborate than stated in Khalaf and Joseph's case, but their statement still indicates that they are engaging in the

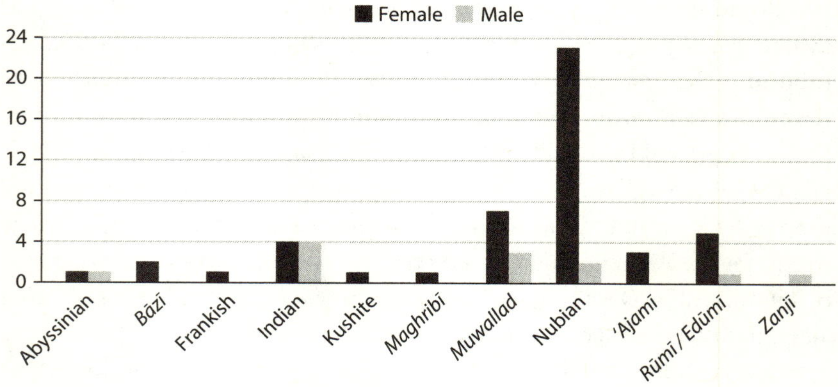

FIGURE 3.2. Enslaved people documented in the Cairo *geniza* documents by gender and type (*jins*), ca. 1000–1250. "Other African" includes a woman called *al-maghribiyya* (Westerner) which may here refer to a region of Libya, and a woman described as a "carob-colored" Christian. See appendixes 1 and 2 for more information.

transaction willingly.[41] While such a clause might seem to be standard language, there is reason to believe that a slave owner might later claim to have acted under duress to challenge a transaction after the fact—either as a crafty stratagem to undo their action, or because they felt that this was indeed the case.[42] Another central issue is the seller's clear title to the enslaved person for sale. In their testimony before the court, Khalaf and Joseph acknowledge that they held joint possession of Ḥidhq, that they sold her to Zayn completely, and that they retained no ownership whatsoever—"not even for a penny." As Yaṣe'a's case underscores, enslaved people changed hands frequently, and it was plausible that a past owner could sue the current one and argue that they retained a partial share. Here the scribe addresses that hypothetical threat by guaranteeing both Zayn's right of complete ownership and the rights of her heirs in perpetuity. Her brothers state that they, and their heirs after them in perpetuity, will be responsible to pay if a past owner who retains a rightful claim to all or a portion of Ḥidhq's ownership comes forward.

Another focus of the bill of sale is the mix of guarantees, indemnifications, and warranties meant to protect sellers and buyers. In Ḥidhq's bill of sale, the scribe uses an elaborate legal formulary drawn from the Babylonian Talmud that is not uncommon among late eleventh- and twelfth-century bills of sale: "This slave girl Ḥidhq is lawfully enslaved, exempt and cut off from free status (or manumission), from accusations, and from the claims of the king and queen. No person has their mark[43] upon her. She is clear from all blemishes, from all boils that may emerge, and from old sores."[44] The first two provisions emphasize that Zayn, the buyer, is purchasing an enslaved woman who has a clear title. The final phrase about blemishes and boils functions analogously to Judeo-Arabic phrasing drawn from Arab-Islamic precedents that scribes also used for their Jewish clients.[45] The most common of these phrases is "like the sale of imported slaves (*bayʿ al-jalb*)." The custom of *bayʿ al-jalb* meant that buyers assumed the risk of all the "defects" that were common among enslaved people.[46]

In the *Mishneh Torah*'s "Laws of Selling," Moses Maimonides writes that sellers must accurately report their enslaved property's blemishes before the sale is concluded. After the fact, he adds, a buyer can only return a person if she is discovered to have blemishes that prevent her from working or that undermine her value as a commodity.[47] Eye diseases were common, for example, and known to afflict enslaved people.[48] Leprosy would be a condition that permitted the buyer to return the person because the condition is repulsive to others and would make the servant unsuitable for the labor of serving food and drink. Bad breath could not be a defect, however. As Maimonides states, "Slaves are not for sex."[49] He continues to explain that sellers are not allowed to return enslaved people who are thieves, gluttons, or prone to escape, since all slaves are presumed to have these tendencies.[50]

Bills of sale written according to Jewish law include the required "symbolic purchase (*qinyan*)." The *qinyan* is a gesture, like the exchange of a token item between the two parties, that marks the execution of the transaction, and it is made by both the seller and buyer.[51] Bills of sale for Jewish slave owners also routinely include language that emphasizes how the document is put in the hands of the buyer as proof of their new ownership. The symbolic purchase and formal granting of the physical bill of sale are what Oded Zinger calls legal "practices of alterity" that "distance what happens in legal institutions from everyday reality" and thus lend Jewish legal institutions an air of authority.[52] Further, as Eve Krakowski demonstrates in her study of Jewish legal documents from the *geniza*,[53] scribes' consistent use of the symbolic purchase, an unambiguously Jewish legal feature, did not undermine these documents' legitimacy and utility in the larger Islamic legal system. To the contrary, scribes used Jewish legal language alongside, and sometimes instead of, Islamic language in documents whose components and purposes were thus legible and useful across the plural legal environments of the medieval Islamic world. This is one reason why Jewish slave buyers could and did take Jewish slave sellers to both Islamic and Jewish courts, where they attempted to return "defective slaves."[54] Jewish documentary practices were also such that Christian slave owners accepted the validity of prior Jewish records when they transacted with Jews in Islamic courts.[55]

Taxes

At first blush in chapter 2, Nathan b. Nahray's worry over taxes he might have to pay for the import of an enslaved girl at the town gate of Malīj prompt a cluster of straightforward interpretive possibilities.[56] His litany of questions implies that he likely simply wanted clear instructions from his senior colleague about how to organize her trafficking and sale. Perhaps he worried about encountering an unscrupulous official who might opportunistically detain or try to extort him.[57] Though all these concerns might have lurked in Nathan's mind, his terse question about how much tax he should expect to pay belies a more complex reality. All slave buyers should have paid taxes on their purchases, and the middlemen who trafficked slaves from as far as western India, through Aden, and on to Cairo were also expected to pay tariffs. Yet slave owners in the local market also sought to avoid paying taxes, and they appear to have been successful more often than not.

Scrutiny of the *geniza* bills of sale corpus shows two main fees that some slave buyers paid: taxes to the Egyptian state and a broker's commission.[58] Payments to the state are usually called *ḥaqq al-sūq* (the market tax) or *ḥaqq al-sulṭān* (lit. the government's tax).[59] The second payment, the broker's fee (*dilāla, juʿl al-dilāla*), is rare in bills of sale for slaves and is found irregularly in other *geniza* records related to commodities transactions.[60] These amounts are not always specified because, at least for the purpose of the bill of sale, it sufficed to make clear which party was responsible to pay them.[61] For commodities such as indigo and sugar, a brokerage fee of around 2 percent was assessed in eleventh-century Ifrīqiyya.[62] It seems that slave sales incurred a two-dinar fee when a broker was used.[63]

Goitein assumed that the brokers' fees were only mentioned if there was an unusual stipulation that necessitated clarification—for example, if the seller was to pay the fee instead of the buyer, as was customary.[64] It was likely, he added, that when the brokers' fees were not mentioned, it was because it was taken for granted as a cost. Or it was omitted because the buyers and sellers knew each other and therefore did not need a broker. Indeed, Egyptian Jews who sought to purchase enslaved people clearly favored working with relatives and known associates, as Khalaf, Joseph, and Zayn did. A recently identified fragment from the papers of the prolific *geniza* scribe Ḥalfon b. Menasse (also Menashshe/Menashe, fl. 1100–38) allows us to take this analysis a bit further.[65]

As scribes routinely did, Ḥalfon kept personal notes about transactions for which he had composed a bill of sale, or planned to do so subsequently. These notes sometimes appear one after the other in pages that were once bound in bifolio notebooks. There are thirty-one such entries by different scribes that pertain to sales and transfers of enslaved people.[66] Such notes are essentially "shadow" bills of sale, as they include most of the contingent information (names, prices, "type" of enslaved person, etc.) that a skilled scribe could then integrate into a formal document with the legal formulas appropriate to the task at hand.[67]

One notebook entry (figure 3.3) of Ḥalfon survives as a small fragment (approximately 5 × 4 cm) that is torn away from a larger sheet of paper. On the left side of the fragment are the hints of further writing that were made illegible when the paper was torn. It reads:

> The sel[ler: . . .
> The buy[er: . . .
> son of [N . . .

Ḥalfon turned the paper 45 degrees counterclockwise and wrote:

> the divorcee
> of Abū al-Bayān the
> scribe.

He turned the paper at an angle again and wrote:

> Like the purchase
> of an imported slave (*shirā' jalb*).
> If anyone then tattles
> to the government, then it will be on
> this buyer.
> Not the seller.

The salient clue found in this terse note—one that Ḥalfon certainly did not intend to be published later—is the phrase "If anyone then tattles to the government," then it will be the buyer's responsibility. What Ḥalfon meant was that the buyer and seller could expect to avoid paying the government's tax (*ḥaqq al-sulṭān* or *ḥaqq al-sūq*) unless someone informed on them or their transaction was otherwise discovered.

A case shows further that slave buyers took advantage of the opportunity to avoid taxes at their own risk. In the fall of 1223, several decades after Ḥalfon's death, the slave owner Abū al-Majd had become exasperated with a woman he

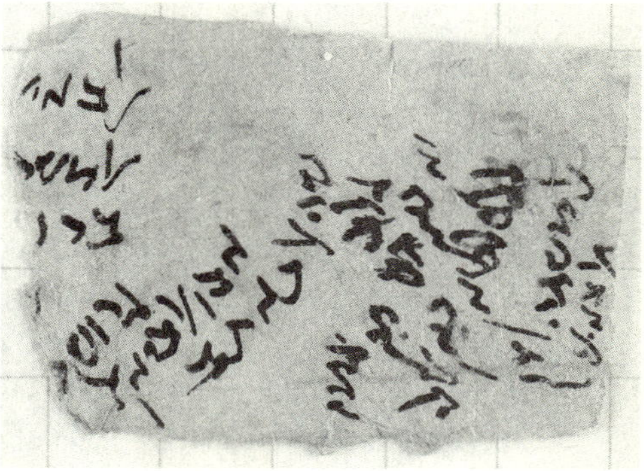

FIGURE 3.3. A note recorded by the scribe Ḥalfon b. Menasse about avoiding tax payments on the sale of an enslaved person, ca. 1100–38. The JTS Library manuscript shelf mark is ENA NS 77.254. Paper. Approx. 4 × 5 cm. Image courtesy of the Jewish Theological Seminary. This image is copyrighted material of JTS and cannot be copied, reproduced, republished, or reprinted by users of secondary materials.

was trying to sell, to no avail, in Fustat.[68] He vented his frustration in a letter to his associate, a jug maker, who was in Alexandria. His *jāriya*'s illness complicated his efforts to find a buyer, not to mention that she resisted being sold.[69] Moreover, bread prices—a barometer of economic conditions—had risen sharply. He explains to his friend that he might ask someone to sell her on his behalf in the countryside (*al-rīf*) or perhaps back in Alexandria. It might also help, he says, if Abū al-Barakāt would come to Fustat to help, for Abū al-Majd was also himself sick due to the persistent cold weather. The matter had become particularly serious and urgent for him because someone had "tattled" on him to a government agency (*al-dīwān*), which then apparently demanded that he not only pay them 52 dirhams (roughly 1.4 dinars) but also sell the woman.[70] It is not clear whether the 52 dirhams were a fine, a bribe, or the regular tax on slave sales that he had tried to avoid.

Abū al-Majd's predicament and complaints underscore larger facts about the slave trade in Egypt. It was primarily a local affair, conducted within social and economic networks that clustered in cities like Fustat, Cairo, and Alexandria but that also connected buyers in these places to smaller Egyptian settlements north and south of the main urban centers. Buyers and sellers in the Jewish community usually did not need brokers unless they ran into unusual difficulty in selling someone.[71] They used word of mouth and letters to advertise that they were looking to buy or sell.

Slave owners also sought out Jewish communal officials whom they considered to be effective middlemen and problem-solvers for facilitating slave sales, as they did for a host of other issues.[72] Jewish leaders were a part of the slave-owning classes themselves. They were also well acquainted with members of the Jewish community and knowledgeable about the law. These officials would not have viewed themselves as professional brokers but, as in the wider transregional mercantile context, the job of the broker was often done by a person who had a hand in many kinds of economic and social roles.

Slave owners also sought to avoid government taxes when possible and seem seldom to have paid them. Abū al-Majd's complaint, and Ḥalfon's note about avoiding taxes, suggest that his experience with the *dīwān* was exceptional, even if it was a risk that lingered in people's minds. Nathan b. Nahray's anticipation that he would need to pay a tax at the city gate in Malīj "or elsewhere" suggests that trafficking in slaves between urban centers made such an expense more likely.[73] Slave owners who bought and sold people within Cairo and Fustat were less likely to have their transactions noticed by the government.[74]

These findings support Jessica Goldberg's conclusions about the relationship between the government and *geniza* merchants with regard to taxes, and they suggest that her claims may also apply to the twelfth and early thirteenth centuries. She argues that taxes on mercantile goods were less important to the eleventh-century Fatimid regime than were the revenues on agriculture and land.[75] It was more important to the Egyptian state for merchants to facilitate the trade of commodities, which it could then consume through purchase or even direct sequestration.[76] Individual slave owners largely benefited from this situation. Two Arabic-script *geniza* bills of sale drawn up likewise omit mention of government taxes, a fact that raises questions. In these two cases, the parties were both Jewish and Christian. Did all slave buyers in Cairo generally avoid paying the government's tax?[77]

Reasons for Buying and Selling Slaves

As Abū al-Majd's predicament shows, it was not always easy for prospective buyers and sellers to find each other. Sometimes, the death or absence of a family member, or an enslaved servant, prompted the household to seek someone for purchase. In one letter, only partially preserved, the writer explains that he and his small children are ill and that there is no one to serve them or give them medicine. He got conflicting advice. One person told him, "Don't buy a slave girl." Yet another person told him, "Buy a slave girl."[78] The ill parent finally resolved to do the latter, but the author had difficulty in accessing the money he needed to purchase a *jāriya*. One purpose of his letter was to enlist the recipient's help in approaching a communal leader (*al-rayyis*) Abū al-Najm to purchase her.[79]

Illnesses, other emergencies, and even business opportunities could create the urgent need for capital that led owners suddenly to seek buyers for their enslaved property. One Jacob b. Joseph [. . .] al-Barqī wrote about the illnesses and poverty of some of his associates during what he described as a harsh winter. Two of them, ʿAwāḍ and his elder daughter, were very ill and had become dependent on public charity for support. ʿAwāḍ sought to sell his *ghulām* but was unsuccessful.[80] Jacob's and his children's predicament shows that what Mark Cohen calls "conjunctural poverty" could force slave owners to sell their enslaved servants just as happened during larger famines, as befell Yaṣe'a and her owner, Leah.[81]

Owners sold enslaved individuals to raise capital for mercantile ventures and for charitable causes. The woman Mubāraka bt. Samuel appeared in court after she had sold her servant for 20.5 dinars and given the proceeds to her brother Faraḥ to use to trade "in the West" (probably Ifrīqiyya).[82] She was in court because her husband Yeshuʿa contested the sale and claimed that she only had the right to give Faraḥ ten of the dinars, as the slave had been part of her dowry (*nedunya*) to which he had a partial legal claim.[83] In court, Mubāraka testified to these details and thus empowered Yeshuʿa to claw back the other 10.5 dinars from her brother. It appears here that this lawsuit was motivated by the husband Yeshuʿa's interests and not a result of collusion between the married couple to manipulate Mubāraka's brother. Farther afield in Almería, Spain, a merchant who was unable to sell a *ghulām* asked his partner for more money so he could pay a silk dyer.[84] These transactions illustrate an important generalization: most slave owners did not purchase people as investments or to turn around quickly for profit. But when the circumstances presented opportunities, or gave them little choice, those same owners could sell enslaved people to generate capital to make investments and to pay off debts.

Dowries, Inheritances, and Gifts

As with Mubāraka bt. Samuel and her husband Yeshuʿa above, the enslaved person-as-capital was a significant part of some wedding dowries.[85] For brides especially, ownership of an enslaved person figured saliently into issues of domestic labor and social status.[86] In an early record from 995, an enslaved woman from the Byzantine realm is part of Sutayt bt. Yaʾīr's trousseau.[87] As in Sutayt's case, the dowries of 85 percent of slave-owning brides included a single person. Two exceptions to this general trend include the enslaved boy Saʿd (Good Fortune) and his unnamed mother, who were included in the same dowry and valued together at 40 dinars.[88] Another extraordinarily wealthy bride received four enslaved girls valued collectively at 100 dinars—two of them personal attendants (*waṣīfatayn*) and two of them servants designated for more menial tasks (*al-jawāri*).[89]

Inheritance bequests were another way that slave owners transferred ownership and intergenerational wealth to others. The *geniza* preserves an abundance of wills, sometimes written while the testator was severely ill and faced an imminent chance of death. In other instances, living testators made inventories of their estates that included enslaved men, women, and children and made provisions for the future. Sometimes, but not always, these inventories specified which family member would inherit a particular person. In 1120, before he left on a business trip, a merchant gave instructions for how his estate should be divided, presumably in the event of his death. He provided that his daughter would inherit two enslaved girls and a share of some real estate.[90] In the mid-thirteenth century, a man willed to one of his sons the enslaved "Black Nubian" woman, who had likely cared for him up until his death.[91] Of the sixteen wills and inventories that include enslaved people, there are six cases in which the heirs are given complete ownership of a person with no attached stipulations.[92]

Some testators decided that their human property should be sold, and the proceeds used for specific reasons. In the twelfth century, a man bequeathed a *jāriya* to his daughter but ordered that his *waṣīf* be sold and the proceeds be used to pay for his burial expenses.[93] The woman Khulla bt. Shabbāt instructed that her *ghulām* be sold and his price be divided between two charitable purposes.[94] In other cases, testators attached conditions that gave enslaved children a say in their futures. One father instructs that, if the *jāriya* bequeathed to a daughter wishes herself to be sold, then the sale's proceeds should remain with his daughter.[95] Other enslaved people are listed as property in estate inventories but without any indication of what their owners planned to do with them.[96]

Wedding dowries and deeds of gift and inheritance are not commonly thought of as evidence for the medieval slave trade. From an enslaved person's point of view, however, they are further evidence of how various contingencies could lead to their sale and resale over time. From the point of view of the slave-owning classes, these legal acts were also part and parcel of the many strategies they used to preserve and transfer wealth and to provide social capital for their children. Together with bills of sale, scribal notebooks, and letters, this evidence also reveals the demographics of domestic slavery in medieval Egypt and illustrates how the slave-owning classes understood who could be lawfully enslaved.

Ethnicity, Skin-Color, and Medieval Racism

Geniza scribes used the Arabic term *jins* to denote what we would today call ethnicity.[97] The term can also be translated as genus, species, family, kind, or type.[98] Scribes recorded a person's *jins* because it was part of how human beings were commodified and identified as legal property that had been lawfully enslaved.[99] Around the turn of the thirteenth century, a Jewish man named Nathanel sold a woman described as "the slave girl of the Nubian type (*al-jāriya al-nūbiyya al-jins*)."[100] A girl named Warda (Rose) was included in a wedding dowry along with a copper vessel and a basin where she is described as "of the slave-born type (*al-muwallada al-jins*)."[101] In many cases, the term *jins* is not explicit, but it is implied, as in the formulation "the Persian (or non-Arab) slave-girl (*al-jāriya al-ʿajamiyya*)."[102] In documents produced by Jewish courts, *jins* may have also been understood as a gesture to Jewish law, which recognized two kinds of slaves—the Hebrew slave (*ʿeved ʿivri*) and the Canaanite ("foreign") slave (*ʿeved kenaʿani*)—and which specified some biblical categories of people as prohibited from marriage with Jews.[103] As a corpus, *geniza* documents provide a relative wealth of data about the *jins* (pl. *ajnās*) of the enslaved population of medieval Egypt (figure 3.2).

Yet an important caveat must accompany how we understand the value and limits of historical sources that report the *jins* of enslaved people. Ultimately, a writer's use of *jins* reflects how he, or another of the enslaved person's handlers, classified the person for sale. Thus, the recorded *jins* cannot invariably be trusted as an accurate statement about that individual's personal history. Two examples underscore the interpretive problems we face in using descriptions of *jins* as historical data. The first is the case of "the *Zanj* slave" and "the lands of the *Zanj*," both terms that *geniza* merchants used.[104] One common understanding of *Zanj* (*zanjī*, *zanjiyya*) is that it means a person from "East Africa"—and indeed it may. Still, medieval writers also labeled enslaved people as *Zanj* who were from other regions of Africa, such as those from the interior of southern and central Africa (from East Africa's inland hinterlands), as well as from northeast Africa (including the Horn).[105] The ambiguity of *Zanj* as an ethnonym should likewise inspire caution about accepting categories like Nubian, *Rumī*, and Indian without taking context into account.

A second reason to regard *jins* data with caution is that slave traders and owners sometimes lied about enslaved people's origins to market them and to protect their investment. There is no explicit evidence in the *geniza* of this practice,[106] though it is documented for the later Mamluk period. In early-fifteenth-century Alexandria, a Venetian man purchased "a female slave of Nubian race, called Mubāraka (Blessed), a Christian woman" and sent her to Venice with a note describing her as "a little slave girl, black, Saracen, about fourteen years old." What would explain this redescription of Mubāraka? Hannah Barker explains that racial and religious categories of enslaved people were dictated by the owners. To wit: "Mubāraka was a Nubian Christian in Alexandria because that categorization made her legally enslaveable in Alexandria, and she was an Arab Muslim in Venice because that categorization made her legally enslaveable in Venice."[107]

For an enslaved person, such deceit and ambiguity could be of utmost consequence. In a fifteenth-century episode, the biographer Muḥammad al-Sakhāwī (d. 1497) explains that though an enslaved concubine was called by the name Jawhara, "[s]he used to say that her name was Fāṭima and that she was *jabartiyya* (a Muslim from the Horn of Africa), and not *ḥabashiyya* (a Christian or 'unbeliever' from the Horn)."[108] What Jawhara/Fāṭima meant was that she, as a Muslim, had been unlawfully enslaved.

Though skepticism of how the slave-owning classes use *jins* categories is warranted, there is also ample evidence that corroborates *jins* data found in *geniza* documents. *Geniza* sources indicate that Nubians made up the largest category of enslaved people by *jins* in Jewish Egyptian households.[109] Arabic writings from outside the *geniza* show that Nubians were enslaved in Muslim households. Such writings also describe the slave trade within Nubia and onward to Egypt and Iraq.[110] The aggregated *jins* data reflects real geographic patterns of enslavement and trade even if it is likely that some enslaved people were misclassified due to fraud or ignorance.[111]

The relative predominance of Nubians (figure 3.2) shows that, though the slave trade to Egypt had an almost hemispheric reach, slavers most intensively exploited the non-Islamic regions of Africa that bordered the country. Nubians are followed in proportion by the *muwallads*.[112] Indians and enslaved people from the Byzantine realm are the next most present groups, making up 9.6 percent and 6.9 percent respectively.[113] After these groups come small proportions of Persians (*'Ajamī*),[114] Beja (*Bāzī*), Abyssinians, and Franks (*Ifranjī*). People familiar with the scholarship on the slave trade in the medieval Mediterranean may be surprised by the relatively low numbers of enslaved people from different European regions, as some have proposed that they were a major export to Muslim lands earlier in the ninth century.[115] This discrepancy illustrates the historical variability of the slave trade.[116]

For bills of sale written according to Jewish law, scribes usually only describe the enslaved person using *jins*. The religion and a physical description of the person are generally not given.[117] In one case there is an indication that the woman for sale is Black, though the word "Black" is not used. In 1231, the perfumer Moses b. Ṭahor purchased the Nubian woman named Abnūsa. The name Abnūsa is the feminized form of Abnūs, which means ebony (or ebony wood), which was black in color and valued by medieval Egyptians for commodities like pens, ink pots, and furniture.[118]

However, when we turn to the informal notebooks that scribes kept, in which they recorded the details of transactions, we find mentions of enslaved people's color, religion, and age. Ḥalfon b. Menasse recorded such cases: the widow Nafīsa sells the girl named Tawfīq (Success) who was "a *jāriya* [. . . *sawiyya*] who had not yet reached maturity";[119] the enslaved woman named Ikhtiṣār (Brevity) is described as "sexually mature (*balūgh*)" and "Black (*sawdā'*)";[120] finally, the "Black Nubian slave (*nūbiyya sawdā'*) called ʿAlam (Banner)" is sold.[121] Another unidentified scribe tersely records details in his notebook for the sale of "Intijāb (Selection) the Black (woman) [. . .] (for) 34.5 dinars."[122] In only one of these four "shadow bills of sale" does the scribe indicate the *jins* of the enslaved person along with her color. Because we lack the formal deeds that would have been composed later on the basis of these notes, it is unclear what *jins* would have been applied to these girls and women in a formal bill of sale. "Nubian" is the most likely answer. The question remains whether scribes labeled enslaved people described as "Black" as "Nubian" regardless of the person's identity or place of enslavement. For the slave trader and owner, the label "Nubian" did the essential work of classifying a person as lawfully enslaved.

In the inheritance deeds that Jews recorded for their heirs, they also described the enslaved people whom they bequeathed to others using a color and religion, but only rarely *jins*. In the first half of the thirteenth century, the man ʿAmram ha-Kohen bequeathed his valuable wardrobe to one of his sons. For the other son he left "the Black slave-girl (who is) of the Nubian type (*ha-shifḥa al-sawdā' al-nūbiyya al-jins*)."[123] Another father, Abū al-Baqā, gives a half share of "the Black (slave-girl)[124] named Misk (Musk)" to his son Mukarram.[125] In a separate deathbed declaration, a sick woman who feared her death was imminent instructs her sister not to sell Saʿāda, her Black (*al-sūdāniyya*) child-nurse, or Saʿāda's son.[126] When a pregnant woman wrote to her uncle, she asked him to purchase a young

"Black (*sawdā'*)" girl for her.[127] The usage of "Black" in these writings varies. At times it is used as an adjective that describes a slave (*jāriya* or *shifḥa*). In two other examples, "Black" is used alone as a noun to signify "slave." While the conflation of "Black" and slave status (or descent from an enslaved parent) has a history that predates this evidence,[128] *geniza* evidence illustrates how this idiomatic usage percolated up and down the registers of the Arabic language, from literature to the everyday writings found in the *geniza*, and through time.[129] The colloquial use of "Black" in notebooks and letters also underscores that, despite the plurality of ethnicities and the variety of skin colors among the enslaved population of medieval Egypt, the visibility and predominance of Black people in slavery shaped the worldview and language of the slave-owning classes.

When we consider this documentary evidence alongside other contemporaneous writings, we find juxtapositions of Nubian, Christian, Black, slave, and even the proto-racial theory of climes. Nāṣir-i Khusraw's description of Nubia notes that the people there have "black skin (*siyāh-pūst*)" and practice "Christianity (*tarsāyī*)."[130] More than a century later, Benjamin b. Jonah of Tudela describes a journey from Aden to Aswan that passed through the lands of Kush and Sebā, which seems here to mean medieval Nubia and Abyssinia (or the Horn of Africa more generally).[131] Among the Kush, he says, is a king called the sultan of Abyssinia (*sulṭān al-Ḥabash*) and a people who are like animals. They eat grass that grows along the Nile. They are naked, lack intelligence, commit incest, and are sexually promiscuous. "Seba is very hot," he adds. People come from Aswan and lure these people into traps. They then enslave them and sell them to Egypt and beyond. He concludes, "These are the Black slaves, the sons of Ḥam."[132]

Benjamin's statement that "Seba is very hot" is not a gratuitous one. This detail, coming as it does between the description of an animal-like people and the arrival of slave traders, would seem to interrupt the logical flow of his story except that it is here a reference to the Greco-Arab theories of environment, bodily humors, and biobehavioral difference. Scholars in the medieval Islamic world drew upon Ptolemaic precedents in their use of seven climes to divide the world into "civilized and uncivilized zones."[133]

Environmental conditions in the different climes were thought to affect the bodily humors. Extremes of hot and cold, and dry and wet, in the climes farthest from the most temperate middle clime purportedly caused an imbalance among the humors. This imbalance, according to one medieval Iraqi epistle, caused "differences in the characters of people, and their natures, their colours, their languages, their customs, their judgements, their beliefs, their actions, their crafts, their methods of planning, and their ways of governance."[134]

Climes and color had both positive and negative associations. Praising the "brownness" of Iraqis, for example, Ibn al-Faqīh al-Hamadhānī (d. early 10th c.) reports in his *Concise Book of Countries*:

> And one of the people of discernment said: "The people of Iraq are people of sound rational thought, commendable desires, and well-balanced characters. They have skill in every craft, with well-proportioned limbs and well-cooked humours. And they have a brown colour, which is the most equitable and balanced of colours."[135]

When viewed through the medieval theories of climes and humors, the names given to some enslaved women, like Sitt al-Sumr (Best of the Brown Women), take on multiple possible meanings related to people's physical appearance and temperament.[136]

In this light, Benjamin's statement that "Seba is very hot" allegedly explains why the people who lived there were like animals. He also references the extreme heat to explain these groups' Blackness, which he linked to the biblical curse of Ḥam's descendants by his father Noah.[137] Benjamin's contemporary, Moses Maimonides, also connected the plight of enslaved people to the so-called curse of Ḥam. In the *Mishneh Torah* he writes, "The sages commanded that one should have the poor and orphans in his household instead of slaves. It is better to use them so that the sons of Abraham, Isaac, and Jacob benefit from his wealth and not the descendants of Ḥam."[138] The instruction to include poor people in one's household as an act of meritorious piety is found in the *Mishnah* (ca. 2nd c. CE), but the opposition that Moses sets between the poor and orphans on the one hand and enslaved people on the other appears to be his addition.[139] His rhetorical flourish also reflects upon a set of centuries-long traditions in Jewish, Christian, and Muslim writings that discuss how Noah cursed the descendants of his son Ḥam (specifically, Ḥam's son Canaan) to serve others as the lowest of slaves after Ḥam saw his drunk father naked inside his tent and told his brothers about it.[140]

There is no mention in the Hebrew Bible of black skin as a punishment for Ḥam's indiscretion. Nor was there then a conflation of Blackness and slave status. David Goldenberg, who has written two books about the history of the so-called curse of Ḥam, shows that rabbinic traditions about the darkening of the skin as a punishment from God for sin appeared in sixth-century sources that themselves rely upon accounts believed to date to the third and fourth centuries.[141] It was only from the ninth century forward that Christian, Muslim, and Jewish writers began to conflate the biblical curse of slavery with a "curse" of black skin, in what Goldenberg calls the "dual curse."[142]

By the time of Moses Maimonides and Benjamin b. Jonah, black skin and slave status had become linked in written and artistic representations—but not invariably so.[143] All people of all colors and types (*ajnās*) were at risk of enslavement somewhere in the known world where they lacked specific protections, or where they were designated as enemies and "others" to be actively captured and then ransomed or enslaved.[144] For proof of this, Egyptians needed only to observe the phenotypical and linguistic diversity of the enslaved people who circulated among them as domestic servants, factotums, soldiers, and more. What unified these groups was their designation as lawfully enslaved human commodities.[145] But the predominance of Black people in the enslaved population at large meant that slavery was still in the process of becoming racialized due to this social reality.

Though scholars have long drawn our attention to the allure of the long-distance trade in luxuries and enslaved people from distant cultures, the local market was actually at the heart of the slave trade. Chapter 3 has shown how this local market was fed both by the trafficking into Egypt of people newly enslaved outside of the *dār al-Islām*, and to a lesser extent by the continued enslavement of children born with slave status. Once inside the Egyptian market, enslaved people were frequently subject to resale and forced transfers through their owners' inheritance bequests, gift giving, and dowry making. Slave owners held and transferred their human property as intergenerational wealth, which they also converted to gold dinars in moments of need and capital opportunity.

This churn generated a large paper trail that illuminates how Jews participated in the local trade within an Islamic society. Trained scribes produced multilingual bills of sale that they tailored to protect the rights of slave owners in Jewish and Islamic courts. Jews preferred to buy and sell enslaved people among themselves, but they also transacted with Egyptian Christians and, rarely, with Muslims. This written output illustrates how jurists, judges, and scribes fashioned a usable Jewish slavery law by turning both to rabbinic and Islamic legal precedents, sometimes adopting Talmudic formularies in lieu of more common Arabic ones, and at other times incorporating Islamic practices into Jewish document production. Slavery is another domain in which Muslim courts and non-Jewish litigants recognized the validity of deeds of sale produced by Jewish courts.[146] Jewish slave owners went to Muslim courts to defend their rights as slave owners in suits against other Jews.

Evidence for the churning local slave trade furnishes ample information about the demographics of domestic slavery. Though the slave trade had a global reach, Nubians were the ones most trafficked to and within Egypt. Scribes were careful to identify enslaved people according to their *jins* because this classification identified a person as lawfully enslaved. In less formal writings, such as letters and scribes' personal notebooks, writers used "Black" as a shorthand for "slave." This finding does not mean that slavery was rigidly racialized in medieval Egypt.[147] Any non-Muslim outside of the *dār al-Islām* was in theory lawfully enslaveable. The conflation of Black and slave does, however, provide a glimpse into the worldview of the Egyptian slave-owning classes whose language choice reflected that Nubians from the "lands of the Blacks" were the most common group of enslaved people. This chapter does not argue that there was necessarily a straightforward continuity in how "Black," "African," and slave status became more tightly intertwined. Rather, the language choice of *geniza* writers in their historical context illustrates how ideas about Blackness were continually (re)interpreted and formed in social conditions that the evidence allows us to describe.[148] The next chapters tighten our focus on how the presence of Nubians and other enslaved people shaped the gendered social world of Jewish households and communities.

PART II

Household Slavery

4

Slavery *lil-Khidma* in the City

Personal Service, Specialized Labor, and Forced Sex

Part 1 of this book began by taking a bird's-eye view of the interregional slave trade to Egypt and how it was composed of different modes of enslavement and trading that operated differently over time. Chapter 3 then narrowed the geographic scope to Egypt and argued that the local trade was the most important market for the preponderance of slave owners, who also acquired enslaved people as inheritances, gifts, and in their wedding dowries. The chapter also illustrated how the language of slave owners, jurists, and narrative writers reflected medieval ideas about race.

Starting with this chapter, part 2 of the book now focuses our attention more tightly on a basic unit of social life—the household—and how it was the primary site of bondage for most enslaved people documented in this book. Like many scholars, I have, with some hesitation, referred to this type of urban, household slavery as "domestic."[1] While this label is partly justified, this chapter will argue that it also unintentionally conceals some central facts about the intertwined lives of enslaved people and their enslavers. Though households had private, inner dimensions, they also required daily interaction with the urban world beyond their walls. Thus, from the enslaver's point of view, an enormous part of an enslaved person's practical and symbolic value came from their usefulness as mobile agents not only within the home but especially outside of it. This chapter illuminates how this was the case through an investigation of "visible" and "invisible" evidence. Chapters 5 and 6 then delve deeper into the practical and symbolic value of slavery for the slave-owning classes by focusing on gendered dimensions of slave ownership. Part 3 of the book, which concentrates on the life histories of enslaved people, will extend the analysis to show how the knowledge and social attachments they made through their urban movement as laborers was one key to how they made lives for themselves.

This chapter adopts the language of *geniza* writers and their contemporaries, who understood what is commonly called "domestic slavery" as slavery *lil-khidma*. *Khidma* is a common Arabic term that has different meanings and connotations related to its root meaning of "service."[2] When Egyptian Jews used the term in relation to slavery, as in a *jāriya lil-khidma*, they used it to describe an enslaved person whose purpose was to serve their owner and their owner's dependents in myriad and variable ways. As such, when Mardūkh b. Mūsā, the Alexandrian merchant, widower, and father, wrote for help finding a *jāriya* after his wife's death, he framed his need plaintively: "I do not have any one to bring me a cup of water. I am in the utmost need of someone to serve me. . . . Please, my lord, secure for me a *jāriya* who is suitable for personal service (*lil-khidma*)."[3] Writers also invoked the term when they wanted to stress that a man had purchased an enslaved woman as a sex slave, as in "she is *not* a slave girl for personal service (*laysa hiya jāriya lil-khidma*)."[4]

Though slavery *lil-khidma* was common in the cities and towns of the medieval Middle East, writers of the era did not delineate its scope or comprehensively describe the quotidian tasks that it involved.[5] One assumes that this is because they largely took the nature of what *khidma* entailed for granted, or they recognized that households and slave owners varied from person to person and locale to locale. The reason that this chapter revisits the ostensibly obvious topic of what domestic labor entailed is that the question of labor is fundamental to a larger aim of the book, and that is to conjure vividly the interagency of slaver and enslaved, and specifically in part 3 of the book to render as fully as possible enslaved people as protagonists in their own life histories.

This chapter has two main sections. The first section analyzes what the prescriptions found in legal and narrative writings from medieval Egypt say about enslaved labor. Ibn Buṭlān's manual for buying slaves and the rabbinic legal materials enable me to sketch out a broad framework for the kinds of work that enslaved people were expected to do. There is some direct documentary evidence from the *geniza* that can be read alongside these, and other sources fill out the picture of what Jewish Egyptian slave owners asked their slaves to do. This is the evidence in which the labor of enslaved people is more or less explicitly named, and thus historically visible.

The research for the second section emerged from my engagement with archaeologists and art historians who have devised new approaches to study slavery and the slave trade. When it comes to the material and visual records, the presence of enslaved people and the evidence of their activities are often "invisible" or ambiguous.[6] In recent decades, slavery scholars such as the archaeologist Paul J. Lane have argued that we should reorient our inquiry away from "confirming the presence of enslaved people to understanding the wider implications of the fact of their presence."[7] Following his and their lead, I have asked how this interpretive reorientation might help us envision slavery as it existed in the households, shops, markets, and alleyways of medieval Fustat and Cairo. This part of the chapter asks readers, to paraphrase Lane, to query the historical implications of enslaved people's presence in and between households and the cityscape. Finally, I argue that the main professions of the slave-owning classes can be analyzed to understand what kinds of labor enslaved people did in medieval Egypt that has long been overlooked or underestimated. Together, the study of house layouts, artisan workshops, and the urban pathways that connected them will illuminate the world of slavery *lil-khidma* and, ultimately, the lives of enslaved individuals.[8]

Descriptions of Enslaved Labor in Narrative and Legal Writings

Ibn Buṭlān, whose coarse stereotypes of Beja women we read in chapter 2, wrote in his slave-buying manual about the kinds of labor that he thought best suited enslaved women of different types (*ajnās*).[9] Though enslaved men (*waṣīfs*) were known to do labor within the household, Ibn Buṭlān recommended that buyers only purchase a woman for jobs like cooking, singing, dancing, and nursing.[10] Some types of women were, however, better for specific kinds of labor. Somalian (*al-Barbariyyāt*) women were thought to be suitable for housework, sex, and childbearing; Black women for wet-nursing; Persians for childcare; Arabs to be singers and musicians; and *Rūmīs* to guard valuable items in a trustworthy manner. In contrast, Indian and Armenian women were considered unruly and thus not well suited for slavery within the household. As the evidence in chapter 3 showed (figure 3.2), most Egyptian slave buyers did not have much of a choice in what type (*jins*) of person they purchased, nor is it clear that they shared Ibn Buṭlān's stereotypes. For present purposes, the use of his generalizations is in the details they provide for the kinds of "personal service (*khidma*)" that slave owners expected their servants to perform regardless of their *jins*.[11]

In addition to describing a broad array of work, Ibn Buṭlān's advice suggests a culture of slavery in which buyers of means would purchase people for highly specialized purposes. The slave owners documented in the *geniza*, however, mostly purchased one enslaved person and used that individual for many diverse purposes. The main terms they used to describe them—*jāriya, waṣīf(a), shifḥa*—did not designate a labor specialization but rather an unfree servant for all manner of *khidma*. There is, however, some evidence for women who were purchased as trained singers. The singing slave-girl (*jāriya mughanniya*) Ṣirf was purchased for 40 dinars (more than twice the normal price of most enslaved girls and women). It was her training and talent that allowed her seller to command such a high price. In addition to her use as an object for his own entertainment, her buyer may have seen her as an investment since singers could be "rented" out as performers. In the record for her sale, the woman ʿAbīr is called both a *jāriya mughanniya* and a professional wailer (*al-nāʾiḥa*) of the type that people would hire for funerals.[12] In English translation, "wailing" does not do justice to the work that the skilled *nāʾiḥa* performed. She gathered information about the deceased and interacted with the mourners. At the appropriate time she incorporated this information into her lamentations.[13] In chapter 7, we will read further about how enslaved people could later use such acquired information to form mental sociospatial maps of the city for their own purposes.

Another labor specialization rarely applied explicitly to enslaved people was "child-nurse (*dāda*)," though it is clear that other women called *jāriya*s were also expected to care for children as part of their duties.[14] *Geniza* documents contain only rare references to wet-nursing by enslaved women. In one fragmentary record, we learn only that a wet nurse was owned by another woman and that a man was interested in purchasing her.[15] In another ambiguous case, the enslaved mother named Jinān (Paradise), a *muwallada*, sold for an exceptionally high price of 34 dinars in the first half of the twelfth century. Her sale forced her separation from a young girl (*ṣabiyya*) named Wafāʾ (Fidelity) who was seemingly her daughter. Wafāʾ was two years old, which is the age at which she might be weaned from her mother's breast. Jinān's high price may indicate her value as a wet nurse to her purchaser's household, as she could have been used by the owner's wife or another relative and also contracted out to nurse other children.[16] In addition to the glimpses of this intimate and essential work that *geniza* documents provide, medieval Jewish law also shows that Jews understood such labor by enslaved women to be a primary benefit to free married women and their households.

Such is the case in Moses Maimonides's legal code the *Mishneh Torah*, where he reiterates the kinds of work that either free wives or enslaved maids (*shifḥa*s) should do within the household.[17] This work included quotidian household labors like baking bread, cooking food, washing clothes, wet-nursing, feeding the husband's riding animal, and either grinding grain or supervising its milling.[18]

Crucially, for every enslaved women that a household owned (or could afford), a wife was expected to do fewer and fewer of these tasks.

Maimonides himself reminded his readers that household work could vary across different local cultures.[19] In some places the main textile work is weaving, in others embroidery. Similarly, Maimonides's rabbinic predecessor, the Iraqi gaon Sherira b. Ḥananya (d. ca. 1004),[20] acknowledged that women in Baghdad did not typically grind grain themselves at home because they had access to communal mills. Women in the villages did, however, continue to grind grain during his lifetime.[21] In any event, slave-buying manuals and the Jewish laws of marriage together provide a basic starting point for connecting a few crucial points. *Khidma* included a tremendous range of work that could benefit everyone in the household regardless of their age and gender. The *khidma* of enslaved women was understood, especially, to alleviate married women of work they would otherwise be expected to do.[22]

This context helps to explain the gendered patterns of both who was enslaved in medieval Egypt and who purchased them (figures 3.2 and 4.1). Approximately three-quarters of the enslaved population documented in the *geniza* was female. Though certain types of enslaved males (*waṣīfs*) could do some of the same labor that females did, there are reasons that explain the roughly three-to-one ratio of women and girls to men and boys that go beyond the stereotype that household labor was feminine.[23] First, women were more vulnerable to enslavement through raiding, kidnapping, and as surviving prisoners of war. Anecdotal evidence also suggests that parents were more likely to sell their daughters than their sons during times of exceptional famine. Thus, enslaved women were simply more likely to be available for sale. A second reason for the greater percentage of enslaved females was that medieval Jewish law and mores dictated that women should not own enslaved men because the women would then own the men's bodies, too. Female ownership of enslaved men was an immodest affront to the gendered social order.[24]

A third reason is sexual slavery. Though slave owners probably used boys and men for sex, there is little documentary evidence of this in the *geniza*. However, the evidence clearly shows that men used enslaved women and girls both for household labor and for sex.[25] Maimonides indirectly acknowledges that household labor led to intimacy and physical proximity, and that people found such interactions sexually arousing. For this reason, the *Mishneh Torah* cautions that only wives can perform certain household labor for their husbands. These tasks included washing her husband's body, making his bed, pouring him a beverage, and just generally "doing his bidding" by fetching things and tidying up around

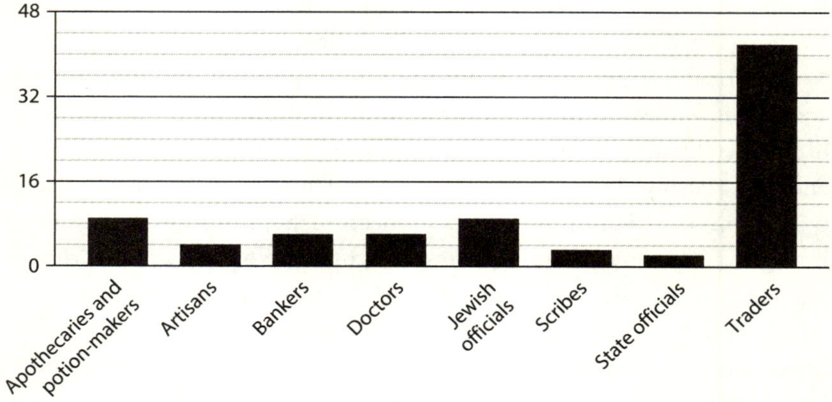

FIGURE 4.1. The professional affiliations of slave-owning men documented in the Cairo *geniza*. See appendix 3.

him.[26] This same logic also explains why Maimonides reasons that menstruating Jewish women should temporarily refrain from this kind of work, for such would tempt the couple to have sex during the wife's time of ritual impurity (*nidda*).[27]

In slave-owning households, enslaved women did not have a choice about whether and when they provided such *khidma*—whether they performed it as a matter of course or only sometimes in their female owners' stead. From their perspectives, such seemingly casual and innocuous interactions were fraught since proximity meant the potential for violence and coercion, including rape.[28] For this and other reasons, the prescriptive advice and laws found in the writings of Ibn Buṭlān and Moses Maimonides are a starting point for sketching the types of labor that enslaved people, and females in particular, were pressed to do in medieval Egypt. Though we lack first-person accounts by enslaved people, we can write them into histories of daily life within the household by using the better documented descriptions of free women's labor, by recognizing how free women's and enslaved females' labor was conflated, and by acknowledging that unfree women and girls were commonly used as coerced purveyors of intimate *khidma*.

Khidma in the City

The site of household labor was not merely *inside* the physical home but also *outside* of it in the city through which free and unfree workers moved. This section of the chapter continues the argument that "assuming the fact" of enslaved people's presence—despite their muted presence in written sources and their

FIGURE 4.2. An unglazed earthenware bread stamp from medieval Fustat, ca. 12th–15th c. © The Trustees of the British Museum. Image IDs 01614093353 and 01614093352. Shared under a Creative Commons Attribution-Non-Commercial-Share Alike 4.0 International (CC BY-NC-SA 4.0) license.

"invisibility" in medieval Egyptian archaeology—will allow us to expand what we know about their lives and the larger Egyptian society.

Members of the slave-owning classes often lived in multiroom dwellings with multiple stories and central courtyards. In some cases, single homes stood alone, though sometimes they shared walls with neighboring structures. In other cases, family groups lived in apartments that were part of large multistory buildings with as many as four or five floors. Archaeologist Matthew Harrison's reconstructions of dwellings in medieval Fustat show that multistory homes had wall flues for the disposal of wastewater and sewage that were connected to subterranean canals.[29] Courtyard fountains and rooftop wind-catchers cooled the home while floor runnels fed water to shrubs. Large kitchens were rare. Instead, small corner nooks were used to prepare bread dough and other dishes that were then taken out of the home to marketplaces where cooks heated the food and bakers placed the dough within large communal ovens or smaller portable ones.[30] Bread stamps (figure 4.2) for the Fatimid period show that people used stamps to identify their dough so they could retrieve the proper loaf after baking, or perhaps have it correctly delivered by a bakery worker.[31] This archaeology of daily life is also the archaeology of slavery. Enslaved people moved throughout the physical home. Over the course of a day, they emptied chamber pots, watered shrubs, and kneaded dough.

Free women's dowry lists provide further, heretofore largely unconsidered, evidence of the material culture of household slavery when studied in light of enslaved people's assumed presence. For not only did some brides bring enslaved servants into their marriages as part of their dowries, as we have already seen, but the household implements included in these same dowries would have been used by free and unfree people alike.[32] Such implements included mixing bowls, pitchers and ewers for liquids, washbasins and buckets, all ordinary items meant to be used both in and outside the household.[33]

While the interior courtyard provided a sense of calm and privacy, the world outside of residential walls buzzed with the activity of enslaved and free people running all kinds of errands. During his visit to Cairo, Nāṣir-i Khusraw was keen to describe the splendor of the metropolis for his readers. In one market he found "rare goods from all over the world" such as tortoise-shell implements, fine crystal wares, elephant tusks, and "much honey and sugarcane."[34] In the food stalls was a marvelous variety of fruits, vegetables, and herbs grown locally and citrus fruits and bananas, olives and dates, basil and pomegranates imported from near and far.[35] Homes and markets were connected by a dense network of alleyways that required continually burning lamps to light the ways of pedestrians and beasts of burden. Water carriers used camels to transport drinking water from the Nile. Households drew nonpotable water for their own use from various wells closer to home using buckets and brass ewers. When the alleyways became too narrow or otherwise inaccessible for pack animals, people carried goods on their backs.[36]

In reading this section of Nāṣir's travelogue, one would not know that circulating among these throngs of people were enslaved men, women, and children. Here the *geniza* records document their presence, as letter writers refer, albeit tersely, to the enslaved servants whom they dispatched to run errands like delivering goods and bags of money.[37] Enslaved people also did the food shopping at different markets around the city. On this point, a seemingly offhand example Maimonides offers in a section of the *Mishneh Torah* on the "Laws of Sales" shines a rare written light on what was a fact of daily life. He explains that it is permissible for a shopkeeper to discount his prices to attract customers. For this purpose, he continues, "a merchant is permitted to hand out roasted seeds and nuts to children and slave girls (*shifḥot*) so that they frequent his establishment."[38] The value of Maimonides's example lies in how ordinary it is. As such, it provides a rare, candid glimpse into how slavery *lil-khidma* fit into the everyday rhythms of urban life. Its details underscore how enslaved people were mobile agents who moved throughout the city, between public and private spaces, and alongside diverse groups of free and other unfree people.

Trades, Professions, and Enslaved Labor

So far this chapter has shown that we can enlarge what we know about the scope of enslaved people's labor (*khidma*), where the physical sites of labor were, and how the nature of quotidian labor shaped the intertwined lives of these unfree workers and the slave-owning classes. We can access another site of enslaved labor that is largely unexplored in *geniza* scholarship on slavery through the study of the professions of slave-owning men. Among the over two hundred individual male slave owners that I have found in the *geniza* corpus, I have identified the occupations for nearly 40 percent of them.[39] Four professional clusters stand out among this group: medical workers, artisans, officials in religious and governmental capacities, and, finally, traders (*tujjār*, sg. *tājir*). The latter group is far and away the most common profession among known male slave owners (see figure 4.1 and appendix 3).[40] The profession of the slave owner is another data point that historians can use to ask questions and draw inferences based on "the assumption of enslaved people's presence." In addition to *khidma*, slave owners had the prerogative to compel their unfree servants to do other kinds of work including professional tasks and, I will argue, as sex slaves.[41] The professions of the slave-owning classes are also an indicator of the connection between slave ownership and socioeconomic class.

The category "medical workers" includes two subgroups that occupied different socioeconomic niches but who likely used enslaved labor in similar ways. The first subgroup, apothecaries, includes men described as pharmacists (*al-ṣaydalānī*), perfumers (*al-ʿaṭṭār*), and potion makers (*al-sharābī*). The second subgroup includes doctors and physicians (*ha-rofe*, *al-ṭabīb*). The domains of scents, drugs, medicines, potions, and healing were interconnected. Aromatic substances like sandalwood, camphor, ambergris, and musk were used to perfume air and body, but they were also common ingredients in medical prescriptions. The commodities that perfumers and pharmacists imported also had cultural cachet that is reflected in the names that these men gave the enslaved women who worked in their apothecaries. The perfumer Seʿadya b. Abraham purchased a *jāriya* named Perfume (ʿAbīr). Another perfumer, Abū ʿAli, owned a woman named Musk (Misk), after another pungent scent.[42]

This chapter argues that the work of the apothecary was also likely the work of his enslaved servants, despite the latter's uncredited role.[43] Cairo's apothecaries buzzed with activity as substances were prepared and combined according to doctor's prescriptions and the recipes that were written in pharmaceutical manuals.[44] A part of one such manual survives in the *geniza* and its contents suggest the sometimes hectic, smoky, and caustic atmosphere of the perfumer's workshop. The Jewish druggist Abū al-Munā Dāwūd b. Abī Naṣr al-Kūhīn composed *The Management of the Pharmacist's Shop and the Rule for the Notables on the Preparation and Composition of Medicines Beneficial to Man* in Fustat in 1260.[45] The labor this manual describes resembles a specific type of cooking, which we know was a type of work expected of enslaved people. One recipe instructs that, to make aloewood syrup in order to treat palpitations, improve digestion, and "gladden the soul," take approximately 169 grams of Indian aloe wood, grind it, soak it in water for a time, cook it over a gentle flame until it has reduced by one-third, strain it through a sieve, add sugar, and cook it slowly until it forms a syrup. Finally, perfume it with musk and it will be ready for consumption.[46]

Other recipes require that someone tend the cooking concoction and skim any foam from the top. There are fruits to be juiced or macerated; silkworm larvae to chop; and many, many ingredients to be crushed, ground, boiled, and simmered for hours on end.[47] Enslaved women followed their owners' instructions and learned these recipes through repetition. Some of them may well have had medical knowledge from their free lives before enslavement.

Apothecary work was a kind of skilled labor, and knowledge of it could be used by enslaved pharmacy workers for their own purposes. Chapter 7 explores the agency of enslaved people in depth, but a brief illustration here helps to connect the dots. Arsenic (*zarnīkh*), for example, was used in cosmetics, for hair removal, and to treat some skin diseases. It was known to be a standard ingredient in the apothecary's inventory such that some landlords expressly prohibited their tenants from using it within their leased properties.[48] Arsenic could be toxic and even deadly when ingested. It was one of multiple common ingredients that could be used deliberately as a poison.

During the Mamluk sultanate in Egypt (1250–1517), the historical period just after this book's focus, chroniclers report that enslaved women used poison to kill their owners. It was rumored that the Sultan al-Ṣāliḥ Ḥājjī (r. 1381–82 and 1389–90, d. 1412) was partially paralyzed during the last years of his life after eating food given to him by his own enslaved women and thought to be poisoned. In his report, the Mamluk historian Ibn al-Taghrī Birdī (d. 1470) suggests that the women's tactics were justified. For after the sultan had been reprimanded for physically and excessively abusing enslaved women, he began to order his musicians to play more loudly so that the screams of the women could not be heard as they were beaten at his behest.[49] Suspicions of poisonings by enslaved women with access to pharmacies were not unique to Egypt, but were also known in Venice during the early fifteenth century.[50]

Enslaved labor in the apothecary is one aspect of what historian Hannah Barker calls the shared culture of slavery in the Christian and Islamic Mediterranean.[51] This particular aspect of slavery is full of historical ironies that reveal the strange entanglements of interagency, the idea that slave owners' and enslaved people's agency were linked. Unfree pharmacy workers were an active part of medieval medical culture as skilled practitioners under the coercive direction of trained artisans, and sometimes with their own indigenous medical knowledge.[52] As trafficked subjects, some of them were transported on boats carrying clay vessels and cloth sacks filled with the exotic *materia medica* that pharmacists imported. As laborers in the apothecary, they would have pulverized and cooked these materials to make the potions that some slave owners consumed, sometimes unknowingly drinking poison, and at other times in hopes of increasing their sexual vigor as they preyed on other enslaved women and girls.[53]

Another subgroup of slave owners whose professions indicate labor done by enslaved people that is otherwise unmentioned in written sources is the artisan-worker. A main form of this work was in various textiles and included professions like the dyer (*al-ṣabbāgh*) and the silk specialist (*al-qazzāz*), who could have been a silk weaver, a silk merchant, or both.[54] Other slave-owning artisans were known as goldsmiths (*al-ṣā'igh*) or candlemakers and sellers (*al-shammāʿ*).[55] Not only were these artisans able to use enslaved women and girls for *khidma* and sex in their homes, they could also compel them to learn and complete the tasks required in their workshops. Another common task for *jāriya*s was as couriers who delivered and collected goods and money on behalf of their owners.[56] Not every slave-owning artisan necessarily used his *jāriya* for deliveries or specialized labor like dyeing, weaving, or making candles. Some artisans did, however, and this fact suggests how historians might use the professions to enlarge how we think about the likely range of enslaved people's quotidian labor.[57]

The third subgroup is the communal and government official, a category in which I include the scribe (*kātib*), judge (*dayyan*), welfare officer (*parnas*), head of the Jewish community (*nagid*), cantor (*ḥazzan*), head of the rabbinic academies (gaon of the yeshiva), and those who served the Egyptian state as courtiers and officials.[58] The scribes documented in the *geniza* were Christians, such as Ḥanūn b. ʿAllūn, who worked in the Fatimid *dār al-dībāj*, a compound known at this time for the silk business, and who purchased a Christian woman from a Jewish merchant who specialized in the sale of purple textiles (*al-arjawānī*).[59] Some slave-owning officials were well known or were members of well-known families. Moses b. Samuel was the son of Samuel b. Ḥananya, who was the head of the Egyptian Jewish community (*nagid*) between 1140–59. Moses was the *nagid*-designate when he owned the enslaved woman Nasrīn in 1148. Zakkār b. ʿAmmār, an eleventh-century *nagid* of the Sicilian Jewish community, which was connected to Egypt through trade and migration, had a large contingent of male slaves (*ghilmān*). Two leaders of rabbinic academies, Joshua b. Dosā (mid-12th c.) in Egypt and Evyatar ha-Kohen Gaon (ca. 1041–1112) in Palestine, also owned at least one *ghulām*, as did an unnamed leader of the community (*al-rayyis*). The judge (*ha-dayyan*) Zakkay, a contemporary of Samuel's, purchased an enslaved woman named Ghazāl (Gazelle).[60]

The frequency of slave owning among this class of men suggests a kind of enslaved labor that we have not considered and that is rarely discussed in historical sources of any kind. The first type of work is clerical and it involved degrees of literacy. An exceptional example of an enslaved woman who could read and write is Taqarrub (d. 1024), who served as a secretary for the Fatimid princess Sitt al-Mulk (970–1023).[61] Taqarrub presented petitions and information to Sitt al-Mulk when she conducted government business after the mysterious disappearance of her brother, the caliph al-Ḥākim.[62] In his slave-buying advice, Ibn Buṭlān indicates that "leading citizens" who have enemies and secrets to hide should be wary of purchasing a *jāriya* who comes from the ruler's palace (*dār al-sulṭān*), "especially if she can write."[63] This statement, considered alongside the prevalence of slave owners who read, wrote, and kept records for a living, suggests that literate women may have been more common among the enslaved population than surviving documents indicate.[64]

The Mercantile Class

Traders (*al-tujjār*) constituted by far the largest subclass of slave owners documented in *geniza*. Traders owned both males and females, though here I focus on the work that merchants forced enslaved women and girls to do. Much of this work was the same kind of labor, *khidma* and errand running, that served other slave-owning men. The greater prevalence of mercantile slave-owners, however, is due to a kind of "work" that is also largely muted in the *geniza* documents. Traders were the most likely class to use women as sex slaves. The next chapter will analyze the consequences of Jewish men's use sexual slavery despite the efforts of Jewish jurists and leadership to discourage its practice. The present discussion focuses on why traders used sex slaves at all.

Traders were more likely than many other groups to have the financial means to afford an enslaved person, and sometimes more than one. Traders could be both stationary, conducting business using letters and their mobile agents, and traveling. Some merchants traveled primarily within Egypt, while others were continually on the move across the Mediterranean and into the Indian Ocean. In their absence, some traveling merchants provided lump, or monthly, sums of money to their families or designated associates with the express intention that the funds be used for an enslaved person's living expenses. For families of a certain socioeconomic class, it was understood that the costs of maintenance for enslaved servants should be included in such payments.[65]

We met one traveling merchant in this book's first pages. Ibn Jamāhir purchased a woman to use for sex while he was traveling and working in the lands of the western Indian Ocean. He got her pregnant and she bore their child. At this point, according to the accusations made by the *ghulām* Ṣāfī, Ibn Jamāhir sold her and their son in Berbera on the north coast of the Horn of Africa.[66] Another traveling merchant well known to *geniza* scholars is Abraham ben Yijū. Ben Yijū (Ibn Yijū) traveled east from Ifrīqiyya to Egypt, Yemen, and, eventually, to the western coast of India, where he lived from 1132 to 1140 and then again from around 1145 to 1149 and where he worked as an exporter of brassware and other goods.[67] After his arrival in India, Ben Yijū purchased a woman named Ashū.[68] She apparently bore his children there. Ben Yijū later freed Ashū, from which point on she is called by a new name, Berakha. When Ben Yijū and his children left India and returned to Egypt, Ashū was not with them.[69]

Ibn Jamāhir and Ben Yijū represent a class of mobile merchants who traveled widely and who had the desire and means to purchase enslaved women. Merchants were not the only class of men who engaged in this durable kind of sexual slavery. About two centuries later, a Muslim jurist best known for his detailed travelogue, Ibn Baṭṭūṭa (d. 770/1368–69 or 779/1377), bought and sold many women throughout the course of his journeys across the Middle East, the Indian Ocean World, and beyond.[70] Ibn Baṭṭūṭa spent six years in Delhi, where he worked as a judge for the sultan. During that time, he married multiple wives and acquired numerous enslaved women by purchase and as gifts. When the time came for him to arrange sea travel from Delhi to China, he requested a private cabin for himself and the enslaved women that he brought for sex and *khidma*.[71]

Because sexual slavery, and the opportunistic sexual exploitation of all enslaved people regardless of their specialized "type," is such a common and durable feature of slavery across time and space, it is easy to take its practice as a historical given. Yet sexual slavery was also understood by medieval writers as a particularly gross form of violence, even if they accepted it as a legal practice and perpetrated it because they could. Given the ambivalence toward sex slavery, it is worth asking why men in every age kept forcing girls and women to do this "work." The answer to this question differs depending upon the historical context.[72] *Geniza* evidence suggests why Jewish merchants across North Africa and the Indian Ocean worlds between the eleventh and thirteenth centuries used sex slaves instead of, and sometimes alongside of, other kinds of sexual relationships.

I start from the assumption that many traders, and men in general, sought sex through multiple avenues: in and out of marriage, with their wife or wives, licitly and illicitly, with prostitutes,[73] with enslaved women (possibly girls) and men (possibly boys), with free men (boys) and women (girls), coercively and with consent, and so on.[74] Of these groups, enslaved girls and women were both constantly vulnerable to sexual predation and the least likely to have protectors. This fact alone does not tell the whole story, however.

When men sought sex outside of marriage, some of them considered the possible consequences for their social and professional reputations. Traders who used prostitutes, for example, found that other merchants told others about it in their correspondence, as information about merchant behavior was a key part of the reputation management that affected business relationships.[75] Among the news that the trader ʿAllān b. Ḥassūn in Aden shared with his uncle and father-in-law ʿArūs b. Joseph in Cairo was a report about ʿArūs's nephew, Joseph.[76] ʿAllān describes the behavior of his cousin Joseph who had, perhaps disingenuously, tried to dissuade him from setting out to sell coral and storax in Sindābūr (near Goa): "Joseph stays in Lakhba with the whores, companions, and a beardless boy who s[. . .]."[77] Here ʿAllān seems to relay such information as a way to impugn his cousin's character in order to manage his business network's reputation and perhaps to advance his own status vis-à-vis Joseph.

Merchants were not the only class of men who used prostitutes. In Alexandria, one Abū al-Ḥasan al-Dimashqī wrote to a Jewish leader (*al-rayyis*) about one of the community's respected elders who was arrested along with a prostitute (lit. a "woman (or girl) worth [less than] a penny") in one of the city's caravansaries, a place that functioned like a hostel.[78] Abū al-Ḥasan indicates that the elder's arrest was partly a result of deceit and was related to a more pervasive atmosphere of "hatred" in the city.

Jewish men who had sex with Muslim women, or even those who were caught in suggestive circumstances, risked running afoul of Islamic authorities and thus facing imprisonment, fines, and corporal punishment. An Arabic-script petition for help in such a case provides details about a man who experienced these consequences firsthand.[79] The petitioner, who probably sought intervention from a state authority,[80] reports:

> [I inform] your lofty presence . . . of what happened last night in the town, namely, that (the official titled) *minḥat al-dawla* apprehended a Maghribī Jewish trader who was with a Muslim woman. They had been drinking together for three days in his compound in this noble month (of Ramaḍān). He (*minḥat al-dawla*) took them, and with them, a Muslim man who owned the wall neighboring (his compound). All of them are in the prison of the chief of police.[81]

Another incident, this time involving a Jewish traveler from Ceuta, in the Maghrib, to Bijāya in Algeria, echoes the circumstances of this man and woman's arrest. In Bijāya this traveler was imprisoned after the town authority (here, *ṣāḥib al-Bijāya*) questioned him about his female companion: How is this woman related to you? The traveler replied that she was his wife. When he could not provide a document that proved this, the *ṣāḥib* confiscated all his belongings and put him in jail.[82] Thus, sex with free women, whether they were sex workers (prostitutes) or not, could lead to a range of bad outcomes, from embarrassment to imprisonment.

Polygyny (plural marriage) was possible for some men in Egypt. Mordechai Friedman's research shows that Jewish men in Egypt, especially during the twelfth century, were legally permitted to take a second wife despite debate among Jewish jurists and variable practices across other medieval Jewish communities.[83] For men primarily interested in sex, but less so in legitimate progeny, plural marriage had complications in addition to its potential costs. To begin with, Jewish law restricted the conditions under which a man could take a second wife. Men needed their first wives' permission to take a second wife and then would need to provide for each wife's separate quarters and maintenance in addition to paying the sums specified in the new wives' *ketubbas*. When a man violated these conditions, the first wife could divorce him and demand all of the payments specified in her *ketubba*, which could entail a considerable expense.[84]

Women and their families also began to tailor their engagement and marriage agreements proactively to prevent men from taking second wives and buying enslaved women of whom the wife or wives did not approve. In his research on the emergence of written engagement contracts, *geniza* scholar Amir Ashur demonstrates that the formalization of these protections coincide with the twelfth-century intensification of merchants' long-distance travel in the western Indian Ocean world and beyond.[85] In other words, the content of Jewish women's engagement contracts reflects the behavior of the growing class of traveling merchants, whose absences strained household life to begin with and whose decisions to purchase enslaved women and sometimes take second wives exacerbated the plight of those left behind.

For some Jewish men, the purchase of an enslaved woman for sex, though discouraged by Jewish law, was an acceptable risk to take. Because Islamic law allowed men to use enslaved women for sex, a Jewish man's sexual use of a slave was not troubling to Muslim authorities unless there were other extenuating circumstances.[86] For a Jewish man, particularly if he was a mobile one, the enslaved woman's lack of status and kin networks made her an easier and more manipulable target than a free woman. The fact that an enslaved woman could be resold without much or any loss of money besides possible brokers' fees was no doubt an added appeal for mobile men of means. For unfree women, the impact of men's calculus was experienced as sexual violence and continual sale and resale in markets throughout the Mediterranean and Indian Ocean worlds.

This chapter is a bridge between part 1 of the book and its remaining chapters. It has refocused our attention from the interregional and local slave trade to the urban households where the lives of enslavers and enslaved people were unequally bound together. It has also critiqued the category of "domestic" slavery that has long been used to describe this system and instead adopted the language of *khidma* used by the slave-owning classes in their own writing on the subject. *Khidma*, or personal service, entailed the types of work inside the home that "domestic" implies. What made slavery *lil-khidma* even more valuable to slave owners, however, was that enslaved people were made to move *within* and *without* the home to do all kinds of labor tailored to their household's needs and desires.

A key mode of interpretation in this chapter followed the idea that scholars of slavery can tell a fuller story by moving beyond the quest merely to identify the presence of enslaved people to understanding "the implications of the fact of their presence." This reorientation recognizes that enslaved people did not leave behind explicit material traces of their slave status in the archaeological record of the medieval Middle East. Instead, they lived and worked where slave owners did, and the material culture of their daily life and work resembled the clothes and implements used by most everyone. This insight has animated the chapter's investigation of the "invisible" dimensions of slavery *lil-khidma* that have been hiding in plain sight in the domestic architecture, dowry lists of household implements, and urban environment of public ovens, food stalls, water sources, and the alleyways that connected them.

The collective biography of the slave-owning classes, especially their gender ratio and professional affiliations, is instrumental in making more visible the daily work of enslaved people and the socioeconomic location of slavery in society at large. Enslaved women worked in apothecaries and other artisan workshops. A small number of them could read and write, and their knowledge enabled their owners to use them in work that required some literacy. The final section of this chapter argued that the prevalence of traders among the slave-owning classes was due to their use of enslaved women and girls as sex slaves.

The rest of the book now employs this chapter's findings to different ends. The next chapter investigates how Jewish men's use of sex slaves created tension within the larger Jewish community and how it bedeviled the leaders and jurists who sought to stop it. These tensions gave rise to masculine competition among Jewish men, both over how slavery should be regulated and who had the power to control it. Chapter 6 explores the ramifications of Jewish women's slave-owning. Free women imagined the enslaved women and girls whom they owned to be like kin to them in a culture within which free women were legally and socially disadvantaged in relation to free Jewish men. The feminine ideals embraced by slave-owning Jews meant that the *khidma* of enslaved people benefited free women in unique ways. The book's penultimate chapter builds on the themes of *khidma*, mobility, and sex work to center the life histories of enslaved women as knowledgeable agents whose experiences, chances, and choices were powerfully shaped, but not fully determined, by these factors.

5

Slavery and Masculinity

THIS CHAPTER RECALLS two main arguments made in previous chapters. Chapter 1 argued that medieval Jewish law in Egypt lacked both a clear framework and coercive mechanisms for effectively regulating Jewish men's use of enslaved women for sex in a larger Muslim society where sexual slavery was legal and culturally accepted. And chapter 4 revealed that Jewish merchants were the single largest class of slave owners in the Egyptian Jewish community, and it explained why merchants, and other classes of Jewish men, chose to use enslaved women for sex even though their jurists and leaders in Egypt sought to forbid the practice. With that in mind, this chapter focuses on the controversies and competitions that emerged in the Jewish community and among Jewish families due to sexual slavery.

Such was the case around the middle of the twelfth century, when a marital dispute erupted in part over a husband's sexual exploitation of his wife's *jāriya*. The details of this case are preserved in two separate petitions that were sent on the wife's behalf to the head (*nagid*) of the Egyptian Jewish community, Samuel b. Ḥananya.[1] The husband, a silk weaver or merchant (*qazzāz*) called Abū al-Faraj, used heavy-handed tactics against his unnamed wife in the apparent negotiations over the terms of their divorce.[2] He was verbally belligerent and pressured her to accept a smaller and delayed marriage gift than they had earlier agreed upon.[3] Though he was supposed to meet his wife's younger brother and return some of her possessions, Abū al-Faraj delayed doing so and recruited other people to support him in his tactics. He also took an enslaved woman who rightly belonged to his wife. In defiance of Samuel's orders, Abū al-Faraj settled this *jāriya* at his sister's house where he reportedly "maintained the slave girl as needed" and "spent more and more of his time with her."[4] Using the modest language of the twelfth century, the petitions' writers made clear to Samuel that Abū al-Faraj was using his estranged wife's *jāriya* as a concubine. As he and his wife came closer to finalizing their divorce, Abū al-Faraj eventually purchased the woman—though in another gesture of disrespect he refused to pay the broker's fee normally incumbent on the buyer.[5]

Abū al-Faraj's actions are a specific example of the larger trend in which some men used enslaved women for sex in defiance of the Egyptian Jewish community's leaders. While no additional known records survive that detail what became of this disintegrating family and the anonymous enslaved woman, other contemporary sources illustrate that Jewish men's sex with enslaved women understandably created household strife that spilled over into the gendered politics of the Jewish community. The Jewish community's failure to clarify and consistently enforce a Jewish law of sexual slavery had a host of unintended consequences that affected both free men, their families, and, of course, the enslaved women.[6] We notice the ambiguity of these laws in the reactions of Jewish Egyptian leaders and laypeople who expressed exasperation and even confusion over how to handle cases in which Jewish men used enslaved women for sex. This ambiguity emboldened some of the Jewish men who used women in this way to do as they wished despite social pressure and Jewish communal authorities' condemnation. For other men, such ambiguity led them and other communal leaders to experiment with different strategies that permitted them to interpret and implement Jewish law so they could legitimize these women and their joint offspring as members of the Jewish community. This ambiguity also amplified the already liminal status of enslaved women and their children, both in law and in daily life.[7] They were more vulnerable to caprice since they did not have any special protections in Jewish law that were analogous to those that mitigated the plight of *umm walad*s (enslaved mothers) in Islamic law and social practice.[8]

This chapter analyzes these disputes and their effects on people's lives. Because they could not prevent the practice, Jewish jurists and leaders chose to make accommodations for the Jewish men who took enslaved women as concubines. Jewish men's competition with each other over the sexual exploitation of enslaved women forced such accommodations and was one way in which they constructed and projected masculinity in a larger society in which they were socially and legally subservient to Muslim men. This competition also reflected, and helped constitute, male privilege and dominance over all women in their households, wives in particular.[9] But dominance over women was not the only way that men portrayed their masculinity. For other men of the slave-holding classes constructed quite different masculine ideals—ones that emphasized charity, circumspection in religious matters, and the manumission of enslaved people as a mode of piety. The culture of male slave-owning illustrates the multiplicity and dialectics of medieval masculinities.

Persistent Controversies over Sexual Slavery

Explicit documentary evidence of Jewish men's use of enslaved women for sex is densest for the roughly one-hundred-year period between the mid-twelfth century and the first half of the thirteenth century. The scant evidence that survives from the eleventh century is consistent with what we know from the later period. In a letter sent to a Jewish leader (*nagid*) in the community of Qayrawān, the author shares news about a visit to Egypt by the Iraqi leader (*nasi*) Daniel b. ʿAzarya (d. 1062).[10] The author reports approvingly that Daniel issued a proclamation that "removed the slave girls from the houses," a statement that *geniza* scholars have interpreted as a condemnation of concubinage.[11] The lack of evidence as yet does not allow us to gauge whether Daniel's proclamation was effective, but we do know that Jewish men bought enslaved women for sex in the second half of the eleventh century and beyond.

The mid-twelfth century is the time of the merchant Ibn Jamāhir, who sold his *jāriya* and their child in Berbera. It is the era of Abraham b. Yijū, who had children with his *shifḥa* Ashū in India.[12] And it is the period when the silk weaver Abū al-Faraj took his wife's *jāriya* as his concubine and defied local Jewish leaders to do so. The latter half of the twelfth century also corresponds with the life of Moses Maimonides in Egypt, whose writings provide a wealth of insight into Jewish slave-owning. In chapter 1, we read about a responsum of Moses Maimonides in which he rejected the applicability of the law of the "beautiful captive woman" when asked about the legality of a Jewish man's cohabitation with an enslaved Christian woman.[13] In the written query sent to Maimonides about this case, the author explains that this slave owner's family found his behavior repugnant. The local community also "gossiped" about him and his *jāriya*. Though Maimonides rejected one legal avenue for resolving this communal crisis, he suggested another accommodation: that it is preferable either for the man to sell the woman or to free her and marry her. He recognizes that such a marriage was technically forbidden since it was clear that the slave owner had been using his *jāriya* for sex, and moreover that the man's behavior was "bad news" and a "corrupted situation." "But," he adds, "*we have ruled in several similar cases* that he should manumit and marry her. And we did so to enable repentance, for we have said 'it is better that he should eat the gravy than the actual forbidden fat.'"[14] As Miriam Frenkel and Moshe Yagur have also concluded, Maimonides's opinion in this responsum, and his claim to have ruled likewise in several similar cases, illustrate how jurists yielded to "a widespread social phenomenon."[15] There is more to say about this case below in this chapter and in chapter 7.

Questions about Concubinage in the Responsa of Abraham Maimonides

For the first part of the thirteenth century, the densest cluster of evidence for sexual slavery in the Egyptian Jewish community comes from the responsa of Abraham Maimonides, the only son of Moses Maimonides. Abraham Maimonides became the head of the Jewish community (*rayyis al-yahūd*) at around eighteen years of age.[16] Like his father, Abraham continued to receive queries about Jewish men who had purchased enslaved women for sex. When asked about the biblical practice of concubinage (*pilagshut*), Abraham's reply echoes what his father wrote in the *Mishneh Torah*: concubines are only permitted to kings; they are forbidden to all other Jews.[17]

Goitein was the first to notice that several responsa about sex slavery in the *geniza* were sent to Abraham Maimonides, and Friedman later published editions of them in his work on Jewish polygyny.[18] For most of these particular responsa manuscripts, only the queries survived. Still, the questions that Jews asked are just as historically valuable as the answers they received. As the historian Pinchas Roth argues in his scholarship on responsa from medieval Provence, queries to legal scholars demonstrate the concerns of the Jewish community as a whole. Their rhetorical composition can reflect a complex mix of preoccupations, motives, and even manipulations.[19] For the Egyptian case, it is noteworthy that Jews preserved these queries and eventually deposited them in the *geniza*, despite the lack of jurists' replies. In this light, the questions posed to Abraham are rich sources precisely because they speak to the attitudes and concerns of Egyptian Jews toward the vexing issue of sex slavery in the first decades of the thirteenth century.

Four queries written and posed to Abraham present a variety of scenarios and questions. A single manuscript page, now in the David Kaufmann Collection in Budapest, contains two queries.[20] The first question begins:

> What do you say . . . in the case of a person who buys a slave woman who is not a slave woman for personal service (*wa-laysa hiya jāriyat khidma*)? He has a wife and (he) is not with her in one town. He rents a house for the aforementioned slave woman, and he lodges her there. This man is not one

who is concerned with religion. He travels for work and then he returns to the slave woman. He has a wife and children in Alexandria. Instruct us whether he is allowed to do this or not.

After leaving a finger-width of space, the writer turns to a second scenario:

Instruct us in the case of a person who has never been married. He purchased a Christian slave woman (*jāriya ʿarela*), converted her, and resides with her constantly—and there is no *ketubba* or betrothal (*qiddushin*). Instruct us. Is [this permitted to him?][21]

A third query, now in the British Library, reads:

Concerning a person who does not have a wife, whether his wife died, or he has never married in his life: he takes a slave woman. She is not a freedwoman and is not betrothed (to him). He resides with her constantly. There is not a single one of his relatives with him in the house—just he and the slave woman, who (has not been) manumitted. Instruct us if he is permitted to reside with her before he frees her and marries her with a *ketubba* and a betrothal (*qiddushin*). And if they have a son, what will (his status) be? What is the solution for this?[22]

The fourth responsum is the only one for which Abraham's response is preserved, and that reply is written in his own hand. This responsum is found on two separate manuscript pages held in the Cambridge University Library's Taylor-Schechter Genizah Collection. These two pages were long separated, by decades and perhaps centuries, until Friedman found that they were originally part of a single sheet of paper (figure 5.1).[23] One can see two sets of handwriting. In semiblock handwriting, an unnamed scribe has composed or copied a legal query about concubinage. The scribe then left a blank space of about six centimeters so that Abraham could later write a response.

After a customary litany of greetings and honorifics for Abraham, the "distinguished master," "the *nagid* of all the *nagids*," and the "powerful hammer," the writer asks Abraham for his opinion:

What do you say . . . concerning a Jew who has a wife and children by her in Alexandria: He discarded her, left, and then bought a slave woman. She was not a slave for personal service (*jāriya lil-khidma*), but rather a concubine (*ama surriyya*), or the lady of the house (*ṣāhibat al-manzil*).[24] He took up with her for a time. When he left—traveling to the Fayyūm—he

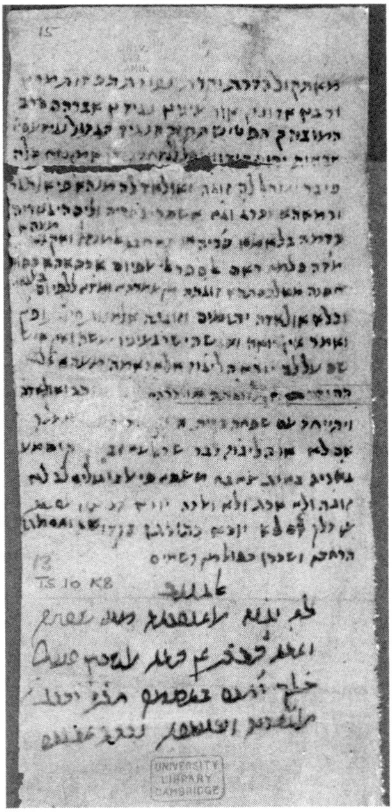

FIGURE 5.1. An autographed responsum of Abraham Maimonides. T-S 6J2.15 + T-S 10K8.13. Paper. 8.5 × 20 cm. Reproduced by kind permission of the Syndics of Cambridge University Library.

clothed her in fine garments the likes of which his wife had never worn. Thus he departed for the Fayyūm with the slave woman, abandoning his children as orphans and his wife like a widow of a living man (*almenut ḥayyut*). As it is said, "No one sees, and every man does as he sees fit. No man pays any heed."[25]

Teach us (the law in this matter): Is he allowed to take up with her without (giving her) a *ketubba* and without paying his wife her delayed marriage gift? For he abandoned his wife and children, and he is alone with a slave woman at home. She is residing with him. Is this allowed, or not? Is it permissible for an unmarried Jewish man to reside with a slave woman, spending the entire day and night with her in the house? And he does not have a wife, a sister, or his children (with him). Teach us if silence concerning this matter is permissible. If not, teach us according to his holy Law and his expansive wisdom. May his reward be multiplied in heaven.

The second semicursive hand belongs to Abraham. He titles his writing "The Response (*al-jawāb*)" and signs his terse response at the end.[26]

> The unchaperoned situation with the slave woman is not permissible. And if it is confirmed that this person did this, (then) pronounce a ban (of excommunication) upon his name until he leaves the slave woman, has sent her out, and has distanced himself from her. Signed—Abraham[27]

These four queries rehearse many of the themes and anxieties that attended Egyptian Jewish men's use of sex slavery. As chapter 4 explained, when a writer states that a man purchased a woman who "was not a slave for personal service (*laysa hiya jāriya lil-khidma*)," especially when he stresses that the man and woman are alone together in a residence, he means that she was purchased for sex. The slave-owning men described in the queries travel for work between, for example, the city of Alexandria and the rural region of the Fayyūm (map 2), which was a center of flax production.[28]

When married men purchase enslaved women for sex they sometimes "abandon" their wives and children, both by residing elsewhere without them and by redirecting material support away from them to the enslaved concubine in the form of rent and fine clothing. Writers mention these details because they had a larger social meaning—they signal the marginalization and humiliation of the abandoned wife and children. As one writer stresses, the traveling merchant put his concubine (*surriyya*) up in her own lodging and then bought her "fine garments (the likes) of which his wife had never worn."[29] The gravity of a wife's circumstances were also greatly exacerbated if her estranged husband did not grant her a deed of divorce (a *geṭ*). She would be, as the query writer states, "a widow of a living man" unable to remarry until she received this written deed. Husbands who had agreed to pay a delayed marriage gift (*me'uḥar*) in the event of divorce might also withhold it and use the *geṭ* as leverage to compel a woman to accept a lower than agreed upon sum.[30]

Notably, the enslaved women in these queries are portrayed largely as accessories to men's misdeeds, but without any expectation that they have legal protections—at least as slaves. The sole preserved response indicates that Abraham viewed the women as a problem to be solved through their sale, that is, by enslavement to another owner. Children born to Jewish men and enslaved women were a different matter. There was great anxiety about the status of these children—a worry that the query writers emphasize as well: "If they have a son, what will (his status) be?" In reading the litany of questions in these queries, we can only appreciate the rhetorical impact that that would have had if we also consider the larger Islamic legal context that we read about in chapter 1, and in particular the rights of the *umm walad* (enslaved mother) and her freeborn, Muslim children. We might then read between the lines of these queries and detect a commentary about the fact that Egyptian Muslims had a law that permitted sexual slavery and provided Muslims with ways to preserve the marriages and protect the children in slave-owning families of men who used enslaved women for sex. The rhetoric of the queries suggests an unstated question:

How do we as Jews in this society confront the dilemmas posed by sex slavery in our own community?

Chapter 1 showed that Jewish law was multivocal on the subject of what to do with Jewish men, their sex slaves, and their children. Some opinions stress unequivocally that such a child would be born with slave status, other rulings permitted accommodations that recognized offspring as legitimate. These queries to Abraham Maimonides seem crafted to elicit a reaffirmation of the accommodation offered by his father Moses Maimonides that we encountered just above. "It is better that he should eat the gravy than the actual forbidden fat." In other words, manumit the enslaved woman and marry her according to Jewish law with a betrothal (*qiddushin*) and a wedding contract (*ketubba*).[31] This solution made the enslaved woman a Jewish wife whose children would be born, unimpeachably, as Jews.[32]

The queries are not only valuable for their rhetorical stances. They also illuminate and corroborate the social history that emerges from documentary *geniza* sources that often lack the context that responsa provide. Recall the case of Abū al-Faraj, his wife, and their enslaved servant, whom we met at the outset of this chapter. The correspondences between this twelfth-century evidence and later twelfth-century and early-thirteenth-century responsa are instructive. When Abū al-Faraj took (and eventually purchased) an enslaved woman, he put her up at his sister's house where he "maintained her as needed" and spent "more and more of his time with her."[33] At the same time, he refused to pay his wife the full delayed marriage gift to which they had agreed. As his wife and her supporters claimed, she was "cut-off" and "desolate." She and their young daughter are "cast to the floor. [Abū al-Faraj] pays us no attention."[34]

Documentary records also illustrate that Jewish courts investigated the timing of enslaved people's manumission and the status of their children. In a case first brought to light by Mordechai Friedman, the traveling merchant ʿEli b. Yefet Ibn al-Wāsitī purchased a Nubian woman in Ashkelon (*ʿAsqalān*) along with the enslaved woman's daughter; the daughter had died some time before this court appearance.[35] The mother's name is partly obliterated where the document is torn in two, so I will call her "Umm Nūbiyya," which can be understood as a Nubian mother or mother of a Nubian girl.[36] By profession and social connections, ʿEli belonged to the slave-owning class. His networks included a welfare official in Fustat as well as other Jewish notables, merchants, and apothecaries in Ashkelon and elsewhere.[37] At some point before 1093, ʿEli had freed Umm Nūbiyya, married her with a *ketubba* and *qiddushin*, and had traveled to Fustat with her. They also had a daughter together named Milāḥ. ʿEli was summoned to the court in

Fustat because he, or someone else in the Jewish community, wanted to establish the legal status of his daughter Milāḥ beyond any doubt of possible slave status.[38] At issue before the court was the timing of Umm Nūbiyya's manumission and the identity of their living daughter. Was she the enslaved child that ʿEli had purchased along with her mother in Ashkelon? Or was she in fact another child born *after* ʿEli freed and married Umm Nūbiyya? The court scribe was also careful to write, perhaps at ʿEli's or the judge's behest, that ʿEli had purchased Umm Nūbiyya "for personal service (*lil-khidma*)." In short, ʿEli had not purchased her to use as a sex slave in Ashkelon.

For the sake of his daughter Milāḥ's social capital and, perhaps most pressingly, her marriage prospects, it was important for ʿEli to prove that Milāḥ was a freeborn Jew. If the court found otherwise, he could have faced pressure to divorce Umm Nūbiyya. Milāḥ herself would need to undergo a formal conversion to Judaism before a Jewish court. Each of these anxieties motivated this family to leave the court in Fustat with written evidence in hand that supported their claims to being lawfully wed after Umm Nūbiyya's manumission and before Milāḥ's birth. In a real sense, these specific concerns led to the creation of the evidence that allows us to know their history.

Medieval Masculinities

We should also consider the possibility that the court was motivated to make an example of ʿEli, and that it did not intend to rule that he divorce Umm Nūbiyya or that Milāḥ had been born with slave status. In such a scenario, the court investigated ʿEli to perform its authority over Jewish men, women, and children, however limited that power was as a *dhimmī* institution. The last section of this chapter argues that controversies over sexual slavery were one domain in which Jewish men behaved according to different masculine ideals.

Modern scholarship on masculinity in medieval societies provides insights into two key themes. First, masculinity is often engendered through competition between men. Second, this competition illustrates that there are multiple forms of masculinity and that these ideals evolve in tension with each other. As the historian Ruth Karras shows in her study of medieval England, political power was so narrowly held in the Middle Ages that it was not a common way for most men to assert their masculinity. As a result, a "core component of medieval masculinity is the need to prove oneself in competition with other men and to dominate others."[39] In England, idioms of masculinity differed across different social cleavages, such as those between noble and peasant, rich and poor, and Christian and Jew. As Karras underscores, patriarchy thus "meant not just the dominance of men over women, but the dominance of a small number of men over most men and all women. It is not always possible entirely to disentangle one form of domination from another."[40]

Michelle Armstrong-Partida's history of "defiant" parish priests in medieval Catalonia illustrates the multiplicity of medieval masculinities. She shows how the Church's campaign to instill celibacy among the clergy precipitated a "crisis of masculinity."[41] This campaign, spurred by the Gregorian reforms of the eleventh and twelfth centuries, sought in part to insulate clergy from the "secular world." Some clergy, the clerical elite in particular, were able to fashion masculine ideals that embraced celibacy and emphasized their roles as "spiritual fathers" who valiantly defended the church from the supposedly morally corrupt laity who were greedy, violent, and captive to sexual desire. These elite clerics could embrace and champion this mode of masculinity because their social world was composed of other men who "shared their views, goals, and elite backgrounds."[42]

"Defiant" parish priests, as "the working class of an international institution," embraced masculine ideals more in keeping with the normative, or hegemonic, masculinity of their environment. For these men, the masculinity of elite clerics would have alienated them from their parishioners on account of its propensity to "[shun] women" and "denigrate" lay masculinity. For these and other reasons, parish priests adapted to forms of lay masculinity that valued "being the head of a household composed of a woman and children, providing for the family, protecting oneself and one's family . . . , dominating socially inferior men, and socializing with male peers to validate one's male status." As heads of households, parish priests rejected celibacy and procreated within concubinous unions that resembled marriage.[43]

Like their lay and clerical counterparts in Catalonia, Jewish men in Egypt were not monolithic in their masculinity, nor in their socioeconomic positions within Egyptian society. Some Jewish slave owners were a part of the community's leadership class—either as leaders themselves or as members of their families. For jurists and communal leaders, their social positions depended more on upholding the power and prestige of Jewish law and the efficacy of their offices. Other slave owners were part of the merchant and artisan classes. While they, too, could be among the community's leaders, a subset of these men was frequently on the move and less likely to be as rooted in a local community. As such, masculine ideals that hinged upon status and prestige in local settings and hierarchies were less appealing or accessible to them. These variable affinities led Jewish men to embrace different forms of masculinity and this brought them into conflicts that the controversies over sexual slavery lay bare. As the sociologist R. W. Connell writes:

> To recognize diversity in masculinities is not enough. We must also recognize the relations between the different kinds of masculinity: relations of alliance, dominance and subordination. These relationships are constructed through practices that exclude and include, that intimidate, exploit, and so on. There is a gender politics within masculinity.[44]

Such gender politics of Jewish masculinities are evident in the rhetoric of our sources. One durable theme is that there are some slave-owning men who can be trusted and deserve the benefit of the doubt. Other men are not trustworthy. This attitude is evident in Moses Maimonides's *Mishneh Torah* regarding slave-owning men who claim that their sons were born to manumitted women (i.e., sons thus born as free Jews and not with slave status). He writes:

> If the man is a scholar or a trustworthy man who is exacting in his strict observance of the commandments, then the son shall inherit from him. . . . (But) if (the father) is a commoner, and needless to say, if he was among those who act freely in this way . . . then (the son) is presumed to be a slave for all purposes.[45]

In one of the responsa queries to Moses's son Abraham Maimonides, the "trustworthy scholar" is implicitly contrasted with the man who uses his *jāriya* for sex and who is thus apparently not "concerned with religion."[46] In Abraham's response to a question about the permissibility of *pilagshut*, he equates, in biblical terms, Jewish men's use of sex slaves with societal disorder through an allusion to the book of Judges: "In those days, there was no king in Israel. Every man did as he saw fit."[47]

Jewish masculinities were also conditioned by the Jews' status as *dhimmīs*. *Dhimmī* status had multiple implications. On the one hand, it meant that the Egyptian state recognized and protected Jews' rights as slave owners. On the other hand, subordination meant Jewish men were limited in how they could perform forms of masculine dominance that were the privilege only of free Muslim men of certain statuses. This subordination hindered Jewish jurists and leaders who sought to establish and enforce the rules of slave ownership. As we have read above, they did not have the coercive power to enforce their own rulings—there were no Jewish police forces, prisons, or other such institutions. One of the strongest tactics available to Jewish leaders was the ban of excommunication, which we saw Abraham Maimonides suggest as an option in one of his responsa.[48] Yet even excommunication in the Egyptian Jewish community had limited effect. Mobility was one factor that complicated a ban's enforcement. Men were known to evade the effect of a ban by moving to a new city.

When Jews sought to enforce bans or to coerce other men to behave in a certain way, they sometimes sought out the Islamic state's help.[49] We read above about a Jewish man who upset his family and the local community by taking a Christian woman as a concubine. This case may never have been recorded for posterity were it not for a heated argument between this slave owner and his irate brother. The brother was upset because his slave-owning sibling lived with his enslaved concubine in the same house as his father's wife and her three young children.[50] The situation led to a vociferous argument between the two brothers but not to any resolution. Incensed, the irate brother reported his sibling to a Muslim judge and alleged that his sibling had converted the enslaved concubine to Judaism.[51] It seems that Muslim judges did not actively seek to investigate the religious status of enslaved people in Jewish household. But when the issue was thrust before them, the judges did not ignore it. The Christian concubine was summoned before the judge, and her testimony surprised everyone. You will read more about her strategic gambit in chapter 7.

While some men performed their masculinity as the judges of Jewish law and the custodians of Jewish institutions, others, like the slave-owning silk weaver Abū al-Faraj and the merchant Ibn Jamāhir, performed theirs by demonstrating that they could defy Jewish communal norms with relative impunity. They did this both by dominating free and unfree women and by intimidating other men. The petitioners who wrote on behalf of Abū al-Faraj's wife stressed that she lacked a strong, male protector who could stand up to her husband.[52] Her father refused to help her, and her brother was "too bashful" to be of much use.[53] Not only did Abū al-Faraj spurn the attempted interventions of appointed mediators, including the head (*nagid*) of the Jewish community, but he then doubled down on his behavior and tactics by spending "more and more time" with his wife's *jāriya* and by withholding money and clothing due to his wife and their daughter.[54] Jewish leaders lacked the coercive tools to force Abū al-Faraj to honor his marriage agreements (in his wife's *ketubba*), let alone to compel him to let go of the woman whom he used as a concubine.

In his defiance of Jewish legal and cultural norms, Ibn Jamāhir borrowed a tactic from the very Jewish judges and leaders who opposed his gross exploitation and abandonment of an enslaved woman. He went to Muslim authorities and asked them to use violence and coercion in his conflict with other Jews with one of their *ghulāms*, Ṣāfī. The other Jewish merchants in the Red Sea port of

ʿAydhāb were sympathetic to Ṣāfī if only because at that time he served the head of the rabbinic academy in Cairo. These merchants are probably the ones who wanted this deposition taken and sent to Fustat. The story told in the deposition illustrates how the politics of masculine competition cut in multiple directions:

> [T]he chief of police sent a herald to assemble the Jews. . . . Some (Jews) hid themselves. Officers escorted some of them (before the chief). When the chief saw that the aforementioned Ibn Jamāhir was incensed, he ordered Ṣāfī to be flogged. Ṣāfī decried and ardently protested (the order) to beat him saying "I am the *ghulām* of the *rayyis*, the head of the rabbinic academy!" Ibn Jamāhir retorted: "I demand justice!"[55] After (the beating), (the chief) ordered (Ṣāfī) to be put in jail. Thus, he was imprisoned in the presence of his adversary (Ibn Jamāhir), who was the plaintiff against him, and in the presence of all of the Jews who had been assembled.

Ibn Jamāhir perhaps did not think anyone back in the Egyptian Jewish community would know that he had fathered a child by an enslaved woman and then sold her in Somalia (Berbera). When Ṣāfī, who was supposed to be subordinate to him, confronted him in ʿAydhāb, Ibn Jamāhir became enraged and brought the power and violence of Muslim authorities down upon the *ghulām*. The fact that some of the other Jewish merchants hid from the police chief's emissary suggests that they did not approve of Ibn Jamāhir and that his use of the police intimidated them. The terse observation that the chief of police jailed Ṣāfī "in the presence of all the Jews" shows that the chief had sought to assemble the Jews not for their legal testimonies but rather as witnesses to Ṣāfī's punishment and humiliation. Ṣāfī withstood a beating and detention that reinforced everyone's place in the intersecting hierarchies of masculinity and the *dhimmī*s' subordination to Muslims. That Ibn Jamāhir, a Jew, had aligned himself with Muslim authorities to get what he wanted was not an anomaly of this system but rather a feature of it.

The *ghulām* Ṣāfī was not a bystander. He knew the unwritten rules of masculine competition and he deployed them rhetorically by shouting (I paraphrase), "How dare you punish me, the *ghulām* of a powerful and honorable man!"[56] There was yet more to this scene. The deposition continues:

> It happened before the slave (*al-ʿabd*) Ṣāfī's beating that one of the (Jewish) Maghribī[57] merchants went to the police chief's house to save the slave (*al-ʿabd*). When Abū Saʿīd Ibn Jamāhir learned that he had requested Ṣāfī's release, he recruited some Muslim associates (*aqwām min al-muslimīn*) and set them

> against this merchant from out of town (*al-gharīb*).[58] They made life difficult for him and threaten[ed him with] a fine and other things[59] after making false accusations against him.[60] Ṣāfī was freed from detention only after paying a fine.[61] This is what happened.

The men who testified for this deposition were not neutral observers, as they are clearly sympathetic to (and perhaps among) the other Jewish merchants in ʿAydhāb who had been coercively "unmanned" by a Muslim chief of police, Ibn Jamāhir, and this merchant's Muslim supporters.[62] In this episode at least, these merchants had chosen or been compelled to align themselves with an alternate mode of masculinity that was rooted in Jewish religious norms and institutions, one that was pitted in this instance against a masculinity of dominion. Their social positions were buoyed by their association with the head of the rabbinic academy in Cairo through their support for his *ghulām* Ṣāfī.

There is no evidence that Ibn Jamāhir suffered any social or other consequences back in Cairo. He was a known figure in elite Jewish communal and mercantile circles.[63] The last thing we know about him was how he died. A few years after this event, Ibn Jamāhir drowned in a shipwreck near the port of Aden. The rabbinical court in Fustat coordinated with the "representative of the merchants (*wakīl al-tujjār*)" in Yemen to settle his estate. In Fustat, Ibn Jamāhir had left behind a widow, a young son, and two minor orphan girls for whom he apparently also provided.[64] Witnesses from Aden testified to the court in Fustat:

> We were indeed fully acquainted with our master and lord Ḥalfon (Ibn Jamāhir). . . . When he was cast up from the sea, we saw him and recognized his appearance . . . his face and nose were intact, without change. We were present as his burial.[65]

Ibn Jamāhir's example illustrates that not only were there multiple masculine ideals, but that the same man could perform according to two seemingly opposed scripts. According to one, he fathered a child by his *jāriya*, left them in a distant land, and then intimidated all those who criticized his behavior. In the other, he, along with his wife, adopted two orphaned children and raised them as an act of piety.[66] Nothing more is known about the history of this specific *jāriya* and her child. Chapter 7 does tell the stories of people like them.

We do not know the names of the other Jewish merchants in ʿAydhāb, nor do we have further records about what motivated them to record the deposition that shines a spotlight on Ibn Jamāhir's violent caprice. Contemporaneous records do illustrate, however, how other Jewish men performed a masculinity of "the scholar and trustworthy man" who acted as "good" slave owners. Some men chose to free their *jāriyas* as an act of piety and as a part of their legacies. One example is the dying man Abū al-Ḥasan, who was confined to his bed when he proclaimed that his two *jāriyas*, Kashf (Discovery) and Gharaḍ (Wish), should be freed "like all proper Jews (*mithla saʾīr kashiri Yisraʾel*)."[67] He then added a provision for the "young girl (*al-ṣaghīra*)" Kashf. She, he instructed, "shall remain with my young sister Sitt al-Riʾāsa until she is old enough to make her own choices (*ilā an tudrik al-mukhayyara*). Then, if she wants to remain, she shall remain. And if she chooses to leave, she shall leave."[68] The open-ended nature of Abū al-Ḥasan's declaration, and the lack of further evidence about Kashf's life, mean that we don't know what choice she eventually made.

The story of another freedwoman suggests one possible trajectory. In the late eleventh century, a dyer known as Ibn al-Watīd freed a woman whom he owned because "he sought recompense from God."[69] In other words, Ibn al-Watīd cast his decision to free his enslaved woman as an act of repentance. The freedwoman, whose slave name is not known, adopted the name Mubāraka.[70] We know about Mubāraka because the welfare official (*parnas*) ʿEli ha-Kohen sought the aid of a Jewish woman in Fustat to find Mubāraka a marital match to "one of our coreligionists (*aṣḥābunā al-yahūd*)."[71] ʿEli subsequently commissioned a scribe to write a deed in which the Jewish woman, identified only as "the mother of Saʿd al-Mulk," vouched for Mubāraka's status as a freed, Jewish woman. He knew that the written evidence would also help him persuade potential grooms of Mubāraka's marriageable status as a freed convert to Judaism.[72]

These men were all a part of the slave-owning classes, either as slave owners in fact or by virtue of their socioeconomic status. And we do not know how they acquired and used enslaved women prior to these single moments when the documents provide these specific snapshots. Abū al-Ḥasan's declaration to manumit Kashf and Gharaḍ so they could be "proper Jews"; Ibn al-Watīd's emancipation of Mubāraka as a supplication for God's recompense; and ʿEli's intervention to find her a groom: all these actions illustrate how men also performed masculinity through piety and in ways that give documentary texture to the topos of the "trustworthy" man, and the "good" slave owner, that we find in legal writings. In an Islamic society and Jewish community where men had power and privilege over all women, and especially over enslaved ones, these men's choices give a fuller picture of the dialectical construction of masculinities.[73]

A central argument of this book is that slave owning was a practice that engendered Jewish culture in medieval Egypt. In this Islamic society, sexual slavery was a legal and sanctioned form of biological and cultural reproduction. Jewish men purchased women for sex, despite the efforts of Jewish jurists and communal leaders to end the practice. This conflict was made more fraught by the principle of matrilineal descent in Jewish law, as well as the legal ambiguities concerning sex with enslaved women. Legal queries sent to scholars show that laypeople had genuine questions about what was permissible and how they ought to respond to Jewish men's use of sex slaves. In intra-Jewish disputes over slavery, and in their bids for Muslim men's interventions, slave-owning and masculinity prove to be domains where the internal dynamics, stresses, and disjunctures of communal boundary making are particularly visible.[74]

Another consequence of Jewish slavery law that becomes especially conspicuous in an Islamic context is that the enslaved concubines of Jewish men lacked clear and specified rights. One outcome was that married men who purchased women for sex often did so at the expense of their wives and children. A second outcome was that enslaved concubines and their children had none of the protections that *umm walad*s and their free, Muslim children did in Islamic law. As the fate of Ibn Jamāhir's concubine and their son shows, enslaved mothers and their children could be sold as "foreign slaves" and, ultimately, with impunity.

Controversies over Jewish men's use of sex slaves shaped the gendered politics of masculinity. One masculine ideal promoted the pious, scholarly, and trustworthy man who was circumspect in his observance of Jewish law. His word could be trusted. When he said that he had first manumitted an enslaved woman before having a child with her, he was to be believed, and his child born a free Jew. Another mode of masculinity is evident in men's strident opposition to the attempted interventions of Jewish leaders. When these men purchased women, they and their offspring by enslaved women were suspect. The behavior of men like the silk weaver Abū al-Faraj defied the norms of Jewish law and piety. He kept his wife's *jāriya* and used her as a concubine despite the interventions of the head of the Egyptian community.

Because Jewish leaders lacked strong coercive power, such heavy-handed tactics forced them onto their back feet and toward compromises. The counsel that Moses Maimonides gave to one such party, discussed above, about how to deal with another Jew and his enslaved concubine, suggests that he was aware of the dialectical construction of masculinity, even if he would have not have described it this way. He advises, "Try to get him to marry her. Do it softly and gently."[75] Maimonides's admonition to Jewish slave owners in the *Mishneh Torah* also points to this masculine dialectic. Though Jewish law allows a slave owner to "have a Canaanite slave perform excruciating labor . . . compassion and wisdom should guide him to be merciful and to pursue justice and not to make his slave carry a heavy yoke, nor cause him distress. He should allow (his slave) to partake of all the food and drink he serves. . . . Similarly, he should not embarrass (a slave) by his actions or words, for the Written Law prescribes (that they perform) service (*'avdut*), not (that they be) humiliated. Nor should one shout or vent anger upon them extensively. Instead, one should speak to them gently, and listen to their complaints."[76]

Jews and Muslims both told themselves stories of "good" and "bad" slave owners.[77] Normative law holds up the "good" slave owner as an exemplar, but this does not mean that the experiences of enslaved people were benign. In my view it is a fuller accounting to stress that exploitation and amelioration were mutually reinforcing over time. Moreover, the slave-owning men studied in this chapter performed according to both opposing ideals depending on the context.

Both the merchant Ibn Jamāhir and Moses Maimonides are cases in point, though in very different ways. Ibn Jamāhir purchased an enslaved woman, used her as a sex slave during his travels, made her pregnant, and then banished the woman and child to Berbera. Back in Cairo, he had a wife, young son, and two adopted orphan girls, the latter whom he supported as an act of piety. What we know about Maimonides through his legal writings on slavery shows that he sometimes sought to mitigate the negative impacts of slavery, though mostly because he cared for Jewish law and community and not because he viewed the Canaanite slave as a person with rights. In a dietary manual that he composed for an Ayyubid dignitary, Maimonides wrote in its introduction that he hoped the advice and recipes provided would make the ruler more virile as he forced himself on his many "slave women (*jawārī*)."[78] This was his rhetorical flourish and not a convention of the genre.

The next chapter shifts the focus to women and how their slave owning engendered certain feminine ideals in Egyptian Jewish culture. The topic of masculinity will remain salient, however. For women, like Abū al-Faraj's wife in this chapter's introduction, had to defend their rights as slave owners against their husbands and other men. Jewish women's slave owning is also a domain into which Muslim authorities could step as part of their own masculine performances vis-à-vis Jewish men, not to mention all women in Islamic society.[79] Part 3 of the book will center the lives of enslaved women and revisit key themes from their points of view. Despite their muted presence in most historical sources, their life histories can still be told.

6

Slavery and Femininity

AS SHE LAY DYING in her bed surrounded by witnesses, the free woman Sitt al-Dalāl painted her relationship with her *jāriya* Munā (Wish) in poignant terms. She said to the assembled group: "I inform you that she, my *jāriya* Munā, has attended graciously to me during this and previous illnesses *in ways that my mother and sister have not done*. Now witness that this *jāriya* shall not be sold, bought, or transferred."[1] It is at such moments of death that we find among surviving documents some of the most intimate portraits of the emotional lives and family relationships of slave owners.[2] The prospect of death did two crucial things: it focused the dying person and her heirs upon the disposition of property and the shoring up of legacies. And it occasioned document creation in the form of wills, inventories, and other written evidence.[3]

Sitt al-Dalāl's recognition of Munā points to a story that has yet to be fully told. While the centrality of enslaved women to global medieval slavery is now widely recognized, scholars have not fully explored how and why free women were themselves a significant part of the demand for slaves.[4] We have already seen in previous chapters that Jewish women were central to the demand for enslaved labor. A pregnant woman in Fustat asked her uncle for help purchasing a Black child. A merchant traveling and working in India sent his wife a six-year-old girl along with red silk and pearl bracelets.[5] Some women received enslaved people as part of their wedding dowries, including one bride of extraordinary wealth who received two maids (*jāriyas*) and two ladies-in-waiting (*waṣīfas*).[6] Women were also active in the local slave market, where they transacted with other Jewish women and men, as well as Christians.[7] In almost all cases, the slaves bought and sold by free women were girls and women.[8]

As chapter 4 illustrates, slavery *lil-khidma* served the interests of free women in the ways one would expect. While men, women, and children all benefited from enslaved people's labor, their labor benefited free women in particular ways.

Freedom from work, especially from labor outside the home, was a marker of social status for free women.

In the hierarchies of subordination that ordered Egyptian society, Jewish women were subordinated as *dhimmīs* and due to their gender in both Islamic society and within Jewish law and culture. Free women did hold power, however, over enslaved women. In this superordinate position, they accrued consequential benefits from slave owning beyond the calculus of household *khidma*. The current chapter focuses on kinds of "work" that have been less studied, which today we might call "emotional" or "affective" labor. Female enslavers expected their slaves to perform for them as caretakers, personal attendants, go-betweens, and even—after an owner's death—as a part of her legacy. Thus, enslaved women were also prevalent in medieval societies because they were a form of intergenerational wealth as well as unfree dependents who could be controlled by free women who relied on them as intimate familiars in ways "analogous to kinship" when other women, like sisters and mothers, might not want or be able to provide support.[9] A focus on the gendered dimensions of slavery thus brings the unequal relationships between free and unfree women to the foreground.

Yet the authority of female enslavers was more fragile than that of their male counterparts. Free women had to defend and assert their rights as slave owners against encroachment by their husbands and sometimes other male relatives. Enslaved women, too, occasionally found ways to resist free women in ways that were less likely to threaten slave-owning men. When they felt compelled to defend their rights as slave owners, free women were motivated not only by their economic interests but also by their notions of feminine honor and to protect their psychosocial worlds. By analyzing why and how women sought to control female slaves, it will become clear that the very notion and exertion of slave-owning power was itself inflected by gender.

This chapter will illustrate how practical realities, feminine ideals, and Islamic patronage culture all shaped free women's demand for enslaved servants. Jews regarded their young slaves not only as practical kin *qua* enslaved people, but also as potential free clients after their manumission. At the same time, the presence of enslaved women in the household was not always an unequivocal boon for the lady of the house, as we have seen in the previous chapter, due to the actions of husbands like Abū al-Faraj who used their wives' own *jāriya*s for sex. Free women also had to defend their rights as slave owners against such incursions, which were sometimes physically violent.

Enslaved Labor and Feminine Honor

Though slave-owning men and women extracted some of the same daily benefits from enslaved women's labor, that labor meant something very different for free women than it did for men, particularly when that work required the worker to leave the home and enter mixed public spaces. The connection between public errands and gendered notions of honor are evident in a medieval rabbinic responsum from the Algerian city of Tilimsān that emphasizes men's anxieties about their wives and children appearing in mixed public spaces. The query's author asks whether Jews are permitted to own enslaved women who refuse to convert to Judaism if there are no other suitable slave women available for purchase.[10] The author explains why the question of purchasing slaves is an urgent one: "Anyone who does not own a maidservant is in great anguish. His children or his wife must bring water upon their shoulders from the springs, wash their clothes, and go to the public ovens with non-Jewish slave women and prostitutes."[11] Though it is the women's labor, it is the men's shame.

A similar anxiety is expressed by the Egyptian Mālikī jurist Ibn al-Ḥājj al-ʿAbdārī (d. 1336–37), who wrote a treatise that enjoined Muslims to adhere more closely to Islamic law and to uphold higher standards of morality. Ibn al-Ḥājj did not fault women who prepared bread at home so long as they did not interact with the baker's helper who came to retrieve the uncooked dough. Elsewhere in his work, Ibn al-Ḥājj, too, singles out public ovens as places where enslaved people and others engaged in "idle talk."[12] Evidence from the *geniza* illustrates that such reservations about women, labor, seclusion, and status were not merely hypothetical concerns. Jewish courts, themselves composed of members of the slave-owning classes, took them seriously and factored these gendered values into their own decision-making. In this context, enslaved women made it possible for others to maintain their modesty and reputations by performing their roles as go-betweens and public errand runners.[13]

Male relatives could pressure and coerce wives and daughters to seclude themselves as a matter of their own masculine honor. Some women chose seclusion for themselves and, likewise, considered it a marker of their feminine honor and class status.[14] We see a clear expression of this in a twelfth-century case concerning a woman in Fustat whose husband had been away from the city for business for several months.[15] One outcome of this case was that the woman was awarded additional financial support from her husband for herself and for "someone to serve her," in this case her *jāriya*. In making their case before the court, the woman's representative identified her as one of "the elite of the city who remain secluded in their homes."[16] Even within the home, enslaved women could be intermediaries between their owners, secluded in their rooms, and other members of the household and their visitors.[17] In this context, enslaved women once again made it possible for others to maintain their modesty and reputations by performing their roles as go-betweens and public errand runners.[18] Within the home, these same women could serve their mistresses as intermediaries between husbands and other family during times of strife. We do not know how enslaved women felt about this, but we do know that this role could put them in harm's way, as we read at the end of this chapter.

Jewish law has long acknowledged the connections between household work, women's class status, and enslaved labor. Recall the list in chapter 4 of women's labors in the *Mishneh Torah* that wives were expected to perform for their husbands.[19] This same list specifies how slave ownership should relieve wives of certain kinds of work. If the wife brings one enslaved servant (*shifḥa*) into the marriage (or the assets to buy one), if the husband has a *shifḥa*, or even if he has the money to purchase a single *shifḥa*, then the wife is exempt from grinding grain, baking, washing, and from feeding straw to riding-beasts. If the wife or husband has (or can afford) two *shifḥa*s then the wife is not required to cook. Maimonides adds, "Nor is she required to breastfeed her son, only to give him to her *shifḥa* for breastfeeding."[20] Unfree women were personal attendants for their mistresses and perhaps even for other "favorite" enslaved women in the same household.[21] This work required close physical interaction and touch and ranged from hairdressing to body-hair removal.[22]

"Cursed Be He Who Separates Her and My Younger Daughter"

Free women were thus attached to enslaved laborers not just because they brought relief from work, but also because this relief brought them feminine honor according to the expectations of their social class. The intimacy of some of this labor also inflected the way that free women understood the importance of enslaved people to their emotional lives and those of their children. The words of another unnamed dying woman, written in a letter to her sister, provide a vivid description of how female enslavers understood these entanglements.[23] The letter writer believed that her death was imminent and provided instructions concerning her two daughters and for three enslaved people: a woman named Saʿāda (Happiness) and her son and a third woman named ʿAfāf (Chastity). Her testimony is urgent, and it brims both with recriminations over past events and anxiety for her children's uncertain futures:

> My lady, my sister, I inform you—may God make me your ransom—that I have fallen seriously ill with remote hope for recovery...
>
> My lady, I hereby relate my will to you, if almighty God decrees my death. Take care of my little daughter and strive to give her an education, although I know that I am imposing on you excessively. For there is—I swear by my father—no money to provide maintenance for her, let alone (for her) education. But she has a model in the saintly lady (our mother). Do not let her appear in public. Do not neglect her nanny (*dāda*), Saʿāda, or her son. And do not separate them from her, because they are fond of her, and I have willed the Black woman (*al-sūdāniyya*) to her.
>
> However, the younger maidservant (*al-waṣīfa al-ṣaghīra*)[24] ʿAfāf shall be given to Sitt al-Sirr—but nothing else—and this only after your (pl.) debts to Abū Saʿd and others have been paid. Cursed be he who acts against my dying wish.
>
> For I have noticed more than once that you favor the elder (daughter) over the younger one. But you know that I took an oath more than once—and the last one in her presence—not to will anything to Sitt al-Sirr, for reasons that cannot be mentioned, but about which you know.
>
> My lady, let Abū al-Barakāt—may I be his ransom—come and attend to me, for I am in distress. Do not act against anything I have mentioned to you all. When it comes to the elder slave woman (*al-jāriya al-kabīra*)—cursed be he who separates her and my younger daughter—(there shall be) no sale or anything else. My lady, only God knows how I wrote these lines!

We know nothing more about this dying woman or her fate. What is striking is her fierce conviction that the enslaved woman Saʿāda is the best available caretaker for her youngest daughter. Her instructions appear to be based on two considerations. First, she believed that there was an intimate, affective connection between Saʿāda (and Saʿāda's son) and the youngest daughter.[25] Second, the author is suspicious of her own female blood relation, her sister, whom she might otherwise have called upon to help raise both of her children.

There are some clues that suggest why the writer distrusts her elder daughter (Sitt al-Sirr) and sister. Even as she assigns her elder daughter Sitt al-Sirr the *waṣīfa* ʿAfāf, she insists that she will be given "nothing else," and ʿAfāf "only after your debts to Abū Saʿd and others have been paid."[26] She justifies her harsh tone by accusing her sister of favoritism, "more than once," toward the elder Sitt al-Sirr over the unnamed younger daughter. To compound this slight, Sitt al-Sirr committed some kind of transgression, "which cannot be mentioned," that only reinforced her mother's decision to curtail her inheritance. Despite her reticence about Sitt al-Sirr's specific misdeeds, the mother's plea that her sister "not allow [the younger daughter] to appear in public" speaks to the values that she wished to impart to her children and that Sitt al-Sirr may have transgressed: that women of their social class used enslaved women to run public errands for them so they did not have to. For a woman who owned two enslaved people (three, if we include Saʿāda's son), it is possible that her disappointment with Sitt al-Sirr's indiscretion was based on the older daughter's breach of this decorum.[27]

Gendered Dimensions of Kinship and Patronage Culture

Another key to understanding the attachment that Jewish women felt for enslaved women such as Saʿāda is found in the deeper currents of kinship practices and cultural values prevalent in the medieval Islamic Middle East. In her study of family structures and relationships in medieval Egypt, Eve Krakowski argues that the most important kinship bonds among Jews were not necessarily between what Pierre Bourdieu would call "official kin," or bonds based on genealogical kinship, but with people outside of her immediate natal family.[28]

Relationships with "practical kin" were based on their usefulness and reciprocity, and not primarily on an idealized set of relations as in "official kinship."[29] In this sense, "practical kinship" comes into being and is perpetuated through meaningful actions on the part of those with working social ties. In instances when official kin could or would not perform the duties that family members required, a female slave owner turned to enslaved women as practical kin. The historian Sally McKee argues that similar phenomena are evident in interactions between enslaved women and their owners in late medieval Italy and Venetian Crete. The "ties analogous to kinship" that McKee observes in Italian and Cretan households bear a striking resemblance to the ways in which Jewish women in medieval Egypt described and relied on enslaved women.[30]

"Ties analogous to kinship" resemble the pervasive patron-client relationships that ordered the medieval Islamic world, which is a topic discussed in chapters 1 and 8. The way that Jewish women viewed their ties to enslaved women does not conform to what normative law would suggest. Islamic law conceives of this patronage as a tie between men and not women. In Jewish law, manumission was supposed to sever all vestiges of the dependency tie between the manumitter and the manumitted. Despite this, *geniza* evidence illustrates that Jewish slave owners, including women, did treat their enslaved and freed people as clients, or at least potential ones.[31]

Young orphans were another group that Jews sometimes thought of as analogous to enslaved girls.[32] Paternal mortality rates were relatively high in the medieval Jewish community, with 40 percent of young, unmarried women identified as orphans.[33] As Mark Cohen notes, Jewish law and custom considered the court to be "the father of orphans," a fact that emphasizes the community's custodianship of them. The death of a father entitled an unmarried orphan girl to communal aid.[34] In both rabbinic texts and *geniza* documents, Jews reasoned that providing a dowry for an orphan so she could marry was regarded as an act of charity equivalent to redeeming a captive.[35] Recall that one reason the Jewish court in Fustat was interested in the death of the slave-owning merchant Ibn Jamāhir was that it intended to use his estate to provide dowries for two orphan girls in his household.[36]

Jewish charitable institutions also aimed to support orphans by ushering them ultimately toward their first marriage. So, too, was the case for some freed women, like Mubāraka in the previous chapter, whom the welfare official ʿEli ha-Kohen sought to marry off to a Jewish man with the help of a local woman.[37] Welfare officials also enlisted the support of free Jewish women to teach orphans domestic skills as well as basic religious precepts and practices. In some circumstances, widows or divorcées would take an orphan into their home. One woman who no longer lived with her absent husband kept an orphan, as she put it, "to keep me company."[38] Individuals made efforts to arrange upkeep for orphans by enlisting the help of others in the community and by arranging lodging.

One of the primary ways that girls and young women—including orphan girls—before their first marriage would have generated some modicum of wealth for themselves was through spinning, weaving, and embroidery. Textiles had practical and monetary value, and they could comprise part of a modest dowry for a prospective bride. In one undated letter, a woman informs the recipient that a grandmother who had been taking care of two orphaned sisters had died and that she (the author) now looked after them. She explains that there is a local woman with no children of her own who could teach the girls, saying that the girls will live alone and support themselves with communal funds: "A place should be rented for them somewhere close to my home . . . and these 2 dinars should be given to the older girl so she can use it [for . . .] maintenance, silk, and other things."[39] Basic instruction in Jewish prayer was also a part of these efforts.[40]

Recognition that these unmarried girls were what Krakowski calls "inherent economic dependents" and at risk of falling into poverty likewise motivated concern for orphans.[41] Thus another strategy for taking care of orphans was to take them in as servants so that they were not solely dependent on charity.[42]

Orphans and enslaved girls both required maintenance costs. A court deposition from 1098 reflects that the sums for their upkeep were not trifling. A dispute over such costs arose when a man named Tiqva b. Amram sued his business associate Shela b. ʿAyyāsh for money he had given him to carry out business on his behalf in Syria and Palestine (*al-Shām*).[43] When Shela came back empty-handed, Tiqva went before a judge and demanded the 48 dinars he had provided. He took the opportunity to request additional "expenses for a *jāriya* of tender age, whom he had brought up for" his associate.[44] In response to the latter accusation, Shela responded: "As for the *jāriya*'s expenses, I left her with them so that they could put her to work (in exchange) for her maintenance and I would be responsible for the clothes alone."[45] When it came to the exchange of service for maintenance, the line between orphanage and enslavement could apparently sometimes be a fuzzy one.

"On the Condition That They Profess the Jewish Faith"

Another exceptional source, also a woman's deathbed declaration, illustrates how the factors discussed above combined to shape how female slave owners viewed themselves and their enslaved property. The testimony of the dying woman, Sitt al-Ḥusn, shows powerfully how one woman sought to construct a legacy for herself within the larger cultural matrix of kinship, patronage culture, and concern for "inherent economic dependents."[46] She was a person of substantial means and left behind considerable property including two *jāriya*s,[47] various shares of real estate, and a sizeable wardrobe. Sitt al-Ḥusn requested that, if proceeds from the sale of some of her real estate were not enough to pay for her burial expenses, then her husband should sell her ornate head-covering (*al-ʿiṣāba*) made up of eleven pieces to pay the balance.[48]

It is unlikely that Sitt al-Ḥusn had surviving children, as no blood relatives besides her second husband are mentioned in her will.[49] In fact, the first parties she names as her heirs are Dhahab (Gold) and Sitt al-Sumr, her "virgin slave girls (*juwārihā* [*sic*] *al-abkār*),"[50] after having freed (*ʿataqat*) the two of them henceforth."[51] Sitt al-Ḥusn gave them, as a legal gift (*wahabat*), one-quarter of a house she owned in partnership with a deceased associate. This quarter share was meant to be an asset and not for them to use as a residence. This much is made clear by a stipulation that she added to her bequest:

> She gave to the community one half of the house in which she had lived, (so that) the two slave girls (could live there) for the rest of both of their (lives)—in

> the part that belongs to the community (and) where the will was witnessed—on the condition that (the slave girls) profess the Jewish faith (*'al tenay an kānū* [*sic*] *yahūd al-hayba*).[52]

Sitt al-Ḥusn's gift of lodging likely made the decision to remain more appealing and practicable for Dhahab and Sitt al-Sumr.

A final condition regarding Dhahab's and Sitt al-Sumr's inheritance appears at the end of the will:

> If something should remain from the income of one-eighth of the aforementioned house (which Sitt al-Ḥusn instructed her executor to sell in order to pay for her burial expenses), it shall be given to the slave girls mentioned above; likewise, (they shall be given) all clothing suitable for women.

Like some of her male counterparts, whom we met in the previous chapter, Sitt al-Ḥusn performs a kind of pious femininity by manumitting Dhahab and Sitt al-Sumr *and* giving them economic capital.[53] Additionally, one half of Sitt al-Ḥusn's house was designated as a pious foundation for Jewish communal charity (*lil-qodesh*).[54] Such a bequest was a charitable act in perpetuity, since the property could be rented and these proceeds administered to aid community members in need.[55]

Evidence of manumission is relatively common in the *geniza* corpus. What is far less common is the evidence that Dhahab and Sitt al-Sumr were also given economic and social capital.[56] They conditionally receive a quarter share in one piece of real estate, which they could presumably sell. In addition to this, their mistress promises them the right to live in one half of another home in perpetuity (which amounted to one room, it seems). Finally, any leftover income from the sale of a third real estate share, along with "all clothing suitable for women" were to be given to them. Clothing could be both a saleable asset, depending on its type and quality, as well as a marker of social status.[57] Sitt al-Ḥusn also bolstered Dhahab and Sitt al-Sumr's status and reputation by asserting that the two girls were "virgins." Normally, when applied to free women, the term serves to assert that they had never before been married. In the context of slavery, the word choice may also have signaled that they had not been exploited for sex and were therefore "chaste."[58]

In the social universe that Sitt al-Ḥusn was soon to leave behind, one conspicuous element was missing from her legacy: offspring. Sitt al-Ḥusn viewed and treated Dhahab and Sitt al-Sumr almost as if they were her daughters, or perhaps as orphans that she had adopted.[59] But these two girls weren't her offspring or orphaned Jews, they were enslaved girls. Sitt al-Ḥusn's stipulation that the girls live as Jews underscores another motivation behind their emancipation. Such a condition meant in part to further ensconce the two girls within the Jewish community where Sitt al-Ḥusn's high status was a kind of social currency that could help ensure them matches to suitable spouses and some modicum of social standing. Still, in the main, this strong inducement to "profess the Jewish faith" underscores how Dhahab and Sitt al-Sumr were part and parcel of Sitt al-Ḥusn's legacy as a wealthy, honorable, and pious Jew.

The conditions and inducements that Sitt al-Ḥusn included in her will recall Abū al-Ḥasan's provisional manumission of the young girl Kashf, which we read about in the previous chapter. Abū al-Ḥasan freed Kashf (and a second woman, Gharaḍ) so that they could live as "proper Jewish girls."[60] Because Kashf was young, Abū al-Ḥasan remanded her to the custody of his sister Sitt al-Ri'āsa until she was old enough to choose for herself whether to remain a part of the household or "to leave." Abū al-Ḥasan and Sitt al-Ri'āsa were part of a slave-owning family. She had also received the woman 'Ūd al-Zān as part of her substantial dowry one year earlier.[61] Their sister, Sitt al-Ḥasab freed a woman named Ṣalaf (Vainglory) in 1157.[62] In Kashf's case, Sitt al-Ri'āsa had, at least when she married, the means to free her and to provide generously for her. There is no other evidence, however, that allows us to know what happened to Kashf.

Free Women Undermined

The history told so far in this chapter has emphasized how free women benefited from slavery and how they, like men, used slavery to fashion their own gendered notions of honor and prestige. This is one part of the story. Another aspect of this history is how male slave owners encroached upon the rights of slave-owning women, and how free women sought to defend their prerogatives, rights as slave owners, and well-being in marriage to slave-owning men.

We read in chapters 4 and 5 about traveling merchants, and men like Abū al-Faraj the silk weaver, whose decisions to use enslaved women as concubines marginalized their wives and children, and even threatened their livelihoods. Concubinage could be both a humiliation and a factor that precipitated a husband's disappearance, often leading him to neglect his family materially as well as emotionally and physically. Mordechai Friedman has shown that prospective brides and their families began to insert new legal language into their wedding documents in response to married men's practice of such sexual slavery and absence. In the twelfth century, the clause "he (the groom) will not keep a slave girl whom she (his wife) dislikes (*wa-lā yubqī jāriya takrahuhā*)" and variants such as "he will not take a slave girl as a concubine (*wa-lā yatasarrā bi-jāriya*)" became so common that they were referred to as "the well-known stipulations for Jewish women (*shurūṭ banot Yisra'el al-ma'lūma*)" and "the well-known stipulations of Fustat (*al-shurūṭ al-ma'lūma bi-miṣr*)."[63] The inclusion of the so-called slave-girl clause could not by itself prevent a husband from retaining an enslaved woman that his wife resented, or from using that person for sex, but it did give wives and their relatives leverage to pressure men to honor their agreements.

The latter dynamic is the likely context behind a fragmentary legal deed in which a husband named Abū al-Makārim agrees to sell the *jāriya* Ghazāl unless she behaves better toward his unnamed wife, who was the daughter of a leader in the Jewish community.[64] Precise details about the events in 1134 that precipitated Abū al-Makārim's actions are lacking. The language of the deed tells a story in which the husband would only "restore" Ghazāl to his "personal service in his household (*khidmat baytihi*)"[65] if the *jāriya* agreed to cease her vexing behavior toward his wife. It seems that Abū al-Makārim wanted to avoid a sale since he had invested in training (*ista'dabhā*) Ghazāl in certain manners and valuable skills.[66] It is not clear what happened next.

In other ways, Jewish law provided husbands with power over enslaved women that legally belonged to their wives. Some of the wife's possessions were considered part of the "iron sheep property (*nikhse ṣon barzel*)."[67] Husbands had the right to use these items, including enslaved human beings, for their own purposes and even profit. Though the bride technically owned her iron sheep property, she required the husband's permission to sell it while they were married. Thus, when Sitt al-Aqrān sold a Nubian woman to another Jewish woman in Cairo in November 1108, the court required the permission and participation of her husband Judah b. 'Allān in the sale.[68] Judah testified that "I am satisfied with the sale of this slave woman . . . I have not retained anything for myself from this sale, nor any claim of grievance." The witnesses to the transaction added that they made a symbolic purchase (*qinyan*) with Judah and recognized that "he executes for (his wife) this sale in this document according to all that was written and de[tailed] above."[69]

Such power asymmetries in Jewish marriage law and practice that disadvantaged women also opened the door for husbands to circumvent their wives' wishes through legal stratagems. Mordechai Friedman discovered a striking example of this in a model legal formulary of the kind that scribes wrote to serve as guides for others in composing certain genres of documents. On the reverse side of a formulary for how to compose a deed of manumission is another formula for how a husband can cancel his wife's manumission of her slave.[70] The hypothetical husband's testimony reads:

> Know that I am deposing a disclaimer before you that my wife so-and-so, daughter of so-and-so, possesses [the daughter of] a foreign slave woman who is a minor and was raised in our house. She wants to emancipate her and free her. But I do not want or desire to free [her]. When she pressed me with her words, I had to mislead her and to act according to her wishes and to mislead the daughter of her slave girl, whose name is so-and-so, that I am making her a free woman. But it is not my intention to manumit or to free her. The deed of manumission that I have written for her is void and like a potsherd thrown in the street (i.e., it is worthless) and is not to be relied upon.[71]

Per the instructions of this formulary, the court should then ratify his testimony and give him a signed copy of it to keep as evidence.[72] Though this case is a theoretical one, it highlights how married men could use the law to undermine their wives for whom slave ownership was a particular kind of social capital. In such an event, a Jewish woman had few good options for overcoming the legal and cultural advantages that men had in Jewish law and the courts. One of the strategies available to her, however, could put a Jewish man and his supporters on the defensive: she could sue him in an Islamic court.[73]

"I Demanded to Return the Jāriya *to Him"*

Ḥasana bt. Menasse ha-Kohen did just this sometime in the winter of 1126–27 when she sued her brother Solomon ha-Kohen, a banker.[74] In an appearance before a Jewish court with her husband El'azar, she testified:

> Six months ago, more or less, I bought from (my brother Solomon) . . . his *jāriya*, known as Iftikhār (Pride), for 17 dinars. He received the money, and I took the *jāriya*. Subsequently, I noticed things about the *jāriya* that required me to appear with the seller (Solomon) before the Muslim judge. I demanded (*ṭalabtu*) to return the *jāriya* to him. We then kept intensely negotiating the issues until several well-meaning mediators intervened between us. They decided that he would pay me one and a quarter dinar and that I would keep the *jāriya* (despite) all of her defects (*'uyūbhā*).[75]

Ḥasana testified that she accepted the agreement and received the one and a quarter dinar (a rebate of around 7 percent of the original price). In return, Solomon, and perhaps the court, insisted that she agree to release him from all future responsibilities for Iftikhār and her defects. If she were to ever make a claim against him, no matter what further defects she discovered, she would have to pay him a substantial fine of 10 dinars, which the Jewish court could take from her "in any manner that it sees fit." In her testimony, Ḥasana does not state the precise nature of the slave's alleged "defects," though she names "flight (*harab*)" and "theft (*sariqa*)" as two examples of the kinds that she would have to accept because of her mediated agreement with Solomon. Elʿazar, Ḥasana's husband, agreed to these conditions as well. Solomon received a copy of the written deposition from the Jewish court to keep as "a title of rights and as proof."[76]

In his studies of Jewish women's use of the Islamic legal system in Egypt, Oded Zinger concludes that women did so because it sometimes provided "a more level playing field for them."[77] These reasons included differences in Islamic law, the greater enforceability of Muslim legal rulings in the Egyptian context, and the opportunity to neutralize the advantage of a legal opponent who might be better connected in the Jewish community. Zinger's research also illustrates how Jewish courts were frequently not sympathetic to women's legal claims. Female litigants could face wider communal pressure to relinquish their rights in particular circumstances. Scribes also "scripted" the women's speech as "screaming," "cursing," and "threatening," in comparison to the speech of men that is described as "complaining" and "beseeching."[78] Though Jewish men sought justice in these Islamic venues as well, they were also generally hostile toward women (and other men) who did the same thing.[79]

It is difficult to be sure about this without more evidence, but Ḥasana's choice to go to a Muslim court in the first place could have been her own tactic to force her brother Solomon to the negotiating table, or at least to take her complaints more seriously. It was their appearance before the Muslim judge that precipitated the intervention of the well-meaning mediators who, it appears, brokered the small refund as a compromise between the two siblings. The large fine that Ḥasana agreed to pay in the event that she tries to sue her brother over Iftikhār's "defects" in the future is likely due to the general hostility of Jewish courts toward Jewish women's patronage of Islamic courts at all.[80]

These dynamics bring us back to questions about the gender politics of masculinity, and they underscore how femininity was implicated in this competition. As Ruth Karras argues, patriarchy "meant not just the dominance of men over women, but the dominance of a small number of men over most men and all women."[81] In the Islamic context where religious identities were a formal part of how different imperial subjects were classified, the *dhimmī* status of Jews was an opportunity for Muslim authorities to display such dominance. Again, Zinger's work is illuminating here:

> Two further explanations [for why Islamic legal institutions were receptive to Jewish women] may be suggested . . . [and] must remain speculative. The first is that subordinating Jewish women was probably not as appealing to the sense of authority of a Muslim official . . . as demonstrating his (and the state's) domination over Jewish men. Thus, by using Muslim legal venues, Jewish women provided Muslim officials an occasion to perform their authority over Jewish men. The second explanation is that assisting Jewish women who felt wronged by their male relatives or by Jewish communal institutions fit well with the self-image of Muslim jurists. By helping the weakest of the weakest, Muslim judges demonstrated the superiority of Islamic justice over that of the *ahl al-kitāb* [the people of the book, i.e., Jews and Christians].[82]

In an Islamic empire characterized by legal pluralism and a hierarchy of subjects based on religious identity, slavery surfaces again as a domain in which power, prestige, and gendered ideals were contested and reproduced. In this regard, female slave-owning could function both as an obstacle to some Jewish men and as a convenient lever for Muslim men whose power and privilege allowed them to set the rules of masculine competition.[83]

A report about a husband who beat of one his household's *jāriya*s is a chilling reminder both of how the violence of slavery is largely muted in the documentary *geniza* and of the particular ways in which all women were vulnerable to the caprice of men.[84] The terse report is found within a legal query to Moses Maimonides as one of several examples meant to elicit a broader legal opinion concerning how divorced couples should divide their property when both the husband and wife are alleged to have violated their marital obligations.

A husband accused his wife of not following the laws of ritual purity. In Egypt, these laws had come under greater scrutiny after a decree, also by Moses Maimonides, that Jewish women who violated them could forfeit the compensation (dower) promised to them in their marriage contracts.[85] In this case, the wife responded that she had not neglected the law. Rather, she states that it was her husband's own fault as he raped her even after she had told him that she had not yet immersed herself, which Jewish law required her to do before she and her husband could have any sexual contact or close interactions that might lead to sex.[86] In his query, the writer continues, "Furthermore, she became ill due to (an abundance) of black bile.[87] Madness and confusion overcame her. It is said that the reason for this was that her husband got angry with one of the *jāriyas* and beat her (the *jāriya*)."[88] The author concludes his presentation of the facts by explaining that the husband then prevented the sick woman's family from caring for her as her illness persisted.

Some of the book's recurring themes come together in this event: the archive's silence about violence against enslaved people, a man's attempt to dominate those around him, a wife's subordination, and a *jāriya*'s even greater subordination and instrumentalization. This chapter has argued that though enslaved women and girls did much of the same kinds of daily labor for all people in the household, slave ownership meant something very different for women than men. Slave-owning women often faced greater social, economic, and legal constraints than their male counterparts. Their seclusion within the home could be forced. Even when it was not, women's public appearances could be monitored and construed as dishonorable. Thus, for slave-owning women, their *jāriyas* and *waṣīfas* represented both economic and social capital. Enslaved women were their factotums within the house and outside of it; they were wealth that could be passed on to future generations or sold to raise capital.[89] And lastly, slave owning meant a woman had someone they could lawfully control, someone who could serve them as both a worker *lil-khidma* and as an "affective laborer" analogous to kin. This is why women experienced a husband's assault of her *jāriya*, or his choice to abscond with her, as attacks on their own persons and limited autonomy.

As with Ibn Jamāhir's concubine, the enslaved woman mentioned in the above query was not herself of particular concern to the writer.[90] He mentions her beating only to explain why the wife had become ill, perhaps by having an acute mental health crisis. The next chapter does something that medieval sources are not apt to do, and that is to put such women at the center of the story.

PART III

The Lives of Enslaved and Freed People

7

Lives in Slavery

THESE ARE THE THREE fragments of information that scribes have left us about Wafā' and her mother Jinān. First, Wafā' and Jinān were born into slavery as *muwalladas*. Sometime in 1141 or 1142, when Wafā' was a mere two years old, a man called Abū al-Ḥasan sold her mother Jinān to Mufaḍḍal b. Abū Sa'd b. Ṣibyān on an installment plan of 2 dinars per month. The seller, however, kept the young child Wafā' for an unknown period of time.[1] Were Jinān and Wafā' permanently separated? Or did they remain in some form of contact?[2] We do not know. Jinān's subsequent fate, in fact, is completely unknown to us.

Second, the child Wafā' resurfaces in a marriage document that lists her as a *waṣīfa* and as one of four enslaved women who were included in the dowry of a wealthy bride.[3] Third and finally, on January 20, 1181, the three daughters of the welfare official (*parnas*) Zayn b. Abū al-Riḍā manumitted Wafā', who was by then roughly forty years old.[4] These three points in time suggest the barest outline of a two-year-old girl's passage through a life in slavery to the moment of her manumission as a middle-aged woman.

Because Wafā' is only identified by her first name (*ism*), there will almost always be some doubt about whether these three mentions of a Wafā' refer to the same person or to two or even three different people with the same given name. In this and other similar cases, however, other clues give us reason to identify all three Wafā's as the same individual. Recall that, because of its density and coherence, the *geniza* attests to a large but interconnected cast of characters in the generations between the late tenth and mid-thirteenth centuries.[5] The scribes who produced documents for others, and kept their own notebooks, make much of this book's history possible. Scribes like Ḥalfon b. Menasse, whose note about avoiding tax payments we read in chapter 3, were themselves nodes of social, economic, and information networks.[6] This role enabled them to facilitate connections between buyers and sellers.

In Wafā''s case it was the father-son scribal duo of Nathan b. Samuel (fl. 1128–53) and Mevorakh b. Nathan (fl. 1150–81) who wrote the documents that attest to her life. Nathan wrote the notes for Jinān's sale when Wafā' was two years old, and he composed the dowry list in which Wafā' was noted as property. Based on what we know about Nathan, Wafā' would have been thirteen years old or younger when she was included as property in the bride's dowry. By the time she was finally freed in 1181, the scribe Nathan was dead. It was his son Mevorakh who had continued in his father's professional footsteps and composed Wafā''s deed of manumission.

Nathan, whose nickname was *al-Nezer* ("the Diadem"), was also the second husband of Sitt al-Ḥusn, whom we met in the previous chapter when she freed her two young *jāriyas*, Dhahab and Sitt al-Sumr. Nathan and Mevorakh surface again as the scribes who produced evidence mentioning two enslaved girls with the same names. Several years before Sitt al-Ḥusn's act of manumission, Nathan recorded testimony about an owner's clear title to a three-year-old *waṣīfa* named Dhahab.[7] Mevorakh recorded a similar testimony, in which two brothers acknowledge that they received payment for a *jāriya* named Sumr.[8] It is far more likely than not that all this evidence refers to the same two girls, who eventually wound up in the possession of Sitt al-Ḥusn.[9] Dhahab would have been around eight years old when she was freed. Sitt al-Sumr's age is harder to determine, but she likely would have been at least five or six years old, for this is the minimum age at which enslavers thought an enslaved girl could be of use to them.[10] Later in this chapter, we will meet another woman, Na'īm (Bliss), whose appearances in a cluster of different documents in the late eleventh and twelfth centuries attest to a life in slavery. Not every enslaved person with the same first name (in the *geniza* corpus) is the same individual, but some of them are.[11]

In addition to using scribal identities to reconnect the fragmented archive for individual lives, this chapter uses two other approaches to make enslaved people more visible as historical subjects despite their oblique and fleeting presence in most *geniza* documents. The first method is a kind of textual assemblage.[12] We have already encountered, for example, an unnamed six-year-old *jāriya* who was trafficked by a Jewish merchant from somewhere in India to his family in Egypt.[13] Though the documentary trail begins and ends with these sparse details, a wider assemblage of texts in Sanskrit, Arabic, and Judeo-Arabic provide evidence that enables us to figure out the histories of young girls like her who were enslaved in India and forcibly sent by sea, land, and river to Egypt. Such assemblages will also enable us to imagine the urban "underworlds" into which enslaved people sometimes disappeared, in which they took refuge, and where they made their own social connections.

A second method is the juxtaposition of individual and collective biographies, itself a kind of assemblage. This approach mines all the surviving documents and responsa that provide the most detailed and coherent narratives about enslaved people as historical actors. While I often cannot, for example, tell you whether a specific enslaved individual gained her freedom, I can tell you that one of every four enslaved people mentioned in the *geniza* was eventually freed.[14] Such careful mining reveals the silences, gaps, and dead ends that frustrate our efforts to make sense of the bulk of the surviving material that is less forthcoming about the actions and decision-making of enslaved people.

The organization of the chapter emerges from this biographical, life-course[15] approach, as it begins with a focus on slavery as a fact of birth and childhood for many people. The chapter then considers how the enslaved people whom the slave-owning classes defined as "mature" navigated the perils and limited opportunities that Jewish and Islamic law afforded them as well as the mobility that their coerced service required. Their stories show how enslaved people gained knowledge and used it to their advantage, and how they formed their own social attachments despite the constraints imposed on them by their enslavers.

Child Slavery

As in Wafā''s case, child slavery was a fact of birth for the individuals described as *muwallad(at) al-jins*.[16] While the circumstances of *muwallads*' births are usually historically opaque, *geniza* evidence offers clues that suggest some were born to mothers owned by Jews. As in Ṣāfī's accusation against Ibn Jamāhir, a plausible explanation is that a slave owner raped the *muwallad*'s mother, or otherwise coerced her to have sex, and made her pregnant. Were the owner a Muslim man, then the child would be free born. Jewish laws of matrilineal descent, however, meant that Ibn Jamāhir's son with his enslaved concubine was also born as "a Canaanite slave" according to medieval Jewish law. In the Egyptian marketplace, they would be labeled *muwallads*.[17] In another case, a pregnant woman named 'Ushshāq was sold by one Jewish woman to another in the second half of the twelfth century.[18] Both women were married, and their husbands gave their formal approval for the transaction.[19] The buyer "inspected (the slave woman), and she was thoroughly familiar with her. She knew of all 'Ushshāq's defects, deficiencies, and maladies—(those) hidden and apparent. She knew that 'Ushshāq was pregnant and she consented to this."[20] These details suggest one plausible scenario. Perhaps the seller's husband Yakhīn had made 'Ushshāq pregnant, and his wife therefore sent her away and finally compelled him to permit her sale.[21] The buyer may have paid a slightly lower price for ʿUshshāq because of the pregnancy, or because the sellers were not in a strong bargaining position, given their circumstances.[22] In any event, the facts of the case indicate that ʿUshshāq's child would be born with slave status and labeled a *muwallad*, who could subsequently be bought and sold along with his mother.

It is possible that ʿUshshāq was able to keep her child, as some families in this era were sold together. In her dowry, one bride received an enslaved woman along with her son Saʿd.[23] Likewise, the Nubian woman Ḥidhq was sold along with her unnamed daughter in 1094.[24] And in the mid-thirteenth century, a woman named Ṭāwūs (Peacock) was sold together with her ten-year-old son Mubārak (Blessed) in Fustat.[25] Another *jāriya*, Fūq (Loving Communion), lived with her mistress just downstairs from that woman's mother, who owned Fūq's daughter.[26]

Families were also broken up through the slave trade. Three minors, a boy and two girls described as *dūn al-bulūgh*[27] (prepubescent, before the age of sexual maturity), were each sold alone in separate transactions. The two girls were Nubians, one *waṣīfa* whose name is lost and the other a *jāriya* named Tawfīq, whose owner thought she was a Christian.[28] In 1152, the Abyssinian *ghulām* Muqbil was also sold before he reached puberty.[29] As far as the slave-owning classes were concerned, puberty was one of the most consequential moments in an enslaved person's natural life cycle besides birth, death, and the minimum age of "usefulness" as a worker (around five to six years old). For enslaved girls, it meant they could become pregnant and that their sexual vulnerability now had consequences for owners.[30] For boys, it meant that they could become a sexual threat within the household.

Like these mothers and children, most enslaved people were not born with slave status as *muwallads* but were violently enslaved in a range of circumstances that I detail in chapter 2. For children captured and trafficked to Egypt, their bondage on a ship and as part of an overland caravan must have been bewildering and terrifying. At one extreme end of the interregional slave trade, some Jewish merchants purchased enslaved people in India, or Yemen, and sent them home with other handlers. This was the tribulation of one six-year-old *jāriya* (figure 7.1).[31] The man who purchased her wrote to his family, probably from Aden or another port in the western Indian Ocean, that he planned to return to the "lands of India,"[32] but that, before his return, he intended to send this child (along with pearl bracelets and red silk clothing) with someone who was traveling with the Kārim merchant flotilla.[33] The fleeting appearance of this child, sparsely described in a tattered fragment, is variously emblematic of the limits of history as a way of knowing about the lives of enslaved people.[34] Four words mark the

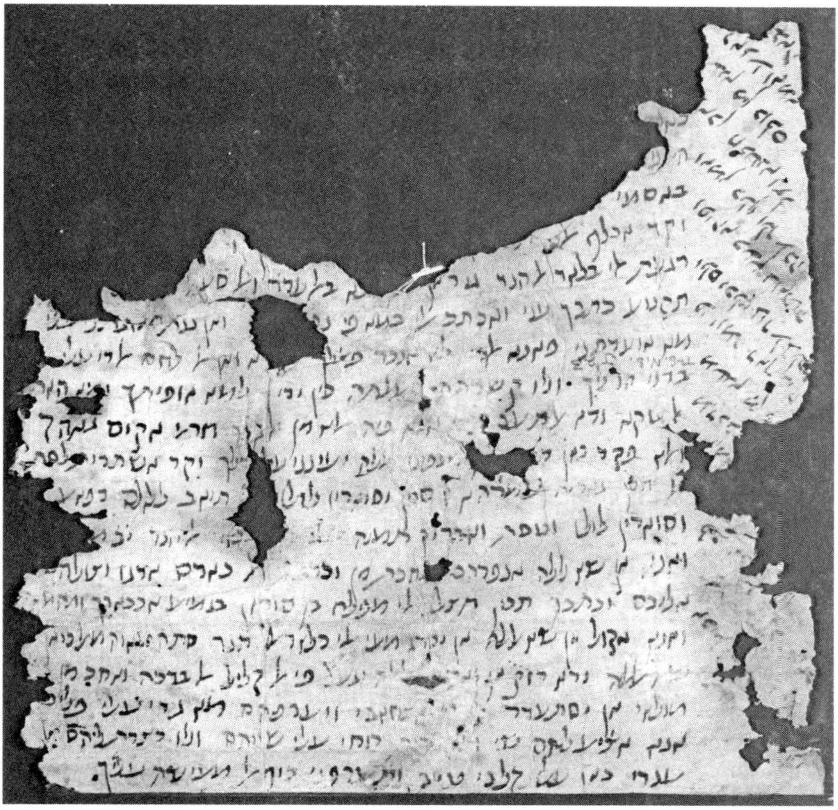

FIGURE 7.1. A twelfth-century merchant's letter sent to Cairo from somewhere in the western Indian Ocean realm that mentions the trafficking of a six-year-old girl, ca. 12th c. T-S NS J23. Paper. 18 × 18 cm. Reproduced by kind permission of the Syndics of Cambridge University Library.

beginning and end of her presence in the written record, nestled as they are in a short list of luxury goods meant for an Egyptian household. Her archival appearance is denuded of the violence and degradation of enslavement.

Though I cannot reconstruct her individual history beyond these sparse details, I can draw from an assemblage of medieval evidence to illustrate how children like her would have experienced enslavement and trafficking. The merchant who acquired this *jāriya* mentions the town of Nahrwāra (modern Anhalwāra) in Gujarat, where some *geniza* merchants had been doing business from at least the late eleventh century. They either purchased enslaved people there or purchased enslaved people in Egypt who were trafficked from India.[35]

There was enslavement and slave trading in medieval Gujarat, as well as in other locations along the western coast of India where local rulers levied taxes on trafficked people.[36] In a medieval Gujarati manual for epistolary and legal writings, the anonymous editor of the *Lekhapaddhati-Lekhpañcāśikā* provides guides for how to write bills of sale for enslaved girls who lost their freedom in different ways. These model documents date to the era when *geniza* merchants were active in the region.[37]

In contrast to the bills of sale drawn up in Jewish and Islamic courts, the Jaina-Gujarati examples describe the violence of enslavement. Two model documents present variations on a common theme. The first recounts that a sixteen-year-old girl named Panutī was captured in warfare and brought to a public market, where a merchant purchased her as a slave (Sanskrit, *dāsī*) to do household labor. The owner was required to provide basic maintenance for her, but he could also bind and beat her if anyone from her family came and tried to redeem her from slavery. Should the girl become so desperate that she killed herself by jumping into a well, the owner would not have to bear this as "a sin" himself.[38]

The second model document narrates, from a slave owner's point of view, how war and famine conspired to compel one ten-year-old girl to submit herself as a slave (*dāsī*) in order to avoid starvation.[39] Her given name was Saṃpūrī. She was a *rājaputrī*[40] girl from the village of Siranāra in Gujarat. Her father Jagaḍa was still alive, but he and the entire family were begging for food due to the chaos caused by plundering armies. They abandoned Saṃpūrī, who set off alone in rags, begging for scraps of food "at every house in every village" and sleeping in temples, monasteries, and alms houses.[41] The bill of sale projects the possible words of the young girl: "Who would be the owner of an orphan like me, the only refuge being death . . . will you keep me as a slave?"[42] Eventually Saṃpūrī fell at the feet of a merchant and beseeched him with folded hands: "I have come voluntarily. Please engage me for the work of a female slave and save me from this terrible famine. I shall work according to your order and, as long as I live, work as a female slave."[43] She promised to do household work and to cultivate the fields so long as she received the minimal maintenance of food, clothing, and footwear. Once the merchant accepted Saṃpūrī's surrender, she was required to make an oath of abject subservience:

> If I . . . commit theft . . . go elsewhere (to beg) . . . (be) tempted or enticed by some man, leave you, or mix with your enemies . . . then on the basis of the deed, you will catch me by my hair, bind and beat me, and again put me to the work of a female slave. . . . If I, (feeling) self-satisfied . . . refuse to perform

> the duties when ordered to do so, you will punish me by kicking and beating me with sticks and torture me to death, for which you, my lord, will be as free from guilt, as had you been absent. . . . If I ever feign stomach ache or commit suicide by jumping into a well or pond or by taking poison, the leading men of the city (*pañcamukhanagara*) should know that you, my Lord, are guiltless, and that I have died in consequence of my own previous actions and due to fate.[44]

The *geniza*'s paper trail tells us that Jewish merchants eventually purchased girls like Panutī and Saṃpūrī and trafficked them to Egypt through the capillary networks of the protoglobal slave trade. The girls were forced onto ships alongside an array of provisions and commodities packed in baskets, bottles, and chests.[45] Passengers on ships in the western Indian Ocean often paid for a cabin (*balīj*) and they kept their enslaved servants (or human cargo to be sold) with them in these small compartments.[46] Within the cabin, she shared space with her handler and bales of goods like indigo and pepper. If the ship's crew followed the Islamic laws of maritime admiralty, there would have been separate toilets outside the cabin for men and women.[47] Yet, to the extent that stories about travel in the medieval Indian Ocean can be taken to reflect plausible dangers, to venture outside the cabin was risky for an enslaved woman. One such tale relates the violent fate of a *jāriya* from Sind (modern-day Pakistan) who took refuge in her cabin from a predatory sailor. During a storm, she left the cabin to cling to the rigging with the other passengers. A sailor (or another passenger) raped her and she fell overboard.[48]

For enslaved people trafficked from India to Egypt, the length of the journey meant that their vulnerability to rape and violence was protracted. The combined maritime and overland travel could easily last two months or longer depending on the season.[49] Ports of call, whether at the edge of the ocean or along the Nile, were places where some children were inspected, marketed, and sold to new owners. The fulcrum of the transoceanic trade in the western Indian Ocean was Aden, and the rulers of the city collected lucrative tariffs on all manner of goods, including enslaved people from India and beyond.[50] Enslaved people who disembarked here, whether from India or East Africa, were beset by all manner of gawkers and hustlers. A traveler in thirteenth-century Yemen, Ibn al-Mujāwir (d. 1292), wrote with disdain about the slave inspections he witnessed in Aden, a report best rendered in his own words:

> The slave girl is fumigated with an aromatic smoke, perfumed, adorned, and a waist-wrapper fastened round her middle. The seller takes her by the hand

> and walks around the souk with her; he calls out that she is for sale. The wicked merchants appear, examining her hands, feet, calves, thighs, navel, chest, and breasts. He examines her back and measures her buttocks in spans. He examines her tongue, teeth, hair and spares no effort. If she is wearing clothes, he takes them off; he examines and looks. Finally, he casts a direct eye over her vagina and anus, without her having on any covering or veil.[51]

Once in southern Egypt, traders and travelers would disembark and trek inland to a town such as Qūṣ from where the group would travel north along the Nile for multiple weeks. Seaborne, riverine, and overland travels were all fraught with physical dangers posed by nature, disease, and opportunistic human predators. The latter "man-made" obstacles included capture and ransom by pirates at sea. On land, pirates became raiding parties and "highway robbers"—as we learn from the last-known letter written by David Maimonides to his brother Moses about his travel across the Eastern Desert between Qūṣ, on the Nile, and ʿAydhāb on the Red Sea coast.[52] He reports that he was separated from his caravan after it was attacked. Once he arrived in ʿAydhāb, he learned that some of his companions had died of thirst, while others were wounded. He also reports that one of his companions sailing the Red Sea had shipwrecked at the Dahlak archipelago.[53] Due to these threats and the sheer physical toll that traveling exerted, men rarely brought their wives and children with them on journeys of any length.[54] Other enslaved women and children had no choice. In short, despite such women and children's seemingly benign appearance in the historical record, their experiences of enslavement and trafficking were far from it.

We have already met different children in previous chapters who were bound to new households once they were forcibly brought to Egypt, or born there as *muwalladas*. Some of their histories flicker in and out of view at critical junctures in their lives. Such is the case with Dhahab and Sitt al-Sumr, whose owner, Sitt al-Ḥusn, freed them and conditionally bequeathed residential rights and clothing to them so they might establish themselves within the Jewish community and eventually marry.[55] Kashf was freed and immediately remanded to the woman Sitt al-Riʾāsa, who was supposed to raise the child as a "proper Jew" until the girl was old enough to choose whether she wanted to remain as part of the household or not.[56] Some enslaved children lived in households with other young people. Such was the case with the son of the Black nurse Saʿāda, whose owner counted on her to raise her youngest daughter. This dying mother willed Saʿāda and her son to her youngest because she thought they were fond of each other.[57] What became of these children? The collective biography of the minors and adults known from *geniza* sources and contemporaneous responsa will sketch out some of the possibilities.

Naʿīm: A Speculative Biography

The people who wrote about enslaved people were not apt to differentiate between them based on age or their stage of life, even after puberty.[58] Instead, the nature of such writing was largely dictated by the occasions and contingencies that led to the creation of a document, or prompted a letter writer to share news or send greetings. Like the lives of Wafāʾ, Dhahab, and Sumr, the life in slavery of a Nubian woman, Naʿīm, generated such a paper trail. But it is an open question of how many records refer to the very same woman. In total there are seven different records, each a product of a separate circumstance, that describe a woman (or women) named Naʿīm who lived in Fustat and Cairo between the late eleventh and late twelfth centuries.[59] There is some chance that these snapshots of human trafficking, destitution, and emancipation illustrate the contours of a long life in slavery.

What follows is partly speculative, with the exception of two records that are definitely the same Naʿīm. Once again scribes and their methods for drawing up bills of sale are a key part of our story.[60] Naʿīm first surfaces in the written record in Fustat when Shemarya b. Ḥalfon sold her to the woman Khāliṣa in 1098 (figure 7.2).[61] Nearly a decade later in the fall of 1107, a Naʿīm appears on a few alms lists as the recipient of bread loaves along with dozens of other poor people (figure 7.3). In these cases, it is unclear what her status was—she is listed only as "Naʿīm." Had her owner died? Or was everyone in her household going hungry? A year later, in November 1108, Naʿīm was sold again in Cairo, by the woman Sitt al-Aqrān to Sitt al-Munā, the widow of Nahray b. Nissim (figure 7.4). What had happened in between her appearance in the bread line of 1107 and her sale in 1108 is also unknown. Did, for instance, the heirs of the deceased owner who died in 1107 finally sell her to Sitt al-Aqrān in 1108?

The next record about her was created when Sitt al-Munā sold Naʿīm in 1115. Sitt al-Munā, the widow of the merchant (and sometimes petty slave trader) Nahray b. Nissim, took the original bill of sale with her to an Islamic court.[62] The scribe flipped over that original bill of sale and wrote a new, supplementary bill of sale for Naʿīm on the reverse side of the paper (figure 7.5).

This supplementary deed (called a *faṣl*) records Naʿīm's purchase by a Christian scribe named Maqāra b. Ḥarūn, who was a former associate of her dead husband. Though the *faṣl* was more commonly used for real estate transactions,

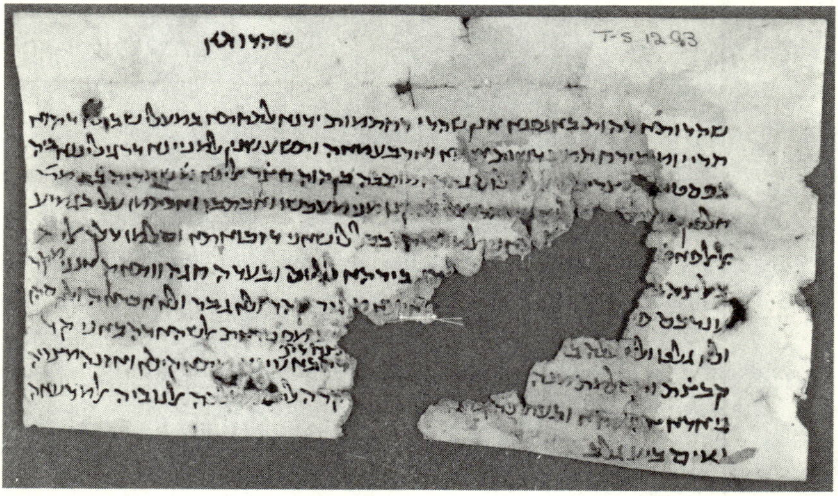

FIGURE 7.2. A bill of sale for the enslaved Nubian woman Naʿīm, 1098. T-S 12.93. Vellum. 22 × 12 cm. Reproduced by kind permission of the Syndics of Cambridge University Library.

its purpose was similar in slave sales.[63] The technique allowed the new owner to acquire both proof of his purchase and proof that the prior owner had herself acquired a clear title from the previous owner. Jewish scribes adopted the idea of the *faṣl* from their Muslim counterparts for their own Judeo-Arabic documents, even when all the transactions were between Jews.[64] For historical purposes, this *faṣl* provides rare, unambiguous proof that allows scholars to trace the sale and movement of enslaved people between households despite the limits and ambiguities of slave-naming practices. The sales of 1108 and 1115 are definitely for the same Naʿīm.

The next time that an enslaved woman named Naʿīm is mentioned in a document is in 1138, when she was contested property in a divorce settlement between the known slave owner and cantor, Shabbetay b. Joseph, and his wife Turfa bt. Abraham.[65] Between 1115, when Maqāra purchased Naʿīm from Sitt al-Munā, we can only speculate about the number of owners she might have had before being bound to Shabbetay and Turfa's household. As is often the case in these disputes, we do not know which spouse was able to claim Naʿīm as their property, and thus the paper trail again goes cold.

One short note, written almost forty years later, suggests another small possibility. On two pages from a notebook in which a scribe, or *parnas*, recorded the names of people who received alms in the form of clothing or dirhams on

FIGURE 7.3. An alms list identifying recipients of bread loaves. Naʿīm's name is the fifth entry in the third column from the right where the scribe notes that she received four loaves of bread (the number indicated by the Hebrew letter *dalet*). T-S K15.50. Paper. 14 × 20 cm. Reproduced by kind permission of the Syndics of Cambridge University Library.

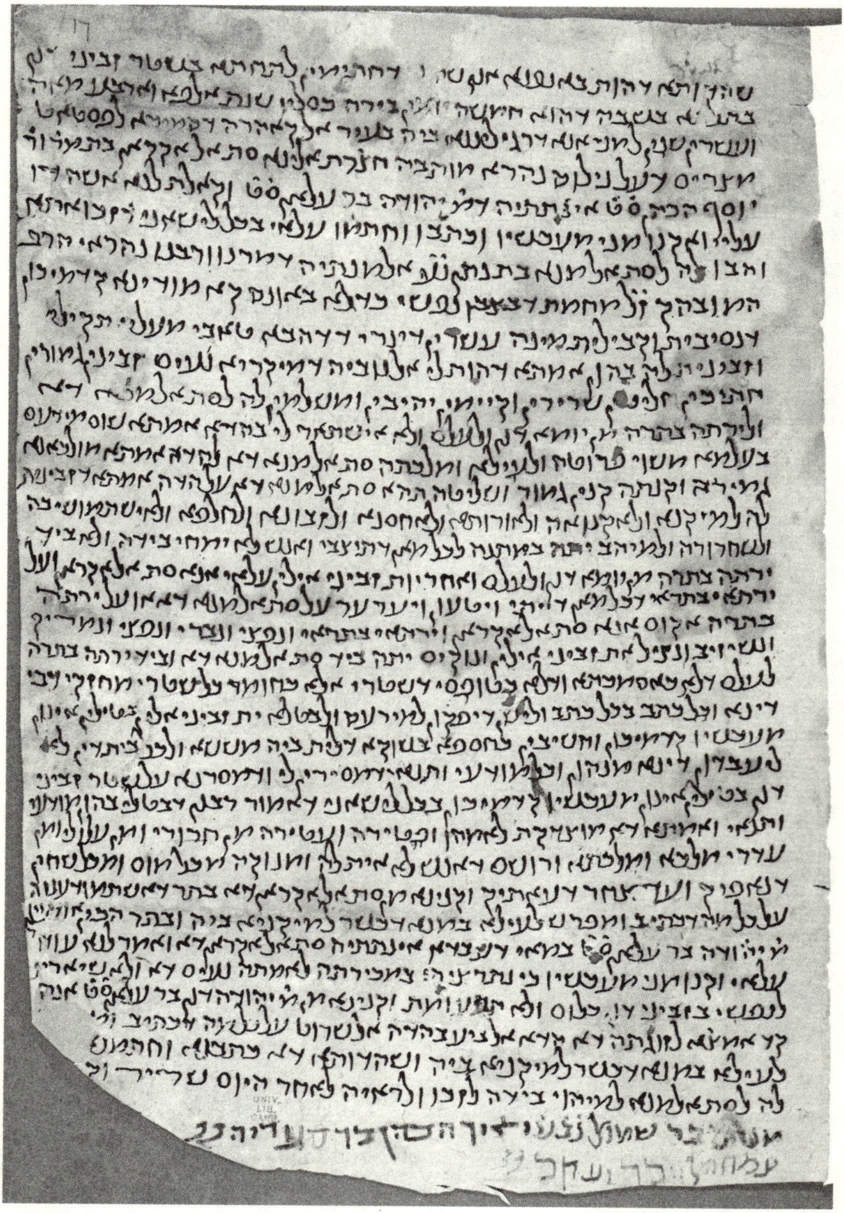

FIGURE 7.4. A bill of sale for the enslaved Nubian woman Naʿīm, 1108. T-S 18J1.17r. Paper. 21.5 × 31.5 cm. Reproduced by kind permission of the Syndics of Cambridge University Library.

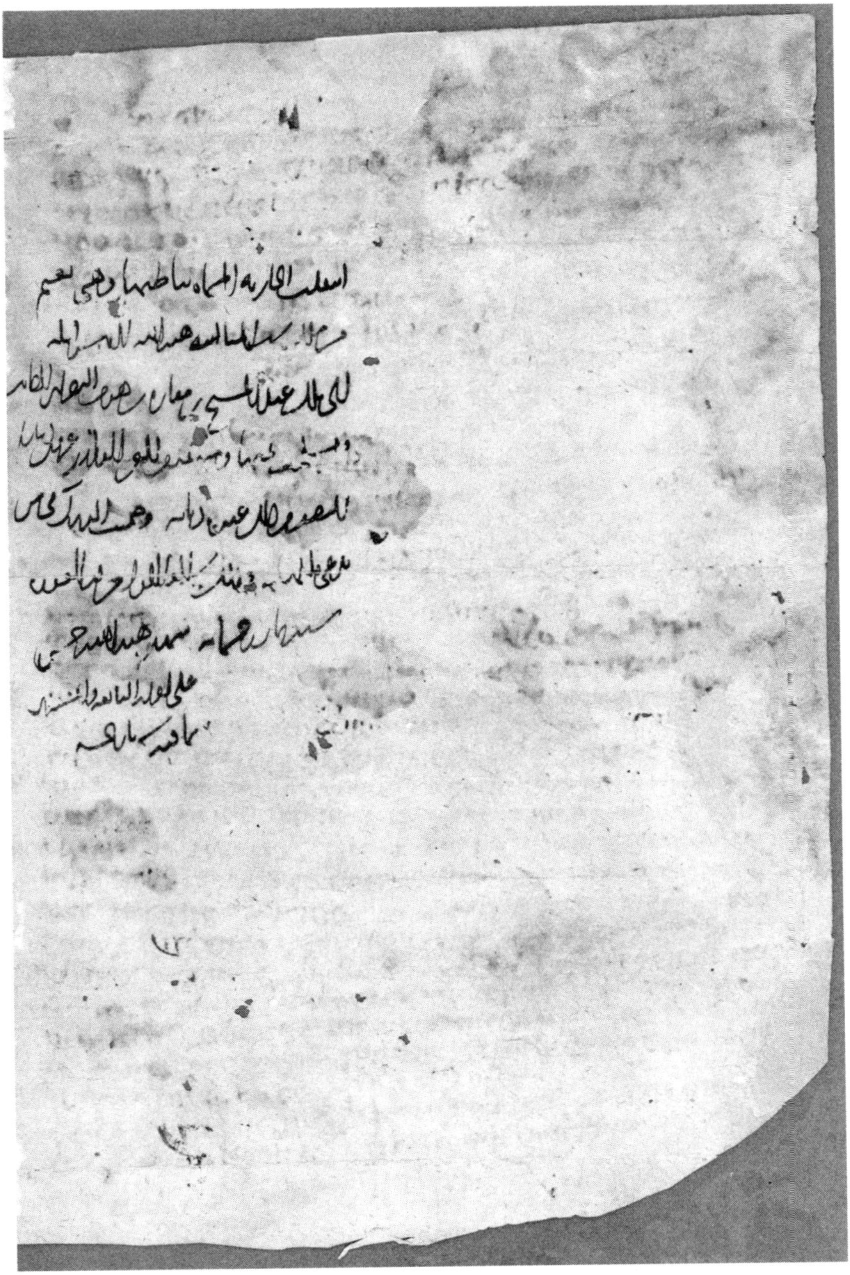

FIGURE 7.5. A supplementary bill of sale (1115) for the enslaved Nubian woman Naʿīm, written on the reverse side of her 1108 bill of sale from a Jewish court (figure 7.4). T-S 18J1.17v. Paper. 21.5 × 31.5 cm. Reproduced by kind permission of the Syndics of Cambridge University Library.

or after December 1176, there are three words and one number on a list of "Dirhams Expended": "Naʿīm. A manumitted *jāriya*. 3."[66] It is improbable that this would be the same Naʿīm, given what little we know about life expectancy in this era.[67] She would have been around ninety years old. Improbable, but not impossible.

As Oded Zinger writes about the study of life histories based on fragmentary *geniza* records: "[T]he incomplete nature of the sources curtails our ability to fully recover the life stories of the people involved. At the same time, it sparks our curiosity and propels our inquiry forward. We use our imagination to offer an interpretation of the partial and convoluted evidence in an attempt to arrive at a general view without reducing the inherent messiness of everyday life."[68] Indeed, Naʿīm's speculative history illustrates the possibilities, methods, and *challenges* of scholarly spadework that can yield evidence, not only for the social history of enslaved people but also for other medieval subjects whose marginal presence in surviving sources has discouraged their study.[69]

Enslaved People as "Theorists of Power"

Much direct evidence for the presence of enslaved people was produced as a result of enslavers' attempts to commodify them. While most of the surviving paper trail mutes and omits the speech and action of enslaved people, sales were also the moments when enslaved people had great potential to resist their enslavement, or at least to shape its terms.

A common way in which enslaved people affected sales was by undermining them. In *geniza* letters, slave owners complained about enslaved people who scuttled potential sales through their outright refusal to be sold. In chapter 3, we learned about a slave owner who had been caught by state authorities trying to avoid paying taxes and fees on the sale of a *jāriya*.[70] Though he tried, he could not find a buyer. As he complains in the margin of a letter, whenever anyone comes to inspect her, she acts terribly until the prospective buyer walks away.[71]

One can hear echoes of this enslaved agency in the cautions given by Ibn Buṭlān in his slave-buying manual. Though slave traders coached, and probably coerced, enslaved women to flirt with potential buyers, the women did not always acquiesce. Ibn Buṭlān instructs buyers looking for enslaved men to find out why their current owner wants to sell them. Has the boy or man been beaten, and why? Is he up for sale because he has undermined his master, or because he constantly complained about his ill treatment and neglect?[72] Ibn Buṭlān's advice acknowledges what the slave-owning classes were rarely apt to write down: that they physically and otherwise abused enslaved people, and that enslaved people did not suffer this abuse passively.[73]

In the Islamic context, buyers were alert to the possibility of a woman's concealed pregnancy, as she would then have rights as an *umm walad* that limited her owner's ability to resell her. Enslaved women knew this, and they sometimes cooperated to mislead buyers. Ibn Buṭlān warns, "Very often (slave girls) will put rags soaked with other girls' blood into their vaginas [to pretend they are menstruating]. The one who should examine them is a woman who is opposed to them foisting someone else's child on you. Order her to palpate their breasts and feel for a pregnant belly."[74]

Women enslaved by Jews did not gain the protections of the *umm walad*, but they did employ their knowledge of Jewish and Islamic law to protect themselves through the laws of the slave market. One way in which enslaved women showed themselves to be what Jennifer Morgan calls "theorists of power" was by recognizing the subordinated position of their Jewish enslavers as *dhimmīs*, and therefore as subordinate to Muslims.[75] The bold and decisive actions of two women illustrate how.

We first met Yaṣe'a in chapter 3 where she appeared as a *jāriya* belonging to a Jewish woman who sold her during a period of famine. In the years that followed, Yaṣe'a was sold several more times until she was caught in an ownership dispute between two Jewish parties. A Jewish court in Alexandria ruled that she should serve both claimants by alternating between their households every month. Yaṣe'a had been with one of her co-owners for only three days when the woman "beat her in front of some Muslims."[76] The author of this report then abruptly switches from Judeo-Arabic to Hebrew, perhaps to emphasize the gravity of the situation: "She left (*yaṣe'a*) the community (*min ha-kellal*)."[77] In this and similar contexts, Jewish writers use this phrase to indicate when a person converted to another religion, or when their religious status in Jewish law changed.[78] Here it is clear that the phrase meant conversion to Islam, specifically. Though the fact is left unwritten, the two Jewish owners sold Yaṣe'a immediately because Jews, as *dhimmīs*, were not allowed to own Muslims.[79] The very reason this historical account exists is because the two rival claimants were subsequently ordered to split the proceeds of the sale, but one of them argued that he was the sole and rightful owner.

I suggest the name "Yaṣe'a" for this woman, although her birth or "slave" name is never mentioned. Yaṣe'a, which translates here as "she left," is the one word out of the more than six hundred in the account that renders her as a subject and actor. Even here the author's choice of words obscures a broader scope of decision-making and action. The beating alone was not what precipitated Yaṣe'a's decision to convert to Islam: it was also the fact that a Jewish woman, a member of a subordinated gender and a subordinated class of *dhimmīs*, upset the social order by publicly performing an act of violence and dominance. The presence of Muslims could have been consequential in different ways. Perhaps they stepped in to shield Yaṣe'a from being beaten. One or more of them could have shared this news with a Muslim authority or could have taken Yaṣe'a to a Muslim court themselves. Yaṣe'a may have counted on the fact that her beating by a Jewish woman would make a judge sympathetic to her. Such a dynamic is apparent in a later, sixteenth-century incident in which an Abyssinian woman told her Egyptian Jewish owner, the head of the state mint, that she was going out to the bath. Instead she took shelter in the house of a Muslim judge and converted to Islam. When her owner came to retrieve her, the judge refused to put her, now a Muslim, under the authority of a Jew.[80] Perhaps Yaṣe'a knew about other such stories from her own time.

A consequence of the writer's use of the euphemism "she left the community" is that Yaṣe'a's actual speech before Muslim authorities goes unrecorded in the responsum query. In the face of the pervasive archival silence that mutes the voices of enslaved people, it is worth noting that her conversion to Islam required her to declare the *shahāda*, a declaration of creed, before a Muslim authority. For the record, we can reconstruct her speech. Yaṣe'a declared before a Muslim judge that "[T]here is no god but God; Muḥammad is the Messenger of God."[81] A judge may also have issued her a written certificate that attested to her status as a Muslim.[82] Yaṣe'a's conversion did not cause her manumission, but it did free her from physical abuse and from being a contested pawn between two feuding slave owners.

Another enslaved woman, whom we might call "Bint Yahūdiyya (Daughter of a Jewish Woman)," was also presented with an opportunity to convert to Islam. Her story is told in a responsum query that we read about in chapters 1 and 5, which describes a case in which a Jewish man used an enslaved Christian as his concubine.[83] The slave owner's brother opposed his behavior and reported him to a Muslim judge. As in Yaṣe'a's case, Bint Yahūdiyya's story was only written down because a dispute between two Jews escalated into a more serious affair of community-wide concern.

The Muslim judge thus summoned the enslaved woman before him and pressed her: "What is your status?"[84] She replied immediately, "I am Jewish." He then gave her a chance to convert to Islam.[85] She replied, "I am Jewish, the daughter of a Jewish woman (*bint Yahūdiyya*)."[86] The reason for her double emphasis, that she is Jewish and born to a Jewish woman, is because of matrilineal descent. She wanted to underscore that she was a freeborn Jew and not a convert whatsoever. Her testimony, if it did not satisfy the judge, at least convinced him that it was best to send her back home with her owner. The Jewish community found the whole incident quite salacious, and they gossiped about it.

Somewhere in this story, someone is lying. When Moses Maimonides read about these events in the query sent to him, he did not think that the woman was "Jewish, the daughter of a Jewish woman." He tacitly accepted the report that she was an enslaved Christian.[87] This means that Bint Yahūdiyya, in her testimony to the Muslim judge, likely invented a Jewish lineage for herself.[88] The immediate consequence was that it perpetuated the status quo. She returned with her owner to his house. We do not know why she did this. Did her owner threaten to harm her if she did not go through with this ruse? Did the *jāriya* calculate that her sale would bring its own set of risks and thus act to integrate herself further into her current household?

Yaṣe'a and Bint Yahūdiyya both made tactical gambits, but to different ends. Yaṣe'a's conversion to Islam dis-integrated her from two households and forced her onto the market where she chose (or was forced) to take her chances amid its uncertainties. Bint Yahūdiyya's claim to Jewish ancestry could have worked in at least two ways, both of which find corroboration in contemporaneous evidence. Her testimony could have precipitated a chain of events that led her owner to free her and marry her, as Moses Maimonides counseled. As we read in chapter 1, and in the next, Bint Yahūdiyya's manumission would have affected her full and lawful conversion to Judaism, and any children she then conceived with her former captor would have been born as free Jews. Moreover, as a bride she would have gained certain economic rights that were enshrined in a written marriage contract. The actions of two men we met in chapter 5, the silk weaver Abū al-Faraj and an unnamed man who housed his concubine in her own apartment in the Fayyūm and lavished her with fine clothing, suggest a second possibility: for some enslaved women, becoming a man's "favorite"[89] concubine could bring them benefits, albeit fragile ones.

Enslaved women, who sought to make the best of largely terrible choices, might choose what most of us think of as the path of "resistance": to flee. Other women might choose to accept an apartment and gifts as valuable benefits. My own thinking on this subject is guided by Sally McKee's insights into sexual slavery in medieval Europe:

> There is also no question that slaves could try to ameliorate their lives by means of sexual service, either offered or conceded. Mitigating circumstances, however, could only alter the fundamental inequity between a master and a

> slave. . . . Whether or not slaves found ways to exert power over their own actions, over their masters, or even over the households in which they lived, sexual relationships between masters and slaves rested on a bedrock of coercion. Coercion defined, prescribed, and fixed all relationships between slaves and their masters and mistresses.[90]

To acknowledge that sex, "offered or conceded," could be a strategy that some enslaved people used to protect themselves is not to blame them for their exploitation or to apologize for sexual predators. Rather it follows a critique, powerfully articulated by Walter Johnson, that historians of slavery have so strongly conflated the "agency" (the personhood and humanity) of enslaved people with resistance alone, that they have missed how enslaved people also cared for themselves and their loved ones by going along, collaborating, and attending to their "bare necessities of life."[91]

Mobility: Networks, Knowledge, and Attachments

How did Yaṣe'a and Bint Yahūdiyya know how to navigate Islamic and Jewish law to force and prevent their respective sales? It is a simple question, but its answers open possibilities for further understanding enslaved people as knowledgeable subjects in their own right. As "theorists of power," enslaved people were shrewd observers of people, both within their own households and among the slave-owning classes at large. Their safety and well-being depended on it. They also required knowledge of social relations, urban geography, and law. One key to enslaved people's acquisition of knowledge was the very mobility that made them useful to slave owners in the first place.[92] As chapter 4 illustrates, *khidma* (personal service) required that enslaved people move inside and outside the home, crossing layered boundaries between private and public spheres and even into parts of the city that members of the slave-owning classes would have avoided altogether.

As mobile agents, *jāriya*s developed mental maps of residential compounds, streets and alleyways, neighborhoods, and the sinuous arteries that connected all of them. Navigation of such spaces required not only knowledge of the city, but also of the people who lived and worked in specific places. The instructions that *jāriya*s received, by word of mouth or perhaps in writing, would have resembled the addresses that letter writers used to help couriers locate recipients. In those days there were no numbered street addresses, but rather instructions like "To Fustat, the House of Exchange, the office of Ibrāhīm b. Isḥāq, the Jewish banker" or to "the Coppersmith's Market." Delivery instructions could also contain provisions for backup recipients. One writer asked to receive a message at "the Perfumer's Market (and) the shop of al-Kohen the Sicilian, or to the Grand Market (and) to the shop of the potion maker Abū al-Faraj."[93] Enslaved factotums constructed their mental maps as they made occasional deliveries and in relation to the locations they knew from their more routine errands at food vendors, public ovens, and water sources. With every resale in the local market, the enslaved factotum was forced to expand her knowledge of residences, markets, and public venues.

Not every contact entailed interpersonal conversations between enslaved people and others, but some of them did. Even silent or terse exchanges provided the chance for observation and eavesdropping. More consequential were the run-ins with other free, freed, and enslaved people who were out and about doing the same work. Every queue for bread, water, and the retailer's attention held the potential for a chance encounter or conversation that might lead to the accumulation of crucial knowledge about individuals, households, neighborhoods, and the workings of slavery throughout.

Ibn Buṭlān himself recognized that enslaved people acquired useful knowledge, and he instructed would-be slave buyers to beware of them accordingly:

> Special precautions for leading citizens (*al-ru'asā'*). They say: leading citizens—anyone with an enemy from whom he fears treason, or whom he fears will come across (his) secrets—should be wary of purchasing a eunuch (*khādim*) or a *jāriya*, especially if she can write and comes from the ruler's palace (*dār sulṭān*)—unless he has had direct experience of her. Also, of purchasing a *jāriya muwallada* from a merchant or an importer (*jallāb*), for this is a trick that has been the undoing of many kings and leading citizens.[94]

One outcome of the local churn—the cycles of sale and resale that enslaved people experienced—was that they acquired technical skills and social knowledge as they changed hands. The *jāriya* in the apothecary learned about healing potions, and poisons. The scribe's *jāriya* may have learned to read and write. The *waṣīfa* who waited on her mistress was familiar with her collection of jewelry and knew where it was kept. Like flies on a wall, enslaved people heard news, gossip, and were privy to otherwise private conversations within their households. These are some of the avenues through which Yaṣe'a, Bint Yahūdiyya, and other enslaved women would have learned how to maneuver Islamic and Jewish law.

Some enslaved people also used mobility to resist their owners and, sometimes, to escape altogether. Along with theft, flight is the most common complaint that slave owners made. The mostly obliterated remnant of one bill of sale explains that the seller provides only a limited guarantee for a *ghulām*, named

Ṣandal (Sandalwood), who had run away (*haraba*) multiple times and who was accused of stealing (*saraqa*).[95] Flight could mean different things, including a temporary or open-ended relocation to known whereabouts. This appears to have been the case when the *jāriya* Tawfīq left her mistress in Alexandria.[96] The woman, identifiable as the mother of Abū al-ʿIzz, wrote to her son primarily because she needed him to buy silk while he was in Fustat. She added, however, that Tawfīq "has gone to my sister's house. Your aunt enticed her (*afsadathā*) until she went to her."[97] In her view, it was the sister who had manipulated Tawfīq and encouraged her to leave. The mother's word choice, that Tawfīq herself "went (*rāḥat*)" to her sister's house, suggests that this *jāriya* made a choice to leave. We are left to guess how (and whether) the sister's inducements for Tawfīq were better for the *jāriya*, or whether they were manipulations within a broader family dispute.

Other women left their owners with no indication that they would ever return. The strongest evidence for this kind of flight dates to the time of civil war, drought, and famine in the eleventh century called "the crisis of al-Mustanṣir's caliphate (*al-shidda al-Mustanṣiriyya*)" by chroniclers of the era.[98] In a letter to her husband, a woman in Fustat conveyed her distress about a group of Easterners (*mashāriqa*), possibly a reference to the Turkish army faction, who tunneled (*naqaba*) into their home and stole 30 liters (2 *wayba*s) of wheat.[99] She reported that amid the chaos "many slave girls (*jawārī*) have run away (*harabū*) with the Bedouin."[100] The family's own *jāriya*, however, did not run away.[101] In assessing this report, we must remember that we hear of these events from a member of the slave-owning classes. Did the women flee with the Bedouin, or were they taken as plunder?[102]

Urban Marronage *in the Underworld*

Two questions attend the flight of enslaved people from their captivity: Where did they go? And, if flight was an option, why didn't more people flee? We know that Tawfīq fled to the house of her owner's sister. In most cases, however, there is no written indication of where people fled, as in the case of the *ghulām* Ṣandal and the *jāriya* Iftikhār. These two eventually came back, however, and this suggests either that they eventually returned of their own volition, or that they were apprehended and forcibly brought back to their owners who might then punish them with beatings, and possibly tie them up with ropes.[103] In both scenarios—"voluntary" return and apprehension—the likelihood is that Ṣandal and Iftikhār participated in a kind of urban marronage within Fustat and Cairo.

Cites across the Islamic Middle East had neighborhoods with reputations as havens for marginalized groups ranging from disabled and impoverished people to organized groups of beggars and tricksters.[104] As the historian Kristina Richardson writes in her study of the Roma in the medieval Islamic world:

> If historians remain sensitive to the meaning embedded in the plans of houses, the orientation of streets, and the paths and gates connecting neighborhoods to surrounding quarters, they can better visualize the construction of minority cultures and their interactions with other settled groups.[105]

In Egypt such neighborhoods and groups are better known from the early Mamluk period, when the Ḥusayniyya and Bāb al-Lūq quarters became known for crime and poverty.[106] In his studies of the crime narratives found in Mamluk-era chronicles, Carl Petry notes that in their descriptions of theft, flight, and even murder by enslaved people, there is a perceptible

> milieu in which slaves had enough autonomous mobility for runaways to stand a reasonable chance of escape or seclusion. This milieu was at least as illustrative of the culture in which these chattel slaves lived and served as it was of their criminal threat to public order more specifically.[107]

Within these neighborhoods there were houses that served as collective residences for poor and transient peoples that were distinct from the *funduqs* that paying customers used for short-term lodgings.[108] One communal compound known from Mamluk Cairo and Jerusalem was the *ḥawsh* (or *ḥūsh*, pl. *aḥwāsh*), which was a single-story mud-brick structure that contained many small rooms organized around a central courtyard with space for both food preparation and a toilet.[109] Another communal home for those who lived at the margins of urban society in Cairo was the *maṣṭaba*, which popular literature portrayed as a place where young men—whom al-Ḥarīrī described in one of his rogue tales as "importune beggars and low artisans"—resided.[110] Other groups were known to find havens in rural districts beyond the city.[111] While the precise locations and composition of these places were different in the pre-Mamluk period, they are an enduring feature of cities in the medieval Middle East. Moreover, at different points in premodern Cairo, enslaved people were associated with these districts and their residential refuges.[112]

Enslaved people like Ṣandal and Iftikhār, in addition to the "many slave girls" who ran away with the Bedouin, could have sought out these communities to hide temporarily or even to attempt an escape from slavery altogether.[113] Though these urban marronages[114] could be havens, they were not utopias. Medieval writers associated them with sexual violence, in particular, and warned readers about predators who drugged "beardless" boys and then raped their stupefied victims.[115] In his *Book of Charlatans*, al-Jawbarī (13th c.) also warned his readers about "pretty women" who adorned themselves and targeted men whom they suspected were "well-heeled and alone." They seduced, drugged, and robbed the men, whom they then stripped naked and abandoned.[116] These dangers, whether perceived or real, suggest one explanation for why we don't read more about flight as a more common and regular strategy used by enslaved people. They had to make their own risk-benefit calculations.

The movement of enslaved people through mixed, public spaces and into the shops and residences of the city also provided them with opportunities to meet one another. These encounters sometimes led to durable interpersonal attachments between enslaved people in different households. This was the case for the woman Ṣayd (Quarry), also called Sitt (Lady) al-Ṣayd, and a *ghulām* who was bound to another household.[117] We know a precious few details about their relationship because Ṣayd's mistress complained about them in two different family letters sent from her home near Qūṣ to Fustat, albeit with fewer details than we would like. Ṣayd did two things that were particularly distressing to the writer.[118] First, she went to a judge and asked him to issue an order that the letter's recipient pay alimony for her (Ṣayd's) children. Second, she told the judge that she was pregnant and that she wanted to marry the *ghulām* of (a man named) Ibn Miṣbāḥ.[119]

Ṣayd sought to provide for herself and her children, not through flight or rejecting the terms of slavery, but by using them to her relative advantage. Ṣayd knew that slave owners were obligated to provide the necessities of life for those they owned. She sought out a Jewish judge (*dayyan*) and persistently pressed him (*taqātalat*) to issue a written order (*farḍ*) that she could use to compel her owner, who was away in Fustat, to provide them more material support (*mūnathum*).[120] Ṣayd also took the initiative to forge her own intimate bonds of kinship with a prospective husband of her choosing, another enslaved person. Her mistresses' complaint that "she (Ṣayd) is pregnant, and she wants to marry the *ghulām* of Ibn Miṣbāḥ"[121] speaks further about a world largely hidden from historians, a world to which the slave-owning classes were largely not privy. What they did observe of enslaved people's intimate lives and kinships they usually did not care to write about, unless it inconvenienced them.

The contingencies that led Ṣayd's history to be so tersely recorded compel us to reconsider the other fragmented histories that appear in this book and that encompass the enslaved life course from birth and childhood into adulthood as a "sexually mature (*balūgh*)" person. Who were the fathers of 'Ushshāq's unborn child, of Jinān's daughter Wafā', and of Ṭāwūs's ten-year-old son Mubārak? And what prospects did these enslaved families have as they were sold and resold from household to household? We aren't able to answer these questions, but Ṣayd's dogged insistence that she make and protect her own family does point us to larger conclusions relevant to slavery studies across time and space.

Natal alienation, dishonor, and "social death"[122] are central to the violence that slavery does to enslaved people, but these characteristics do not invariably define them or delimit the scope of their actions.[123] In the documentary corpus that furnishes much of the evidence for this book, this violence is largely muted. This chapter uses an assemblage of texts to bring more light from narrative and legal sources that allows us to imagine both the violence of human trafficking and the quotidian lives of enslaved people that exist beyond the margins of the documents.

Another salient storyline is that, though natal alienation and social death were strategies and outcomes favored by enslavers, enslaved people resisted and overcame them through their own volition. Enslaved people knew, and learned, how to navigate the profound power asymmetries that conditioned their lives. They acquired knowledge, skills, and their own social ties in slavery through the labor and movement that their enslavers required of them.

The final chapter of the book focuses on the lives of a group of enslaved people in Jewish households who experienced passage through the liminal states of alienation and social death toward integration as freed converts to Judaism. Many of these freed people chose to remain in the Jewish community, where they married other Jews, became the parents of Jewish children, and built their own mercantile careers in the footsteps of their former owners.

8

Freed People and the Jewish Community

WHEN ABRAHAM B. Aaron freed the woman Nāshiya in 1176, he stated before witnesses (figure 8.1):

> I, Abraham ha-Kohen, son of Aaron ha-Kohen, (and by) any other name under which I am known, hereby declare, out of my own free will, without any coercion, thoughtlessness, or error, but being in full possession of my mental faculties, that I am freeing you, Nāshiya, you who were my slave beforehand. Hereby, I am freeing you; now you are free; now you belong to yourself; you are permitted to join the Jewish community (*be-qahal de-Yisra'el*), to adopt a (new) name as a Jew (*be-Yisra'el*), and do what you like as do (all) free persons. Neither I, Abraham ha-Kohen, nor my heirs after me, nor any (legal representative) of mine has any rights to you or to your offspring, whom you will establish among the Jews (*be-Yisra'el*). The document is for you a bill of manumission from me and a deed of freedom according to the law of Moses and the Jews (*ke-dat Moses ve-Yisra'el*).[1]

Nāshiya is one of over fifty freed people who can be identified in the *geniza* corpus. Like most of the enslaved and freed people whose collective history is told in this book, there is only a single surviving record that attests to her life. Consequently there are many questions about her that we would like to have answered. Questions like: How was Nāshiya forced into slavery, and for how long did Abraham own her before he freed her? What was her life like as an enslaved woman and as a freedwoman? Did she choose a new name and decide to remain as a part of the Jewish community in Egypt? Did she marry and/or have children? And what would the prospects have been for a child born to a former slave? As seen in the previous chapters, we find that in the one

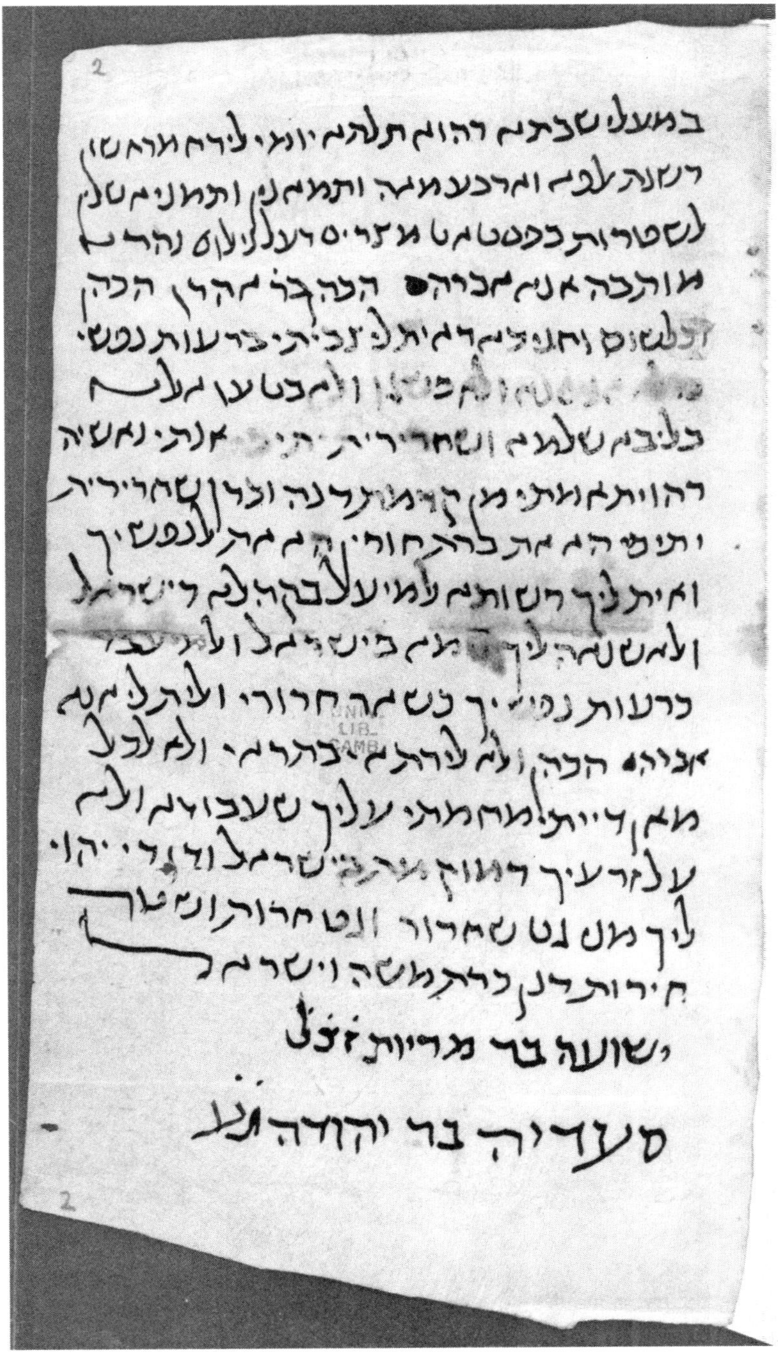

FIGURE 8.1. A signed deed of manumission for the freedwoman Nāshiya, 1176. Vellum? 9.5 × 17 cm. T-S 8J12.2. Reproduced by kind permission of the Syndics of Cambridge University Library.

record about her, Nāshiya does not speak. Still, this chapter is about people like her.

By the numbers, around one-quarter of the enslaved people documented in the *geniza* corpus were eventually freed.[2] In a few cases, the trajectories of women like Wafā' and Dhahab, whom we read about in the previous chapter, are visible as they moved through life with slave status until they were eventually freed. But in most cases, specific enslaved individuals cannot be identified or matched with specific freed people for a few main reasons. One reason is naming. As Nāshiya's deed of manumission indicates, freed people often adopted new names and relinquished their slave names, though this was not always the case.[3] The second reason is that, once they gained their freedom, an unknown number of enslaved people left the Egyptian Jewish community and thus largely disappear from the written records preserved in the *geniza*. Third and finally, whether or not their owners ever planned to free them, enslaved people died for the same reasons that all people did—illness, epidemics, and old age. Still, an important conclusion emerges from patterns of enslavement and manumission shown in this book's appendixes: emancipation was not uncommon, but it was more likely that a person born, or forced, into slavery died without ever attaining freed status and its protections, opportunities, and greater dignities.

This chapter tells the history of the freed people who remained a part of the Jewish community in Fustat, and sometimes farther afield in Sicily and Ifrīqiyya. There were different pathways toward freedom. The best documented one was through a formal process such as Nāshiya's that culminated in the newly freed person receiving a written document that was meant to be safeguarded as proof for themselves and their offspring. The freed people who chose to remain in the Jewish community did so as converts to Judaism. In most respects, the evidence we have of their lives shows that they participated in society as freeborn Jews did. They married other Jews and owned real estate. They had Jewish children. They got divorced. They were involved in legal cases involving inheritances and business partnerships. In large measure, we are only able to identify them as freed people because slavery had eradicated their natal patrilineal genealogy, and the labels of "freedman" and "freedwoman" were used as substitute patronymics of sorts.

As a group, and from what we can know from a few individual biographies, the history of freed people in the Jewish community illustrates how most of these subjects forged their life paths not by rejecting their pasts as slaves, or even by repudiating their connections to the former enslavers. Instead, they used the limited benefits that accrued to them precisely because of their formerly enslaved status and participated in society with a new social position, articulated using the vocabulary of "freed person" (i.e., not simply "free"). In the second generation, their children were only sometimes associated with descent from a "freed person," and, in the third generation, there were no traces of this past found in how grandchildren were known.[4] Thus, "freed" status served as a generational bridge toward assimilation as Jews in Arab-Islamic society. This process was itself inflected by Islamic law and social practices. The two worked in tandem.

From the perspective of free and freed Jews, the erasure of slavery's history was probably viewed as a welcome success. In historical perspective, there is another story to tell. The successful assimilation of freed people, and the elision of enslaved pasts from their descendants' genealogies, worked over the centuries to conceal the presence of a coercively integrated multiethnic diaspora at the heart of one of the most vibrant Jewish communities of the Middle Ages.

Becoming a Freed Person

For people enslaved and then freed by Jews, their experiences of slavery and freedom were conditioned by the medieval Jewish laws that effectively regarded slaves as "partly" Jewish and freed people as a type of convert to Judaism. These laws, analyzed in chapter 1, held that when a Jew purchased an enslaved person, he was supposed to have the slave undergo a ritual immersion in water.[5] Enslaved men were supposed to be circumcised.[6] All slaves, regardless of gender, were expected to obey the same commandments that applied to Jewish women, such as eating kosher food and observing the Sabbath.[7] If the slave went through with the immersion, and accepted the commandments, then she was no longer considered an "idolater," but neither was she considered Jewish.[8] Rather, she entered a new, liminal status somewhere between gentile (non-Jew) and Jew until her manumission, at which point she became a Jew and a part of the larger Jewish community.[9] Freedmen, due to their gender, took on the commandments of Jewish men and were permitted, as their bills of manumission sometimes stated, to study Torah and to teach it to their sons.[10] The Aramaic legal formulas found in Nāshiya's and other freed people's deeds of manumission make clear that emancipation was meant to be complete and unconditional.

As we have seen in earlier chapters with Jewish men who took enslaved concubines, not all slave owners chose to follow this formal process. Some men tried to prove, or convince others, that they had already freed their former slave before marriage and child birth, but they were not always able to prove it. These dynamics were part of a larger phenomenon that Moshe Yagur calls "sociological conversion, one in which daily interaction, social bonding, and the forming of family units mattered more than court sessions, rabbinic procedures, and the written law."[11] When Jewish men treated a freedwoman and his children by her as if they were free Jews, or when they used an enslaved woman as a concubine, this forced Jewish leaders to respond and to find accommodations that allowed them both to preserve their own authority and to preserve families that were living according to Jewish law, or that might be persuaded to do so.[12]

Many Jews did follow the law and the formal procedures for freeing enslaved people. Deathbed declarations that freed enslaved people, such as Sitt al-Ḥusn's in chapter 6 for Dhahab and Sitt al-Sumr, were regarded as legally binding no matter the language in which they were uttered. It was incumbent upon the heirs of the deceased, however, to make sure that a written deed of manumission was correctly executed and placed in the hand of the freed person.[13] When an enslaved person received a deed of manumission (*geṭ shiḥrur*),[14] Jewish law held that he or she was supposed to go through a ritual immersion once again to mark the passage from "liminal Jew" to "fully Jewish." As Yagur emphasizes, the enslaved and freed person is made passive in this legal process.[15] They receive freedom and are converted to Judaism, but their acceptance or rejection of Jewish status is not recorded in manumission deeds.[16]

In practice, the former slave owners recognized that their former slaves had a choice to make. As Abū al-Ḥasan said on his deathbed after he freed the young girl Kashf: when she gets older, she can choose "to remain" with his sister, Sitt al-Riʾāsa, or Kashf can choose "to leave."[17] Sitt al-Ḥusn also tacitly acknowledged that Dhahab and Sitt al-Sumr had a choice to make about whether they would continue to live as Jews or not—their receipt of real estate and clothing was contingent on their choice. This chapter tells the histories of the people who chose to stay. Their presence in the Jewish community generated a paper trail due to their roles as spouses, parents, divorcées, business partners, and so on.

There are at least fourteen manumission deeds, or remnants thereof, preserved in the *geniza*—preserved because they were important for freed people and their immediate heirs to keep as proof of their freed status and the free, Jewish status of their children.[18] Evidence of most freed people comes from how they are described in a variety of letters, wedding documents, legal records, and various lists. Sometimes freed people are identified by their personal name, and occasionally the name of their former owner. In other cases, they are only called "the freedman" or "the freedwoman," using the gendered Hebrew terms *meshuḥrar* and *meshuḥreret* (fem.) and the Arabic ones *al-ʿatīq(a)*, *al-maʿtūq(a)*, and *mawlā*.[19]

Marriage, Divorce, and the Risk of Poverty

Marriage to a free person was the most common visible strategy that freed women used to gain security and social standing after their manumission.[20] We read in chapter 5 about the Nubian woman Umm Nūbiyya, who married the merchant ʿEli b. Yefet and had a daughter with him after another of her children, an enslaved girl, had died.[21] We have also seen how some slave owners provided economic and social capital to the people whom they freed so they would have better prospects in marriage. In 1124 the freedwoman Tawfīq, possibly the same Nubian woman whose owner thought she was a Christian in 1100, married a Jewish man and came to own a share of a house.[22] Tawfīq's capital may have come from her former owner, who provided her with the real estate so she could have a better chance both of finding a good marital match and of having a better chance of stability and relative prosperity in that marriage.[23]

We know more about the wealth of the freedwoman Munā, whose dowry was worth 120 dinars when she married in 1184. This sum exceeded the dowries of the two other free brides whose marriages were recorded alongside hers in the same court register.[24] The wardrobe Munā brought with her likewise befit a woman of means and honor. When she woke and donned one of her *jūkhāniyya*s (a common dress with long sleeves), she could choose from a multicolored array of them, made from the finest Egyptian *Dabīqī* linen. There was a white dress, another in green, one in a sumptuous pomegranate red, and a second white dress with decorated bands. And when Munā wrapped her shawl around her shoulders to keep warm, she fastened it with its own gold pin.[25] For dressier occasions, she had a matching two-piece ensemble made up of a silk headdress and waist-wrap (*khaṣī*).[26] Munā's wardrobe was not extraordinary, but it was certainly "fine clothing," the likes of which most women could not afford.[27] Consider the entirety of the clothing that belonged to one *jāriya* named Misk. Her wardrobe was recorded in the estate inventory of her recently deceased owner. All of Misk's clothing could fit wrapped up in her sleeping carpet and included a belt, two cloaks, one robe, one dress, and a pair of mismatched socks.[28]

The economic and social capital that Munā received from her former owner facilitated her marital match to a man with social standing in the Jewish community, a welfare officer (*parnas*). His status and connections proved crucial when her wealth was threatened by officials in the Ayyubid sultanate. Mūna had given a large loan to a professional perfumer (*ʿaṭṭār*). When the perfumer died, the Office of Inheritances (*dīwān al-mawārīth*) sought to seize his estate and Mūna's capital with it.[29] Through her husband and other connections, Munā had access to well-placed Jewish "elders (*sheikhs*)." The elders asked a Muslim judge to intervene, and they paid him a handsome sum to do so. Indeed the judge protected enough of the perfumer's estate so that Munā recouped 23 dinars, which was more than enough gold to purchase her own *jāriya* if she wished.[30] In contrast to Munā's sizeable dowry of 120 gold dinars, when another slave owner freed the *jāriya* Mubāraka in this same era, he provided her with a dowry roughly equivalent to only 3.75 dinars.[31] The small size of her dowry may explain why she married a dyer (*al-ṣabbāgh*).

Freedmen also found marriage matches in the Jewish community, had children, and established themselves in a trade. Of course, unlike freedwomen, freedmen did not receive dowries. Instead, they were expected to offer a marriage payment and to promise a delayed marriage gift. Freedmen had to generate their capital through their own labor and initiative, though they sometimes received inheritances and possibly gifts in cash and kind. When Salāma (Health) the freedman married in 1111, he promised his bride a combined marriage gift of 13 dinars, 3 of which were due at the time of marriage.[32] His wife's dowry held typical items like clothing and furnishings. It also included 14 dinars in cash, which is listed as "half the price of a house (*dār*)," presumably for the couple to use for their joint residence.[33] Not all married couples, free or freed, could expect to have their own residence, or part of one.[34] A scribe's terse and partly obliterated note indicates that another freedman offered an immediate marriage gift of [4] dinars to his new wife and expected to live with her in the house (*dār*) of Ibn Jamāhir, the same merchant whom Ṣāfī accused of abandoning his concubine and their child.[35]

Freed people also got divorced, as happened to Umm Nūbiyya in the late Fall of 1154.[36] One benefit of marriage and divorce was the financial safety net that it was supposed to provide. Ibtidā' had married the merchant Abū al-Murajjā b. Nathan and they had a daughter together, named Fakhr.[37] Upon their divorce, Abū al-Murajjā agreed to pay alimony (*mezonot*) of 30 dirhams per month (less than a dinar), due on the first of the month, "for his daughter who he had put in the custody of Ibtidā' the freedwoman, his divorcée."[38] The most likely scenario is that Abū al-Murajjā was pressured by Ibtidā' to pay this extra alimony before he left on a mercantile venture, since he would not be present to care for Fakhr directly. Thirty dirhams per month was not a great sum, so Ibtidā' must have had other wealth from her dowry and marriage gifts, or possibly from other sources of income like rent payments or investment returns.

Whether free or freed, poverty was a chronic condition for some freed people and a latent threat for many more of various social classes.[39] Impoverished freed people found themselves in line for alms with other poor people who hoped to receive bread flour, clothing, or a handful of silver coins. This was the case with the woman Sarab (Flowing Water), who received the same kind of dress (*jūkhāniyya*) as the free widow and orphans who stood in line with her, though not one as fine as any of Munā's dresses.[40] That same year Sarab queued again with other free women for small cash donations that they could use for daily necessities.[41] The 5 dirhams that Sarab received were taken from a charitable fund that was raised through donations; enslaved and freed people are also found in donor rosters for different purposes. The freedman Bandār (Harbor), who appears to have died in Sicily in the tenth century, left various funds in his will for the local poor and also for the poor of Jerusalem.[42] A *ghulām*, Ṣāf, gave 2 dinars to a collection for a widow, a collection that was organized by his owner, who was a merchant.[43] What we do know about the fortunes of freed people shows that their lives largely resembled those of free people in their variety and in many of the factors that shaped their life chances.

Naming, Genealogy, and Clientage

Though the Jewish law of manumission was supposed to sever all ties of dependency between the former slave and the former owner, in practice the erstwhile connection between the two parties remained a part of how freed people were identified and known to others. The behavior of former slave owners, however, shows that they sometimes thought of freed people as their clients in ways that resemble Islamic law. The most common evidence for this is naming practice. In legal documents, freed people required a kind of surname in addition either to the personal name they retained, or to the new one they chose. While manumission freed the person, it did not restore their natal genealogy. There is one deed of manumission, written by the merchant Abraham b. Yijū for the woman Ashū in India, that gives the freedwoman both a new name (Berakha) and a patrilineal genealogy as the daughter of the biblical patriarch Abraham.[44] There is no evidence, however, that this symbolic patronymic was used elsewhere outside of ritual purposes.

Instead, the name of the former owner was sometimes used as a substitute *nasab*. When she married a free man in 986, one bride's wedding contract calls her Mu'tazz (Proud) "the freedwoman (*meshuḥreret*) of Moses b. Palṭi'el."[45] When Munā, whom we encountered earlier in this chapter, was married, she was identified as "Munā, the bride, the freedwoman (*ha-meshuḥreret*) of Ibn Futayḥ."[46] Nearly twenty years later, long after she had made the transition from newly freed person to married woman, she was not identified with her former owner any more, but only by the legal name "Munā the freedwoman and wife of Abū al-Faraj b. al-Tinnīsī the welfare official (*al-parnas*)."[47]

Freedmen, too, used their former owners' names as part of their legal identification, as with "Mukhtār the freedman (*ha-meshuḥrar*) who was the *ghulām* of our lord Evyatar ha-Kohen Gaon"—the latter the head of the Palestinian rabbinic academy after it had been forced to relocate from Jerusalem to Tyre and then to Tripoli in Lebanon.[48] In the second generation, a significant change occurred, and the Jewish children of freed men gained their own natal patronymic. In these cases, the names of their fathers' former owners were dropped, and the fact of their fathers' slave-past was subsequently omitted altogether. Thus, the second wife of Abraham b. Yakhin was called in their prenuptial agreement, "Sitt al-Dalāl the virgin daughter of Joseph the elder (*ha-zaqen*), (may his) e(nd be) g(ood), the freedman (*ha-meshuḥrar*)."[49] When they divorced years later, she was listed simply as "Dalāl the daughter of Joseph."[50]

Formerly enslaved men also adopted the vocabulary of freedom and clientage, but they did so for their own purposes, typically emphasizing that manumission created a new bond of dependency between themselves and their former owner. The freedman (*'atīq*), named Faraj (Relief), had been the *ghulām* of the merchant Barhūn al-Tāhirtī, whose family was involved in pan-Mediterranean commerce and was a politically well-connected one in eleventh-century Ifrīqiyya. Faraj traveled to Egypt to meet with one of the Tāhirtī family's then somewhat estranged business partners, the merchant Joseph b. 'Awkal, a man well known to historians of the *geniza*.[51] A freedwoman, only identified as "the wife of Suqayr," who had also belonged to the same Barhūn, had married and immigrated to Egypt. In the last year or so, she had died, and Faraj knew that she had named him one of her heirs. Was she Faraj's mother, a sibling, or had they bonded through their shared experiences of enslavement? We do not know. No letters had arrived from Egypt to Ifrīqiyya with updated news about the freedwoman's estate. This silence had left Faraj to stew in his own juices of suspicion and to worry about his inheritance. Finally, he realized he needed to act. With a letter from two respected Jewish merchants, Faraj approached the Ibn 'Awkal clan, one of the most well-known Jewish mercantile families in Fustat, to help him secure the bequest. When he arrived in Fustat, the freedman presented the letter, written by the nephews of his former owner (Barhūn), that relates many of the salient details that illuminate his own history.[52]

It appears that Faraj's meeting with Joseph b. 'Awkal was fortuitous for the freedman, though the matter of his inheritance is not mentioned again in surviving correspondence. In a later letter from Faraj himself to Joseph and his sons, he writes to thank Joseph for sending him pearls that had brought him "profit and blessing."[53] He reports that he had sent textiles from the same shipment to Iberia ("al-Andalus"), where he apparently hoped for better market conditions. Above all Faraj wanted the Ibn ʿAwkals to send him more pearls. If you must, he writes, wait until the pilgrims return from Mecca, because they will bring pearls back with them to sell. And if there is money left over after buying pearls, then purchase and send high-quality indigo.[54]

Faraj had mastered the epistolary niceties and vocabulary of patronage that were expected by his Egyptian partners. Faraj was deferential but also ingratiating, as Joseph was the senior partner in their relationship. So he writes, "But you, my master, are alone competent to decide . . . be patient with me for I am a burden on you." In his closing salutation, Faraj closes his letter: "From (your) grateful Faraj, the client (*mawlā*) of Barhūn."[55] While a free merchant would write his full name with his patrilineal genealogy, Faraj substituted an analogous one created by his manumission, "client of Barhūn," in lieu of his own birth father's name, which he had been forced to relinquish through enslavement. He styled himself with one of the most prestigious credentials he had: he was the client of a Jewish patron known to his associates, the head of another mercantile family like the one with whom he was doing business.[56] Faraj reasoned that, in his case, claiming to be the client of Barhūn gave him social capital he could use.

In practice, Jewish writers used the Hebrew *meshuḥrar* (freedman) and *meshuḥreret* (freedwoman) analogously to the Arab-Islamic term *mawlā*. Yet *mawlā* implied something more: an enduring patron-client bond (*walāʾ*) in Islamic law that was meant to provide mutual benefits to both parties. The freed client (*mawlā*) could call on the reputation and assistance of his patron (also called a *mawlā*), and the patron retained inheritance rights to the estate of his freed client. In the Jewish laws of manumission there is no similar provision that grants the manumitter a claim to the property of the manumitted person. Still, patron-client relationships were a part of the ambient culture of slavery in the Islamic Middle East, and both groups, freed people and their former owners, sometimes used the language and Islamic law of *walāʾ* to their advantage.

Freedwomen are never called *mawlā*s in *geniza* documents, as the freedman Faraj called himself. But at least one free Jewish man, the son of a deceased, former slave owner, tried to use the Islamic laws of clientage (*walāʾ*) to his own benefit by pursuing the estate of a freedwoman.[57] These events unfolded in the town of Minyat Ghamr, north of Fustat in the Nile Delta. There a lady died, one identified only as the freedwoman (*ʿatīqa*) of a deceased Jewish elder (*shaykh*). This *ʿatīqa* had formed ties with other women in Minyat Ghamr, and a group of the locals (*ahl al-balad*) had buried her. Furthermore, she had left a bequest of 102 dirhams (worth approximately 2.5 dinars) that she designated for a group of townswomen. These women were about to donate the money to "the needs of the city" when their plan was suddenly interrupted. The son of the freedwoman's former owner, named Abū al-Ṭāhir, learned of this bequest and went to the local Jewish judge to complain. Abū al-Ṭāhir argued to the judge that *he* was the rightful heir to the freedwoman's bequest according to Islamic law. Indeed, Islamic law did permit the male descendant of the former owner to inherit from his father's *mawlā*.[58]

Abū al-Ṭāhir's tactic intimidated the Jewish judge, who was sympathetic to the freedwoman's wishes but was also worried by Abū al-Ṭāhir's intimations that he would take the matter to Islamic authorities. The judge did not want to issue a judgment on his own authority alone, so he wrote to Abraham Maimonides, who was head of the Egyptian Jewish community at this time. In his letter, the judge gave a few reasons in support of Abū al-Ṭāhir's claim to the money: "He has debts to Muslims and his tax farm has collapsed. . . . [He] is beloved by the people . . . and he is able to act regarding what he says (i.e., appealing to Muslim courts)."[59] Abraham Maimonides replied to the local judge with a ruling that thrust the matter back into his hands:

> (Jewish) law provides that (the estate) of a convert who does not have heirs is derelict. Whoever first seizes (the inheritance) becomes its rightful owner. Since the women who (now) have the money do not want it, it is permissible to give it to the aforementioned (Abū al-Ṭāhir) with their permission. The needs of the city have nothing to do with it. Peace.[60]

The likely outcome of this case was that the local Jewish judge favored Abū al-Ṭāhir's claim, whom he called the "lord (*sayyid*)" of the deceased woman. In Jewish law, this statement is erroneous.[61] His word choice was instead a subtle indication that he was persuaded (or perhaps intimidated) by the claim based on the Islamic laws of clientage and inheritance. As in the case of sex slavery, Jews like Abū al-Ṭāhir wanted to enjoy what they saw as the benefits of Islamic slavery law. But they wanted to exercise these rights through Jewish law and institutions when possible.[62]

Integration, "Oblivion," or, How to Assimilate a Multiethnic Diaspora

From the point of view of medieval jurists and many among the slave-owning classes, the integration of Munā, Faraj, and other freed people into the Jewish community in Egypt and beyond was a success story. It was a demonstration of piety to free an enslaved person, to induce them to accept their conversion to

Judaism, and to support their establishment with social and economic capital. Moreover, the successful and public integration of freed converts was a sign to all Jews that Jewish law and leadership provided workable pathways for sanctioning how their congregations used slavery to various social, economic, and reproductive ends. If the law had been followed, and if the freed person had lived according to Jewish laws and customs, there was no dishonor in freed status or in being descended from a freed person.

In practice, however, Egyptian Jews sometimes showed ambivalence toward the presence of freed slaves in their family lineages. A recent discovery by Moshe Yagur illustrates how one Jewish family sought to excise the history of slavery from genealogical memory.[63] Yagur was the first to decipher and publish a tattered bill of manumission for the woman Saʿāda. Saʿāda's owner, the merchant Abū al-Maʿālī al-Levi b. Khalaf al-Dajājī, freed her in Fustat in 1198.[64] What remains of the deed itself conforms to the legal formulas common to this type of document: Saʿāda is declared to be free in perpetuity according to "[the law of M]oses and Isra[el.]" What is unusual about the deed is that a scribe wrote a note on the back of it that attested to Saʿāda's proper actions and behavior as a freed convert to Judaism. She had immersed herself in a ritual bath at the "synagogue of the Iraqis" (one of a few synagogues in medieval Fustat) and had learned from those present about the commandments that were incumbent on her as a Jewish woman.[65] What happened on this autumn day in October was that Saʿāda went through the final rituals of her proper conversion to Judaism.

Yagur recognized that Saʿāda's former owner, Abū al-Maʿālī,[66] is likely the same man mentioned in a separate memorial list of the Khalaf al-Dajājī al-Levi family. This list shows that Abū al-Maʿālī had two wives and that the first of them was a freed slave woman (*shifḥa meshuḥreret*) who bore him a daughter and son. From his second wife, his cousin, he had a son named Abū Saʿīd. What is strange about this list is that only the name of Abū al-Maʿālī's son by his freeborn cousin is identified. The name of his first son, born to a freedwoman, is omitted from the family's genealogy.[67] When the scribe composed this memorial list, he chose to consign the name of the son born to the freedwoman Saʿāda to historical "oblivion."[68] Over time, the willful erasure of slavery's trace from family genealogies worked together with the natal alienation of enslavement and the naming practices for freed slaves to mute the role of slavery and enslaved people in the articulation and reproduction of Jewish culture and community.

Freed people were a type of convert to Judaism. Jewish law and religion rendered them passive in the process, but Jews recognized that the freed person had an active choice to make after this conversion. They could remain in the Jewish community, or they could leave. This chapter has told the histories of the freed people who chose to remain. Their stories illustrate how freed status was not simply the opposite, or negation, of slave status. Rather, freed people's life chances were shaped both by the circumstances of their manumission (namely the socioeconomic status of their former owners) and by their use of the rights, protections, and strategies employed by free people. Freedwomen like Munā and Mubāraka acquired dowries and entered marriage agreements with, respectively, wealthy and relatively poor Jewish men. Their different paths were largely determined by the wealth and choices of the person who had freed them. Though Jewish law did not recognize anything like patronage (*walāʾ*) in Islamic law, former owners like Abū al-Ṭāhir and freed people like Faraj sometimes acted according to its scripts.

No matter their previous religion or ethnicity, freed people became the Jewish mothers and fathers of Jewish children. For medieval Jews, this was a positive outcome, even if it took ongoing work and supervision to ensure that Jewish slave owners followed the laws of slavery. In the second generation, the children of freed people might still be known as the daughter or son of a freedman, but by the third generation the traces of slavery had been "disappeared" from their names and genealogies. Over the course of generations and centuries, two processes continued alongside each other. In one process, Egyptian slave owners continually purchased enslaved people newly imported from beyond Egypt's borders and those who were born locally with slave status. In the second, the laws and practices of Egyptian slave owners effectively muted the centrality of slavery, and its violence, in their society's biological and cultural reproduction.

Conclusion

DURING THE FESTIVAL of Passover, Jewish slave owners in Cairo annually retold the story of the biblical Israelites' enslavement in Egypt. In his guidance for how fathers should teach their children about this holiday's meaning, Moses Maimonides explains:

> It is a commandment to inform one's sons even though they do not ask. As it is said, "You shall tell your son . . ." (Exodus 13:8). A father should teach his son according to the son's knowledge. How is this applied? If the son is young or foolish, he should tell him: "My son, in Egypt, we were all slaves *like this female slave or this male slave.* On this night, the Holy One, blessed be He, redeemed us and took us out to freedom."[1]

Given what we know about the history of slavery in Egypt during Maimonides's lifetime, his instructions suggest the likelihood that enslaved Nubians stood by during the festive meal ready to serve cups of wine along with the ritual foods that commemorated the Israelites' exodus from Egypt. For modern readers, this scene turns the story of Passover on its head with its seemingly casual and unironic involvement of enslaved servants at a celebration of liberation from bondage. In the Middle Ages, however, this scenario did not present a paradox. Slavery was a universal danger, and most peoples were both among the enslaved and the slave-owning classes somewhere in the world.[2] In the face of this persistent threat, it was indeed a miraculous relief to be slave owners and not slaves themselves.

Though Maimonides could not have known it, the Jewish community where he lived and worked would be among the generations of Egyptian Jews whose discarded writings today comprise arguably the densest cache of documentary records for the social and cultural history of slavery in the medieval Islamic Middle East. This accidental archive is now called the Cairo *geniza*, and in this book I have used it to illustrate how the slave trade operated, how slavery shaped daily life and culture, how people experienced enslavement, and, sometimes, how they entered the Jewish community through manumission.

My analysis moves from a macro-level examination of legal systems and transregional trade, then homes in on urban households and, finally, narrows to the micro-level of enslaved and freed people's biographies. The shifting scale makes clear how slavery and the slave trade were embedded across the domains of medieval society, from geopolitics to the most intimate moments of life. Other legacies of slavery and medieval Jewish history emerge only when we move across these scales and consider how the parts fit together as a whole.

Slavery Law and the Slave Trade

As we have seen in chapter 1, the interplay between Islamic and Jewish slavery laws shaped, in tandem, the practice of slavery among Egyptian Jews. Jewish slave-owning underscores a trade-off inherent in the *dhimmī* status of Jews and Christians in Islamic lands. As *dhimmī*s, Jews were protected from enslavement *and* empowered to use enslaved non-Muslims as they wished. They could also patronize Muslim courts and other venues to defend their rights as slave owners. The only significant limitation on Jewish slave-owners was that Jews could not own enslaved Muslims because such dominance turned the societal hierarchy upside down. Within these broad contours, Jews were allowed to conduct their affairs as slave owners in their own courts. Most of the time, Muslim rulers did not notice, or perhaps did not care, about the enslaved people who became converted Jews through purchase and manumission.

Sex slavery was a crucial way that Islamic and Jewish slavery law differed. In Islamic law, it was lawful for a man to use an enslaved woman for sex, and any children were born as free Muslims. The enslaved mother also gained the protection of the law of the *umm walad* that held she could not be sold by her owner after their child's birth and that she became free upon her owner's death.[3] In contrast, Jewish jurists like Moses Maimonides ruled that it was not permissible for a Jewish man to have sex with an enslaved woman. If he did, he was supposed to sell her and "distance himself from her immediately." Moreover, following laws of Canaanite slavery, any children born to him by his enslaved concubine were considered non-Jewish slaves. Accordingly, both the mother and child could be sold to the ends of the earth.

Though these Jewish legal principles were ostensibly straightforward, their implementation was anything but simple. First, as *dhimmī*s, Jewish leaders did not have at their disposal certain coercive tools, like armed police and prisons, that they might have used to enforce their rulings. Second, as Eve Krakowski observes in the context of rabbinic maturity laws for adolescent girls, Jewish law did not invariably determine what Jews did in all aspects of family law. Jews structured parts of communal life "according to social mores closer to those recognized by their Muslim (and Christian) contemporaries,"[4] and they wanted to participate more broadly in "ordinary" Egyptian culture.[5] Still, they preferred to do that through Jewish courts and institutions and by using "the technical elements of rabbinic law."[6]

Yet a subset of men continued to use women as sex slaves, despite its prohibition in Jewish law. Jews and their local leaders knew that precedents for sexual slavery existed in Jewish law and tradition, and they asked jurists why these principles were no longer applicable in their time and place. For his part, Maimonides used one responsum to encourage leaders to find accommodations that steered these men toward marrying their concubines despite the letter of Jewish law. Other jurists before and after him were unyielding. And in many cases, Jewish men's use of concubines led to acrimony, divorce, family abandonment, and deep communal consternation. In terms of the legal context for understanding the social history of slavery among Egyptian Jews as I have laid out here, *dhimmī* status, the interplay of legal systems, and the ambiguity of the Jewish laws of sex slavery loom large.

As with slavery law, part 1 also illustrated why the slave trade needs to be historicized with greater attention to its historical variability. Chapter 2 shows that the transregional slave trade to Egypt (1000–1250) operated in distinct modes—diplomatic, state-sponsored, and mercantile. I parsed the slave trade into different modes to show that it was historically dynamic over time and to underscore that there is little evidence for largescale (wholesale) trading by merchants. State embassies, especially in the first half of the eleventh century, often brought lavish gifts of slaves to facilitate the establishment, renewal, or continuance of diplomacy. While some of these slaves might reach the larger local market for resale, the ruling dynasty and their bureaucracy had the reputation for retaining vast numbers of them. More importantly, this kind of slave trading should not be assumed to be a perennial, or even a regular, source of enslaved people for any market. Even durable diplomatic agreements, like the so-called *baqṭ* between Islamic Egypt and Christian Nubia, fell into periods of desuetude. Nubia and other polities sent gifts of slaves to the Fatimids through their own volition, not because they were coerced by the caliphate.[7]

Another mode of the interregional slave trade was the state-sponsored trade for enslaved soldiers. Narrative sources, to the extent that their precise numbers can be believed, give the impression that such trafficking could involve large numbers of people when it was a state priority. Crucially, sovereigns leant their authority and resources to both diplomatic and state-sponsored slave trading. In an era before there was insurance for slave traders, the loss of significant numbers of enslaved people would have been ruinous for most merchants without state backing.

There is scant evidence in our period for the existence of a wholesale slave trade organized by regular merchants that moved large numbers of people together by ships or overland caravans.[8] Instead, the documentary sources show that individual merchants trafficked small numbers of enslaved people, usually just one person, as a part of their larger businesses in a mix of other commodities. The overall flow of enslaved people to medieval Egypt moved through a diffused capillary network. Those capillary networks could converge at waypoints, such as on the Red Sea island of Dahlak Kabīr, at the Egyptian-Nubian border, or in Egyptian towns and cities like al-Bahnasā, Cairo, and Alexandria. But they flowed in and out of these nodes in a decentralized manner. The absence of evidence does not mean there was never a ship or caravan dedicated to enslaved people, but this was not the primary way that most enslaved people were trafficked to Egypt in the period between 1000–1250.

My study of the decentralized mercantile slave trade led me to critique how some long-cited evidence for the transregional slave trade in the Middle Ages has been interpreted. Specifically, medieval reports about the ninth-century Rādhānite merchants have been used to posit a vast interregional slave trade. I do not doubt that the Rādhānites traded in slaves or that there was some kind of transregional slave trade in the ninth century. Were the Rādhānites agents of a slave trade that routinely trafficked large groups of people across Afro-Eurasia? Or did they transport and trade small numbers of enslaved people alongside their mixed cargo of furs, swords, and other goods? This is an ambiguity that I cannot resolve, but I do not think its implications should be ignored. The answers have bearing on the assumptions that guide how historians interpret other evidence and use it to reconstruct the slave trade.

Despite the clear impact of the transregional slave trade on the demographics of Egypt's enslaved population, chapter 3 shows that the most documented slave trade was the local resale market. Most slave owners purchased enslaved people locally and from someone they knew or found through their own personal networks. Informal intermediaries like relatives and business associates made these connections in addition to designated brokers and local slave dealers (*al-nakhkhāsūn*).

Sales were not the only way that enslaved people changed hands. Owners commonly bequeathed slaves to their heirs and included them as part of their daughters' dowries. Although gifts, bequests, and dowries have not always been studied as a part of the slave trade in the medieval Middle East, they reveal how slave owning was a form of intergenerational wealth for the slave-owning classes. From the point of view of an enslaved person, sales, gifts, dowries, and bequests could all lead to the repeated dislocations that they experienced throughout their lives in bondage.

As a corpus, the *geniza* documents also reflect the demographic makeup of Egypt's enslaved population. It comprised mostly girls and women who were Nubians and *muwallad*s, though Indians, other Africans (Abyssinian, Beja, Zanj, and Maghribī), and people from Byzantium were also a significant presence. These writings illustrate that, though the slave trade was near hemispheric in its reach, enslavers most intensively exploited northeast Africa, and Nubia in particular, for exports to Egypt.

The preponderance of Nubian and other peoples from what medieval Arab authors called the "lands of the Blacks (*bilād al-sūdān*)" shaped the language that slave owners used to describe enslaved people. While "Black" was not recognized as one of the official "types" (*ajnās*, sg. *jins*) of lawfully enslaved people that were written in bills of sale, Black was used as a shorthand for slave in letters and in scribes' personal notebooks, where writers also conflated Black and Nubian. Even though slavery was not racialized in medieval law, and despite the varied makeup of the enslaved population at large, the slave-owning classes in Egypt linked Blackness and slavery, and they used racist stereotypes shaped by the theory of climes to justify the enslavement of the Black peoples who lived in northeastern Africa especially.[9]

While the conflation of Black and slave may seem to fit into the long arc of slavery's global history, this development was a historical contingency and not an end point. Later, during the fifteenth century in Mecca, for example, the shorthand for slave woman was Abyssinian.[10] The language that writers used to describe enslaved people provides snapshots of how slavery's social history and medieval ideas of race were mutually reinforcing, but in a historically variable way. My thinking on these subjects follows recent scholarship on medieval race by Geraldine Heng and Rachel Schine, which focuses on processes of racialization as opposed to the idea that race has a fixed, substantive content.[11] They emphasize the strategic work that people make race do in specific times and places. This way of understanding race is relevant to scholars working on *geniza* documents and other corpora of contemporaneous Arabic documents. What might the language used in everyday writings tell us about the contingent histories of racial thought and its uses?

Slavery for Personal Service and Urban Society

Part 2 of the book narrows to focus on the households and neighborhoods of Cairo, which were primary sites of slavery *lil-khidma*, or slavery for personal service, as *geniza* sources denote what is traditionally called domestic slavery. I adopt the language of slavery *lil-khidma* in lieu of domestic slavery to emphasize an essential point: enslaved people moved between domestic and public spaces. Their mobility made them valuable to their owners and opened up a wider world of action and interconnection for them as well.

In searching for ways to historicize slavery *lil-khidma* in medieval Cairo more finely, I turned to the professions and gender of slave owners as indicators of otherwise hidden labor patterns (appendix 3). All free people in slave-owning households benefited from the work done by their slaves, though not all in the same ways. The ratio of slave-owning men to slave-owning women was roughly three to one. Male slave owners clustered in particular professions, namely apothecaries, doctors, officials, and merchants. Professional data also provides more context for the practice of sex slavery among Jewish men in Egypt. Merchants, especially traveling ones, were far and away the largest group among the slave-owning classes. Many of these men owned *ghulāms*, enslaved male factotums who traveled and conducted trade. The merchants were also the class of men most likely to buy and sell female slaves expressly for sex, though all enslaved people were vulnerable to sexual exploitation.

Another site of enslaved labor was in the apothecary. Work there entailed many of the same tasks as food preparation, so it was not a stretch for a slave-owning pharmacist to compel his *jāriya* to work at home and in his shop. Scribes and other officials likewise wanted enslaved workers who could read and write to aid in their daily tasks in addition to household labor. Though we know that enslaved people did these kinds of work from other historical contexts, chapter 4 demonstrates that slave labor was more varied and widespread in medieval Egypt than has been recognized. This world of work matters not only because it points to the larger economic and social location of slavery in this society. The details of work are also crucial to understanding the daily life of enslaved and freed people. Labor was part of how they experienced life. My hope is that the methods and sources that the chapter uses to illuminate this hidden history spur further research that will expand our understanding of the skilled and knowledgeable people who were subjugated in slavery.

Scholars of medieval slavery have long recognized that the gender of enslaved people affected their experiences of slavery. Part 2 emphasizes that slave owning also shaped gender roles and ideals in Jewish culture. Chapter 5 focuses on male slave-owning and particularly on the implications of sex slavery. Controversies among Jews about whether sex slavery was permissible, and how to mitigate its negative impacts, were factors in the construction and performance of different masculine ideals. Some men, like the merchant Ibn Jamāhir and the silk weaver Abū al-Faraj, were callous and brash in their use of enslaved women for sex and antagonistic toward Jews, leaders and laypeople alike, who rebuked their behavior. These men's acts of dominance over enslaved women were, as Ruth Karras and Miriam Frenkel argue, also linked to men's dominance over all free women and other men more generally.[12] The men who opposed Ibn Jamāhir and Abū al-Faraj performed a masculinity that resembles what Oded Zinger calls "the masculinity of belonging" in which "[b]eing a man meant belonging to a variety of social networks and fulfilling the obligations that such belonging entailed."[13] In the context of slavery, this meant standing up to domineering slave owners whose sexual exploitation of enslaved women undermined the economic security and social status of Jewish women and children. Men could also perform this masculine ideal by manumitting and providing for freed people, and by advocating for them in their search for Jewish spouses. Slave owning illustrates the existence of multiple masculine ideals that were defined in relationship to one another.[14]

Moreover, the same man could perform according to both scripts, depending on the context. Ibn Jamāhir, who "banished" his *jāriya* and their son to the Horn of Africa, also provided for orphaned children back in his Egyptian home, an act of charity that Jews understood as analogous to caring for enslaved servants. Egyptian Jews also had a notion of social class that gave the benefit of the doubt to men who were thought to be generally circumspect in Jewish law, and they contrasted such exemplars with "the commoners" who were "not concerned with religion." Thus, some slave-owning men were likely to find their behavior scrutinized more than others. It bears emphasis that the durability of slavery over the long durée was buoyed by masculine ideals, as well as stories of "good" and "bad" slave owners. These ideals and categories led away from a broad structural critique of slavery as a widespread practice because they shifted the blame for its evils on to the shoulders of the men who corrupted the institution through their caprice and impiety.

Masculine competition also shaped the relationship between Egyptian Jews and Muslim authorities. As *dhimmīs*, Jewish men's masculinity was constrained by their legal subordination to Muslims. Relatedly, the authority of Muslim leaders was reinforced, as Zinger argues, not only by their dominance over all men but also through their own role as protectors of "the weak," including Jewish women.[15] This dynamic is evident in the case of a Jewish woman who used Muslim courts to defend her rights as a slave owner when she felt she had been defrauded by a seller.

Chapter 6 studies the slave-owning women who belonged to a class that *geniza* writers called "the elite of the city." Since Jewish women were subordinated as both Jews and on account of their gender, their slave owning represented an uncommon domain in which they theoretically had the most power. Slave owning relieved free women of the unpaid household work that was expected of women. It enhanced their feminine status, as slave owning allowed them to avoid public appearances that could be construed as dishonorable for women. Free women also relied on their enslaved maids to provide affective labor through caregiving, both for themselves and their own children. Free women's relationship to slavery was also particularly fraught since a husband's slave owning could be both a boon and a threat to his wife's interests. When their husbands took enslaved concubines, they sometimes redirected economic resources to these slave women. This behavior was both economically threatening and potentially humiliating.

Like their male counterparts, slave-owning women performed according to multiple scripts of dominance and magnanimity depending on how their circumstances and outlooks fluctuated over time. They could beat enslaved people with relative impunity, and, as they approached the end of their lives, they could choose either to free someone or to bind them more tightly to their heirs in servitude. Slave-owning women might also perform according to feminine ideals of piety and charity, like caring for orphaned and freed girls.

The Lives of Enslaved and Freed People

The final part of the book presses against the limits of what the *geniza* can tell us about the lives of individual slaves, who often seem to be like a needle in a haystack. The overwhelming majority of people documented in the *geniza* appear only once, and in the span of a few words. Chapter 7 suggests methods for assembling dossiers from disparate *geniza* records for women like Wafāʾ and Naʿīm, who I suggest are the same individuals—even if naming patterns for slaves mean that there will almost always be some doubt. It is possible that future historical research using social network analysis may put such informed conjecture on firmer ground.[16]

While recognizing such persistent challenges, part 3 constructs a collective biography of more than two hundred individuals from their births with slave status, or enslavement as young children, into their adolescent and adult lives (appendixes 1 and 2). The most important age thresholds in the life cycle of enslaved people were around two years old, when they could be weaned from their mothers; six years old, when they were deemed useful for service; and then their age of sexual maturity (*bulūgh*), at which point they became adults whose ages were no longer reported. This long, undifferentiated phase of life continues until manumission or death while still enslaved.

Part 3 recasts topics and themes from earlier chapters from the points of view of enslaved people. One such case is the trafficking of a young Indian child from western India to Cairo. In the span of four partly effaced words in a single merchant letter, she flickers in and out of view. Chapter 7 narrates the stories of girls like her by assembling and analyzing a range of evidence including a medieval Sanskrit epistolary manual, Arabic travelogues and popular literature, and other merchant letters from the Egyptian ports of call through which she would have passed en route to Cairo. The interplay of Islamic and Jewish slavery laws also returns as a salient force. Enslaved women knew, or quickly learned, how their Jewish slave owners were constrained by Islamic slavery law. When they appeared before Muslim judges, slave women belonging to Jews made choices that sometimes forced their sales and, in other instances, shielded their owners from legal jeopardy. We cannot know these women's precise motivations, but their choices show how enslaved people shaped their own futures in specific moments.

Chapter 7 revisits the theme of mobility, but this time to focus on its implications for the lives of slaves. I read characteristically terse references in *geniza* letters about enslaved people's disappearances alongside Kristina Richardson's recent history of the Roma people in Cairo's "underworld" to argue for the existence of a kind of urban marronage through which those runaways found temporary refuge.[17] Mobility also led to interactions through which slaves in Jewish households formed attachments to other enslaved people, some of whom sought to marry each other.

For every four enslaved people documented in the *geniza*, there is one freed person mentioned.[18] Chapter 8 is the collective biography of the freed people who chose to stay in the Jewish community after their manumission. As Moshe Yagur has shown in his recent work on the history of religious conversion to Judaism, enslaved and freed people were a specific kind of convert.[19] As Jews, freed people largely made their way in life as their freeborn counterparts did. It mattered immensely whether freedwomen were manumitted with gifts of economic capital. Cash, textiles, and real estate allowed some freedwomen to obtain more valuable dowries that in turn helped them make more favorable marriage agreements with Jewish men.[20] They could also use this capital to form business partnerships, make loans, and so forth.

Freed people of all genders benefited from ongoing associations with men who were socially well positioned and willing to serve as their advocates. In the case of the freedman Faraj, his prospects were shaped by the skills and relationships he had acquired as the *ghulām* of a merchant family in Ifrīqiyya. As he turned his sights on economic opportunities in Egypt and the pearl trade from Arabia, he found it advantageous to assert his status as the client (*mawlā*) of his former owner in order to insert himself into profitable relationships with other freeborn Jewish merchants.[21]

Even though manumission was most consequential for the former slave, it served the interests of the broader Egyptian Jewish community. First, in the relationships between former owners and freed people, we again see how free Jews wanted to enjoy the benefits of the larger Egyptian culture, but in a Jewish idiom. Thus, even though Jewish law envisioned a complete break between manumitted slaves and their former enslavers, those owners sometimes wanted to maintain such ties for their own benefits, similarly to the Islamic laws of clientage (*walāʾ*). Second, naming practices and the laws of slavery worked over two to three generations to obscure, and even actively erase, the presence of enslaved people in family genealogies. From the perspective of the community, this assimilation and erasure were success stories as it suggested to the slave-owning classes that Jewish law provided a workable pathway for mitigating slavery's harms and for growing the ranks of the Jewish community. In historical perspective, the same process helps explain why those harms have often been ignored.

Slavery, Jewish History, and a Medieval Nubian Diaspora

This book is also a slow-moving history of a largely African diaspora, predominately Nubian, that was partly assimilated into the heart of one of the most vibrant Jewish communities of the Middle Ages. This history emerges through thinking across the different scales of the book. It also prompted me to consider some unexplored connections at the intersections of Jewish history and *geniza* studies with the other fields such as Nubian studies and, more broadly, African history.

The violence of slavery also inheres in how it is remembered. Memories of enslavement remain a part of modern Nubian identity formations, the pathos of which are heightened by the modern dispossession and marginalization of Nubians in modern Egypt, especially after the completion of the Aswan High Dam marked the flooding of the Nubian heartland.[22] In his novel *Dongola*, Idrīs ʿAlī (d. 2010) narrates the modern-day alienation of the Nubian Egyptian protagonist ʿAwaḍ Shalālī, whose recollections juxtapose the glory of Nubia's medieval past and the "disgrace (*waṣma*)" of Nubians' enslavement to Egyptians from the Middle Ages down to the modern era.[23] Early in the novel, ʿAwaḍ sets out to discover what became of his cousin, who had been arrested, and later killed, due to his revolutionary ideals—namely that Nubia should secede from Egypt. When ʿAwaḍ encounters the Egyptian police, they deride him on account of his Blackness and taunt him as "the son of a slave."[24] On his train journey from Cairo to his Nubian homeland near Aswan, ʿAwaḍ ruminates on history:

> The country road intermittently ran parallel to the tracks. This was the road used for invasions when they headed south in search of ostrich feathers, musk, crocodile skins, livestock, and the gold they snatched from the arms and necks of women. But the true and real aim of the campaigns was always to take prisoners. They exported them for sale and as gifts to the vast Islamic state because they loved the strong slaves (*raqīq*) of Nubia. Perhaps they used them to build citadels and fortresses and sent them to their deaths in hopeless wars.[25]

In ʿAwaḍ's narration, slavery remains a durable and painful symbol of Nubia's long and ongoing subjugation to "the north," to Egypt. Though it has been hiding in plain sight for decades, this connection between the records preserved in a medieval synagogue and the historical memory of the Nubian people in contemporary Egypt and Sudan lingers in my mind as an unfinished story.

When I began research for this book, I sought to put the lives of enslaved people at its center. As my work progressed, I realized that I could not avoid also writing the history of the slave-owning classes, who were themselves central to the Jewish community at large. What, then, are the significances of Jewish slave-owning in the medieval Middle East? I offer three conclusions. First, slave owning was a durable form of Jewish power that Islamic law empowered Jews to wield over others. This power was, of course, relative. Jews did not dominate the slave trade by any stretch of the imagination. Nor is there any evidence that they owned people in greater proportions than their Muslim and Christian counterparts.[26] Jews were, one might say, ordinary slave owners in the context of medieval Egypt.[27] They exploited enslaved people and occasionally freed them just as

Egyptian Muslims and Christians did. Sex slavery caused a different set of problems for the Jewish community than it did for Muslims, but it was still a part of a common culture.

Second, slave owning illustrates how Jewish power and privilege were not simply the opposite of Jewish subordination. Rather, these two phenomena were intentionally linked. By allowing *dhimmī* subjects to dominate non-Muslim slaves, *and* by curtailing their power in certain conditions, Muslim authorities established and reinforced the larger political and social order. I leave it to other scholars to determine whether similar patterns pertained to relationships between Jews and the state in Iberia, across Europe, and in other Islamic lands.

Third, slave owning shaped the formation of medieval Jewish culture. In her study of medieval Islamic slavery law and marriage, the scholar Kecia Ali argues that slaves are omnipresent in medieval texts not only because they were ubiquitous in society, but also because they were "useful to think with" and "central to jurists' conceptual world."[28] Scholars of late Second Temple and rabbinic Judaism have recognized this, too.[29] The *geniza* and contemporaneous sources studied in this book illustrate further how medieval Jewish culture and law were articulated, not only in light of slave labor and the status threat of enslaved women to free women and families, but also through the writings and actions of the slave-owning classes. Though enslaved people were a minority of society, in the Jewish community they were frequently found among the families of the head of the Jewish community, the leaders of the rabbinic academies, and the circle of Moses Maimonides.[30] As the historian Lev Weitz argues, these phenomena have parallels in the Syriac Christian communities of the medieval Middle East.[31] There is more to uncover about these societies as a whole by considering the slave-owning histories of Jewish, Syriac Christian, and Coptic Christian populations alongside each other.[32]

It also mattered in medieval Jewish law that most of the enslaved people in medieval Egypt were mostly black- or dark-skinned, and Nubian more specifically. As the scholar David Goldenberg shows, Maimonides tacitly acknowledged the presence of Kushites and their marriages into the Jewish community when he explicitly identified them as exempt from a list of foreign nations prohibited from marrying Jews.[33] Maimonides's inclusion of Black Kushites in the *Mishneh Torah* departed from earlier rabbinic precedents where they are not named. Jewish writers of the era understood "Kush" to be a land that comprised medieval Nubia and Abyssinia, and *geniza* scribes also used "Kushite" as an official type of enslaved woman.[34] By creating a new accommodation for Kushites in Jewish marriage law, Maimonides's accommodation signals the agency and legacy of the enslaved Nubians, Abyssinians, and Beja who were forcibly integrated into the Egyptian community, who sometimes married into it, and who became the mothers of Jewish children.

In Jewish historiography, there is a standard vocabulary for acknowledging the presence of Jews who are Ashkenazi (from Central Europe), Sephardic (from Iberia), Mizrahi ("Easterners," including those from modern Islamic lands), and so on. Yet there is no vocabulary that accounts for the presence of the specifically Nubian, *muwallad*, and many other people whose fragmented histories have been told here and who were a part of Jewish history in one of its preeminent settings. Yet to reckon with the centrality of slavery in the elaboration of medieval Jewish culture, and with the very identity formation of Jews within their communities and imperial contexts, requires that we acknowledge and incorporate their coerced presence. There is no comprehensive accounting of medieval Jewish history without them.

APPENDIXES

Preface

None of these three appendixes is definitively comprehensive of the documentary *geniza* for their subjects, as researchers continue to make new discoveries in the geniza. Each appendix does approach exhaustion for the sources (between the tenth and mid-thirteenth centuries) known to me before the summer of 2024. Appendixes 1 and 2 include enslaved and freed individuals from the published responsa of Moses and Abraham Maimonides who are discussed in the book, but I did not use those works for the slave owners in appendix 3.

These appendixes are the basis for figures that I cite in the book, such as the proportion of enslaved women to men and the rate of manumission.[1] I emphasize, however, that these appendixes are not meant to be a precise census. There is often ambiguity about whether a slave name that appears across numerous documents refers to the same person or multiple, different individuals (e. g., Ghazāl, Ḥidhq, Naʿīm). I also note when the legal status of a specific person is ambiguous—they could be enslaved, freed, or free. The purpose of the appendixes is to make the research that undergirds this book more widely accessible.

People with known names are mentioned in alphabetical order. Names that begin with an *ʿayin* are ordered according to their second letter. When an enslaved or freed person's name is in quotation marks (e.g., "Bint Yahūdiyya"), it indicates that I have adopted this as a nickname for them in the book when their actual name is unknown or illegible in the sources. Anonymous people are mentioned at the end of the appendix and at the end of each subsection in appendix 3. Entries marked with a caret (^) indicate that the precise legal status of the person is ambiguous (e.g., enslaved, freed, or free). Entries marked with an asterisk (*) indicate that the person is also documented as a freed person and appears in appendix 2. Though all the freed people mentioned in appendix 2 were previously enslaved, they are only listed in appendix 1 if they are mentioned as a slave in a historical source. *Geniza* documents in round parentheses may contain references related to the same individual.[2] All dates, when known, are CE.

Appendix 1: A Snapshot of Enslaved Individuals Documented in the *Geniza* Corpus (994–1260) and the Responsa of Moses and Abraham Maimonides

The final two entries in appendix 1 (nos. 172–73) come from a reference to two groups of seventy enslaved people who were part of a diplomatic gift discussed in chapter 2. This source does refer to an actual shipment of a group of enslaved people, but I am skeptical that the given figures are accurate. I have excluded these groups from the overall totals that I mention in the book.

1) ʿAbīr (Perfume) 1. A singing slave-girl (*jāriya mughanniya*). 1156. RNL Yevr.-Arab I 1700.15v.
2) ʿAbīr 2. A Persian (*ʿAjamiyya*)[3] *jāriya*. Ca. 1150–81. T-S 8J8.4.
3) Abnūsa (Ebony). A Nubian *jāriya*. 1230. Mosseri VII 58.1, (T-S 8J8.16, T-S NS J449).
4) Abū al-Faraj. A *ghulām*. ENA 3153.6v.
5) Abū al-Munā. A *ghulām*. 12th c. MS Heb. b 13/50.
6) ʿAfāf (Chastity). A *waṣīfa*. ENA NS 48.6.
7) ʿAlam (Banner) 1. A [N]ubian woman. Ca. 1100–38. Mosseri VII, 69.2.
8) ʿAlam 2. A *waṣīfa muwallada*. T-S 10J11.31.
9) ʿAlam 3. A *jāriya*. 1133. T-S 13J2.20.
10) ʿAlam 4. A Nubian *jāriya*. 1137. T-S 20.41, (T-S NS 342.121).
11) ʿAlam 5. A "black" Nubian woman. Ca. 1100–38. T-S NS 342.121, (T-S 20.41).
12) ʿAnbar (Ambergris). A Nubian *mamlūk*. 1245. Or. 5566B.15.
13) Ashū/Berakha (Sanskrit, Quick).*^ A *shifḥa* and Tuluva woman.[4] 1132. D 55.10.
14) B-M-[.]. A *Rūmī mamlūk*. T-S AS 147.8.
15) Bakhtiyār. A *ghulām* mentioned in a letter written in Aden. 1139. T-S 24.64.
16) Balagh (Balūgh) al-Munā (Attainment of Desire). A *jāriya*. T-S NS J409.
17) Bidʿa/Ghazāl 5 (Innovation/Gazelle). A woman known by two different names was sold. 1149–50. T-S NS 311.23v.
18) "Bint Yahūdiyya" (Daughter of a Jewish Woman). Moses Maimonides, *Responsa*, no. 211.

19) Bomma (Bama). An Indian *ghulām*. 1130s–1146. T-S 6J4.14 + T-S 18J2.7 (T-S 12.416 is a partial copy of this letter), T-S 20.137, T-S NS J240 + T-S 20.137 (T-S NS J241 and T-S NS J1 are copies), ENA 3616.19 + Or. 1081 J3, T-S 24.64, T-S 18J4.18 (partial copy in T-S NS J21 + T-S 8.19), NLI 577.3/6, and Halper 472.
20) Dalāl (Flirtatious, Coquettishness, possibly Ḥalal, "Praise"). A *jāriya*. 1128–53. T-S J1.29.
21) Dhahab 1 (Gold).* A "virgin" *jāriya*. Ca. 1140–59. T-S 13J22.2, (T-S 12.140, 1135), (T-S AS 157.314, no date).
22) Dhahab 2. A *mamlūka* and *muwallada*. Married to the *mamlūk* and *muwallad* Muwaffaq. T-S NS 157.58.
23) Ḍiyā' (Light). A *jāriya* and *muwallada*. 1226. T-S 6J1.7 + T-S 13J4.2, Or. 1080 J273.
24) Durrī (Radiant). A *ghulām*. Late 12th c. T-S K6.177, (T-S K6.149).
25) Faraj (Relief).* A *ghulām*. Ca. 1020. T-S 12.175, T-S 8.12.
26) Fayrūz (Turquoise) 1. The *mamlūk* of a merchant in Yemen. 1150. ENA 1822a.75.
27) Fayrūz 2. A *waṣīf* and *muwallad*. 1175. MS Heb. b 13/39.
28) Fūq (Loving Communion).[5] A *jāriya*. 1143. T-S 13J3.3.
29) Fūq's daughter. 1143. T-S 13J3.3.
30) Gharaḍ (Wish).* A *jāriya* and freedwoman. Ca. 1160. T-S Misc. 24.137.4.
31) Ghazāl 1 (Gazelle). Called both a *jāriya* and a *shifḥa*. 1134. Or. 5566C16, (ENA 4011.62), (T-S NS 311.23v).
32) Ghazāl 2. An Indian *jāriya*. 1155. ENA 4011.62, (Or. 5566C.16), (T-S NS 311.23v).
33) Ghazāl 3. A woman sold during the tenure of the *nagid* Samuel b. Ḥananya. Ca. 1140–59. T-S NS 311.23v,[6] (Or. 5566C.16), (ENA 4011.62). See also Bid'a/Ghazāl.
34) Ghazāl 4. An *'Ajamiyya* woman named in a note that seems to be related to a slave sale. T-S NS 342.141.
35) Ghazāl 5. Greetings are sent to a so-named woman or girl in a letter. Possibly mid-12th c. JRL A 284.
36) [Ḥ]-L-L. A *jāriya* purchased by a brother for his sister. ENA 4100.18.
37) Ḥidhq (Dexterity) 1. A Nubian *jāriya* and mother of a daughter. 1094. T-S 20.93b, (T-S 16.188).
38) Ḥidhq 1's daughter. A Nubian or *muwallada*? 1094. T-S 20.93b.
39) Ḥidhq 2. A Nubian *jāriya* (also called an *amta*). 1105. T-S 16.188, (T-S 20.93b).

40) Ḥidhq 3. A "westerner" (*maghribiyya*), possibly indicating Libyan (or the Fezzān more specifically). 1104. T-S 8J5.5 (2v).
41) Iftikhār (Pride). A *jāriya*. 1126–27. T-S Misc. 23.8.
42) Ikhtiṣār (Brevity). An enslaved woman described as "black" and sexually mature. 1100–38. T-S NS 184.31, (T-S NS 224.53).
43) Intijāb (Selection). A *jāriya* described as "black." 12th c. T-S NS 320.126.
44) ʿIzz (Honor). A *jāriya*. 1128–53. T-S J1.29.
45) J-Ḥ-W[.].[7] An enslaved girl or woman who was sold. Ca. 1100–38. T-S 16.225.
46) Jinān (Paradise). A *muwallada* and mother of Wafāʾ (see below). 1142. F 1908.44SS.
47) Jawhar. A *ghulām*. 1139. Aden. T-S 24.64.
48) Kashf (Discovery).* A "young" *jāriya*. Ca. 1160. T-S Misc. 24.137.4.
49) Kitmān (Secrecy). A *jāriya muwallada*. 1091. ENA 4020.47v.
50) Milḥ (Salt) 1. A Nubian jāriya. 1084. T-S 18J1.12, (ENA 4011.48).
51) Milḥ 2. A Nubian jāriya. 1100–01. ENA 4011.48, (T-S 18J1.12).
52) Misk (Musk) 1. A *jāriya*. 1164–65. T-S 13J37.12r, T-S 13J37.12v.
53) Misk 2. A "black" *jāriya*. T-S NS J32.
54) Mubārak (Blessed) 1.*^ Probably a *ghulām* or freedman. 1104. ENA 2727.28.
55) Mubārak 2. A ten-year-old boy and son of Ṭāwūs (see below). 1241. T-S 16.20.
56) Muhja (Life Blood or Heart). A Beja (*Bāziyya*) *jāriya*. Ca. 1216. ENA 2559.6, RNL Yevr. 669.3.
57) Munā (Wish).*^ A *jāriya*. 1230. T-S Misc. 25.107. (Munā 1 in appendix 2.)
58) Muqbil (Fortunate). A prepubescent (*dūn al-bulūgh*) Abyssinian *ghulām*. 1152. T-S 13J8.3.
59) Muwaffaq (God Made You Successful, Lucky). Ẓarf's son. Mid-11th c. T-S 16.15.
60) Nadd (Incense). A *jāriya*. 1156. RNL Yevr.-Arab I 1700.15v, RNL Yevr.-Arab I 1700.22v, (T-S 13J33.10).[8]
61) Naʿīm (Bliss). A Nubian *jāriya*. (1098), 1108, 1115. (T-S 12.93), T-S 18J1.17r + v, (Halper 342), (T-S K15.39; T-S K15.50); (T-S NS 324.132d).[9]
62) Nashū (Nushuww, Young Girl).* A *waṣīfa*. Ca. 1126. T-S 16.44 + T-S 12.613, ENA NS 16.11.
63) Nasrīn (Wild Rose) 1. A *jāriya* whose sale was used to fund a campaign for the ransom of Jewish captives. 1170. T-S NS 309.12, (T-S 13J3.7; T-S NS J357).

64) Nasrīn 2. A *jāriya* sold by son of the *nagid* Moses b. Samuel to a banker. 1148. Fustat. T-S 13J3.7, (T-S NS 309.12, T-S NS J357).
65) Nasrīn 3. A *jāriya* who is listed as property belonging to the woman Sutayt b. Nadiv. T-S NS J357, (T-S 13J3.7, T-S NS 309.12).
66) Nisā' (Sitt al-Nisā', the Best of Women). A *waṣīfa*. 1128–53. T-S J1.29.
67) Nujūm (Stars).* An *Edūmiyya shifḥa*. Mid-11th c. T-S J3.44.
68) P[D-N]. An Indian *waṣīf*. 1194. MS Heb. b 12/32.
69) Qaḍīb (Poised, from staff or rod, straight like a rod). A Persian (*'Ajamiyya*) *jāriya*. 1158. T-S NS 320.17.
70) Qawām (Well-Proportioned). A Christian, "carob-colored" *jāriya*. 1090. T-S Ar. 42.174.
71) Rahaj (Discord)[10] 1. A Nubian *jāriya*. 1134. T-S 13J2.20, (ENA 4011.63).
72) Rahaj 2. A *jāriya*. 1152. ENA 4011.63, (T-S 13J2.20).
73) Rahaj 3. A *waṣīfa*. 1182. MS Heb. f 56/46v.
74) [Ra]sm (Drawing). A *jāriya*. 1129–30. ENA 4020.63.
75) Rayḥān (Basil) 1. A Nubian child and brother to Shamīma (see below). No date. JRL B 7005.2.
76) Rayḥān 2.^ A factotum of the Fatimid caliphate. Not clear if he was enslaved or freed when mentioned here. 1141. Or. 1080 J258.
77) Riḍā (Contentment, Delight). A *shifḥa*. T-S 16.15.
78) Sa'āda (Happiness, Prosperity, Good Fortune) 1. A Black (*sudāniyya*) mother and enslaved child-nurse (*dāda*). ENA NS 48.6.
79) Sa'āda 1's son. ENA NS 48.6.
80) Sa'āda 2. A *jāriya*. Ca. 1190–1212. T-S 10J17.3, (T-S 13J3.16, T-S 18J1.f30).
81) Sa'āda 3. A *jāriya*. 1198. T-S 13J3.16, (T-S 10J17.3, T-S 18J1.30).
82) Sa'āda 4. A Beja (*Bāziyya*) *jāriya* and *amta*. 1190. T-S 18J1.30, (T-S 10J17.3, T-S 13J3.16).
83) Sa'd (Good Fortune). A boy included with his mother in a dowry list. 1100–38.[11] Or. 10653.5.
84) Sa'd's mother. Included in a dowry list with her son Sa'd. 1100–38.[12] Or. 10653.5.
85) Ṣāf (Pure). A *ghulām* who gave a donation to a widow. MS Heb. d 66/78.
86) Ṣāfī (Pure) 1. A *ghulām*. 1144. T-S 12.582, (MS Heb. d 66/78).
87) Ṣāfī 2. A *ghulām*. 1161. MS Heb. d 66/78, (T-S 12.582).
88) Ṣalaf (Vainglory).* An Indian *jāriya*. Possibly the same as the Ṣalaf in appendix 2. 1100–38. T-S 16.239, (T-S 10J28.16).
89) Ṣandal (Sandalwood). A *ghulām*. ENA 2727.37.
90) Saraf (Extravagance). Part of a bride's dowry. T-S 12.635.

91) Ṣirf (Unadulterated). A *jāriya mughanniya* (enslaved singer). 1093. T-S NS 320.5.
92) Ṣayd (Quarry) 1. A *jāriya*. Ca. 1159. T-S 10J7.6(2v) sec. d, (L-G Arabic II.129, Or. 1080 J25).
93) Ṣayd 2. A *mamlūka*. L-G Arabic II.129, Or. 1080 J25, (T-S 10J7.6(2v) sec. d).
94) Sha'af (Burning Desire). A *jāriya* who belonged to Fāṭima, a Muslim woman. T-S AS 202.415.
95) Sha'al (Firebrand). A *jāriya* and a*mta*. 1108. T-S 18J1.16, (Or. 1080 J 49).
96) Sha'ath (Unkemptness). A Nubian *jāriya*. 1044. T-S 16.134.
97) Shamīma (Bouquet). A Nubian child and sister to Rayḥān 1 (see above). JRL B 7005.2.
98) Sumr (Sitt al-Sumr, the Best of the Brown Women). A *jāriya*. Ca. 1140–59. T-S AS 147.23, T-S 13J22.2.
99) Sutayt (Little Lady). A girl of ambiguous status. Ca. 1060. ENA 2808.52.
100) Ṭāhir (Pure). A *ghulām*. 1050. MS Heb. a 2/19.
101) Tawfīq (Success) 1. A Nubian *jāriya* thought to be a Christian. 1100. MS Heb. b 12/20, (T-S 320.29, T-S NS 320.15, ENA 4020.11).
102) Tawfīq 2. A *jāriya* and *amta*. Late 11th c. T-S NS 320.15, ENA 4020.11, (MS Heb. b 12/20, T-S 320.29).
103) Tawfīq 3. A prepubescent *jāriya* [*Fara*]*sāwiyya*.[13] 1100–38. T-S 320.29, (T-S NS 320.15, ENA 4020.11, MS Heb. b 12/20).
105) Tawfīq 4. A *jāriya*. Ca. late 12th c. Halper 400.
106) Tawfīq 5. A Nubian *jāriya*. 1233. T-S Ar. 39.245.
107) Ṭāwūs (Peacock) 1. *Jāriya* and mother of Mubārak. 1241. T-S 16.20, (T-S AS 148.15, ENA NS 72.18).
108) Ṭāwūs 2. A Nubian *jāriya*. 1250. T-S AS 148.15, (T-S 16.20, ENA NS 72.18).
109) Ṭayyib (Pleasant). A *ghulām*. 1051. MS Heb. a 3/13.
110) 'Ūd al-Zān (Beech Wood). Part of a woman's dowry. 1156. RNL Yevr.-Arab I 1700.25v.
111) "Umm Nūbiyya."[14] A Nubian woman and mother of an enslaved child. She was later freed and gave birth to a free Jewish daughter. 1093. T-S Misc. 27.4.23 + 29.
112) Umm Nūbiyya's daughter. A Nubian or *muwallada*? Died before 1093. T-S Misc. 27.4.23 + 29.
113) 'Ushshāq (Sitt al-'Ushshāq, Best of all Lovers). A pregnant *jāriya*. T-S 13J6.7.

114) Wafā' (Fidelity).* The daughter of Jinān and a *waṣīfa*. A *muwallada* after her mother? Ca. 1140–53 with slave status. F1908.44SS, (T-S J1.29).
115) Walā' (Loyalty).^ Mentioned in a letter. Or. 1080 J71.
116) Warda (Rose). A *muwallada*. Dowry. T-S Ar. 30.73.
117) Waṣl (Tryst). A *jāriya*. ENA 3030.6.
118) "Yaṣe'a" (She Left). Freimann and Goitein, *Responsa*, no. 98.
119) Zahr (Blossom). A *waṣīfa*. 1146. MS Heb. d 66/48 + 47.
120) Ẓarf (Elegance). A *shifḥa*. Mid-11th c. T-S 16.15.
121) Anonymous 1. The *jāriya* of Abū Sa'īd b. Maḥfuẓ, known as Ibn Jamāhir. 1141. T-S 12.582.
122) Anonymous 2. The son born to Anonymous 1 by Abū Sa'īd b. Maḥfūẓ. 1141. T-S 12.582.
123) Anonymous 3. A Nubian woman and mother of Shamīma and Rayḥān. JRL B 7005.2.
124) Anonymous 4. A boy who died young. 1080. F1908.44GG.
125) Anonymous 5. A *jāriya* with a "defect" in her eye. 1134. T-S Ar. 29.49.
126) Anonymous 6. A Nubian *jāriya* whose name is only partly legible (l. 4). 1227. ENA 2558.14v.
127) Anonymous 7. A "black *waṣīfa* of the Nubian type (*jins*)." Ca. 1238–48. T-S 10J6.7.
128) Anonymous 8. An Abyssinian *jāriya* and *amta* who was blind in one eye. 1260. T-S 6J1.32.
129) Anonymous 9 (possibly Abnūsa).[15] A Nubian *jāriya*. Early 13th c. T-S 8J8.16, (T-S NS J449, Mosseri VII, 58.1).
130) Anonymous 10 (possibly Abnūsa). A Nubian *jāriya*. Early 13th c. T-S NS J449, (T-S 8J8.16, Mosseri VII, 58.1).
131) Anonymous 11. A prepubescent (*dūn al-bulūgh*) Nubian *jāriya* and *waṣīfa*. 1126. PER H 23.
132) Anonymous 12. A *jāriya*. 11th c. AIU VII.E.131.
133) Anonymous 13. An *'abd*. Ca. 1137–47. T-S 16.345, Or. 5542.17 (a copy of T-S 16.345).
134) Anonymous 14. A Frankish *jāriya*. Ca. late 11th or early 12th c. DK 228.3.
135) Anonymous 15. A *jāriya* mentioned in a letter from Ashkelon to Fustat. Ca. 1060. DK 230.4.
136) Anonymous 16. A Christian *jāriya* was mentioned in a query to Abraham Maimonides. Unclear if this woman is part of a hypothetical case, or whether she was a specific individual. Early 13th c. DK 231.2.

137) Anonymous 17. A *waṣīfa* was greeted in a letter. Ca. early 12th c. DK 238.3.
138) Anonymous 18. A *ghulām* was put up for sale. Early 12th c. ENA 2738.23.
139) Anonymous 19. A *jāriya* was sold in Alexandria. Ca. 1060. ENA 2805.23.
140) Anonymous 20. "The *jāriya* of Rav Nissim." ENA 3153.6.
141) Anonymous 21. A *jāriya*. 1100–38. ENA 4010.13v.
142) Anonymous 22. An *ʿabd*. 1152. ENA 4045.9.
143) Anonymous 23. A *jāriya*. 1100–38. ENA 4101.3b + JRL B 7252.1
144) Anonymous 24. A *jāriya*. Mid- to late-11th c. F 1908.44HH.
145) Anonymous 25. A *ghulām*. Mid- to late-12th c. F 1908.44i.
146) Anonymous 26. A *jāriya* (Kushite) valued in a dowry for 30 dinars. Mid- to late-11th c. Halper 341 + Halper 348.
147) Anonymous 27. The *ghulām* of Ibn Miṣbāḥ. 12th or 13th c.? L-G Arabic II.129.
148) Anonymous 28. A *waṣīf*. Or. 1080J25.
149) Anonymous 29. A *shifḥa* sold for 21 dinars in Cairo. 1207. MS Heb. c 28/1.
150) Anonymous 30.^ A *jāriya* or the money to purchase a *jāriya* was included in a dowry. 1186. MS Heb. f 56/54v, sec. b.
151) Anonymous 31. The *ghulām* of Abū al-Azhar was mentioned in a letter. 11th c. Or. 1081 J24.
152) Anonymous 32. A Christian *jāriya* was mentioned in a query to Abraham Maimonides. Unclear if this woman is part of a hypothetical case, or whether she was a specific individual. Early 13th c. Or. 1080 J281.
153) Anonymous 33. A *jāriya*. T-S 10J9.32.
154) Anonymous 34.^ A *jāriya* (ambiguous, could be enslaved or free). T-S 12.382.
155) Anonymous 35. A *jāriya* was described as "lost from (her mistress's) house." 1157. T-S 12.585v.
156) Anonymous 36. A *jāriya Rūmiyya* was part of a marriage dowry. Ca. 994–95. T-S 16.70.
157) Anonymous 37. A *jāriya* was sold. 1119. T-S 18J1.19.
158) Anonymous 38. A *jāriya* whose previous sale was discussed. 1216. T-S 8J8.5.
159) Anonymous 39. A Zanj *ʿabd* whose death was reported in a letter. Mid-12th c. T-S Ar. 35.14.
160) Anonymous 40. An Indian *ʿabd* and merchant's factotum. Mid-12th c. T-S Ar. 35.14.

161) Anonymous 41. An Indian *jāriya* was mentioned because her son, a Jew, was accused of harassing people in the Perfumer's Market and during the Sabbath. The son's legal status was not mentioned, and he was likely a freed or free person. This also suggests the possibility that Anonymous 41 was freed at some point. T-S Ar. 41.49.

162) Anonymous 42. A *jāriya* was promised by her owner to his first wife in the event of his death. Ca. 1066–1108. T-S AS 164.218 + T-S NS J490.

163) Anonymous 43. The "*jāriya* of (the man) Mukhtār" was listed as a recipient on an alms list. Ca. 1107. T-S J1.4, T-S K15.39.

164) Anonymous 44. A *jāriya* was purchased. 1100–38. T-S NS 184.59.

165) Anonymous 45. A *jāriya* appeared to be the subject of a Mamluk-era petition. T-S NS 306.70.

166) Anonymous 46. A *jāriya* belonging to "the wool merchant (*al-ṣawwāf*)." 1041. MS Heb. b 11/5v.

167) Anonymous 47. A six-year-old *jāriya* was trafficked from the western Indian Ocean region to Cairo. 12th c. T-S NS J23.

168) Anonymous 48. A *jāriya* named Ṭ[. . .].ENA NS 72.18.

169) Anonymous 49. A *jāriya* who became a pawn in a marital dispute. Ca. 1140–59. DK 232.1, T-S 10J17.22.

170) Anonymous 50. The daughter of the *jāriya* Anonymous 48. 1140–59. DK 232.1.

171) Anonymous 51. The *jāriya* of Saʿāda al-Nadiv. 1126. T-S NS 320.7.

172) Anonymous 52. The *jāriya* of Ibn Ṣiriyya. 1126. T-S NS 320.7.

173) Anonymous 53. The *jāriya* of Ibn [. . .]. 1126. T-S NS 320.7.

174) Anonymous 54. An *amta* whose name was not known (*amta pelonit*) by the scribe when he drafted the bill of sale. Ca. early 13th c. T-S 13J8.11.

175) Anonymous 55. A *jāriya* was the subject of a legal dispute over the terms of her sale. 1134. T-S Ar. 29.49.

176) Anonymous 56. A *jāriya* who was beaten by her mistress's husband. Moses Maimonides, *Responsa*, no. 234.

177) Seventy *jāriya*s who were reportedly sent by the Ṣulayḥids to the Fatimids as part of a diplomatic gift and who were kidnapped by al-Bulyanī. T-S AS 149.3.

178) Seventy eunuchs (*ustādh*s) who were reportedly sent by the Ṣulayḥids to the Fatimids as part of a diplomatic gift and who were kidnapped by al-Bulyanī. T-S AS 149.3.

Appendix 2: A Snapshot of the Freed People Documented in the *Geniza* Corpus (994–1260)

1) Akramiyya (Most Noble). A freedwoman. 1217. ENA 2559.13, T-S 13J3.26.
2) Bandār (Harbor). A freedman (*ha-meshuḥrar*). 10th c. T-S 16.133.
3) Berakha/Ashū*^ (Blessed). The freedwoman (*ha-meshuḥreret*) of Abraham b. Yijū who had the slave name Ashū.[16] 1132. IOM D 55.10.
4) Dhahab 1.* A freed *jāriya*. Ca. 1140–59. T-S 13J22.2.
5) Dhahab 2. A freedwoman (*ha-meshuḥreret*). Ca. 1242. T-S NS J226v.
6) Faraj.* The freedman (*al-ʿatīq*) and client (*mawlā*) of Barhūn al-Tāhirtī. Early 11th c. T-S 12.175, DK 246.1 (1015 CE), and T-S 8.12.
7) Gharaḍ.* A *jāriya* who was freed by her dying owner. 1160. T-S Misc. 24.137.4.
8) Hind (India). A *jāriya* who was freed. T-S Ar. 50.71 + T-S Ar. 50.80.
9) Ibtidāʾ (Novice). A *meshuḥreret* and mother of Fakhr (a free girl). 1154. Or. 10588.3.
10) Kashf.* A *jāriya* who was freed by her dying owner and put in the custody of his sister until she was old enough to decide whether she would "stay" or "leave." 1160. T-S Misc. 24.137.4.
11) Khalaf. A *meshuḥrar* and husband of a Jewish woman. Late 12th c. T-S 10J17.16.
12) Makhlūf (Worthy Successor). A man freed by a woman. 1085. T-S Misc. 36.151.
13) Mevasser (Bearer of Good News). A *meshuḥrar* who formed a business partnership with two merchants and formerly named Bishāra. 1092. T-S 8J4.11 + T-S NS J6 + T-S 8J4.12, ENA 972.3.[17]
14) Miriam. A freedwoman received 10 dirhams per month as part of an agreement. 1100. T-S J1.11.
15) Mubārak 1. The *meshuḥrar* and *mawlā* of Joseph b. Josiah. 1080. T-S 20.47b.
16) Mubārak 2.*^ His personal status is ambiguous. He appears to have been either an enslaved *ghulām* or a freedman who worked for a Jewish merchant. Ca. 1104. ENA 2727.28.
17) Mubāraka 1. A freed *jāriya* who was betrothed to a dyer. 1191 (possibly 1201). T-S AS 145.1.
18) Mubāraka 2. A freedwoman from the lands of Rūm (*bilād al-Rūm*) who sought to marry a Jewish man. 1091. T-S NS 321.54.

19) Mubāraka 3. A freedwoman. Ca. 1029–30. T-S NS 320.63.[18]

20) Mukhtār (Chosen One). A *meshuḥrar* who had been the *ghulām* of the gaon Evyatar ha-Kohen. Late 11th or early 12th c. T-S 10J23.1.

21) Munā 1.*^ A *jāriya* whose dying owner declared that Munā should not be bought or sold after her death. It seems that the owner meant to free Munā, but the phrasing is ambiguous. 1230. T-S Misc. 25.107.[19]

22) Munā 2. A *meshuḥreret* who married a *parnas* with a sizeable dowry and was known to have given a loan to a perfumer. 1184. MS Heb f 56/53, MS Heb c 28/54 (1203).

23) Munjib (Noble). A *ghulām* was freed by the woman Sitt al-Gharb. Ca. 1140–59. T-S 13J30.7 + T-S NS J614.[20]

24) Muwaffaq. A *meshuḥrar* who was mentioned as the father of a divorcee. 1172. T-S 10J2.15.

25) Muʿtazz (Proud). A freedwoman who married. 986. T-S 16.105.

26) Naʿīm.*[21] A *jāriya maʿtūqa* who appeared on an alms list as a recipient of 3 dirhams. 1176. T-S NS 324.132c.

27) Nāshiya (Sweet Scent, or Nubile). An *amta* who was freed. 1176. T-S 8J12.2.

28) Nujūm.* An *Edūmiyya* woman who was freed after she had variously been used as collateral, given as a gift, and otherwise changed hands among family members and their associates. 11th c. T-S J3.44.

29) Nushuww.* A *maʿtūqa* and former *waṣīfa* who inherited part of a house from her former owner. A man promised to "marry her and never divorce her," but it is not clear that the marriage took place. Ca. 1126. T-S 16.44 + T-S 12.613, ENA NS 16.11.

30) Saʿāda 5. A freed *shifḥa* (also called an *amta*) and *meshuḥreret* who married and had a son and daughter. Ca. 1200. T-S 12.872, T-S Ar. 6.28.

31) Ṣalaf.* An *amta* who was freed, and possibly the same Ṣalaf listed in appendix 1. 1157. T-S 10J28.16, (T-S 16.239).

32) Salāma (Health). A *meshuḥrar* and a groom. 1111. T-S 24.5.

33) Sarab (Flowing Water). A *maʿtūqa* who appeared on an alms list as a recipient of clothing and cash. Ca. 1182–84. T-S K15.13, T-S 8J5.14, T-S NS 324.132.

34) Sitt al-Rūm (Best of the Romans).[22] A freed *shifḥa* who later appointed her own legal representative. 1070. T-S 12.8 + T-S 10J4.9.

35) Sumr.* A freed *jāriya*. Ca. 1140–59. T-S 13J22.2.

36) T-K(h)-Ā-T]. A freed *amta*. 1110. T-S 8J12.1

37) Ṭarā'if (Rare Treasures). A *shifḥa* freed by Abraham b. Isaac in Jerusalem. 1057. Manuscript shelf-mark lost (ENA 19?).[23]

38) T-W-[..] (Tawfīq?). A freed *amta*. Ca. 1166–67. T-S NS J484.

39) Tawfīq 6. A *meshuḥreret*, the wife of Levi b. Namer, and property owner. Possibly the same as Tawfīq 1, 2, or 3. 1124. Heid. Or. 79.

40) Umm Baqā (Mother of Baqā). A *ma'tūqa* who received clothing as alms. 1183. T-S Ar. 52.247, (T-S NS 324.132).

41) "Umm Nūbiyya."* A Nubian freedwoman who was purchased by a Jewish merchant in Ashkelon along with her daughter. Her daughter died. After her owner freed and married her, Umm Nūbiyya had another daughter named Milāḥ. 1093. T-S Misc. 27.4.23 + T-S Misc. 27.4.29.

42) Wafā'.* The enslaved daughter of Jinān* and later a freed *amta*. 1181. T-S 8J12.3.

43) Yakhīn. A *meshuḥrar* and father of "'Alī Abū al-Ḥasan, the one called Thabāt." T-S AS 211.101-116.[24]

44) Yosef (Joseph). Called "master and lord (*mar ve-rav*) Joseph, the elder (*ha-zaqen*), the freedman (*meshuḥrar*)" in his daughter's prenuptial agreement. 1124. T-S NS 259.37 + T-S 8J5.3, ENA 972.8 (his daughter's divorce deed from 1145 in which he is simply "Joseph").

45) Anonymous 57 (continued from appendix 1). The freedman (*'atīq*) of Ibn Faḍl is mentioned in a letter that was sent from Libya (Tripolitania) to Egypt. 1089. T-S 18J3.19.

46) Anonymous 58. Fragment of a deed of manumission. Gender of freed person uncertain. 13th c. T-S 8J12.4.

47) Anonymous 59. A woman was freed. Fragment of a deed of manumission. T-S AS 152.393.

48) Anonymous 60. The freedwoman (*meshuḥreret*) and former *jāriya* of Jāliyya bt. Aaron ha-Kohen. T-S NS 320.7.

49) Anonymous 61. A woman was freed. 1100–38. T-S NS J152 + T-S NS J110.

50) Anonymous 62. A freed (*ma'tūq*) *ghulām muwallad*. 1231. ENA 2538.1.

51) Anonymous 63. The freedman of Mevasser b. Yefet. Late 10th or early 11th c. T-S K25.66.

52) Anonymous 64. A freedwoman who bequeathed her estate to a group of women in the town of Minyat Ghamr. Ca. 1213–37. T-S 8J16.4.

53) Anonymous 65. A *maʿtūq* who made a donation. Ca. 1225. T-S Ar. 7.13.
54) Anonymous 66. An *ʿatīq* was mentioned in a letter. Ca. late 11th/early 12th c. Mosseri VII, 160.1.
55) Anonymous 67. An *ʿatīq* was called the friend (*ṣadīq*) of the *rayyis*. 1230s. T-S NS J29.
56) Anonymous 68. A *meshuḥrar* who married. Mid-12th c. T-S K15.65.

Appendix 3: A Snapshot of the Slave-Owning Classes

This is a register of people who were slave owners, middlemen in transactions for enslaved people, and those who exerted control over enslaved individuals in some manner, even if their legal slave ownership cannot be confirmed. Husbands of slave-owning women are thus included when they are mentioned in documents as having authority over an enslaved person who was their wife's property.[25] Likewise, wives who had enslaved servants to wait on them while their husbands were away traveling are listed, even though it is not always clear who was the legal owner.

The appendix supports the arguments made in chapter 4 that the professional and gender identities of the slave-owning classes are two factors that illustrate the broad outlines of how slavery fit into the society, culture, and economy of medieval Egypt. Sometimes, the profession and gender of a given slave owner may indicate work that an enslaved individual would have been asked to perform, even though direct written descriptions of this work is generally absent from the *geniza*.[26] Reasons for the preponderance of merchants among the slave-owning classes are also discussed in chapter 4.

This appendix only includes individuals who are documented in the Cairo *geniza* documents. It does not include slave owners mentioned in the book who are documented in contemporaneous sources from outside of the *geniza*. When the gender and profession of the slave owner is known, they are provided.[27] When there is ambiguity about a slave owner's identity, profession, or another piece of information, I have indicated this with a question mark (?). Shelf marks are provided for sources that substantiate an individual's connection to the slave-owning classes, but they are not necessarily comprehensive of all sources related to that individual. Further research will undoubtedly uncover more information about individual owners who are listed below, including about their professional activities. Entries marked with a caret (^) indicate that there is ambiguity about the named person's connection to slavery.

Slave-Owning Men

TRADERS AND BANKERS

1) Abū ʿAlī al-Tājir [. . .] b. Nathan. Trader. Sold the Indian woman Ghazāl to Abū al-Faḍl Elʿazar b. [. . .]. 1155. ENA 4011.62.
2) Abū al-Azhar. Trader. Mentioned as the owner of a *ghulām*. 1030. Qayrawān. Or. 1081J24.
3) Abū al-Bayyān al-Tājir Moses ha-Levi. Trader. Bought the *ʿAjamiyya* woman Qaḍīb from Sitt al-Dalāl bt. Abū al-B[. . .] b. Saʿdān. 1157–58. T-S NS 320.17.
4) Abū al-Faḍl al-Tājir Elʿazar b. [. . .]. Trader. Bought the Indian woman Ghazāl from Abū ʿAli [. . .] b. Nathan. 1155. ENA 4011.62.
5) Abū al-Fakhr al-Tājir Joseph b. Yeshuʿa b. Solomon. Trader. Sold the woman Saʿāda to Abū ʿAlī Yefet b. Ḥalfon. 1190. Cairo. T-S 18J1.30.
6) Abū al-Ḥasan ʿAlī b. Jaʿfar. Trader? Mentioned in a letter as the owner of the *ghulām* Bakhtiyār. 1139. Aden. T-S 24.64.
7) Abū al-Ḥasan al-Ṣayrafī b. Munajjā. Banker. Bought the woman Nasrīn from Moses b. Samuel ha-Nagid. 1148. Fustat. T-S 13J3.7.
8) Abū al-Ḥasan al-Ṣayrafī Solomon ha-Kohen ha-Talmid b. Menasse ha-Kohen. Banker. Sold the woman Iftikhār to his sister Ḥasana. 1126/27. Fustat. T-S Misc. 23.8.
9) Abū al-Mufaḍḍal al-Ṣayrafī b. Abū al-[Ḥas]an. Banker. Sold an Indian *waṣīf*. 1194. Fustat. MS Heb. b 12/32.
10) Abū al-Murajjā b. Nathan. Trader. Had a daughter, Fakhr, with the freedwoman Akhtharā. 1154. Fustat. Or. 10588.3.
11) Abū Isḥāq Abraham b. Peraḥya b. Yijū (Ibn Yijū). Trader. Freed Ashū/Berakha. Owned the *ghulām* Bomma (Bama). Ca. 1131–56. Ibn Yijū traveled, but his slave owning is documented during his time in India. See the references for Ashū/Berakha and Bomma/Bama in appendix 1.
12) Abū al-Riḍā. Trader. A father who gave his daughter Sittūna two *waṣīfas*, among other items. 1120. T-S NS J185.
13) Abū Saʿīd Ibn Jamāhir Ḥalfon b. Shemarya ha-Levi. Trader. Accused by the *ghulām* Ṣāfī of banishing a *jāriya* and her son to Berbera. Ca. 1144. ʿAydhāb. T-S 12.582, T-S K15.65.
14) Abū Zikrī Judah b. Menasse Ṣayrafī. Banker or son of a banker. Possible part-owner of the *ghulām* Jurj? 11th–12th c. T-S 13J28.2.

15) Abū Zikrī Kohen. Trader. Purchased an enslaved woman with his business associate, Khiyār b. Nissim. 1134. T-S NS 321.7a.
16) ʿArūs b. Joseph. Trader. Purchased the enslaved woman Qawām. 1090. Cairo. T-S Ar. 42.174.
17) Barhūn al-Tāhīrtī. Trader. Mentioned by his own freedman (*mawlā*), Faraj, in a letter. Ca. 1020. Qayrawān. T-S 8.12. DK 246.1
18) Ḍāfīr (or Ẓāfir). Trader. Mentioned in a letter as the owner of the *ghulām* Jawhar. 1139. Aden. T-S 24.64.
19) ʿEli b. Yefet b. al-Wāsitī. Trader. Purchased "Umm Nūbiyya" and her daughter. Freed and married Umm Nūbiyya. 1093. Ashkelon. T-S Misc. 27.4.23 + T-S Misc. 27.4.29.
20) Faraḥ b. Joseph b. Faraḥ. Trader. Mentioned to "our *ghulām*, Jurj" in a business letter. 11th–12th c. Alexandria. T-S 13J28.2.
21) Ḥalfon ha-Levi b. Nethaniel Abū Saʿīd b. Hibat Allāh al-Dimyāṭī. Trader. Was unsuccessful in acquiring a *waṣīf* from the *bilād al-Zanj* via his colleague Khalaf b. Isaac in Aden. Ca. 1132, 1140. Egypt. T-S Misc. 28.256.
22) Ibn Abī al-Zift. Trader. Mentioned in two letters as the owner of a *ghulām* involved in trade with *geniza* merchants. Ca. mid-11th century. Tinnīs. T-S 8.18, T-S 13J25.14.
23) Ibn Faḍl. Trader? Mentioned as the former owner of an *ʿatīq*. 1089. Libya. T-S 18J3.19.
24) Ibn al-Ṣāhila. Trader. Owned the *ṣabī* Salār. Ca. 1025. Alexandria. T-S 13J17.3.
25) Ibn al-Tabār. Trader? Owner of the *ghulām* Ṭāhir. 1050. Alexandria/ Fustat. MS Heb. a 2/19.
26) Ibrahīm. Slave trader (*al-nakhkhās*). Involved in the sale and transport of a *waṣīfa*. 12th c.? Fustat or Alexandria. T-S 8J10.9.
27) Ismāʿīl b. Fāṣid.[28] Trader. Congratulated by his brother-in-law on the acquisition of a *ghulām*. 1176. Aden. F 1908.44i.
28) Khalaf b. Isaac. Trader. Reported that he was unsuccessful in purchasing a *waṣīf* for his Egyptian colleague Ḥalfon ha-Levi b. Nethaniel (see above). 1140. Aden. T-S Misc. 28.256.
29) Khalaf b. Mūsā Ibn al-Ṣāʾigh. Trader. Owned the *ghulām* Ṭayyib. 1051. Ifrīqiyya. MS Heb. a 3/13.
30) Khiyār b. Nissim. Banker/Trader. Served as the middleman in the purchase of an enslaved woman for his associate Abū Zikrī Kohen. 1134. T-S NS 321.7a.

31) Ma'ānī (poss. Ma'ālī) b. Khalaf al-Dajājī ha-Levi. Trader. Freed Sa'āda. Probably married her and had two children by her. 1198. Fustat. T-S 12.872, T-S Ar. 6.28.
32) Maḥrūz b. Jacob. Trader. Sent an *'abd* to his associate Sulaymān b. Abū Zikrī. Ca. 1137–47. Aden. T-S 16.345, BL Or. 5542.17 (copy of T-S 16.345).
33) Mardūkh b. Mūsā. Trader. Sought to purchase a *jāriya* for personal service. 1047. Alexandria. T-S 12.254.
34) Nahray b. Nissim. Trader. Bought, sold, and/or transported individual enslaved people for his associates. 1065. Fustat. F 1908.44HH, T-S 8J27.5, ENA 2805.23.
35) Nathan b. Nahray. Trader. Bought, sold, and/or transported a *jāriya* on his cousin Nahray b. Nissim's behalf. 1065. Alexandria. F 1908.44HH, T-S 8J27.5.
36) Shela b. 'Ayyāsh. Trader. Owned a young *jāriya* whom he left with his business partner, Tiqva b. 'Amram. 1098. Damietta and Fustat. T-S 8J4.14.
37) Sulaymān b. Abū Zikrī. Trader. Received an enslaved man from his associate Maḥrūz b. Jacob. Ca. 1137–47. Fustat/Cairo. T-S 16.345, BL Or. 5542.17 (copy of T-S 16.345).
38) Tiqva b. 'Amram. Trader. Used his business partner's (Shela b. 'Ayyāsh's) young *jāriya* while the partner was away. 1098. Fustat. T-S 8J4.14.
39) Yeshu'a b. Ishmael. Trader. Bought, sold, and/or transported a *jāriya* on his partner Nahray b. Nissim's behalf. Ca. 1060. Alexandria. ENA 2805.23.
40) Yeshu'a ha-Kohen b. Jacob. Trader. Owner of the *ghulām* Fayrūz. 1150. Dhu Jibla, Yemen. ENA 1822a75.
41) Yūsuf b. Shu'ayb Abū Jacob (Ya'aqov) Joseph b. Saul Ibn al-Naghira.[29] Trader. Sought unsuccessfully to sell a *ghulām*. Ca. 1138. Almería (Spain). T-S 12.285.
42) Anonymous 69. [. . .] ha-Kohen [. . .] al-Ṣayrafī. Banker or son of a banker. Sold the woman Bid'a/Ghazāl. 1149–50. Fustat. T-S NS 311.23v.
43) Anonymous 70. Trader. Sent his wife a six-year-old *jāriya* from the realm of the western Indian Ocean. 12th c. T-S NS J23.
44) Anonymous 71. Trader? Mentioned his or the family's *jāriya* in a letter. T-S NS J453.

45) Anonymous 72. Trader? Wrote about an enslaved Frankish woman. DK 228.3.
46) Anonymous 73. Trader? Received a letter with query about a transaction involving an enslaved Frankish woman. DK 228.3.
47) Anonymous 74. Trader? Designated the price of a *jāriya* for his daughter's benefit. Mentioned a transaction for multiple *jawāri* [*sic*], but the full context is difficult to decipher due to the document's physical deterioration. Ca. 1100. T-S 13J14.4v, ll. 4–5, 16.

ARTISANS

48) Abū al-Faraj al-Qazzāz. Silk weaver (and/or merchant). Took a woman who is owned by his wife and used her as a sex slave. Later purchased her. 1140–59. Cairo/Fustat. DK 232.1, T-S 10J17.22.
49) Abū al-Ya'qūb Joseph b. Samuel b. Naḥūm. Goldsmith. Owned two *jāriyas* at the time of his death. 1114. Cairo and Fustat. T-S 8J5.1a.
50) Ibn al-Watīd. Formerly a dyer. Freed a woman who came to be known as Mubāraka. 1091. Fustat. T-S NS 321.54.
51) "The Wool Merchant (*al-ṣawwāf*)." His *jāriya* appeared in a draft account as having paid rent. 1041. MS Heb. b 11/5v.

DOCTORS AND APOTHECARIES

52) Abraham b. Araḥ. Son of a candle and potion maker. Inherited, along with his brother El'azar, an unnamed *jāriya* from his father. 1108. Cairo. T-S 8J4.21.
53) Abū 'Alī al-'Aṭṭār. Apothecary. Sold the *jāriya* Misk to Abū al-'Alā. 1165. T-S 13J37.12r.
54) Abū al-Faḍā'il Yequti'el b. Moses. Physician. Sold the *waṣīf* Fayrūz to Judah b. El'azar. Ca. 1175. Fustat. MS Heb. b 13/39.
55) Abū al-Fakhr al-'Aṭṭār Ibn al-Amshāṭī Se'adya b. Abraham. Apothecary. Bought the *jāriya* 'Abīr from Abū al-Ḥasan b. Abū al-Yaman. T-S 8J8.4.
56) Abū al-Ḥasan al-Levi al-'Aṭṭār Yefet ha-Levi b. Nadiv ha-Levi. Apothecary. Purchased an Indian *waṣīf* from Abū al-Mufaḍḍal al-Ṣayrafī b. Abū al-[Ḥas]an. 1194. Fustat. MS Heb. b 12/32.
57) Abū al-'Izz b. Abū 'Imrān al-Sharābī. Potion maker or son of a potion maker. Bought a *jāriya* from Abū al-Ḥasan al-Melammed. 1217. T-S 8J8.5.

58) Abū al-Riḍā ha-Levi al-Ṭabīb. Physician. Left the *jāriya* Misk to his daughter ʿImrān at the time of his death. 1172. Or. 1080 J142 + T-S Misc. 25.53.
59) Al-Asʿad al-Mutaṭabbib. Physician. Owned and freed the woman Akramiyya. 1217. Fustat or al-Maḥalla. T-S 13J3.26, ENA 2559.13.
60) Araḥ al-Shammāʿ. Candle and potion maker. Bequeathed an unnamed *jāriya* to his two sons. 1108. Cairo. T-S 8J4.21.
61) Elʿazar b. Araḥ. Son of a candle and potion maker. Inherited, along with his brother Abraham, an unnamed *jāriya* from his father. 1108. Cairo. T-S 8J4.21.
62) Elʿazar b. Joseph al-Ṣaydalānī. Apothecary or son of an apothecary. Sold the Nubian woman Milḥ to Abū ʿAlī Yefet b. Menasse. 1084. Fustat. T-S 18J1.12.
63) Elʿazar ha-Levi. Physician. Bought the *jāriya* Sumr. Mid-12th c. Cairo. T-S AS 147.23. Possible connection to T-S NS 297.279.
64) Moses ha-Talmid b. Ṭahor. Apothecary. Purchased the *jāriya* Abnūsa from Nathan b. Joseph. 1230. Mosseri VII 58.1.
65) Solomon b. Semaḥ. Physician. Bought the Maghribī woman Ḥidhq from Joseph b. ʿEli. 1104. Cairo. T-S 8J5.5 (2v).
66) Ṭuviyya (Toviyahu) ha-Rofe b. Yefet. Physician. Frees a *Rūmiyya* woman. 1110. Cairo. T-S 8J12.1.
67) Yeshuʿa b. Judah. Physician. Purchases the woman Muhja. 1217. Fustat. Yevr. IIIB 669.3r.

OFFICIALS IN GOVERNMENT OR THE JEWISH COMMUNITY

68) ʿAbd al-Masīḥ b. Maqāra b. Harūn, a Christian. Scribe. Bought the Nubian woman Naʿīm from Sitt al-Munā. 1115. Cairo/Fustat. T-S 18J1.17v.
69) Abū ʿAli Yefet ha-Parnas [b.] Shemarya. Communal welfare official. Sold the woman Rahaj to Abū Iṣḥāq Abraham b. ʿAm[ram]. 1151/1152. Fustat. ENA 4011.63.
70) Abū al-Barakāt Judah b. Elʿazar. Scribe. Bought the *waṣīf* Fayrūz from Yequtiʾel b. Moses. 1175. Fustat. MS Heb. b 13/39, (RNL Yevr.-Arab I 1700.15v).[30]
71) Abū al-Ḥasan ʿAlī b. Hilāl (ʿEli b. Hillel). Government official. His niece in Fustat asked him to purchase "Black" girl for her. 1100–38. al-Bahnasā. T-S 13J21.18.

72) Al-Bulyanī (or al-Bulyanā). Fatimid military officer or local leader? Led raid of a large transport of enslaved women and eunuchs bound for the Fatimid state. 1062–72. T-S AS 149.3.
73) Evyatar ha-Kohen Gaon. Religious leader. Former owner of the freedman Mukhtār. 11th/12th c. Fustat. T-S 10J23.1.
74) Ḥanūn b. ʿAllūn, a Christian. Scribe. Sold an enslaved woman to ʿArūs b. Joseph. 1090. Cairo. T-S Ar. 42.174.
75) Joshua b. Dosā. Head of the rabbinic academy in Egypt. Owner of the *ghulām* Ṣāfī. 1141. Fustat/Cairo. T-S 12.582.
76) Moses b. Samuel ha-Nagid. Son of a *nagid* (head of the Jewish community) and *nagid* designate. Sold the woman Nasrīn to Abū al-Ḥasan al-Ṣayrafī b. Munajjā. 1148. Fustat. T-S 13J3.7.
77) Shabbetay b. Joseph. Religious official. His wife had the woman Naʿīm in her dowry. 1100–38. Fustat/Cairo. Halper 342.
78) [. . .] Zakkay ha-Dayyan [b. Moses]. Judge. Bought the woman Bidʿa/Ghazāl from a banker. 1149–50. Fustat. T-S NS 311.23v.
79) Zakkār b. ʿAmmār. *Nagid.* Had a large contingent of *ghilmān*. 1069. Sicily. T-S Misc. 28.235.
80) Anonymous 75. "The parnas" (a communal welfare official). Owned an unnamed woman who appears on an alms list. T-S Misc. 28.184.
81) Anonymous 76. "*Al-rayyis* (head of the Jewish community)." Owner of the *ghulām* Durrī. T-S K6.177.

OTHER MEN

82) Abraham b. ʿAm[ram]. Bought the *jāriya* Rahaj from Abū ʿAlī Yefet b. Shemarya. 1151/52. Fustat. ENA 4011.63.
83) Abraham b. Isaac. Freed the woman Ṭarā'if. 1057. Jerusalem. ENA 19? (lost).[31]
84) Abraham ha-Kohen b. Aaron ha-Kohen. Freed the woman Nāshiya. 1176. Fustat. T-S 8J12.2.
85) Abraham b. [. . .]. Sold the *ghulām* Ṣandal for 11 dinars. Alexandria. ENA 2727.37.
86) Abū [. . .] Bought Intijāb. 12th c. T-S NS 320.126.
87) Abū al-ʿAlā al-Levi. Bought the woman Misk 1 from Abū ʿAlī al-ʿAṭṭār and later sold her to his own wife. 1165. T-S 13J37.12r + v.
88) Abū ʿAlī Yefet b. Ḥalfon. Bought the woman Saʿāda from Abū al-Fakhr al-Tājir Joseph b. Yeshuʿa b. Solomon. 1190. Cairo. T-S 18J1.30.

89) Abū ʿAlī Yefet b. Menasse. Bought the Nubian woman Milḥ from Elʿazar b. Joseph al-Ṣaydalānī. Fustat. T-S 18J1.12.

90) Abū al-Baqā Ibn al-Muṣinn. Inherited a half share in the woman Misk 2 from his wife. T-S NS J32.

91) Abū al-Barakāt b. Ibn Shaʿyā. Bought the girl Tawfīq from Nafīsa bt. Kathīr b. al-Ṣafūri. 1100–38. T-S NS 320.29.

92) Abū al-Barakāt [Yef]et b. Moses. Sold the woman Saʿāda to Sitt Qaḍīb bt. Abū al-Bayān. 1198. T-S 13J3.16.

93) Abū Faḍl, probably the brother of Daniel b. Ṭuviyya. His household slaves were greeted in a letter. 1167. Probably Fustat/Cairo. T-S 13J33.10 (RNL Yevr.-Arab I 1700.15v, RNL Yevr.-Arab I 1700.22v).

94) Abū al-Faḍl b. Abū al-ʿAlā. Bought an unnamed, partially blind Abyssinian woman from Mūsā al-Kohen al-Bilbaysī b. Abū al-ʿIzz. 1260. T-S 6J1.32.

95) Abū Faḍl Joseph b. Moses ha-Kohen. Together with his brother, Abū Saʿd Ḥalfon, sold the woman Ḥidhq to their sister, Zayn Sitt al-Dār. 1105. Cairo. T-S 16.188.

96) [A]bū al-Faraj. Sold the *Bāziyya* woman Muhja to the daughters of the son of Jacob. Ca. 1216. ENA 2559.6.

97) Abū al-Far[aj] Yeshuʿa ha-Levi. Sold a female slave to Abū al-Riḍā Solomon. 1100–38. T-S 16.225.

98) Abū al-Faraj b. Abū Mufaḍḍal al-Marāwiḥī. Bought the Nubian woman Ṭāwūs from Sulaymān b. Abū ʿAlī. 1250. T-S AS 148.15.

99) Abū al-Faraj b. Hilāl al-Maṣrī. Freed the woman Mubāraka who was then betrothed to a Jewish man. 1191 (possibly 1201). Aleppo. T-S AS 145.1.

100) Abū al-Faraj b. Jalātī(?). Purchased and later sold Nadd. 1156. RNL Yevr.-Arab I 1700.15v, RNL Yevr.-Arab I 1700.22v.

101) Abū al-Faraj Yeshuʿa b. Mevasser (known as Ibn al-ʿAni). Sold the Abyssinian *ghulām* Muqbil, a minor, to Moses b. ʿAwāḍ. 1152. Alexandria or Damietta. T-S 13J8.3.

102) Abū al-Ḥasan al-Melammed. Teacher. Sold an enslaved woman to Abū al-ʿIzz b. Abū ʿImrān. 1217. T-S 8J8.5.

103) Abū al-Ḥasan b. Abū al-Yaman. Sold the *jāriya* ʿAbīr to Abū al-Fakhr al-ʿAṭṭār Ibn al-Amshāṭī Seʿadya b. Abraham. 1150–81. T-S 8J8.4.

104) Abū al-Ḥasan 1. Freed two people, Gharaḍ and Kashf, and placed Kashf in the care of his sister, Sitt al-Riʾāsa. Ca. 1160. T-S Misc. 24.137.4.

105) Abū al-Ḥasan 2. Sold the woman Jinān but kept her daughter Wafā'. 1142. F 1908.44SS.

106) Abū al-Ḥasan b. Yahboy. Received the three-year-old *waṣīfa* Dhahab from his sister, the mother of Abū al-Ḥajjāj. 1145. Fustat. T-S 12.140.

107) Abū al-Ḥasan Solomon ha-Kohen b. Menasse ha-Kohen. Gave the Nubian *jāriya* Rahaj to his wife. 1134. T-S 13J2.20.

108) Abū 'Im[rān b.] Ukht al-Ḥ[akīm]. Owned and freed the woman Sitt al-Rūm. Ca. 1070. Alexandria. T-S 12.8 + T-S 10J4.9.

109) Abū al-Majd. Complained that the woman he owned refused to be sold. T-S 13J36.11.

110) Abū al-Majd b. Jacob. Along with his brother, sold the girl Sumr, whom they inherited from their uncle, to their other uncle, El'azar ha-Levi. Mid-12th c. Cairo. T-S AS 147.23.

111) Abū al-Makārim Joseph b. Samuel. His wife had the woman 'Ūd al-Zān in her dowry. 1156. RNL Yevr.-Arab I 1700.25v.

112) Abū al-Makārim b. [. . .], son-in-law of Maṣliaḥ ha-Kohen Gaon. Owned, or had authority over, the woman Ghazāl. 1134. Or. 5566C16.

113) Abū al-Manṣūr al-Dimāshqī El'azar b. El'azar. Inherited the woman Rahaj from his wife and bequeathed her to his two daughters, Ḥasab and Khifā'. 1182. Fustat. MS Heb. f 56/46v.

114) Abū Manṣūr Semaḥ b. Yefet Abū 'Alī. His bride Sitt al-Khāṣṣa had the woman Zuhr as part of her dowry. 1146. Fustat. MS Heb. d 66/48 + 47.

115) Abū al-Ma'ālī. Listed as owner of the *ghulām* Ṣāf. 1161. Fustat/Cairo. MS Heb. d 66/78.

116) Abū al-Mufaḍḍal. Sold an unnamed enslaved woman as part of settling his dead father's estate. 1150. T-S 13J5.3.

117) Abū Naṣr b. Abraham. Asked his brother Hilāl for help purchasing a *waṣīfa*. Alexandria. T-S NS J16. AIU, VII.E.8 (now lost).[32]

118) Abū Naṣr ha-Kohen El'azar b. Yahyā. His bride, Sitt al-Ma'ālī, had a *jāriya* in her dowry. MS Heb. f 56/42.

119) Abū al-Riḍā Solomon [.] Bought a female slave from Abū al-Faraj Yeshu'a ha-Levi. 1100–38. T-S 16.225.

120) Abū Sa'd Baghdādī. Listed as the owner of an enslaved woman. T-S 16.219v.

121) Abū Sa'd Ḥalfon b. Moses ha-Kohen. Together with his brother, Abū al-Faḍl Joseph, sold the woman Ḥidhq to their sister, Zayn Sitt al-Dār. 1105. Cairo. T-S 16.188.

122) Abū Ya'qūb Isaac al-Nafūsī. Mentioned as the owner of a *ghulām* named Faraj. 1065. Alexandria. MS Heb. b 3/26.

123) Abū Ya'qūb Joseph b. Ephraim. Bought the *jāriya* Milḥ from Joseph b. Nathanel. 1100. Fustat. ENA 4011.48.

124) Abū Ya'qūb Joseph b. Nathanel. Sold the *jāriya* Milḥ to Joseph b. Ephraim. 1100. Fustat. ENA 4011.48.

125) Abū Zakariyyā Judah b. Joseph ha-Kohen. Party to the sale of a slave. AIU, VII.E.8 (now lost).[33]

126) Abū Zikrī Yaḥyā. Bought the Nubian woman 'Alam from Sitt al-Milāḥ. 1100–38. Fustat. T-S 20.41.

127) 'Amram ha-Kohen b. Abū al-Majd Ibn al-Ṣanānīrī. Bequeathed a Nubian woman to his son. 1238–48. Fustat. T-S 10J6.7.

128) (Son of) 'Amram ha-Kohen b. Abū al-Majd. Inherited a Nubian woman from his father. 1238–48. Fustat. T-S 10J6.7.

129) David ha-Levi b. [. . .] Sold an unnamed woman. Fustat/Cairo. T-S 13J7.15.

130) El'azar b. Yefet. Sold the woman Ṭawūs and her son Mubārak to Solomon b. Ṣedaqa. 1241. Fustat. T-S 16.20.

131) 'Eli b. Qimoy. His wife Sutayt had a *Rūmiyya* woman as part of her dowry. 995. T-S 16.70.

132) Ezra b. Mevorakh. Bought an enslaved woman from Shabbetay b. Judah. 1119. Fustat. T-S 18J1.19.

133) Fadā'il al-[. . . . .] b. Jacob. Bought the woman Ṣayd from [Ibn] 'Imrān b. Mardūkh. ca. 1159. T-S 10J7.6(2v), sec. d.

134) Faraḥ b. Samuel al-Qābisī. Purchased a *jāriya* from his sister Mubāraka. Fustat. T-S 10J9.32.

135) [Ibn] 'Imrān b. Mardūkh. Sold the woman Ṣayd to Fadā'il al-[. . . . .] b. Ya'aqov. Ca. 1159. T-S 10J7.6(2v), sec. d.

136) Jacob b. Abraham b. 'Allān. Part of a case involving the *shifḥa* Ẓarf and her son Muwaffaq. T-S 16.15.

137) Jacob b. David. Owner of a Nubian woman who took care of his three children. Ca. 1044. Alexandria. T-S 16.134.

138) Joseph [. . . .]. Bought an enslaved woman from an unknown seller. 1100–38. T-S NS 184.59.

139) Joseph b. Bishr ha-Kohen Ibn Qurayẓa. Received the woman Nujūm as a gift and then freed her. 11th c. T-S J3.44.

140) Joseph b. 'Eli. Sold the Maghribi woman Ḥidhq to Solomon b. Semaḥ. 1104. Cairo. T-S 8J5.5(2v).

141) Joseph b. Josiah. Former owner of the freedman Mubārak. T-S 20.47b.
142) Joseph b. Samuel. Bought the woman Ḥidhq and her daughter from Yaḥyā ha-Kohen. 1094. Fustat. T-S 20.93b.
143) Joseph b. Solomon. His wife Karīma had a Kushite woman as part of her dowry. 1070. Halper 341 + Halper 348.
144) Joseph b. Solomon. Purchased the woman Tawfīq for his daughter Sitt al-Ahl. Fustat. T-S NS 320.15, ENA 4020.11 (a copy).
145) Joseph ha-Levi b. Berakhot. Involved in a lawsuit over the sale of a woman. T-S NS J319 + T-S NS 190.108.
146) Judah b. Moses Ibn Sighmār. His wife wrote to inform him that the family's *jāriya* ran away. 1070. Fustat. Or. 1080 J71.
147) Labrāṭ b. Moses Ibn Sighmār.^ Wrote in a letter that his *ṣabiyya* (ambiguous legal status) sends greetings to the recipient. 1061. al-Mahdiyya. T-S 16.179.
148) Ḥalfon b. Seʿadya. Bought an enslaved person from Nethanel b. Ḥalfon. MS Heb. d 68/106.
149) Haṣan Yefet ha-Levi known as Ibn al-Batnūnī. Bought an enslaved woman from Samuel ha-Levi. 1208. Cairo. MS Heb. c 28/1.
150) Hiba b. Elʿazar. Sold the woman Nasrīn and donated 9 dinars to Moses Maimonides for a campaign to ransom Jewish captives. 1170. al-Maḥalla. T-S NS 309.12.
151) Hilāl b. Abraham. Asked by his brother Abu Naṣr for help purchasing a *waṣīfa*. Fustat. T-S NS J16.
152) Hillel b. Berakhot. Bought the woman Ḍiya from the agent Isaac b. Judah. 1226. Fustat. T-S 6J1.7 + T-S 13J4.2, Or. 1080J273.
153) Hoshaʿana. The *ghulām* of Hoshʿana was listed as a recipient on an alms list. First half of 12th c. T-S K15.48.
154) Ibn al-Ṣīriyya. Listed as the owner of a deceased enslaved woman. 1126. Fustat. T-S NS 320.7.
155) Ibn Futayḥ. Listed as the former owner of the freedwoman, Munā. 1184. Fustat. MS Heb. f 56/53.
156) Ibn Miṣbāḥ. Owned a *ghulām*. Ca. 12th/13th c. Quṣ? L-G Arabic II.129.
157) Makhlūf b. Jacob. Sold the woman ʿAlam to Sitt al-Riḍā bt. Mufarraj. T-S 10J11.31.
158) Menass[e ha-Kohen] b. Jacob. Freed the woman T-W-[..] (Tawfīq?). Cairo. T-S NS J484.
159) Menasse ha-Kohen b. Seʿadya Abū al-Ḥasan b. al-Maṣmūda. Sold the woman Shaʿal to Ṣedaqa b. Judah. 1108. Fustat. T-S 18J1.16.

160) Meshullam b. Hiba Ibn al-Shawaykhiyyā. Sold the woman Kitmān to Moses ha-Kohen b. Ghālib. 1091. Fustat. ENA 4020.47v.

161) Mevasser b. Yefet. Freed an unnamed person. Late 10th c. T-S K25.66.

162) Mevorakh. Sold a *jāriya* to one Yequti'el. ENA 4010.13v.

163) Moses b. ʿAwāḍ (known as Ibn al-Raqqāʿī). Bought the Abyssinian *ghulām* Muqbil, a minor, from Abū al-Faraj Yeshuʿa Mevasser. 1152. Alexandria or Damietta. T-S 13J8.3.

164) Moses ha-Kohen b. Ghālib. Bought the woman Kitmān from Mushallam b. Hiba. 1091. Fustat. ENA 4020.47v.

165) Moses b. Mevasser. Sold the woman Rabāb and her son. T-S NS 342.87.

166) Moses b. Palṭi'el. Owned and freed the woman Muʿtazz. 986. Fustat. T-S 16.105.

167) Moses ha-Talmid. Bought Abnūsa from Nathan b. Joseph. 1230. Mosseri VII 58.1, T-S 8J8.16, T-S NS J449.

168) Moses b. Yefet. Bought the woman Tawfīq from Sayyida bt. Ṣedaqa. 1100. Fustat. MS Heb. b 12/20.

169) Mufaḍḍal b. Abū Saʿd b. Ṣibyān. Purchased the woman Jinān. 1142. F 1908.44SS.

170) Mufaḍḍal b. Jacob. Along with his brother, sold the girl Sumr, whom they inherited from their uncle, to their other uncle Elʿazar ha-Levi. Mid-12th c. Cairo. T-S AS 147.23.

171) Mukarram b. Abū al-Baqā Ibn al-Muṣinn. Received a half share in the woman Misk 2 as a gift from his father Abū al-Baqā Ibn al-Muṣinn. T-S NS J32.

172) Mukhtār. Listed as the owner of a *jāriya* who appears as a recipient on several alms lists. Ca. 1107. Fustat. T-S J1.4, T-S K15.39,T-S K15.50, T-S Misc. 8.25.

173) Mūsā al-Kohen al-Bilbaysī b. Abū al-ʿIzz. Sold an unnamed, partially blind Ethiopian woman to *mawlā al-rayyis* Abū al-Faḍal b. *mawlā al-rayyis* Abū al-ʿAlā. 1260. Not specified. T-S 6J1.32.

174) Nathan b. Joseph.[34] Sold the *jāriya* Abnūsa to Moses ha-Talmid b Ṭahor. 1230. Mosseri VII 58.1, T-S 8J8.16, T-S NS J449.

175) Nethaniel b. Ḥalfon. Sold an enslaved person to Ḥalfon b. Seʿadya. MS Heb. d 68/106.

176) Samuel ha-Levi. Sold an enslaved woman to Ḥasan Yefet ha-Levi. 1208. Cairo. MS Heb. c 28/1.

177) Ṣedaqa b. Judah ha-Zaqen. Bought the woman Sha'al from Menasse ha-Kohen b. Se'adya. 1108. Fustat. T-S 18J1.16.
178) Ṣedaqa ha-Levi b. Moses. Sold the woman Tawfīq to Joseph b. Solomon, who purchased her for his daughter Sitt al-Ahl. Fustat. T-S NS 320.15, ENA 4020.11 (copy).
179) Shabbetay b. Judah. Sold an enslaved woman to Ezra b. Mevorakh. 1119. Fustat. T-S 18J1.19.
180) She'erit, the father of Abū al-Ṭāhir. Owned and freed an unnamed woman. 1213–37. Minyat Ghamr. T-S 8J16.4.
181) Shemarya b. Ḥalfon. Sold the Nubian woman Na'īm to Khāliṣa bt. [. . .] 1098. T-S 12.93.
182) Sibā'a b. Rajā. Purchased Nadd. 1156. RNL Yevr.-Arab I 1700.22v.
183) Simḥa ha-Kohen. Mentioned the family's *jāriya*. Alexandria. T-S 13J24.10.
184) Solomon. Former owner of the freedwoman Dhahab. Ca. 1242. T-S NS J226v.
185) Solomon b. Nathan. Sold a minor Nubian girl to his wife, Libwa. 1126. Fustat. PER H 23.
186) Solomon b. Ṣedaqa. Bought the woman Ṭāwūs and her son Mubārak from El'azar b. Yefet. 1241. Fustat. T-S 16.20.
187) Sulaymān b. Abū 'Alī. Sold the Nubian woman Ṭāwūṣ to Abū al-Faraj b. Abū Mufaḍḍal al-Marāwiḥī. 1250. T-S AS 148.15.
188) Ṭāhir b. al-Ghuzzī. Mentioned as the owner of the *jāriya* Sa'āda. Qaylūb. T-S 10J17.3.
189) Yaḥyā ha-Kohen b. Samuel. Sold the woman Ḥidhq and her daughter to Joseph b. Solomon. 1094. Fustat. T-S 20.93b.
190) Yefet b. Joseph. Freed the woman [W . . .], who was renamed Mubāraka upon her manumission. 1030. Cairo. T-S NS 320.63.[35]
191) Yequti'el al-[K(h) . . .] Bought a *jāriya* from one Mevorakh. ENA 4010.13v.
192) Yeshu'a b. Hillel Ibn Zikr. Sold the woman Ḍiya through his agent Isaac b. Judah. 1226. Fustat. T-S 6J1.7 + T-S 13J4.2, CUL Or. 1080 J273.
193) Yeshu'a ha-Levi. Bequeathed the girl Sumr to his nephews Mufaḍḍal and Abū al-Majd b. Jacob. Mid-12th c. Cairo. T-S AS 147.23.
194) Yeshu'a, husband of Mubāraka bt. Samuel. Sued his wife and brother-in-law for the profits from the sale of an enslaved woman. Fustat. T-S 10J9.32.

195) Anonymous 77. Sold a *waṣīf* and bequeathed a *jāriya* to his daughter in his will. 1100–38. Cairo. MS Heb. f 56/12.

196) Anonymous 78. Sold the woman Muhja to Yeshu'a b. Judah. 1217. Fustat. Yevr. IIIB 669.3r.

197) Anonymous 79. Gave instructions for recipient of a letter to purchase him a *jāriya*. MS Heb. d 66/14.

198) Anonymous 80. A *waṣīfa* was part of a dead man's estate. Ca. 1207. T-S 13J3.19v.

199) Anonymous 81. Left an *'abd* and a *jāriya* to his wife in his will. 1219–20. Fustat. T-S NS J347.

200) Anonymous 82. Wrote about the services his servant Mubārak (probably a *waṣīf*, *ghulām*, or freedman) provided for him during their travels. 1104. Acre. ENA 2727.28.

201) Anonymous 83. A man respectfully called "our lord" was mentioned as the owner of the *ghulām* Abū al-Munā. Ca. 12th c. Ashkelon. MS Heb b 13/50.

202) Anonymous 84. "The Convert (*al-ger*)." Identified as the owner of the *jāriya* Mubāraka in an alms list. 1107. Fustat. T-S K15.113.

203) *Anonymous 85*. Ibn [. . .]. Bought the *ghulām* Ṣandal for 11 dinars. Alexandria. ENA 2727.37.

204) Anonymous 86. Brother of Umm Abū al-Ḥasan. A *jāriya* was part of his estate after his death. Fustat. T-S 8J7.10.

205) Anonymous 87. Husband of Sutayt bt. Nadiv. Bequeathed the *jāriya* Nasrīn to his wife. T-S NS J357.

206) Anonymous 88. Ibn [...]. Listed as the owner of a deceased enslaved woman. 1126. Fustat. T-S NS 320.7.

207) Anonymous 89. "Al-Nezer (the diadem)." Involved in the sale of a *waṣīfa*, seemingly as the purchaser. Fustat. T-S 8J10.9.

208) Anonymous 90. Owner(s) of Fāḍila? The *jāriya* Fāḍila was mentioned in a legal record. T-S NS J401e.

209) Anonymous 91. Paternal uncle of Joseph and Nissim b. Berekhya. Freed the *ghulām* Faraj. 11th c. Qayrawān. T-S 12.175.

Women Among the Slave-Owning Classes

210) Bahiyya bt. Ibn 'Awkal. Gave the *Edūmiyya* woman Nujūm as a gift to Joseph Bishr ha-Kohen. 11th c. T-S J3.44.

211) Fakhr bt. Abū al-Surūr. Bequeathed the woman Rahaj to her husband El'azar b. El'azar. 1182. Fustat. MS Heb. f 56/46v.

212) Fāṭima bt. 'Arabiyya. Owner of the *jāriya* Sha'af. T-S AS 202.415.

213) Furs bt. Zayn b. Abū al-Riḍā. Freed the woman Wafā', whom she had jointly owned with her two sisters. 1181. Fustat. T-S 8J12.3.

214) Ḥasab bt. El'azar b. El'azar. Inherited (along with her sister, Khifā') the woman Rahaj from her father. 1182. Fustat. MS Heb. f 56/46v.

215) Ḥasana bt. Menasse ha-Kohen. Bought the woman Iftikhār from her brother Abū al-Ḥasan al-Sayrafī Solomon ha-Kohen. 1126–27. Fustat. T-S Misc. 23.8.

216) 'Imrān bt. Abū al-Riḍā ha-Levi. Inherited the woman Misk from her father. 1172. Or. 1080 J142 + T-S Misc. 25.53.

217) Jāliya bt. Aaron ha-Kohen. Listed as the owner of a deceased freed woman. 1126. Fustat. T-S NS 320.7.

218) Karīma bt. Nuṣayr. A Kushite woman was part of her dowry. 1070. Halper 341 + Halper 348.

219) Khāliṣa bt. [. . .] Bought the Nubian woman Na'īm from Shemarya b. Ḥalfon. 1098. T-S 12.93.

220) Khulla bt. Shabbāt. Sold a *ghulām* at the time of her death. Ca. 1135. T-S 10J7.10.

221) Khulla bt. Joseph ha-Kohen. Sold an enslaved woman. T-S Ar. 29.49. Ca. 1134.

222) Khifā' bt. El'azar b. El'azar. Inherited (along with her sister Ḥasab) the woman Rahaj from her father. 1182. Fustat. MS Heb. f 56/46v.

223) Labwa. Purchased a minor Nubian girl from her husband Solomon b. Nathan. 1126. Fustat. PER H 23.

224) Michal bt. Yeshu'a. Part of a case involving the *shifḥa* Ẓarf and her son Muwaffaq. T-S 16.15.

225) Mubāraka bt. Samuel al-Qābisī. Owned a *jāriya* as part of her dowry and sold her to her brother Faraḥ. Fustat. T-S 10J9.32.

226) Mudallala bt. Solomon. Freed the man Makhlūf. 1085. Fustat. T-S Misc. 36.151.

227) Nafīsa bt. Kathīr b. al-Ṣaffūrī, widow of Jacob ha-Kohen Ibn al-M['-W-Ṣ-..] Sold the girl Tawfīq to Abū al-Barakāt b. Ibn Sha'yā. 1100–38. T-S NS 320.29.

228) Nasab bt. Zayn b. Abū al-Riḍā. Freed the woman Wafā', whom she had jointly owned with her two sisters. 1181. Fustat. T-S 8J12.3.

229) Sa'āda al-Nadīv. Listed as the owner of a deceased enslaved woman. 1126. Fustat. T-S NS 320.7.

230) Sāda bt. Zayn b. Abū al-Riḍā. Freed the woman Wafā', whom she had jointly owned with her two sisters. 1181. Fustat. T-S 8J12.3.

231) Sayyida bt. Ṣedaqa Ibn Ṭayyib. Sold the woman Tawfīq to Moses b. Yefet. 1100. Fustat. MS Heb. b 12/20.

232) Sitt al-Ahl bt. Abū al-Munā al-'Aṭṭār. Purchased the woman Fūq with money from her mother. 1143. Fustat or al-Maḥalla. T-S 13J3.3.

233) Sitt al-Ahl bt. Joseph b. Solomon. Her father purchased the woman Tawfīq for her. Fustat. T-S NS 320.15.

234) Sitt al-Aqrān b. Joseph ha-Kohen, wife of Judah b. 'Allān. Sold the Nubian woman Na'īm to Sitt al-Munā. 1108. Cairo. T-S 18J1.17.

235) Sitt al-Dalāl bt. Ḥananel. Freed or bequeathed the jāriya Munā. 1230. Fustat. T-S Misc. 25.107.

236) Sitt al-Dalāl bt. Abū al-B[. . .] Ibn al-[. . . .] b. Sa'dān. Sold the *'Ajamiyya* woman Qaḍīb to the trader Abū al-Bayyān al-Tājir Moses ha-Levi. 1157–58. T-S NS 320.17.

237) Sitt al-Fakhr bt. 'Amram ha-Levi. Married to Abū al-Faraj Yeshu'a b. Yoshiyya. Purchased an enslaved woman. Ca. 1134. T-S Ar. 29.49.

238) Sitt al-Fakhr bt. Jacob ha-Kohen. Bought the pregnant woman 'Ushshāq from Sitt al-Ḥusn bt. Abraham. T-S 13J6.7.

239) Sitt al-Fakhr bt. Ṭuviyya. Reported to her husband that their *jāriya* had been "lost" from the house. 1157. Fustat. T-S 12.585.

240) Sitt al-Gharb bt. Abū al-Faraj Ibn Semekh al-Da'wa, wife of the scribe Nathan b. Samuel (*ha-Nezer*). Mid-12th c. Freed the *ghulām* Munjid. T-S 13J30.7 + T-S NS J614.

241) Sitt al-Ḥasab. The woman Sha'al was part of her dowry. 1146. Or. 1080J49.

242) Sitt al-Ḥasab bt. Shela ha-Levi. Owned and freed the woman Ṣalaf. T-S 10J28.16.

243) Sitt al-Ḥusn bt. Abraham, wife of Yakhin. Sold the pregnant woman 'Ushshāq to Sitt al-Fakhr bt. Jacob ha-Kohen. T-S 13J6.7.

244) Sitt al-Ḥusn bt. Sa'āda. Sitt al-Ḥusn freed the girls Dhahab and Sitt al-Sumr. Ca. mid-12th c. T-S 13J22.2.

245) Sitt al-Nasab bt. Isaac Abū al-Munā. Sold the *jāriya* 'Alam, who was part of her *ketubba*. Received the Nubian *jāriya* Rahaj from her husband Abū al-Ḥasan Solomon ha-Kohen b. Menasse ha-Kohen. 1134. T-S 13J2.20

246) Sitt Qaḍīb Sāda bt. Abū al-Bayān. Bought the woman Saʿāda from Abū al-Barakāt [Yef]et b. Moses. 1198. T-S 13J3.16.

247) Sitt al-Khāṣṣa bt. Abū al-Barakāt b. Joseph al-Lebdī. The woman Zuhr was part of her dowry. 1146. Fustat. MS Heb. d 66/48 + 47.

248) Sitt al-Maʿālī bt. Abū al-Ḥasan al-Simsār. Had an unnamed *jāriya* as part of her dowry. MS Heb. f 56/42.

249) Sitt al-Milāḥ wife of Isaac b. Moses. Sold the Nubian woman ʿAlam to Abū Zikrī Yaḥyā. 1100–38. Fustat. T-S 20.41.

250) Sitt al-Munā b. Nathan, widow of Nahray b. Nissim. Bought the Nubian woman Naʿīm from Sitt al-Aqrān in 1108. Sold her to the Christian scribe ʿAbd al-Masīḥ b. Maqāra b. Harūn in 1115. Cairo. T-S 18J1.17r + v.

251) Sitt al-Riʾāsa 1. The woman ʿŪd al-Zān was part of her dowry. 1156. RNL Yevr.-Arab I 1700.25v, (T-S Misc.24.137.4). Probably the same woman as no. 252.

252) Sitt al-Riʾāsa 2. Took custody of the young girl Kashf from her brother Abū al-Ḥasan. Ca. 1160. T-S Misc. 24.137.4, (RNL Yevr.-Arab I 1700.25v). Probably the same woman as no. 251.

253) Sitt al-Riḍā bt. Mufarraj b. Khalaf. Bought the woman ʿAlam from Makhlūf b. Yaʿaqov. T-S 10J11.31.

254) Sitt al-Sirr. Inherited the woman ʿAfāf from her mother. ENA NS 48.6.

255) Sittūna. Her father, Abū al-Riḍā, gave her two *waṣīfa*s. 1120. probably Cairo/Fustat. T-S NS J185 c + d.

256) Sutayt bt. Nadiv. Inherited the *jāriya* Nasrīn from her husband. Late 11th c. T-S NS J357.

257) Sutayt bt. Yaʾīr. A *Rūmiyya* woman was included in her dowry. 995. T-S 16.70.

258) Turfa bt. ʿAmram. The woman Naʿīm was part of her dowry. 1100–38. Halper 342.

259) Zayn Sitt al-Dār. Bought the woman Ḥidhq from her brothers. 1105. Cairo. T-S 16.188.

260) Anonymous 92. Sitt al-Ḥ[. . .] Sent a six-year-old girl (*jāriya*) from India by her husband. 12th c. Western India. T-S NS J23.

261) Anonymous 93. Sitt al-[. . .], daughter of Maṣliaḥ ha-Kohen Gaon b. Solomon and wife of Abū al-Makārim. Owned (or at least used) the woman Ghazāl, though her husband Abū al-Makārim had control of the enslaved woman during their marriage. 1134. Or. 5566C16.

262) Anonymous 94. Widow of Abū ʿAlī Yefet Ibn al-Ṣabbāgh. Bequeathed part of a house to the freed *waṣīfa* Nushuww. ENA NS 16.11, T-S 16.44 + T-S 12.613.

263) Anonymous 95. Wife and daughter. Females. Inherited a *jāriya* from their dying husband and father. Ca. 1100. T-S 13J14.4.

264) Anonymous 96. Wife of Abū al-Baqā Ibn al-Muṣinn. Bequeathed a half share in the woman Misk to her husband Abū al-Baqā Ibn al-Muṣinn. T-S NS J32.

265) Anonymous 97. Wife of Abū al-Faraj al-Qazzāz. Owned a female slave. 1140–59. DK 232.1, T-S 10J17.22.

266) Anonymous 98. Wife of Mukarram b. Abū al-Baqā Ibn al-Muṣinn. Received a half share in the woman Misk from her mother, who was the sister-in-law of her father-in-law. T-S NS J32.

267) Anonymous 99. Inherited an *ʿabd* and a *jāriya* from her husband. 1219–20. Fustat. T-S NS J347.

268) Anonymous 100. Wife of Judah b. Moses Ibn Sighmār. Reported that the family's *jāriya* had run away. 1070. Fustat. Or. 1080J71.

269) Anonymous 101. Younger daughter of unnamed woman. Younger sister to Sitt al-Sirr. Inherited the woman Saʿāda and Saʿāda's son from her mother. ENA NS 48.6.

270) Anonymous 102. A bride who had two *waṣīfa*s and two *jāriya*s as part of her dowry. 1128–53. Fustat. T-S J1.29.

271) Anonymous 103. Received maintenance from her traveling husband for herself and her female servant. T-S NS J401k.

272) Anonymous 104. The *jāriya* Bal[ū]gh al-Munā was a part of her dowry. 1230. T-S NS J409.

273) Anonymous 105. Bequeathed two separate enslaved women to her children. ENA NS 48.6.

274) Anonymous 106. Reported that the woman Ṣayd wanted to marry the *ghulām* of Ibn Miṣbāḥ. Ca. 12th/13th c. Quṣ. L-G Arabic II.129, Or. 1080J25.

275) Anonymous 107.^ Mentioned that Sutayt (probably an enslaved woman) ran errands for the household. Ca. 1060. Fustat. ENA 2808.52.

276) Anonymous 108. Bride of [. . . Yefet] ha-Levi. Had the Indian woman named Ṣalaf as a part of her dowry. 1100–38. T-S 16.239.

277) Anonymous 109. Bride of Moses b. Jacob. The woman Saraf was a part of a woman's dowry. T-S 12.635.

278) Anonymous 110. A boy, Saʿd, and his mother were a part of her dowry. 1175. Or. 10653.5.

279) Anonymous 111. Sought to purchase a *shifḥa*. JRL B 3311.

280) Anonymous 112. Reported that her children and the family's *jāriya* were ill. MS Heb. d 76/60.

281) Anonymous 113. Sold a *Rūmī* man to her son. 12th c. T-S AS 147.8.

282) Anonymous 114. Daughter of Ṣadoq. Sold the woman Intijāb. 12th c. T-S NS 320.126.

283) Anonymous 115. Daughter of Ḥalfon b. Menasse. Asked her uncle to buy her an enslaved girl. 1100–38. Fustat and al-Bahnasā. T-S 13J21.18.

284) Anonymous 116. Sister-in-law of Abū al-Baqā Ibn al-Muṣinn. Owned a half share in the woman Misk, which she later bequeathed to her daughter. T-S NS J32.

285) Anonymous 117. Mother of Abū al-Ḥajjāj Joseph b. Elʿazar. Gave the three-year-old *waṣīfa* Dhahab to her brother Abū al-Ḥasan b. Yahboy. 1145. Fustat. T-S 12.140.

286) Anonymous 118. Mother of Abū al-ʿIzz b. Bishr. Owned the woman Tawfīq, possibly jointly with another family member. Alexandria. Halper 400.

287) Anonymous 119. "Sitt al-Ṣaghīra (the younger lady)." Mentioned in a letter as the owner of the *jāriya* Misk. T-S 10J11.11.

Slave Owners of Unknown Gender

288) Anonymous 120. Sold an enslaved woman to Joseph [. . .]. T-S NS 184.59.

289) Anonymous 121. Bought an unnamed woman from David ha-Levi. No date. T-S 13J7.15.

NOTES

Notes on the Text

1. Zinger, *Living with the Law*, xi–xii, provides further helpful context.

2. Foreman et al., "Writing About Slavery"; Johnson, "On Agency." See also the discussion in Rinehart, "Reparative Semantics."

3. On converting Seleucid years to the Common Era, see Goitein, *MS*, 1:355.

4. Ibid., 1:363.

Introduction

1. T-S 12.582. Hebrew translation in Goitein, "African Port of 'Aydhāb," and the English in Goitein, *Letters of Medieval Jewish Traders*, 335–38. Fauvelle-Aymar, *Golden Rhinoceros*, 106–10. 'Aydhāb was destroyed by the Mamluk sultanate's forces in the fifteenth century. The site is now in a disputed region along the modern Egyptian-Sudanese border. Peacock and Peacock, "Enigma of 'Aydhab."

2. This leader is Joshua b. Dosā. See Goitein, *Letters of Medieval Jewish Traders*, 336–37.

3. ". . . [your] s[on]" or perhaps [her] s[on]." T-S 12.582, l. 6. Goitein refers to this woman as "an abandoned concubine" following his translation of lines 6–7. I prefer "banished" based on the use of *anifta-hā* (you banished her). Goitein, *Letters of Medieval Jewish Traders*, 335–38. Friedman, *Dictionary of Medieval Judeo-Arabic*, 532. Following Shaun Marmon, I use the term concubine sparingly, unless the woman is expressly described as such. As Marmon stresses, any enslaved woman was vulnerable to sexual exploitation, even when she is not called specifically a concubine. The deposition from 'Aydhāb calls Ibn Jamāhir's banished woman a *jāriya*, the most common word used in this era to note a "slave girl" or woman. Idem, "Intersections of Gender, Sex, and Slavery."

4. T-S 12.582, ll. 6–7.

5. See further in this chapter for discussion about this storage room, called a *geniza*, and the sources cited in 28n. The papers were stored with the intent that they would later be given a ritual burial, ostensibly because they contained the written name of God and were not to be desecrated by profane destruction. Rebecca Jefferson's recent research illustrates that there were in fact many *genizot* (pl. of *geniza*) in Cairo and across the Middle East. See idem, *Cairo Genizah* and esp. her epilogue, 189–90.

6. Yagur, "Sa'āda the Enslaved Woman."

7. Hoyland, *In God's Path*, 79; Gilli-Elewy, "Provenance of Slaves"; Robinson, "Slavery in the Conquest Period."

8. Freamon, *Possessed by the Right Hand*, 20n1 and 20–87.

9. These connections and their bibliography are discussed throughout the book. Two additional and relevant sources are Silverstein, "From Markets to Marvels"; Rustow, "Kalah in the Lands of Java."

10. For some examples, see the relevant chapters in Perry et al., eds., *Cambridge World History of Slavery*; Pargas and Schiel, eds., *Global Slavery*; Zhang, "State and Slavery."

11. Eltis and Engerman, "Dependence, Servility, and Coerced Labor," 2. Enslavement as a universal threat is a central argument in Barker, *That Most Precious Merchandise*, 3, 10, 13, 31–8, 209.

12. Culbertson, ed., *Slaves and Households*; Franz, "Slavery in Islam," 61, 69, 91 passim.

13. Franz, "Slavery in Islam," 99, 101.

14. See the discussion in chap. 4 and the sources cited there.

15. Rowson, "Traffic in Boys"; Anooshahr, "Military Slavery," 365.

16. An additional exception is less clear cut. See Talbi, "Law and Economy in Ifrīqiya." Cf. Franz, "Slavery in Islam," 100–2, and Wickham, *Donkey and the Boat*, 159, 173.

17. Popović, *La Révolte des Esclaves* and its English edition Popović, *Revolt of African Slaves*; Talhami, "Zanj Rebellion Reconsidered"; Campbell, "East Africa"; Franz, "Slavery in Islam," 100–10; Ali, "Zanj Revolt"; Richardson, "Boundaries of Blackness." My own analysis is in Perry, "Slavery and Agency," and idem, "Slavery and the Slave Trade."

18. Urban, *Conquered Populations*, 106, 111–15, 125–27; Robinson, "Statistical Approaches," esp. 19–20.

19. Gordon, "Introduction," 4; Dann, "Between History and Historiography." See also Ruggles, "Mothers of a Hybrid Dynasty"; Richardson, "Singing Slave Girls"; and Ballan, "Borderland Anxieties."

20. On these developments, see Gordon, *Breaking of a Thousand Swords*; Franz, "Slavery in Islam," 110–20, and the literature cited in nn207–8. Cf. La Vaissière, *Samarcande et Samarra*. Robert Hoyland notes evidence of enslaved people serving in the army during the eighth century. Idem, *In God's Path*, 164–67.

21. Jackson, "Turkish Slaves"; Tor, "*Mamlūk* Loyalty"; idem, "Mamluks in the Military"; and Anooshahr, "Military Slavery." For the Fatimid period and Egypt, see Bacharach, "African Military Slaves"; Lev, "Army, Regime and Society"; idem, *State and Society*; and Zouache, "Remarks on the Blacks."

22. Sassanian: Lerner, "Seal of a Eunuch." Byzantine: Magdalino, "Paphlagonians"; Tougher, "In or Out?"; idem, *Eunuch*. Thanks to Lora Webb for these references. Islamic: Marmon, *Eunuchs*; Trabelsi, "Eunuchs, Power, and Slavery"; El-Cheikh, "Servants at the Gate"; El-Azhari, *Queens, Eunuchs and Concubines*; Montpetit, "Eunuchs."

23. Marmon, *Eunuchs*; Tolino, "Eunuchs in the Fatimid Empire."

24. Gordon and Hain, eds., *Concubines and Courtesans*.

25. Abbott, "Women and the State," esp. 351, 368; Gordon and Hain, eds., *Concubines and Courtesans*; Nielson, *Music and Musicians*.

26. Ibn al-Sāʿī, *Consorts of the Caliphs*; Gordon, "Place of Competition"; idem, "ʿArib Al-Ma'muniya"; Caswell, *Slave Girls of Baghdad*; Gordon and Hain, eds., *Concubines and Courtesans*; Kapitaikin, "David's Dancers"; Ettinghausen, "Early Realism," 162.

27. Perry, "Historicizing Slavery," esp. 133, 136, and the sources cited there.

28. The history of the Cairo *geniza*'s "discovery," dispersion, and collection is itself an object of study and one that requires ongoing investigation. Hoffman and Cole, *Sacred Trash*; Jefferson, *Cairo Genizah*; Rustow, *Lost Archive*. See also Cohen, "Geniza for Islamists."

29. This figure is subject to change as investigation of the *geniza* is ongoing. For recent figures, see Rustow, "Jewish Communal History" and idem, *Lost Archive*. The bulk of the manuscripts are not documentary, but rather biblical, liturgical, and rabbinic writings as well as works of literature, poetry, philosophy, medicine, and magic. See Ben-Shammai, "Medieval History"; Saar, "Geniza Magical Documents"; Chipman, "How to Read a Medical Prescription."

30. Wagner and Connolly, "Code-Switching."

31. Rustow, *Lost Archive*.

32. Rustow, *Heresy*, xx–xxi and n6.

33. Such joins are indicated in the notes by a plus sign (+) between the distinct shelf-marks that libraries use to identify manuscripts. Lior Wolf et al., "Identifying Join Candidates"; Choueka, "Computerizing the Cairo Genizah."

34. On *geniza* scholarship, see especially works cited by Assaf, Goitein, Friedman, Gil, Frenkel, and Yagur. Scholars of Arabic documents have also produced groundbreaking work on the history of slavery. E.g., Little, "Purchase Deeds for Slaves"; Rāġib, *Actes de vente*; Bruning, "Slave Trade Dynamics; idem, "Voluntary Enslavement"; idem, "Islamic Tombstones for Slaves." Khan's *Medieval Nubia* was published as I was completing this book, and I have not yet comprehensively integrated its findings or published sources into my research.

35. Goldberg, "Use and Abuse of Commercial Letters." See also Rustow, *Heresy*, xxi, and idem, *Lost Archive*, 1–2.

36. See especially the responsa of Abraham Maimonides studied in chap. 5 and published in Friedman, *Jewish Polygyny*, chap. 10. Other responsa are found in modern editions that are based on earlier manuscripts from the *geniza* and other collections.

37. See the discussion in chaps. 1, 5, and 7 of a responsum of Moses Maimonides published in Maimonides, *Responsa*, 2:373–75, no. 211.

38. Twersky, *Introduction to the Code*; idem, "Some Non-Halakic Aspects"; Cohen, *Maimonides and the Merchants*, 4–5.

39. Recently, Mark Cohen has shown the value of the *Mishneh Torah* for social and economic history of "everyday Jewish life in the Islamic world," especially when read alongside documents from the Cairo *geniza*. Cohen's insight holds for the history of slavery as well. Idem, *Maimonides and the Merchants*, 5.

40. See especially the discussion in chaps. 4 and 7.

41. The Hungarian scholar Vilmos Steiner published in 1909 a document about the slave-owning silk weaver Abū al-Faraj that features in chap. 5. See Steiner, *Három arab kézirat*. The earliest essays that focus on slavery and the slave trade are Assaf, "Slaves and the Slave Trade" (1939); and Assaf, "Slaves and the Slave Trade" (1940). The 1939 essay is republished in Assaf, "Slaves and the Jewish Trade in Slaves" (1965).

42. Goitein, *MS*, 1:130–47. This 1967 publication is a revised version of an earlier work: Goitein, "Slaves and Slave Girls." Brief discussions of slavery are numerous in his additional publications and other parts of *MS*. Volume 6 of *MS* (edited by Paula Sanders) is a comprehensive index and a guide to those references.

43. Today much of this archive is available through the Princeton Geniza Project's website.

44. The works of Goitein and other scholars are cited more comprehensively in the book's bibliography. A recent triple issue (vol. 32, nos. 2–4) of the journal *Jewish History* (2019) provides a view of the state of the field.

45. Friedman, "Monogamy Clause"; Friedman, "Master and Slave Girl"; Friedman, "Pre-Nuptial Agreements"; Friedman, "Polygyny in Jewish Tradition"; Friedman, *Jewish Polygyny*; Ashur, "The India Trade"; Ashur, "Protecting the Wife's Rights"; Ashur, "Engagement and Betrothal Documents."

46. Frenkel, "Slavery in Medieval Jewish Society"; Krakowski, *Coming of Age*; Zinger, *Living with the Law*; Zinger, "'She Aims to Harass Him.'"

47. Ghosh, "Slave of MS. H.6."; Ghosh, *Antique Land.* Goitein and Friedman, *India Traders*; Goitein and Friedman, eds., *Abraham Ben Yijū.* Cf. Gamliel, "Aśu the Convert."

48. Yagur, "The Community's Borders"; Yagur, "Religious Identity."

49. Cohen, *Poverty and Charity*; Cohen, *Voice of the Poor.*

50. Margariti, *Aden*; Goldberg, *Trade and Institutions*; Ackermann-Lieberman, *Business of Identity*; Ackerman-Lieberman, "Legal Writing"; Ackermann-Lieberman and Yildirim, "Slavery, Slave Trade"; Goldberg, "Goitein's *A Mediterranean Society.*"

51. Rustow, *Heresy*; Rustow, "Jewish Communal History"; Rustow, "Formal and Informal Patronage"; Rustow, *Lost Archive.*

52. Goitein, *MS*, 1:140, 211, and Goitein and Friedman, *India Traders*, 17. Gil and Frenkel see some evidence for what we might call Jewish "wholesale" slave trading in the 9th c. See Gil, *Jews in Islamic Countries*, 607–14, esp. 607, and Frenkel, "Slave Trade," esp. 143–50. I critique how the evidence for the Jewish Rādhānite traders has been interpreted. See chap. 2. On this topic for medieval Europe, see Toch, "Jewish Slave Trade."

53. They were wholesale traders of other commodities like flax and olive oil. I emphasize that this conclusion is based on reading the evidence. It is not that wholesale slave trading by individual Jews is unthinkable in every era. See the sources cited in the next note.

54. There is quite limited evidence for Iraq. See the responsum of Naḥshon Gaon (ninth century) discussed separately in Frenkel, "Slave Trade," 146. For Iberia see Bensch, "Prizes of War," 78, and Ray, *Sephardic Frontier*, 65.

55. Toch, "Jewish Slave Trade."

56. Toch, "Jewish Slave Trade."

57. Faber, *Jews, Slaves, and the Slave Trade*; Friedman, *Jews and the American Slave Trade.*

58. Ward, "Skin in the Game."

59. Two recent works that address these medieval-modern malconnections are Albin et al., eds., *Whose Middle Ages?*; Whitaker, *Black Metaphors.*

60. Arabic sources that predate the *geniza* materials also hint at a mode of decentralized slave trading that historians have overlooked. Bruning, "Slave Trade Dynamics."

61. Perry, "Goitein."

62. The regional trade, as opposed to interregional (long-distance) trade, and commodities like flax were the mainstays of *geniza* merchants' business in the eleventh-century Mediterranean. Goldberg, *Trade and Institutions*, 20, 56–57, 276–79 passim.

63. Yerushalmi, "Servants of Kings," and the sources at 272n28; Abulafia, "Servitude of Jews." On *dhimmī* status: Cohen, *Crescent and Cross*, esp. 52–74; idem, "Islamic Policy"; Levy-Rubin, "*Shurūṭ ʿUmār*"; idem, *Non-Muslims.*

64. Yerushalmi, "Servants of Kings"; Rustow, *Heresy*, esp. 67–133; idem, "Limits of Communal Autonomy."

65. Schorsch, *Jews and Blacks*, 3. See also the discussion in the conclusion. National historiographies have downplayed the role of medieval slavery in nation-building and empire-building. For one example, see Wyatt, "Slavery in Northern Europe."

66. Wasserstein, "Samuel ibn Naghrīla"; Targarona, "Ibn Naghrella, Samuel."

67. Ibn Buṭlān warned of fraud by slave traders. Lewis, ed., *Islam*, 233–34. See also Ibn al-Mujāwir's observation in chap. 7.

68. See the sources cited in chap. 1, 71n.

69. Barker, *That Most Precious Merchandise*; Bruning, "Slave Trade Dynamics."

70. Joseph Miller focused on how marginal actors used slavery as a strategy to challenge the dominance of other groups in society. I use slave trading and slave owning as a strategy in a broad set of senses. Miller, *Problem of Slavery*. Jeff Fynn-Paul proposes that the emergence of "slaving" and "non-slaving" zones in the greater Mediterranean, including the Islamic world, can be explained partly by differences between "organized" and "disorganized" states. Fynn-Paul, "Empire, Monotheism and Slavery"; idem, "Introduction." I argue that historians need to consider the political economies of "non-slaving" zones to understand why polities like Nubia and some Beja tribes supplied enslaved people to Egypt. It was not due to disorganization or because they were forced to do so for most of the period before 1250.

71. See the discussion in chap. 2, and Perry, "Western Indian Ocean," esp. 135–48.

72. Spaulding, "Medieval Christian Nubia"; Makki, "Spatial Ecology of Power."

73. Robinson, "Statistical Approaches"; Urban, *Conquered Populations.*

74. Despret, "Interagency"; Schiel et al., "Slaves, Horses, and Dogs"; Wagner, "Slave Voices."

75. Despret, "Interagency," 44.

76. Hanß and Schiel, "Semantics, Practices and Transcultural Perspectives," 17–20; Walter Johnson, "Agency."

77. Krakowski, *Coming of Age.*

78. Karras's works are numerous. See esp. idem, *Boys to Men*. Blumenthal, *Enemies and Familiars*, esp. chap. 5. Blumenthal's book also models an integrative approach to the study of medieval slavery that cuts across scales from the interregional slave trade, to the household, and finally to microhistories of individual enslaved people's lives. Armstrong-Partida, *Defiant Priests*. Note also Oded Zinger's analysis of Jewish masculinity based on *geniza* documents in idem, *Living with the Law*, 149–50, which I discuss further in this book's conclusion.

79. Foucault, "The Subject and Power," 219–26. Glymph, "Paper Tracings."

80. Johnson, "On Agency."

81. Fontaine, "Early Medieval Slave-Trading"; Raffield, "Slave Markets"; Lane, "Slavery in Africa." Cf. Alexander, "Islam, Archaeology, and Slavery."

82. Lane, "Slavery in Africa," 541.

83. Endelman, "Defense of Jewish Social History."

84. Hartman, "Venus in Two Acts."

85. On "pulses," see Reilly, *Slavery, Agriculture, and Malaria*, 134.

86. Spaulding, "Medieval Christian Nubia."

87. I retain lowercase black when it is used as an adjective, as with skin color. I capitalize Black when a source uses it as a type of person or group of people, or when it is used in *geniza* writings to denote a slave. See the examples in chap. 3.

88. In this regard, historian Moshe Yagur's work is foundational: idem, "Sa'āda the Enslaved Woman," and idem, *Crossing the Line*. Goitein was sensitive to some of these themes, though he sometimes downplayed the violence that attended what he viewed as medieval Jews' humanistic tendencies. Perry, "Goitein."

Chapter 1. Jewish Slave-Owning in an Islamic Society

1. Cohen, *Under Crescent and Cross*; Levy-Rubin, *Non-Muslims*; idem, "*Shurūṭ 'Umar*." Jews use Islamic courts: Zinger, "'She Aims to Harass Him'"; idem, *Living with the Law*. Petitions to *maẓālim* tribunals (including ones by Jewish petitioners): Rustow, "Fatimid Petition"; Tillier, "Mazalim"; Rustow, *Lost Archive*.

2. Franz, "Slavery in Islam," 52–53 and 69; Urban, *Conquered Populations*, 6–9. On slavery in the Quran: Brockopp, "Slaves and Slavery." Freamon emphasizes the Quran's "emancipatory ethic" in idem, *Possessed by the Right Hand*, 10, 96–97, 118, 131–32, 137, 139, 156, 163 passim. See also see Schacht, *Introduction to Islamic Law*; Brunschvig, "'Abd"; Katz, "Concubinage, in Islamic Law"; idem, "Gender and Law"; Marmon, "Domestic Slavery"; Ali, *Marriage and Slavery*; idem, "Concubinage and Consent"; Osswald, *Islamiche Sklavenrecht*; Brown, *Slavery & Islam*; Marmon, "Intersections of Gender, Sex, and Slavery."

3. Aristotle: Franz, "Slavery in Islam," 68, and the sources cited in n42. For a broader view of ideas about slavery in Greek and Roman antiquity, see Garnsey, *Ideas of Slavery* and esp. 107–27 on Aristotle.

4. "Theoretically" in the sense that slave traders sometimes violated this law. Evidence of this violation is limited in the period of this study but increases during the late medieval and early modern period. See Hunwick, "Aḥmad Bābā"; Brown, *Slavery & Islam*, 89–90; Hagedorn, *Domestic Slavery*, 56.

5. Hogendorn, "Hideous Trade," 140–42; Tougher, "In or Out?," 150, 152n4, 155n79; idem, *Eunuch*, 64.

6. On the origins of the *umm walad* laws, see Schacht, "Umm Al-Walad"; Brockopp, *Early Mālikī Law*; Mirza, "Remembering the Umm al-Walad"; Urban, *Conquered Populations*, 7, 77–78, and 106–31; and Katz, "Concubinage, in Islamic Law."

7. Paternity denied: Marmon, "Intersections of Gender, Sex, and Slavery," 195–98, 208–9, and Powers, "Kadijustiz or *Qāḍī*-Justice?"

8. Brunschvig, "'Abd."

9. Enslaved people marry: Raziq, "Un document." In the *geniza* records, Alan Elbaum recently discovered a marriage contract in Arabic script between enslaved people. T-S NS 157.58. The verso contains text from a Passover *haggada*.

10. Rāġib, *Actes de vente*, 1:13–133. See also Marmon, "Intersections of Gender, Sex, and Slavery," 207–12.

11. Published Islamic manumission documents: Khan, *Early Islamic Khurasan*, 152–65.

12. Manumission and piety: Lewis, *Race and Slavery*, 5–6; Brunschvig, "'Abd." For the Jewish context, see *BT*, *Giṭṭin*, 37b and *MT*, *Hilkhot 'avadim* (Laws of Slavery), 9:6. Manumissions could be undermined: de la Puente, "Islamic Law" and see the discussion in chap. 6.

13. Heffening and Endress, "Tadbīr"; Brunschvig, "'Abd."

14. *Kitāba* and the laws of *umm walad*: Brockopp, *Early Mālikī Law*.

15. Brockopp, *Early Mālikī Law*.

16. The meaning and practice of *walā'* and *mawlā* vary across historical contexts. See Crone and Wensinck, "Mawlā"; Urban, *Conquered Populations*, 20–24. The later Ottoman context: Zilfi, *Women and Slavery*, 134–35; Aykan, "Freedom, Kinship, and the Market"; Y. Frenkel, "Slavery in 17th-Century Ottoman Jerusalem," 240–41.

17. Goitein, *MS*, 1:145. Goitein argues that the legal position of Jewish freed slaves was different from that of their counterparts in Islamic law. For one thing, Jewish masters did not retain or gain any rights to their freed slaves' property, person, or offspring. While Jewish law may be clear on this subject, social practice did not always conform to these prescriptions. See chaps. 6 and 8.

18. *Dina de-malkhuta dina*. Elon, *Jewish Law*, 1:64–74. Ackerman-Liberman argues that scholars should not assume that this principle was always followed, especially in commercial law. See idem, *Business of Identity*, 10, 330n50.

19. See especially the analysis of Yaṣe'a's conversion to Islam in chap. 7.

20. Slaves obligated in the same commandments as Jewish women: *BT*, *Yevamot*, 45b, *Ḥagiga*, 4a; *MT*, *Hilkhot 'avadim*, 5:5. Jewish law exempted women and enslaved people from commandments that were required to be performed at appointed times. *BT*, *Qiddushin*, 29a.

21. T-S 18J1.17r, published in Perry, "Aramaic Bill of Sale." See also chap. 3.

22. Manumission is discussed esp. in chap 8. See also Goitein, *MS*, 1:144–47; Yagur, *Crossing the Line*, esp. chap. 1; idem, "Religious Identity," esp. chap. 2 and the document descriptions, transcriptions, and Hebrew translations on 278–348. An English translation of one deed of manumission from the *geniza* (T-S 8J12.2) is in Goitein, *MS*, 5:149–50. See figure 8.1 and the discussion in chap. 8.

23. Biblical writings justify and describe the enslavement of Canaanites, but the term "Canaanite slave" was only coined in the postbiblical period. Marienberg, "'Canaanites.'" "Canaanite" is one of the types of enslaved people suggested by Hai Gaon in his manual of legal formularies. Assaf, ed., *Book of Formularies*, 28. See also *MT*, *Hilkhot 'avadim*, 5–9.

24. *MT*, *Hilkhot 'avadim*, esp. 1–4.

25. These two categories resemble what Orlando Patterson calls the "intrusive" and "extrusive" modes of slavery. However, in contrast to Patterson's analysis, the biblical "Hebrew slave" is better understood as an "extrusive" example of an insider with a fallen status. What medieval jurists thought of as the Canaanite slave corresponds better to his "intrusive" model. Patterson, *Slavery and Social Death*, esp. 38–45.

26. *MT*, *Hilkhot 'avadim*, esp. 5–9. In theory, owners were required to free their Canaanite slave if they caused certain types of physical harm, such as cutting off a slave's finger or blinding them. Enslaved people could also purchase their freedom. *MT*, *Hilkhot 'avadim*, 5–8. Neither of these phenomena are documented in the *geniza*.

27. The precise timing of Hebrew slavery's disappearance remains unclear. See also *MT*, *Hilkhot 'avadim*, chap. 1, and esp. 1:10, on the obsolescence of Hebrew slavery and the Jubilee year in medieval Jewish law. Cf. *MT*, *Hilkhot 'avadim*, 9:4.

28. Lemche, "Manumission"; Hezser, "Slavery and the Jews," 443.

29. For the *geniza* period, Yagur, "Religious Identity"; idem, "Community's Borders"; idem, *Crossing the Line*. For antiquity, see Hezser, "Slavery and the Jews," 441–44. Historian Evyatar Marienberg shows that enslaved people and servants were called "Canaanites" in medieval Europe. Idem, "'Canaanites.'"

30. See Finkelstein, *Conversion*, esp. 108–58 and the sources cited there. Yagur, "Religious Identity"; idem, "Community's Borders"; idem, *Crossing the Line*.

31. *Geṭ shiḥrur* and *sheṭar ḥerut* are commonly used in bills of manumission from the *geniza*. See, for example, T-S 8J12.1, T-S 8J12.2, T-S 8J12.3, T-S 8J12.4, T-S 10J28.16, and the ninth-century formulary partially preserved in T-S NS 211.1 + T-S J3.16 and cited in David, "Formulae," 172–75.

32. T-S 8J12.2. See the discussion in chap. 8.

33. For a concise summary of this legend, its treatment in gaonic responsa, and a short bibliography, see Wacholder, "Halakhah," 99–101; Gil, *Jews in Islamic Countries*, 58–81; Franklin, *This Noble House*, 58 passim; Shweka, "Bustanay." See also 40n in this chapter.

34. *BT*, *Giṭṭin*, 81b. Translation from Wacholder, "Halakhah," 100. Brody, *Teshuvot Rav Natronai*, II:397–98, n6.

35. Wacholder, "Halakhah," 100. See Brody, *Teshuvot Rav Natronai*, II: 397–98. Responsum no. 261 and especially 398n6.

36. Wacholder, "Halakhah," 100. Wacholder identifies Aaron as "[a]nother Sura Gaon," but I have not found evidence of a Suran Gaon with the name Aaron. See "Chronology of the Geonim" in Brody, *The Geonim of Babylonia*, 344–45. There is a Pumbedita Gaon, Aaron b. Joseph (943–60). See also Brody, *Teshuvot Rav Natronai*, II:397–98 and n 8. On Aaron Gaon, see Franklin, "Ibn Sarjado, Aaron (Khalaf)."

37. Brody, *Teshuvot Rav Natronai*, 2:399, no. 262; Nissim b. Ḥayyim Moda'i, *Teshuvot Ha-Geonim: Sha'are Ṣedeq*, pt. 3, sec. 5, no. 38. On Natronai's historical context, see Brody, *Teshuvot Rav Natronai*, 1:69–94 and esp. 70n12 on his linguistic milieu. Translation based on Frenkel, "Slavery in Medieval Jewish Society," 255.

38. Chwat, "Al-Fāsī." "The Rif" is an acronym for Rabbi Isaac al-Fāsī (d. 1103).

39. Joseph Qaro, *Kesef Mishneh*, *'Avadim*, 9:1. The responsa of later Iberian jurists (late thirteenth and fourteenth centuries) show that Jewish men, particularly in the Christian kingdoms of Aragon and Castile, experimented with a variety of extramarital sexual relationships, including those with single Jewish women, single Muslim women, and enslaved women. Assis, "Sexual Behaviour," and Kanarfogel, "Rabbinic Attitudes," 17–26.

40. The *geniza* contains two copies of a responsum that discuss the same case. The first is T-S 13G1. Solomon Schechter indicates that T-S 13G1 is more complete than the edition in *Sha're Ṣedeq*. See Schechter, "Saadyana." Schechter also publishes here T-S 8G1, another copy of the same responsum as T-S 13G1. The second document is T-S NS 298.6 + ENA 4012.1 + BL Or. 5552.4. Gil believes that these three fragments are in the hand of Sahlān b. Abraham, the head of the Iraqi congregation in Fustat (ca. 1034–49/50). See Gil, *Kingdom of Ishmael*, I:1–10; Rustow, "Sahlān ben Abraham." The last fragment contains the date 1352 of the Seleucid era corresponding to 1040–41. George Margoliouth notes that BL Or. 5552.4 presents a different narrative of the story in which Bustanay only has one wife, the slave woman granted him by Caliph 'Umar al-Khaṭṭāb. A salient detail remains the same: Bustanay did not emancipate her

before she gave birth to his children. This version of events omits the later conflict between Bustanay's children over who are rightful heirs. See Margoliouth, "Some British Museum Genizah Texts," 303.

41. Brody identifies two responsa attributed to Natronai b. Hilai in the Taylor-Schechter Geniza New Series collection. See T-S NS 288.18 and T-S NS 298.71, identified in Robert Brody, ed., *Hand-List*, 175, 194.

42. Scholarly literature about Moses Maimonides is vast. Two scholarly biographies are Kraemer, *Maimonides*, and Stroumsa, *Maimonides in His World.*

43. *MT*, *Hilkhot mechira* (the Laws of Sale), 15:12: *she-ayn ha-'avadim le-tashemish ha-miṭa.*

44. *MT*, *'avadim*, 9:1.

45. *MT*, *'avadim*, 9:2.

46. *MT*, *Hilkhot Issurei bi'a* (Laws of Forbidden Intercourse), 12:11–16.

47. Slave owners in Islamic law also owned their female slaves' sexual organ. Ali, *Marriage and Slavery*, 183.

48. *MT*, *Hilkhot 'avadim*, 9:6.

49. Some biblical scholars argue that the Hebrew term *pilegesh* (pl. *pilagshim*) should be left untranslated because its meaning varies. See Stone, "Marriage," and Scott-Patterson, "Compendium Pilegesh(ium)."

50. *MT*, *Hilkhot melakhim u-milḥamot* (Laws of Kings and Wars), 4:4. See also the discussion of conscript labor and the taking of women and children as war captives in *MT*, *Hilkhot melakhim u-milḥamot*, chaps. 4–8. In his time, Maimonides defined the *pilegesh* in comparison with a wife following the tradition of the Babylonian Talmud. Wives had both a betrothal (*qiddushin*) and a wedding contract (*ketubba*) that gave them certain rights in marriage and divorce. The *pilegesh*, in contrast, has neither betrothal nor a *ketubba*. The king acquired the *pilegesh* through force and for himself alone (*be-yiḥud*). *MT*, *Hilkhot melakhim u-milḥamot*, 4:4; *BT*, *Sanhedrin*, 21a. Cf. *YT*, *Ketubbot*, 5:2, and *Yevamot*, 2:4.

51. Deuteronomy 21:10–14; *BT*, *Yevamot*, 47b–48a; *MT*, *Hilkhot melakhim u-milḥamot*, 8:2–9. On this law, see Finkelstein, *Conversion*, 148–58; Friedman, *Polygyny*, 335–36; Yagur, "Captives, Converts, and Renegades"; idem, "Shaving Hair"; Rey, "Reexamination"; Yagur, *Crossing the Line*, 216.

52. The monthlong waiting period was probably also prescribed so any pregnancy might be known during that time. Rey, "Reexamination," 45.

53. Maimonides, *Responsa*, 2:373–75, no. 211. This case is discussed further in chaps. 3 and 7.

54. Maimonides, *Responsa*, 2:373–75, no. 211.

55. See the ruling of Abraham Maimonides in his responsum as analyzed in chap. 5.

56. *MT*, *Naḥalot* (Laws of Inheritance), 4:6.

57. The ban (*ḥerem*), or excommunication, was one tool that Jews could use as a penalty. See further discussion about excommunication as a tool to punish Jewish slave owners in chap. 5. The nature of power in the Jewish community of Fatimid Egypt and the efficacy of the ban are central themes in Rustow, *Heresy*, chap. 8, and esp. xviii, 204–6, and 205n12. See also the discussion about the limited power of Jewish institutions in Egypt to enforce rulings about marriage and family law, see Krakowski, *Coming of Age*, 252–53, and Zinger, *Living with the Law*, 12, 21, 144, 151–53 passim.

58. Goitein, "Interplay," 72, 75; Friedman, *Jewish Polygyny*, 32–34.

59. Krakowski, *Coming of Age*, 4, 299–303. Oded Zinger's findings are also relevant here. Even though Egyptian Jews had access to Islamic courts, they preferred Jewish legal institutions as their "first port of call." Idem, *Living with the Law*, 12, 145–46.

60. Specifically, the mercantile class that was the largest class of Jewish slave owners. See chap. 4 and figure 4.1, and note Rustow, "Genizah and Jewish Communal History," 301, 309–11.

61. See further discussion about Ibn Jamāhir's confrontation with other Jewish merchants in the introduction and in chap. 5.

62. El-Leithy, "Coptic Culture and Conversion," 383; Shenoda, "Displacing *Dhimmī*," 594. Regarding slavery and concubinage in Syriac Christian communities, see Weitz, *Between Christ and Caliph*; idem, "Slavery and the Historiography of Non-Muslims."

63. El-Leithy, "Coptic Culture and Conversion," 383.

64. El-Leithy, "Coptic Culture and Conversion," 383–84 and 384n41.

65. El-Leithy, "Coptic Culture and Conversion," 385–89.

66. El-Leithy, "Coptic Culture and Conversion," 383.

67. *MT*, *Hilkhot ʿavadim*, 6–7, deal extensively with how such writs should (and should not) be written. Divorce deeds and writs of manumission share many features. See David, "Formulae of the Bill of Divorce."

68. As Zinger notes, Copts in Egypt did not maintain a system of courts. Instead, they used documents produced by Muslim notaries. Idem, *Living with the Law*, 154–55, 214–15n43–44.

69. T-S 18J1.17v, published in Perry, "Supplementary Deed of Sale"; T-S Ar. 42.174, published in Khan, ed., *ALAD*, no. 56, pp. 262–63, and ʿAodeh, "Eleventh Century Letters," no. 5, pp. 219–20.

70. Oded Zinger, "'She Aims to Harass Him.'"

71. al-Maqrīzī, *Ittiʿāẓ al-ḥunafāʾ*, II:53; Walker, *Caliph of Cairo*, 65–66.

72. This woman, Raṣad, gave birth to the future caliph al-Mustanṣir. Calderini, "Sayyida Raṣad." And see chap. 2.

73. Baron, "Ghetto and Emancipation"; Biale, *Power and Powerlessness*; Yerushalmi, "Servants of Kings"; Rustow, *Heresy*, esp. part 2 of the book and in xvii–xix, xxxvxxxiii, 347–55; idem, "Limits of Communal Autonomy"; idem, *Lost Archive*, esp. 253–54, 265–67, 403–4. On the reception of Baron's scholarship including and beyond "Ghetto and Emancipation," see Engel, "Colleague Not a Sacred Authority" and the other essays in the same issue of *AJS Review*. This book builds on Baron's and Yerushalmi's arguments by arguing that Jewish subordination and privilege were often linked, and Jews exercised power within this framework. Jewish slave-owning illustrates this dynamic. See also Schorsch, *Jews and Blacks*, 3. There is also an analogy to be made with Jews and Whiteness in the United States as a force that alternates between empowering some Jews and imperiling them. See Dollinger, *Black Power, Jewish Politics*, 65, 100–1; Goldstein, *Price of Whiteness*.

Chapter 2. Parsing the Slave Trade to Egypt

1. Jawhar: Monés, "Djawhar al-Ṣiḳillī" and the sources cited there. The Fatimid army: Yaacov Lev, "Army, Regime and Society"; Zouache, "Remarks on the Blacks."

2. Founding of Fatimid Cairo: Raymond, *Cairo*, 31–79.

3. Bacharach, "African Military Slaves"; Lev, "Army Regime, and Society"; Zouache, "Remarks on Blacks."

4. Cortese and Calderini, *Women and the Fatimids*, 78. Gift of slaves to al-Ḥākim: Ibn ʿIdhārī al-Marrākushī, *Al-Bayān al-mughrib*, 1:261. Gift to al-Ẓāhir and his reciprocity: al-Qaddūmī, *Book of Gifts*, 104–5.

5. Gift from Denia: al-Qaddūmī, *Book of Gifts*, 113. On the gift from Yemen, see this chapter.

6. It was probably Constantine IX. An Ottoman-era copy of an eleventh-century source provides the basis for al-Qaddūmī's translation. The identity of the original author is disputed. See al-Qaddūmī, *Book of Gifts*, 11–13. This manuscript states that Michael sent the gift in 444 AH/1053 CE. See idem, *Book of Gifts*, 110. Constantine still ruled at this time. Later Mamluk-era sources confused the dates for the reigns of Constantine IX and Michael VI: Mathew Barber, "Reappraising the Arabic Accounts," 191–93.

7. Al-Qaddūmī, *Book of Gifts*, 110–11.

8. See Ibn Buṭlān's remark about the danger of purchasing enslaved people who had worked in the palace in chap. 7.

9. See introduction 70n and the sources cited there. Enslaved people as strategists are studied in chap. 7.

10. This is a variation on a larger historiographical tendency that Hannah Barker calls the "black box problem." See idem, "The 14th-Century Tatar-Circassian Shift?"

11. Al-Musabbiḥī, *Akhbār Miṣr*, 34; Beshir, "New Light."

12. Here, "origins" in Islamic history. There is a longer history of Egyptian-Nubian diplomacy and other entanglements: Burstein, "Hellenistic Fringe," 41; Edwards, "Slavery and Slaving," 82–87.

13. Halm, "Nubische Baqṭ," 68–69.

14. Halm, "Nubische Baqṭ," 69. The governor was ʿAbd Allāh b. Saʿd b. Abī Sarḥ (d. 656–58?). See Becker, "ʿAbd Allāh b. Saʿd."

15. Løkkegaard, "Baḳṭ"; Sijpesteijn, "Baqṭ"; Shinnie, "Christian Nubia"; Adams, "Baqt Treaty"; Spaulding, "Medieval Christian Nubia"; Edwards, "Slavery and Slaving."

16. Evidence in the Qaṣr Ibrīm letter indicates that the Nubians had state archives. See Hinds and Sakkout, "Letter from the Governor of Egypt."

17. Spaulding, "Medieval Christian Nubia," 579–80.

18. Hinds and Sakkout, "A Letter"; Fauvelle-Aymar, *The Golden Rhinoceros*, 29–35. My translation is based on the edition of Hinds and Sakkout.

19. On the date, see Munro-Hay, "Kings and Kingdoms of Ancient Nubia," 104. Cf. Vantini, *Oriental Sources*, 130n11.

20. As translated in Vantini, *Oriental Sources*, 420.

21. Bruning, "Slave Trade Dynamics," 685–88.

22. al-Maqrīzī, *al-Khiṭaṭ*, 1: 369–72. Halm, *Nubische Baqṭ*, 88–89. See also al-Maqrīzī, *Ittiʿāẓ al-ḥunāfāʾ*, 2:222.

23. al-Masʿūdī, *Murūj al-dhahab*, 2:126, 129–31. See the translation of the relevant passage in Halm, *Nubische Baqṭ*, 87.

24. al-Musabbiḥī, *Akhbār Miṣr*, 11–12. Beshir, "New Light," 16.

25. In the area of Wādī al-ʿAllāqī to be more specific. Power, *Red Sea*, esp. 158–75; Weschenfelder, "Integration of the Eastern Desert"; Bramoullé, "Les ports du pays beja."

26. Garcin, *Centre Musulman*; Loiseau, "L'histoire désurbanisée."

27. T-S AS 149.3. I made small changes to Goitein's translation in *MS*, 5:69. Goitein wrote to Claude Cahen in late July 1975 after he first read this document in Cambridge. Cahen passed on Goitein's reply to Jean Claude Garcin, who replied in September 1975. Their correspondence can be read in PGP under the above shelf mark.

28. Sayyid, ed., *Fatimids and Their Successors*, 84–94 (Arabic), English summary by Walker and Pomerantz in the same volume, 50–52. See also Qutbuddin, "Idrīs ʿImād al-Dīn."

29. ʿAlī was the founder of the Ṣulayḥid dynasty and a religious emissary (*dāʿī*) of the Fatimid-Ismāʿīlī caliphate. See Smith, "Ṣulayḥids."

30. I am preparing an article that analyzes this *geniza* letter alongside the report in *ʿUyūn al-akhbār* in greater detail.

31. Sayyid, ed., *Fatimids and Their Successors*, 88 (Arabic), 51 (English summary).

32. Al-Qaddūmī, *Book of Gifts*, 116–17, 229–31.

33. Bruning, "Slave Trade Dynamics," 686. See also 20n in this chapter.

34. A recent history of the Crusades: Cobb, *Race for Paradise*. A study based on *geniza* sources: Brendan G. Goldman, "Arabic-Speaking Jews in Crusader Syria." Warfare during the Crusades did generate captives who could be enslaved or ransomed: Friedman, *Encounter Between Enemies*; Smith, "Business of Human Trafficking." I have not found a connection between the Crusades and the origins of enslaved people in Egyptian Jewish households, but this topic still needs to be studied fully.

35. The *hadiyya* is a gift given with the expectation of reciprocity. Another type of gift (*hiba*) is given without the expectation of reciprocity. See al-Qaddūmī, *Book of Gifts*, 4–5; Rosenthal et al., "Hiba"; Bellefonds, "Hiba."

36. The *baqṭ* was a historical precedent that Islamic jurists used to think through different legal questions. The *baqṭ*'s durability in legal discourse, however, does not indicate the persistence of this historical agreement's actual practice over time. On the legal discussion: al-Khalidi, "The Baqt Treaty Under Islamic Law."

37. In his attempts to build a census for the slave trade out of Africa and to Egypt, the historian Ralph Austen recognizes the limits of the premodern evidence and notes that the data for the *baqṭ* are "problematic." He thus does not use reports of it to extrapolate the volume of trade to Egypt per annum. Austen, "Mediterranean Islamic Slave Trade," 215, 216, 219, 220. Following Benjamin Reilly, we might say that the slave trade to parts of the Islamic imperium "pulsed," or waxed and waned, over time: Reilly, *Slavery, Agriculture, and Malaria*, 134. I do not have confidence that the sources currently permit a census such as scholars of early modern slavery have been able to create. I therefore argue instead for deeper historical contextualization and description of the evidence that we do have. See my discussion of reports about the numbers of enslaved soldiers in the Fatimid army and then about the Rādhānites later in this chapter. For an incisive critique that cautions us not to let the enumeration of bodies overshadow our attention to the "pained intimacy" of slavery and its afterlives among the descendants of enslaved people, see Johnson, "Markup Bodies."

For my tentative thinking about the enslaved population as a proportion of the Egyptian community in Cairo, see 26n in the conclusion.

38. The state sought men, but it seems likely that women and children would have been trafficked alongside them. In the later Mamluk-period, slave traders who dealt in boys destined for military slavery also traded in girls. See Barker, "Reconnecting with the Homeland."

39. See the discussion in the introduction.

40. Lev, "Army, Regime and Society," 340.

41. The Ayyubid army was also multiethnic, but these sultans preferred Turkish and Kurdish troops: Bacharach, "African Military Slaves," esp. 486–91.

42. Bacharach, "African Military Slaves," 483–84; Zouache, "Remarks on Blacks," 33.

43. Zouache, "Remarks on Blacks," 33.

44. Bacharach, "African Military Slaves"; Lev, "Army, Regime, and Society"; Zouache, "Remarks on Blacks," 36.

45. Robinson, "Slavery in the Conquest Period," 160, 162n19.

46. Bacharach, "African Military Slavery," 477–80, 493n25.

47. Zouache, "Remarks on Blacks," 26.

48. Bacharach, "African Military Slavery," 483.

49. Bacharach, "African Military Slavery"; Zouache, "Remarks on Blacks." Further analysis of how enslaved Blacks were racialized in medieval Egypt is in the next chapter.

50. On this decentralized trade, see further discussion in this chapter.

51. See the sources cited in 28n. Al-Masʿūdī reports that boats from Egypt and Nubia converged at the island of Philae (Bilāq) for the exchange of the *baqṭ* in 943. Idem, *Murūj al-dhahab*, 2:129–31; Halm, "Nubische Baqṭ," 87.

52. Campbell, "East Africa," esp. 289–95; Jankowiak, "Slave Trade in the Saqaliba."

53. Maritime salvage: Goitein, *Letters of Medieval Jewish Traders*, 189; Margariti, *Aden*, 100, 167, 169–75, 193, 200, 202–3.

54. Medieval maritime laws of jettison accounted for a person's ability to swim: Khalilieh, "Slaves' Juridical Status at Sea," 92.

55. Pearson and Richardson, "Insuring the Transatlantic Slave Trade"; Barker, "Risk of Birth."

56. Risk-management strategies among *geniza* merchants are discussed extensively in Goldberg, *Trade and Institutions*. See also Udovitch, *Partnership and Profit*; Ackermann-Lieberman, *Business of Identity*; Cohen, *Maimonides and the Merchants*.

57. T-S 16.163. Goitein, *Letters of Medieval Jewish Traders*, 130; Gil, *Kingdom of Ishmael*, 3:245–53; idem, "Jewish Merchants," 299; Goldberg, *Trade and Institutions*, 170.

58. Barker, *That Most Precious Merchandise*, 183, 262n273.

59. An exceptional record from the Fatimid period: Richards, "Fragments of a Slave Dealer's Day-Book." Earlier evidence for ʿAbbasid Egypt: Bruning, "Slave Trade Dynamics."

60. A single letter sent to the merchant Joseph b. ʿAwkal (active ca. 990–1030) asks him to send a *jāriya*: Paris, AIU VII.E.131. Ibn ʿAwkal: Elinoar Bareket, "Ibn ʿAwkal Family"; Goldberg, *Trade and Institutions, 38–39, 308–9, 310–11 passim.*

61. Frenkel, "Slave Trade." Scholarship on Nahray and his cohort is relatively extensive: Ackerman-Lieberman, "Nahray ben Nissim," and the sources cited there; Goldberg, "Use and Abuse of Commercial Letters"; idem, *Trade and Institutions*; idem, "Mercantile Letters."

62. There is little indication in *geniza* documents that buyers and sellers frequently went to urban marketplaces where enslaved people were present and for sale. For a likely exception,

see 4n in chap. 5. The sole known mention of a *dār al-raqīq* (slave market) in the *geniza* is in DK 370. This document is a list of names and numbers, perhaps indicating amounts of donations, etc., that mentions Ḥasan of *dār al-raqīq*. *Dār al-raqīq* here most likely indicates the location of Ḥasan's residence or workplace to identify him. In the 1004 CE decree of the Fatimid caliph al-Ḥākim, he forbade slave traders from selling slaves to *dhimmī* groups. The reports about this decree do not mention physical slave markets: al-Maqrīzī, *Itti'āẓ al-ḥunafā'*, 2:53; Walker, *Caliph of Cairo*, 65–66. Al-Shayzarī's twelfth-century *ḥisba* manual mentions that the slave dealer (*al-nakhkhās*) must be upright because he is occasionally alone with enslaved women in his home. See idem, *Islamic Market Inspector*, 102–3.

63. T-S 12.254, right margin, l. 5 through top margin, l. 3. Thanks to Oded Zinger for his personal communication in which he suggested the connection between Mardukh's oath and his search for an enslaved woman. On the meaning of *lil-khidma* when used to describe the labor of enslaved people, see chap. 4.

64. See chap. 1.

65. T-S 12.254, right margin, l. 5, through the top margin, l. 3. Beginning l. 9 of the top margin, Mardūkh reiterates that he has no one to watch his house, fetch him water, or greet guests at his door. Goitein, *MS*, 1:126, 135; 2:589n1. Yagur critiques Goitein's argument that "the Jewish Quarter" in Alexandria should not be understood as a physical place. Goitein, *MS*, 2:589n1; Yagur, "Living in the City," 435–37. Evidence that Alexandria may have had a "Jewish neighborhood": Frenkel, "*The Compassionate and Benevolent*," 38; Yagur, "Living in the City," 434. A list of Mardūkh b. Musā's letters: Goldberg, "Use and Abuse of Commercial Letters," 147–48n111.

66. Frenkel, "Slave Trade," 148–49.

67. F 1908.44HH (also F 34, cited as G. W. XXXIV) and T-S 8J27.5: Gil, *Kingdom of Ishmael*, 4: 421–28, nos. 423 and 424. Partial translations in Frenkel, "Slave Trade," 148–49.

68. F 1908.44HH; Frenkel, "Slave Trade," 148–49.

69. ENA 2805.23, ll. 13–19 and verso, ll. 9–11. Gil, *Kingdom of Ishmael*, 3:20–24, no. 310; Frenkel, "Slave Trade," 148–49. Goitein's draft translation is available in PGP at this shelf mark.

70. T-S 13J21.18: In the hand of Ḥalfon b. Menasse, who wrote it on behalf of his daughter. Goitein, *MS*, 1:135, 265; 2:377, 610; 3:22, 231 and 4:349; Zinger, "Women, Gender, and Law," 60, 259, and 420.

71. A *jālib* is someone who imports slaves and animals for resale. There is ambiguity about who precisely has the enslaved people for sale: *wa-qad sami'tu anna 'indakum minhum kathīr*. It is likely that *'indakum* here indicates "you all," meaning "you people in Bahnasā." See Alan Elbaum's notes in PGP for T-S 13J21.18. See also Bruning, "Slave Trade Dynamics," 691–95 and then 706–9 for his edition of P.CtYBR inv. 2667, in which a ninth-century Egyptian man, who appears to be a *jālib* (importer) or *nakhkhās* (slave trader), reports on the sales, and lack thereof, of his "many" enslaved servants and eunuchs.

72. Freer 1908.44SS. Edited and translated in Gottheil and Worrell, eds., *Fragments from the Cairo Genizah*, 218–25. See the revised edition in Frenkel, "Slave Trade," 156–58.

73. T-S Misc. 28.256. Goitein and Friedman, *India Traders*, 452–55; Frenkel, "Slave Trade," 149–50.

74. There is a great deal written about both the meaning of the geographical term and ethnonym "Zanj" and the ninth-century "Zanj rebellion." See Talhami, "Zanj Rebellion

Reconsidered"; Tolmacheva, "Definition of the Term Zanj"; al-Ṭabarī, *The History*; Campbell, "East Africa"; Ali, "Zanj Revolt in the Abbasid Caliphate"; Grant, "Entangled Symbols" and the sources cited there.

75. Cf. T-S AS 166.174 + (?) T-S AS 167.24. In these two tattered fragments (possibly once part of the same letter), Abū al-Munā b. Yaʿaqov al-Isrāʾīlī al-Ḥāfiẓ al-[. . .] writes to Abū ʿAlī b. ʿAṭāʾ al-Isrāʾīlī about a Zanzibari ship that had not yet arrived. He also mentions an enslaved servant-girl (*waṣīfa*) who has not been found. The fragmentary state of the letter makes it difficult to confirm whether Abū al-Munā means that he has not been able to buy a *waṣīfa* from the Zanzibari ship. My thanks to Amir Ashur for bringing this recent discovery to my attention and to him and Alan Elbaum for sharing their preliminary edition in PGP.

76. T-S 16.345 and BL Or. 5542.17: Two copies of the same letter. Goitein and Friedman, *India Traders*, 480–84.

77. Sassoon 713v, ll, 11–12. Hirschberg, "The Almohad Persecutions," 143.

78. T-S NS J23: Partial translation in S. D. Goitein, "New Light," 179. Goitein and Friedman, *Maḍmūn*, 126n4, 138n57.

79. T-S NS J23. Goitein, "New Light," 178–79. Before the thirteenth century, the *kārim* referred to a convoy of ships traveling between Egypt and the ports of the western Indian Ocean and carrying merchants of various religious backgrounds. Margariti, *Aden*, 152–54. In the Mamluk period, the term *kārim* came to designate an actual merchant consortium that played a great role in Indian Ocean commerce. Later Mamluk *kārim* merchants were known to transport slaves to Egypt from the Red Sea and Indian Ocean trading spheres: Sato, "Slave Traders and Kārimī Merchants,"154.

80. For more on the names that slave owners gave enslaved people, see appendixes 1 and 2; Perry, "Daily Life of Slaves," 75–82; Dirbas, "Naming of Slave Girls."

81. T-S 8J10.9. Goitein, *MS*, 1:452; Goitein's description on his notecard no. 8795 and his transcription are in PGP. The translation is mine.

82. The nickname the "Diadem (*al-Nezer*)," as short for honorifics like "the Diadem of the Scholars," or "the Diadem of the Academy," is not uncommon in *geniza* documents. Some individuals known to be nicknamed the "Diadem" belonged to slave-owning families if they didn't own enslaved people themselves. E.g.: the scribe Nathan b. Samuel, "the Diadem," in T-S 13J22.2, in which another man named Judah ha-Kohen is called "the Diadem of the Scholars." The identity of this specific "Diadem" in T-S 8J10.9 is not known. T-S NS 321.7a: a merchant's account book from 1134 mentions payment to a man named *al-Nezer*, whom Goitein identified as ʿEli b. Nathanel. In this same notebook, there is a credit listed for "the banker" for "the balance of the price of the slave girl." Goitein, *Letters of Medieval Jewish Traders*, 299–304.

83. *Tanḥadiru* is the second-person masculine singular meaning "go down (the Nile River)." Blau, ed., *Dictionary*, 114.

84. Another letter that mentions a delivery "to the Diadem" and a Joseph: ENA 1822a.73.

85. Al-Shayzarī, *Islamic Market Inspector*, 102–3.

86. Richards, "Fragments of a Slave Dealer's Day-Book"; al-Shayzarī, *Islamic Market Inspector*, 102–3.

87. T-S Ar. 50.85 + T-S NS J584. Join made by Alan Elbaum, who also brought their contents to my attention. The judge is called Abū al-Faraj. The broker is Abū al-Munā b. Ṣāʿid. This case is discussed in more detail in the next chapter.

88. P.JoySorrow 34. Partial translation and analysis in Bruning, "Slave Trade Dynamics," 695–96.

89. Guo, *Commerce, Culture, and Community*, 218–19.

90. Marek Jankowiak, "Slave Trade in the Saqaliba," 170.

91. T-S Misc. 28.256. See the sources cited in 73n in this chapter. After 1250 CE, an Ottoman-era *geniza* letter may refer to the trafficking of a large group of enslaved people: MS Her. b 13/45. An Ottoman-era ledger documents several slave sales: T-S K25.140.1.

92. T-S 13J21.18. See 70–71n in this chapter.

93. ʿAbbasid-era Egyptian evidence shows how buyers used letters and personal networks to organize discrete transactions from locations known to have larger slave markets. Bruning, "Slave Trade Dynamics," 690–99.

94. Islamic conquests: Robinson, "Slavery in the Conquest Period." Ghaznavids: Bano, "Slave Markets in Medieval India." Mongols: Biran, "Forced Migrations and Slavery."

95. Bano, "Slave Markets," 355, 370n3.

96. Enslaved people were captured and trafficked from Libya (the Fezzān region in particular) and from as far away as Lake Chad. Pre-Ottoman *geniza* evidence does not suggest that these regions were significant as sources for enslaved people in Egypt compared to the Nile valley below Aswan. In T-S 8J5.5 (2v), an enslaved woman is called a *maghribiyya* (a westerner). This identifier is relational and thus ambiguous. It may indicate an origin from the near west of Egypt (e.g., the Libyan desert) and not from the far Maghrib (i.e., the zone from Tunisia to Morocco). Brett, "Ifriqiya as a Market"; Savage, "Berbers and Blacks"; Lev, "Army, Regime, and Society," 339–40; Maceachern, "State Formation and Enslavement"; Mattingly et al., "Origins and Development of Zuwīla."

97. Power, *Red Sea*, esp. chap. 4.

98. Nāṣir-i Khusraw, *Book of Travels*, 51–52. While the translation renders "Greek," a more accurate translation for "Rūmī" is the more cumbersome "from the Byzantine realm." The juxtaposition of "Nubian" and "Greek" here may mean "Black" and "White (or light-skinned)." My thanks to Hossein Samei for this suggestion.

99. Nāṣir-i Khusraw, *Book of Travels*, 85–86.

100. On the timing of Benjamin's visit, see Benjamin of Tudela, *The Itinerary of Benjamin of Tudela*, ix, 69n4, 70; David, "Benjamin ben Jonah of Tudela." On Benjamin's sense of geography: Fauvelle-Aymar, "Desperately Seeking."

101. Benjamin of Tudela, *Itinerary*, 62 (Hebrew), 68 (English). I made some changes to Adler's translation.

102. For example, this topos is present in al-Idrīsī's writings about the Lamlam and other African peoples. Levtzion and Hopkins, eds., *Corpus of Early Arabic Sources*, 108, 109, 112.

103. In chap. 7, I analyze this and similar evidence of enslaved people's appearances before Islamic and Jewish judges.

104. CUL Or. 1080 J30. Goitein, *MS*, 1:136, 433; 3:39, 435; Zinger, "'She Aims to Harass Him,'" 192; Yagur, *Crossing the Line*, 86.

105. Makki, "Spatial Ecology of Power." Similar dynamics prevailed elsewhere: E. Savage, "Berbers and Blacks"; Maceachern, "State Formation and Enslavement."

106. Medieval Islamic maps routinely label the Eastern Desert region as the lands of the Beja: Pinto, "Capturing Imagination"; idem, *Medieval Islamic Map*, esp. 187–218.

107. Baadj, "Political Context of the Egyptian Gold Crisis"; Ruffini, "History of Medieval Nubia"; idem, "Documentary Evidence and the Production of Power."

108. Ibn Sulaym's reports about Nubia survive via al-Maqrīzī's writings. Kheir, "Contribution to a Textual Problem."

109. Kheir, "Contribution," 47.

110. Kheir, "Contribution," 47.

111. Kheir, "Contribution," 47.

112. Kheir, "Contribution," 54.

113. Kheir, "Contribution," 73. Ibn al-Furāt (citing Ibn Duqmāq) claims that Nubian slaves sold for 3 dirhams because there were so many of them produced by a Mamluk attack on Dongola (Dunqulā): Vantini, *Oriental Sources*, 536.

114. P.QI.3.36 (1191 CE). Translated in Browne, *Old Nubian Texts III*, 50–53. Khan's recent publication, *Arabic Documents from Medieval Nubia*, offers a new wealth of material on this subject that needs to be integrated into this history.

115. P.QI.4.67. Translated in Ruffini, *Qaṣr Ibrim IV*, 78–86.

116. Kheir, "Contribution," 60, 61, 63, 65.

117. Kheir, "Contribution," 42–43, 63–64. On al-Maqrīzī and the *baqṭ* see Spaulding, "Medieval Christian Nubia"; Khan, "Medieval Nubia," 4–11.

118. Gift sent by Ibn Mukārim Abū Yazīd: see 24n, 25n in this chapter.

119. Kheir, "Contribution," 55; Weschenfelder, "Integration of the Eastern Desert," 226.

120. Ibn Buṭlān: Schacht, "Ibn Buṭlān"; Conrad, "Ibn Buṭlān in Bilād al-Shām." Ibn Buṭlān's writings circulated among Jews in medieval Egypt and were deposited in the *geniza*: Baker, "Note on an Arabic Fragment."

121. Ibn Buṭlān, *Risāla jāmiʿat al-funūn al-nāfiʿa*, 375–76. Translation from Lewis, *Islam* 2:249.

122. T-S 18J1.30, l. 11: *wa-jins-hā Bāziyya*

123. ENA 2559.6.

124. Kheir, "Contribution," 51, 59. Kheir writes "Baza." It is Bāza. See al-Maqrīzī, *al-Khiṭaṭ*, 354, 359.

125. Famine was also linked to the enslavement of previously free people in India, where Jewish merchants purchased enslaved people: Perry, "Slavery and the Slave," 142–45.

126. Al-Musabbiḥī, *Akhbār Miṣr*, 11–12. Al-Maqrīzī incorporated al-Musabbiḥī's entry into his own account of Fatimid rule, *Ittiʿāẓ al-ḥunafā'*, 2:134. See also al-Maqrīzī, *al-Sulūk*, 6:113–14.

127. Al-Baghdādī, *Physician on the Nile*, xxvi–xxv, xxix, 139, 143, 153–54. A letter from the *geniza* suggests that cannibalism was also known or rumored to take place in Alexandria. Al-Baghdādī, *Physician on the Nile*, xxvi–xxvii. A legal query sent to Abraham Maimonides references years as *tilka al-ayyām* (those days) and alludes to the social disorder that followed: Freimann and Goitein, eds., *Abraham Maimuni*, no. 98, a source discussed in chaps. 4 and 7.

128. Under normal conditions, an enslaved child would sell for twelve to twenty times as much.

129. Al-Baghdādī, *Physician on the Nile*, 153–54. Quotations are from Mackintosh-Smith's heartrending translation.

130. For an earlier period: Schneider, *Kinderverkauf und Schuldknechtschaft*; idem, "Freedom and Slavery."

131. Schneider, "Freedom and Slavery," 381–82.

132. I quote here the "literal" (his own word) translation of Charles Pellat in his article "Al-Radhaniyya."

133. McCormick, "New Light on the 'Dark Ages,'" 49.

134. Delvaux, "Transregional Slave Networks"; Roach, "People Trafficking Princes."

Chapter 3. Everyday Human Trafficking and the Racialization of Slavery

1. Freimann and Goitein, eds., *Abraham Maimuni*, no. 98. Partial English translations in Perry, "Conversion," 144–45; Frenkel, "Slave Trade," 151–52. "Yaṣe'a" is the Hebrew verb meaning "she left." See more about Yaṣe'a's life and the rationale for my use of this nickname in chap. 7.

2. The names Leah and Reuben are often used in medieval responsa as pseudonyms for women and men, respectively, when the identity of a person is unknown or intentionally concealed, or for a hypothetical actor in a contrived scenario.

3. Famine: Freimann and Goitein, *Abraham Maimuni*, 149n2. See the discussion of famine and enslavement in chap. 2.

4. The query explains that there were no Jews who had the means to purchase Yaṣe'a when Leah needed to sell her. Leah thus sold her to "the Christians." Subsequently a person "redeemed" Yaṣe'a from "the Christians" and "returned" her to Leah, seemingly as an act of charity. Some Jewish slave owners preferred to sell their slaves to other Jews because they viewed them as "partial Jews." On this aspect of Jewish law and its dynamics, see chaps. 1 and 8. See also Yagur, "Religious Identity"; idem, "Captives, Converts, and Concubines," 101–6; idem, *Crossing the Line.*

5. The circumstances that forced Yaṣe'a's sale to a Muslim are discussed in chap. 7.

6. Unknown owner to Leah to "Christians" to Leah (via an intermediary) to Leah's two daughters to Leah's freedman to Reuben to Reuben jointly with his sister-in-law (one of Leah's daughters) to a Muslim owner.

7. On Islamic and Jewish slavery law, see chap. 1.

8. The *muwallad*s are discussed further in chap. 3 as one of the main "types" of enslaved people documented in the *geniza* (figure 3.2). *Muwallad*s could also be trafficked into and out of Egypt for sale. Thus, their classification emphasizes their legal status at birth as enslaved and does not necessarily indicate their place of birth. For this reason, I avoid the translation "houseborn (or in French as *née à la maison*)": Goitein, *MS*, 1:138–39; Rāġib, *Actes de vente*, 1:8, 40. In *geniza* documents, scribes use the term *muwallad* as a *jins.*

9. A minority of records list Cairo as the location of sale. For example, see T-S 18J1.17r, T-S 16.188, and MS Heb. c 28/1.

10. See chap. 3, 29n and the appendixes of this book for the shelf marks related to the sales of enslaved people. The two Arabic-script documents are T-S 18J1.17v and T-S Ar. 42.174. A corpus of Arabic-script bills of sale for enslaved people: Rāġib, *Actes de vente.*

11. Many of these were first identified by Goitein in idem, *MS*, 1: 137–47, 431–37.

12. On the speech of enslaved people, see chap. 7.

13. Assaf, "Slaves and the Slave Trade"; idem, "Book of Formularies"; Weiss, "Formularies Reconstructed" (in two parts, 1973–74); Ackerman-Lieberman, "Legal Writing in Medieval

Cairo"; and Perry, "An Aramaic Bill of Sale." Though Egyptian Jews used the Hebrew Bible to think through slavery law, they do not draw from the biblical text in bills of sale. Legal writings do use biblical texts to explicate slavery law and rhetorically to criticize the behavior of slave owners. See the discussion in chap. 5.

14. "Splendor of the Dynasty" was an honorific used to describe other individuals during this same era. My thanks to Yusuf Umrethwala for sharing with me his research on Fatimid state officials in the *geniza* corpus. In a badly faded note, another of Moses's daughters, ʿĀliya, is identified as the seller of something for 15 dinars. Possibly an enslaved person (*ja*[. . .]). T-S NS 204.14v.

15. "[O]ur customary method of counting": the Seleucid calendar, which is commonly found in *geniza* documents. See Goitein, *MS*, 1:355. This date converts to Tuesday, January 10, 1105 CE.

16. Ṣoʿan Miṣrayim, a biblical toponym mentioned in Numbers 13:22 that is here used to mean Fustat. Alexandria was frequently called No' Amon.

17. On the "symbolic purchase," see the discussion later in this chapter and 51n.

18. The *asmakhta* (nonbinding promise) is not binding because its intent is ambiguous. See the examples given by Maimonides in *MT, Hilkhot mechira*, 11:2–7. One purpose of the *qinyan* was to remove potential ambiguity. Ibid., 11:2, 7. The *lo ke-tufsay de-sheṭaray* (not like a fill-in-the-blank form) clause aims to prevent the seller from claiming that he signed a document composed of legal formularies that he did not understand. *BT, Bava Batra*, 44b; Olszowy-Schlanger, *Karaite Marriage Documents*, 258.

19. "Exempt from . . . the claims of the king and queen": ll. 23–25 are based on *BT, Giṭṭin*, 86a. See Perry, "Aramaic Bill of Sale." Cf. *MT, Hilkhot mechira*, 15:13. The enslaved person who is a known criminal loses all his value because the king may arrest and kill him.

20. Here: *Rusham* (or *rosham*). From *rushama, reshom*, meaning mark, impression, or incision that indicates the owner of an enslaved person. Sokoloff, *Babylonian Aramaic*, 1067.

21. This chapter does not provide a comprehensive analysis of the technical features of bills of sale. For such studies, see Little, "Six Fourteenth-Century Purchase Deeds"; Rāġib, *Actes de vente*; Perry, "Aramaic Bill of Sale"; idem, "Supplementary Deed." See also Wakin, ed., *The Function of Documents in Islamic Law*; Geoffrey Khan, ed., *ALAD*, 7–55; Ackerman-Lieberman, "Legal Writing"; Krakowski's "Rabbinic Law on the Page and on the Ground," in idem, *Coming of Age*, 95–106, and there "Anatomy of a Legal Document."

22. Enslaved people were bought and sold in other Egyptian cities and towns, but *geniza* bills of sale from these latter places are uncommon. T-S 13J8.3: a partially obliterated bill of sale lists its location as "on the shore of the sea [. . .]," which is probably the city of Alexandria. Another *geniza* document that uses this phrase suggests Tyre is another possibility (T-S 8J4.18).

23. Oxford: MS Heb. b 13/39. Thanks to Alan Elbaum for bringing this unusual detail to my attention. "Informal" Jewish courts in private homes: Ackerman, "Methodological Essay," 430. Medieval Arabic writings suggest that sales could be conducted in different locations, including private homes: Barker, "Purchasing a Slave," 9.

24. Seleucid calendar: Goitein, *MS*, 1:355.

25. Both men are first called by their Arabic *kunyas*, which identify them as "the father of Saʿd (Abū Saʿd)" and "the father of al-Faḍl (Abū al-Faḍl)." The *kunya* is not always to be taken literally. See Schimmel, *Islamic Names*, 4–8.

26. The Hebrew Yosef and the Arabic Yūsuf are spelled the same in Judeo-Arabic. The Arabic names that Jews used, in addition to their Hebrew names, have many components. Schimmel, *Islamic Names*; Lindsay, *Daily*, 173–78.

27. *Mithqāl*, equivalent to one dinar, is also used. On currencies used in *geniza* documents, see Goitein, *MS*, 1:359–361.

28. T-S 18J1.30: 22 dinars are credited to the account of the merchant Abū al-Fakhr Yeshuʿ[a] b. Solomon. Yeshuʿa testifies that he released the buyer, Abū ʿAlī Yefet b. Ḥalfon, from his right to receive full and complete payment (in cash). T-S 13J3.16: Sitt Qaḍīb Sāda bt. Abū al-Bayān pays seven of twelve *mithqāl*s (equivalent to dinars) to Abū al-Barakāt [. . .] b. Moses. She agrees pay the remaining five *mithqāl*s in the Hebrew month of Sivan (two months after this sale in the month of Nisan).

29. These figures come from a sample of thirty-eight documents including bills of sale, scribal notebook entries, and declarations of prices in legal documents. More precisely the average price is 20.375 dinars. The highest price is for ʿAbīr, a singing slave-girl (*jāriya mughanniya*) and professional wailer (*al-nāʾiḥa*). See chap. 4, 12n. The lowest price is for the Abyssinian *ghulām* named Muqbil. See T-S13J8.3 and his mention in chaps. 3 and 7. These figures for prices exclude the valuations of enslaved people included in wedding dowries, which can range from 20–80 dinars. For the sources and prices given in Goitein, *MS*, 1:434n64, the following documents (listed from highest to lowest price) may be added. 40 dinars: RNL Yevr.-Arab I 1700.15v; 34 dinars: F 1908.44SS; 27 dinars: RNL Yevr. III B 669.r; 25 dinars: T-S 13J7.15 and Or. 1080J273; 22 dinars: T-S 18J1.30, ENA NS 72.18, T-S Ar. 39.245; 21 dinars: T-S 18J1.16, T-S Ar. 42.174; 20 dinars: ENA 4011.48, ENA 4020.11, T-S 13J3.7, T-S 16.188, T-S 18J1.17r + v (two separate transactions), T-S AS 157.314; 19.5 dinars: MS Heb. b. 12/32, T-S 10J7.6(2v), sec. d; 18.75 dinars: T-S NS 320.29; 17 dinars: T-S AS 147.8v; 16 dinars: T-S Misc. 23.8; 15.5 dinars: RNL Yevr.-Arab. I 1700.15v and 1700.22v; 15 dinars: T-S 18J1.12; 12 dinars: MS Heb. b 13/39; 11 dinars: ENA 2727.37; 10.5 dinars: T-S 8J8.4; 10.25 dinars: T-S 13J8.3. T-S NS 320.15 is a copy or version of ENA 4020.11.

30. See the dataset created by Maya Shatzmiller, "Measuring the Medieval Economy," at https://www.medievalislamiceconomy.uwo.ca/.

31. *Dūn al-bulūgh*: PER H 23; T-S 13J8.3; T-S NS 320.29. An enslaved Nubian woman named Ḥidhq is sold along with her daughter in 1094: T-S 20.93b. It is possible that this Ḥidhq is the same woman that Khalaf and Joseph sold to their sister Zayn (without her daughter) nearly a decade later. Further discussion of child slavery and the biographies of enslaved individuals is in chap. 7.

32. T-S Ar. 54.78. Sometimes writers used different terms to describe the same enslaved person: a woman is called a *waṣīfa* and a *jāriya* in T-S 10J9.32.

33. T-S K25.62. Identification by Alan Elbaum.

34. As translated and quoted in Franz, "Slavery in Islam," 77. See also ibid., 99; Marmon, "Domestic Slavery," 1–8.

35. *MT*, *Hilkhot ʿavadim*, 9:8.

36. On naming practices for enslaved people, see chap. 2, 80n.

37. Names are not a required element specified in Hai Gaon's book of legal formularies: Assaf, "Book of Formularies."

38. I translate *Rūmī(iyya)*, as from the Byzantine realm. This has also been understood as Greek, or Greek-speaking. We might also understand it simply as Roman, and in this historical

context as applying to eastern Romans, or those from the medieval Byzantine empire and its hinterlands (thus, realm). See the discussion in Schine, *Black Knights,* 320, and there in n18. Bāzī(iyya): see chap. 2.

39. The use of "Black" alongside *jins* and religion is discussed further in this chapter.

40. Ushshāq: T-S 13J6.7. Muqbil: T-S 13J8.3. "[C]arob-colored" woman: T-S Ar. 42.174. Published in ʿAodeh, "Eleventh Century Letters," 219–20, and Khan, ed., *ALAD*, 262–63; Perry, "Aramaic Bill of Sale," 452n7.

41. More elaborate coercion clauses: e.g., T-S 18J1.12, ll. 7–8 and MS Heb. b 12/20, ll. 8–10.

42. T-S K27.45 (now T-S NS 246.28). Goitein, *MS*, 2:341–42, 602n42. Published in Friedman, "Master and Slave Girl."

43. Here: *Rusham* (or *rosham*). From *rushama, reshom*, meaning mark, impression, or incision that indicates the owner of an enslaved person. Sokoloff, *Babylonian Aramaic*, 1057.

44. "[A]nd from old sores": there are no signs of previous outbreaks that might indicate the presence of leprosy or another condition. *BT, Giṭṭin*, 86a. Perry, "Aramaic Bill of Sale."

45. Islamic law, too, provided for guarantees against "defects" in enslaved people: Rāġib, *Actes de vente*, 2:70–92.

46. *Bayʿ jalb* (also sometimes *bayʿ al-jalb*): Goitein, *MS*, 1:140, 435; Rāġib, *Actes de vente*, 2: 90n944. Used in *geniza* bills of sale: MS Heb. b 12/20, ll. 15–17; T-S 10J11.31; T-S 8J5.5; T-S 13J3.7; T-S 13J8.3; T-S 18J1.12; T-S 18J1.30; T-S AS 147.8. Written rarely as *shirāʾ al-jalb*: T-S 18J1.19; ENA 77.254.

47. *MT, Hilkhot mechira,* 15:12–13. See also 15:3, 10.

48. T-S 6J1.32 (1260 CE): An Abyssinian woman has "whiteness" in her left eye, perhaps a corneal leukoma as noted in PGP.

49. See chap. 1, 43n.

50. *MT, Hilkhot mechira,* 15: 13.

51. "Symbolic purchase," or *qinyan* (also transliterated as *kinyan* in secondary literature): Goitein, *MS*, 2:42, 328–30, 334, 3:70, 84–85; Krakowski, *Coming of Age*, 104–5 and nn102, 104. See Lieberman, "Methodological Essay," esp. 434n8, and note that *qinyan* also has the more general meaning of acquisition in certain contexts. Ibid., 429. There is some evidence that the requirements for a *qinyan* could differ according to local customs. See Zinger, *Living with the Law*, 201n6.

52. Zinger, *Living with the Law*, 33.

53. Krakowski, *Coming of Age*, esp. chap. 2. See also Krakowski and Rustow, "Formula as Content"; Lieberman, "Methodological Essay on Commercial Contracts."

54. Such a case is analyzed in chap. 6.

55. Perry, "Aramaic Bill of Sale" and idem, "Supplementary Deed" illustrate one such case. A Christian scribe purchases the woman Naʿīm from a Jewish woman. His deed of purchase, written in Arabic script and according to Islamic legal conventions, recognizes the validity of the Aramaic bill of sale held by the Jewish vendor.

56. T-S F 1908.44HH. Discussed in chap. 2.

57. Jewish merchants in Egypt generally operated freely. There were instances where state officials impeded them. For example, see a merchant's petition to a Fatimid official in Khan, *ALAD*, 334–36, and see Goldberg, *Trade and Institutions*, 168–77, on government sequestration of goods, exorbitant taxation, and other merchant hazards.

58. Goitein, *MS*, 1:339–34.

59. *Ḥaqq al-sūq*: T-S NS 320.17 (1157–1158) and T-S 20.41 (1147). *Ḥaqq al-sulṭān*: T-S NS 320.50c (1143). These are all Fatimid-era documents. A bill of sale from the Ayyubid period (1198) uses *rasm al-sūq* (market duties): T-S 13J3.16. The scribe added an unusually extensive formulation in a bill of sale for the Abyssinian boy Muqbil (T-S 13J8.3): *Musallima khārij ʿan al-samsara wal-maks wal-wājib wal-juʿl fa-inna jamīʿ dhālik lāzim lil-mushtarī mar Moses al-madhkūr dūn al-bāʾiʿ.* (Paying tax on the brokerage, the tax, the duty, and the fee—all of these are required of the buyer, the aforementioned lord Moses, and not the seller.) Some fragmentary bills of sale also indicate taxes. E.g., "[. . .] *al-sūq*" in T-S 13J7.15.

60. Goitein, *MS*, 1:160–61, 185, 445n6, 449n25. Brokers' fees mentioned in *geniza* bills of sale for slaves: T-S 13J3.16, T-S Ar. 42.174 (an Arabic-script document).

61. T-S 13J3.16 is a legal agreement made after a slave sale to clarify a payment plan. In this agreement, the buyer agrees that she will pay the *rasm al-sūq* and the *dilāla* (broker's fee). The amounts are not specified.

62. Goitein, *MS*, 1:185. See MS Heb. a 2/11.

63. Check Goitein, *MS*, 1:140, 160–61.

64. Goitein, *MS*, 1:185. For an example of the seller assuming taxes and the brokers' fees, see RNL Yevr.-Arab I 1700.15v. The woman sold here for 15.5 dinars is named Nadd. Her owner resold her for 17.5 dinars inclusive of tax and broker's fee. From this we might infer that the tax and broker's fee amounted to 2 dinars in the first sale. Second sale: RNL Yevr.-Arab I 1700.22v.

65. ENA 77.254. Thanks to Alan Elbaum for bringing this record to my attention and for sharing his translation of the salient lines. Zinger is currently preparing a monograph that uses social network analysis to study Ḥalfon's scribal activities.

66. Perhaps the largest complete notebook of this type dates to 1156 and is held by the Russian National Library in St. Petersburg. The owner of this notebook recorded slave sales among the many other transactions and agreements about which he took notes and for which he drafted documents. Menahem Ben-Sasson and Oded Zinger plan to publish their edition and translation of this source.

67. See also Rustow's description of "phantom" documents in *Lost Archive*, 90–95, 250–51, 263, 266, 272 passim.

68. T-S 13J36.11. In explaining that someone "tattled" on him, the writer uses the same Arabic root (*gh-m-z*) as Ḥalfon did in his note almost a century earlier. See the transcription in PGP as well as Goitein, *MS*, 1:111, 142. Frenkel, "Medieval Alexandria," 22.

69. T-S 13J36.11, ll. 19–20. Sales presented enslaved people with limited opportunities to undermine the transaction. See the discussion in chap. 7.

70. The exchange rate fluctuated over time. Here I have used the rate of 36 dirhams per dinar. On the exchange rate of dirhams for dinars, see Goitein, *MS*, 1:368–92.

71. See chap. 2, 87n, and the case of Abū al-Faraj and his wife, as discussed in chap. 5.

72. See T-S Ar. 50.85 + T-S NS J584. See also T-S 12.327, discussed further in this chapter.

73. See also Goitein, *MS*, 2:289.

74. Enslaved people appear in Muslim courts when these authorities learn from informers of potential legal infractions. See not only the case of Abū al-Majd, but also sources discussed

in subsequent chapters including Or. 1080 J30, Moses Maimonides responsum, no. 211, and Abraham Maimonides responsum, no. 98.

75. Goldberg, *Trade and Institutions*, 165–66, 351.

76. Goldberg, *Trade and Institutions*, 351. The threat of sequestration also suggests why Jews found utility in the Aramaic legal formula from the Babylon Talmud that guaranteed that the person for sale was free from the demands "of the king and queen." See the text of the bill of sale for Ḥidhq in this chapter and the sources in 19n.

77. T-S Ar. 42.174 and T-S 18J1.17v. The latter is a supplemental bill of sale (*faṣl*) and does not include all of the legal clauses that other Arabic-script bills of sale contain. The Arabic-script bills of sale in Rāġib's corpus were written in cities and towns outside of Fustat/Cairo, and they do not indicate that taxes were paid invariably. For his discussion of taxes on slave and animal sales, in general, see Rāġib, *Actes de vente*, 2:54. Commission fees were paid in some instances: P. Cam. Michaéhlidès inv. B 152, l. 4 and P. Caire Mus. Isl. Inv. 21191, l. 7. Published in Rāġib, *Actes de vente*, 1:13–14 (no. IV), 21–22 (no. VIII), and see Rāġib's discussion of commission (*juʿl*) in idem, *Actes de vente*, 2:50–52.

78. T-S 12.327, ll. 5–6.

79. See Alan Elbaum's description in PGP for T-S 12.327. It seems that Abū al-Najm or another person owes the author 5 dinars that he hopes to use toward the purchase of an enslaved person. "The *rayyis* Abū al-Najm" is mentioned in a list that Goitein dated to ca. 1175. See T-S NS 321.14. Two other names mentioned below the main text of the letter and in a different, smaller hand are: Solomon ha-Levi bar Moses *ha-shishi* and [. . .] Moses b. ʿAmram. On the family of Moses *ha-shishi*, see 490n84 in Friedman, "Maimonides, Zuta, and the *Muqaddams*." On the variable Judeo-Arabic spellings of *al-rayyis*, *al-raʾīs*, and so on, see Zinger, *Living with the Law*, xi.

80. ENA 2738.23v, ll. 10–12. See Alan Elbaum's summary in PGP and Goitein, *MS*, 4: 263, 448n8.

81. "Conjunctural" as compared to "structural" poverty: Cohen, *Poverty and Charity*, 26, 42–53, 65–68 passim. Famine: see also the discussions in chap. 2.

82. T-S 10J9.32, 1r. Goitein, *MS*, 3:23n48, 183n119.

83. For an explanation of Jewish marriage law including dowries (and *nedunya*), see Zinger, *Living with the Law*, vii–ix. For marital disputes over dowry assets, see Zinger, *Living with the Law*, 93–94, 193nn80–81.

84. T-S 12.285. See the edition in Goitein, Friedman, and Ashur, *Ḥalfon*, 177–81. Friedman, "An India Trader's Partnership," 79.

85. To date there are at least thirteen marriage records that list one or more enslaved women as part of a bride's dowry.

86. Slavery and wives' domestic labor: see chap. 6.

87. T-S 16.70: A *jāriya rūmiyya* is valued at the incredibly high price of 80 dinars, which is roughly four times the typical sale price. Transcription in PGP based on Goitein's unpublished edition. Goitein, *MS*, 1:138, 433, 3:373, 414, 4:380, 388, 430. See also the numerous references in Bareket, *Jewish Leadership in Fustat*.

88. BL: Or. 10653.5. The document is torn away on its right side and the portion that listed Saʿd's mother's name is missing except for its last letter, a *he*. Together, mother and son are valued at 40 dinars. The bride's name is not mentioned in the surviving fragment. Based on

this document's Hebrew formulary, Goitein argues that the document was drawn up in a Qaraite court. See S. D. Goitein, "Geniza Papers of a Documentary Character," 40; idem, *MS*, 1:138, 434n54.

89. *Waṣīfatayn* is the dual-form of *waṣīfa*. T-S J1.29. Goitein, *MS*, 1:135, 432. Goitein's translation is in *MS*, 4:322–25. See also Goitein and Friedman, *India Traders*, 301n6, 414n4; Krakowski, *Coming of Age*, 31; Goitein and Friedman, *Joseph Lebdī*, 270, and *Maḍmūn*, 120.

90. T-S NS J185c + d. Goitein notes the detail about the two *jāriyas* without qualification. In the photograph of the document in FGP, the relevant phrase is partly obliterated: *wal-dār [wal-jā]riyatayn illadhī lī*. See line 3 in section d. The merchant Abū al-Riḍā also specified an inheritance for his son. He also borrowed 25 dinars against his daughter's dowry and bridal clothing as capital for his mercantile ventures. See Weiss, *Ḥalfon*, 361–62; Goitein, *Index Cards*, nos. 12073–74.

91. T-S 10J6.7. See Goitein, *MS*, 5:135, 543n41. Ashur, "Engagement and Betrothal Documents," 33n104, 55n11; Krakowski, "Female Adolescence," 88, 257. Rivlin, *Inheritance and Wills*, 403–5, 455.

92. These are: MS Heb. f 56/12; MS Heb. f 56/17; T-S 10J6.7; T-S 8J4.21; T-S NS J185 c + d; and T-S NS J347. See also the case of a wealthy woman who wanted to clarify that her husband, who at the time was abroad on business, did not own any part of her *jāriya* named Fūq in chap. 7.

93. MS Heb. f 56/12. A *jāriya* is also bequeathed, but the sale is for the *waṣīf*. It was not uncommon to designate money, or the sale of property, to pay for burial expenses. See T-S 13J3.3 and T-S 13J22.2.

94. T-S 10J7.10. Rivlin, *Inheritance and Wills*, 371–73. My thanks to Rachel Richman for bringing this case to my attention and for sharing her revised edition of this document. It is unusual, and forbidden in the *Mishneh Torah*, for a mature woman to own an enslaved male. See the discussion in chap. 1 and *MT, Hilkhot 'avadim*, 9:6.

95. T-S 13J14.4. Goitein, *MS*, 1:142. Other inheritance cases are discussed in parts 2 and 3 of the book.

96. Two *jāriya*s are part of a goldsmith's estate (1114): T-S 8J5.1a-d. The woman Misk is listed in an inventory along with her modest possessions (1172): Or. 1080J142 + T-S Misc. 25.53 and see the discussion in chap. 8. See also the enslaved women mentioned in: T-S NS J357; T-S 13J3.19v, l. 1; T-S 12.491; MS Heb. f 56/17; and Mosseri VII 129.2.

97. The study of race in premodern history has a long "lineage," as Margo Hendricks and Dorothy Kim note. See Kim's article and its bibliography: idem, "Critical Race." See also Heng, *Invention of Race*; Armstrong-Partida, "Race, Skin Colour, Enslavement and Sexuality." A critique of Heng's approach to the racialization of Jews in medieval England is Pearce, "Inquisitor and the Moseret." For further reception of Heng, *Invention of Race*, see the essays in *Cambridge Journal of Postcolonial Inquiry* 9 (2022): 110–72, which includes Heng's response to Pearce. On race in premodern Arabic literature and the Middle East, see the article and bibliography Schine, "Translating Race"; idem, "Race and Blackness"; idem, *Black Knights*; and Urban, "Race, Gender and Slavery."

98. See the discussion of the medieval Arabic vocabulary of "race-making" in Schine, *Black Knights*, 9–11. In the modern era, the term *jins* is used increasingly to denote someone's sex: Najmabadi, "Genus of Sex."

99. On the laws of enslavement, see chap. 1.

100. Nubian: T-S 8J8.16, a bill of sale.

101. Slave-born: T-S Ar. 30.73v and S. D. Goitein notecard no. 101265 in PGP. On the *muwalladūn/āt* in an earlier era of Islamic history, see Urban, *Conquered Populations*, 15n19, 142, 145, 169n9, 176–78, and Urban, "Race, Gender and Slavery," 7. Urban's work shows that *muwallad* meant people born into slavery, who were viewed as "mixed race" though they could also be part Arab.

102. *'Ajamiyya*: T-S 8J8.4, a bill of sale for the woman 'Abīr. On the term *'Ajamiyya*, see chap. 3, 114n.

103. On Jewish slavery law, see chap. 1. Prohibited marriages: Goldenberg, "'It Is Permitted to Marry a Kushite.'"

104. *Bilād al-zanj*: T-S Misc. 28.256. *Al-'abd al-zanjī*: T-S Ar. 35.14.

105. Talhami, "Zanj Rebellion Reconsidered," 443–61; Tolmacheva, "Toward a Definition"; Campbell, "East Africa." On enslaved people captured in the hinterlands of East Africa, see Moorthy-Kloss, "Slavery in Medieval Arabia."

106. These tensions most frequently turned on the issue of whether a man who claimed that his enslaved woman was a domestic servant while he was actually suspected of using her, against Jewish law, as a sexual slave. See the discussion in chaps. 1 and 5. MS Heb. b 12/20: A bill of sale (1100). The seller states that she is selling the enslaved Nubian named Tawfīq, whom she thinks is a Christian (*wa-aẓunnuhā tarsāwiyya*). Goitein understood *tarsāwiyya* as an Arabization of the Persian *tarsā*: idem, *MS*, 1:136.). In his eleventh-century description of Nubia, Nāṣir-i Khusraw describes the people there as *tarsāyī* (Christian). See idem, *Book of Travels*, 82. In a Slack communication, Alan Elbaum expresses doubt about this interpretation. As Elbaum and Yusuf Umrethwala note, there are locales named Tirsā in Giza and the Fayyūm and the *nisba* al-Tarsāwī al-Fayyūmī is known. Their suggestion is sound onomastically, but I am not able to explain why the scribe of MS Heb. b 12/20 would call a Nubian woman *al-Tirsāwiyya* (meaning from Tirsā, Egypt). Nubia was, however, a Christian kingdom. See also the discussion in this chapter at 119n.

107. Barker, *That Most Precious Merchandise*, 40.

108. Al-Sakhāwī, *al-Ḍaw al-lami'*, vol. 12, no. 93. Hagedorn, *Domestic Slavery in Syria and Egypt*, 56. On the use of the terms *jabartiyya* and *ḥabashiyya* in the context of medieval slavery, see: Erlich, "Jabarti"; Loiseau, "Abyssinia at al-Azhar," 62–64, 69–76; Moorthy-Kloss, "Slaves at the Najahid and Rasulid Courts," 88–89.

109. Goitein, *MS*, 1:137.

110. Rāġib, *Actes de vente*, vol. 1, nos. VII, IX, X, XI. See the discussion in chap. 2.

111. The *jins* distribution of enslaved people found in Fatimid and Ayyubid Egypt reflects this particular historical context, though there would be some overlap with Muslim societies in Syria, Iraq, and Yemen. In his model document for a bill of sale, the eleventh-century Iraqi gaon Hai b. Sherira (d. 1038) provides examples of the kinds of enslaved people that were, presumably, common in late-tenth-century and early-eleventh-century Baghdad. They are "Indian (*Hindu'a*), Canaanite, Roman (*Rum'a*), Libyan (*Lub'a*), or East African (*Zang'a*)." Assaf, "*Book of Formularies*," 28. Hai's inclusion of "Canaanite" reflects the use in medieval Jewish law of this *jins* to indicate a "foreign" slave, generally. I do not know of a slavery document (e.g., a bill of sale) that uses "Canaanite" to describe a person. Scribes did use other

anachronistic categories such as Edomite and Kushite, see further in this chapter at 113n and in the conclusion at 34n. On translating *Rūm'a* as Roman, or from the Byzantine realm, see chap. 3, 38n.

112. The relative prominence of *muwallads* shows that enslaved women gave birth to children with slave status, perhaps more than many scholars have recognized. See the discussion in chap. 2. Urban does focus on the *muwalladūn/āt*: idem, *Conquered Populations*.

113. *Edūmiyya* (Edomite) is a Judeo-Arabic calque of the Hebrew/Aramaic *Edomi*, which is used to identify Rome and, in this case, Byzantium.

114. *'Ajamiyya* can also have the more general meaning of "non-Arab." Bosworth, "'Ajam"; Schine, *Black Knights*, 249, 319.

115. McCormick, "New Light on the 'Dark Ages.'" See also the discussion in chap. 2.

116. Reilly, *Agriculture and Slavery*; Delvaux, "Transregional Slave Networks."

117. In their legal queries to Jewish Egyptian jurists, writers used "Christian" to describe enslaved women instead of identifying them by one of the *jins*-types (Nubian, *Rūmiyya*, etc.) found in bills of sale. In multilingual responsa (Ḥebrew and Judeo-Arabic), writers use the term *'arela* (lit. uncircumcised one) to describe Christians. *Jāriya 'arela*: DK 231.2 (alt: xxv), edited in Friedman, *Jewish Polygyny*, 322–24. *Shifḥa 'arela*: Blau, ed. *Responsa of Moses Maimonides*, no. 211. These sources are discussed further in chap. 5. Whether these Christian women were African or European is unclear. African Christians who hailed from Christian polities (Nubia and Ethiopia) were more common, but European women were bought and sold as slaves. For a fascinating tale about a Frankish woman who was enslaved in early thirteenth-century Palestine and later trafficked to Egypt, see "The Merchant's Tale," as told in Cobb, *Race for Paradise*, 169–71, 303n2. An Arabic-script deed from a Muslim court shows that the Jewish merchant and purple-dyer 'Arūs b. Joseph purchased a "carob-colored [i.e., dark brown or black] Christian (*naṣrāniyya*) woman" from the Christian scribe Ḥanūn b. 'Allūn in 1090: T-S Ar. 42.174. 'Arūs b. Joseph al-Arjawānī is a merchant who appears in many *geniza* documents. For some notes on his biography, see Goitein, "Portrait of a Medieval India Trader."

118. Mosseri VII 58.1v. Ebony-wood (*abnūs*) commodities: T-S 6J5.20 (pens); ENA 2591.13 + ENA 2591.12 (ink wells); T-S 10J12.10v (a stool or chair, *kursī*). On ebony as "a stand-in for skin color," see Schine, *Black Knights*, 257–58.

119. T-S NS 320.29. Goitein, *MS*, 3:331, 501n81. The first two letters of the adjective describing *jāriya* are unclear. Cf. Weiss, "Ḥalfon," no. 197, p. 311, where Weiss reads "*jāriya M-S-Ā-V-Y-H*." Alan Elbaum proposes [. *r*]*sāwiyya*, which better fits the handwriting. The first letter is not legible as a Hebrew *tav* (T), though it is possible that *tarsāwiyya* was intended, or that the scribe made a mistake. What suggests this possibility is the fact that there is a Nubian woman named Tawfīq about whom the seller remarks, "I think she is a Christian (*tarsāwiyya*)." This Tawfīq's sale was in 1100. See the discussion in this chapter at 106n. Ḥalfon's note about Nafīsa's sale of Tawfīq is undated though he was known to be active between 1100 and 1138. Another possible reading is [*F-R*]-*S-Ā'-wiyya*, which may correspond to the Nubian city of Faras, or the Persian province of Fars, despite the nonstandard spelling. Note the common occurrence of the toponym Faras in Pierce, "Nubian Toponyms," 42, 49–50.

120. T-S NS 184.31.

121. T-S NS 342.121.

122. T-S NS 320.126. "The Black (*al-sawdā'*)," which indicates that Intijāb is female. The fact that the price is 34.5 dinars suggests that Intijāb was probably sold along with a child. Or that she had other training or capacity that made her especially valuable. For example, she might have been a wet nurse. See chap. 4, 15n, 16n. The end of the line in T-S NS 320.126 that mentions Intijāb is mostly illegible and so it is difficult to confirm these details.

123. An alternate translation could be "the slave of the Black Nubian type (*jins*)." T-S 10J6.7. *ha-shifḥa*: the definite Arabic adjectives Black and Nubian modify the Hebrew definite article *ha-* used here with the Hebrew *shifḥa* (enslaved woman). See also Goitein, *MS*, 5:135, 543; Amir Ashur, "Shiddukhin," 33n104, 55n11; Rivlin, *Inheritance and Wills in Jewish Law*, 403–5.

124. See the next note.

125. T-S NS J32, right margin: here someone has added a note, written perpendicular to the main text, that reads *al-sawdā' ismuhā Misk. Al-sawdā'* (the Black) modifies *al-jāriya* (the slave girl). Abū al-Baqā had inherited his half-share of Musk from his deceased wife. The other half-share of Musk belonged to Mukarram's wife, who had inherited it from her mother, who was the deceased woman's sister. See Goitein, *MS*, 1:142, 435; 2:531; 3:32, 434. See also Frenkel, "*The Compassionate and Benevolent*," 131, and idem, "Jewish Community of Aleppo," 1:169. Musk: T-S 8J18.29. "Al-Mukarram the son of the Kohen Abū al-Baqā" is the addressee of a letter that dates to the era of Abraham Maimonides's role as leader (*nagid*) of the Egyptian Jewish community (1213–37). Goitein, *MS*, 1:349, 490; 2:193, 561.

126. ENA NS 48.6. See the discussion of this evidence in chap. 6 and the sources cited there. To my knowledge, this is the only description of a Black person using the adjectival suffix *-ī* (masc.) or *-iyya* (fem.), which here indicates the *nisba* of Arabic names, the component that indicates a person's origin or ancestry in some way. E.g., *nūbiyya* translates to "Nubian," or "Nubian woman."

127. T-S 13J21.18. This case is also discussed in chap. 2.

128. Bruning, "Slave Trade Dynamics," 685n13, 690n50, 695.

129. For one recent example, Rachel Schine argues that the "blackness" of several heroes in medieval Arabic epic literature was used to "weave aspirational histories of the Muslim world community." See idem, *Black Knights*, 7 and passim.

130. Nāṣir-i Khusraw, *Book of Travels*, 41 (English), 86 (Persian). See also chap. 2, 98n, where Nāṣir-i makes the juxtaposition between black (Nubian) and white (*Rūmī*) slaves.

131. Benjamin here uses biblical toponyms to describe the region. Isaiah 43:3: God gives Israel "Egypt as ransom for you, *Kush* and *Seba* as an exchange for you." Psalms 72:10: "Let the Kings of Tarshish and the islands pay tribute, kings of Sheba and Seba offer gifts." For a critical analysis of the geography and travel described in this leg of Benjamin's journey, see Fauvelle-Aymar, "Desperately Seeking the Jewish Kingdom of Ethiopia."

132. Adler, *Itinerary*, 68 (English), 62 (Hebrew).

133. Olsson, "The World in Arab Eyes," 489. Olsson underscores differences between how Ptolemy and later Arab writers theorized the climes and mapped them onto the known world. Ibid., 491–99. See also Barker, *That Most Precious Merchandise*, 39–60; Schine, "Translating Race," 338–39, 346, 350, 357; Ballan, "Borderland Anxieties"; Armstrong-Partida, "Race, Skin Colour, Enslavement, and Sexuality." Schine also pushes the analysis of medieval race-thinking beyond climatic theory and the Hamitic curse: idem, "Conceiving the Pre-Modern Black-Arab Hero" and idem, *Black Knights*, 13, 31, 229–72.

134. From *Rasā'il ikhwān al-ṣafā' wa-khillān al-wafā'* as quoted in Olsson, "World in Arab Eyes," 488.

135. Ibn al-Faqīh al-Hamadhānī, *Mukhtasạr Kitāb al-Buldān*, 161–62, as translated and discussed in Olsson, "World in Arab Eyes," 490.

136. Sitt al-Sumr: T-S 13J22.2. Sumr (possibly the same person): T-S AS 147.23. Sumr's life history is discussed in chap. 7. A woman described as "carob-colored" (dark brown?): T-S Ar. 42.174.

137. Goldenberg argues that Benjamin is *not* making a reference to the curse of Ḥam in this statement, and that "black Africans" are indeed intended. See Goldenberg, *Black and Slave*, 75, 114–15. The apposition between "black slaves" and "sons of Ḥam" suggests to me that he is drawing a connection between the two.

First, as Goldenberg shows, Benjamin and other medieval writers did not use "Africa" or "Africans" to refer to the continent and its peoples. The Arabic term Ifrīqiyya referred more narrowly to the region that roughly corresponds with modern-day Tunisia. The people who lived in the region that Benjamin describes belonged to groups that he mentions in the text: Nubians, Kushites, Abyssinians, and those from biblical Seba (perhaps itself a reference to Nubia). Second, the theory of climes shaped Benjamin's views. The "sons of Ḥam" came to live in parts of the world where conditions were believed to cause blackness.

The more important point to Goldenberg here is that Benjamin and Maimonides were not invoking the "dual curse," meaning an interpretation of the curse of Ḥam that understood it to refer to both slave status and "blackening." The biblical curse emphasized slavery, but not "blackening" as the punishment. Benjamin presents the people in the region as "Black slaves" who descend from a lineage cursed with slave status and whose location caused their blackness and allegedly backward behaviors. Benjamin does not mean that he viewed Black-skinned people as the only ones cursed with slavery.

138. *MT, Hilkhot mattenot 'aniyyim* (Laws of Gifts for the Poor), 10:17. See Goldenberg, *Black and Slave*, 114–15 and there in n24. As with Benjamin's reference to the "sons of Ḥam," Goldenberg reads Maimonides's mentions of "the descendants of Ḥam" to mean "Black Africans" and not to be a reference to the curse of Ḥam. Maimonides likely completed the *Mishneh Torah* in the decade after Benjamin traveled through Egypt. See also the discussion in the previous note.

139. *M. Avot*, 1:5.

140. Genesis 9:18–25.

141. David M. Goldenberg, *Black and Slave*, 44–45. See also Goldenberg, *The Curse of Ham*.

142. Goldenberg, *Black and Slave*, see esp. 5, 87–95, 102–45.

143. Michael Gomez, *African Dominion*, 43–57.

144. Barker, *That Most Precious Merchandise*, 3, 13, 209. On enslavement and ransom in the context of conflicts between Christian and Muslim forces, see Fancy, *Mercenary Mediterranean*; idem, "Captivity, Ransom, and Manumission."

145. See Michael Gomez, *African Dominion*, 51–52.

146. On the interplay between Jewish and Islamic law, see chap. 1.

147. The *geniza* evidence ca. 1000–1250 supports Barker's findings for the later Mamluk era and the Italian-Egyptian slave trade from the Black Sea and non-Islamic Africa. Barker, *That Most Precious Merchandise*, chap. 2 and esp. 59–60.

148. On this topic, see Epstein, *Speaking of Slavery*; Davis, *Inhuman Bondage*, esp. 48–102; Epstein, "Attitudes Toward Blackness."

Chapter 4. Slavery *lil-Khidma* in the City

1. Historian Kyle Harper has critiqued use of the term "domestic" slavery and shown that it included different types of labor across different domains in the Roman context: Harper, *Slavery*, 101. In his analysis of Islamic contexts, Franz has emphasized that enslaved people, despite how they and their locations are described, likely engaged in a broad range of labors that defy easy categorization: Franz, "Slavery," 99, 101, on enslaved people in an oasis economy.

2. As Katz notes, *khidma* also has moral and spiritual resonances. The phrase *khidmat al-bayt* more narrowly denotes housework. See the extensive discussions of *khidma* in idem, *Wives and Work*, 7, 30–31, 51–52, 122–23 passim.

3. T-S 12.254, right margin, l. 5ff. Mardūkh's search for an enslaved woman is discussed in chapter 2.

4. Emphasis mine. See the discussion in chap. 6.

5. Textual silence about domestic slavery: Gordon, "Preliminary Remarks," 71, 80–81; idem, "Slavery in the Islamic Middle East," 340. Silence about domestic and women's labor in general: Shatzmiller, *Labour*, 347; idem, "Women and Wage Labour"; Marmon, "Domestic Slavery," 9; Katz, *Wives and Work*, 28–33. Female labor in the Fatimid world at large: Cortese and Calderini, *Women and the Fatimids*, 201–3.

6. On the difficulty of pinpointing evidence of slavery in Islamic and African contexts: Alexander, "Islam, Archaeology and Slavery"; Lane, "Slavery in Africa." Slavery in medieval manuscript illustrations: Balafrej, "Domestic Slavery," and idem, "Automated Slaves." The "invisibility" of the slave trade in medieval Europe: Fontaine, "Early Medieval Slave-Trading"; Raffield, "Slave Markets." See also Biermann and Jankowiak, eds., *Archaeology of Slavery*; Gruszczyński et al., eds., *Viking-Age Trade*; Sutherland, "Study of Slavery," e12633.

7. Lane, "Slavery in Africa," 541.

8. See the discussion in Richardson, *Roma*, 63, and the discussion in chap. 7.

9. Ibn Buṭlān, *Risāla*, 371–78; Mez, *Renaissance of Islam*, 160–62; Lewis, *Islam*, 2:245–51; Cortese and Calderini, *Women and the Fatimids*, 204–5. Another medieval slave-buying manual: Barker, "Purchasing a Slave." An epistolary and documentary manual from medieval Gujarat also provides lists of labors that enslaved women were expected to do as enumerated in model bills of sale. See the discussion in chap. 7.

10. In contrast, another manual of slave-buying advice in a Mirror for Princes advises that men can do cooking and domestic labor if they are "clean in face and body," among other qualities. See the *Qābūs-nāma* of Kai Kaʿus in Levi and Sela, eds., *Islamic Central Asia*, 95–100.

11. Cortese and Calderini, *Women and the Fatimids*, 204.

12. In *geniza* documents, a singing slave-woman is called a *jāriya mughanniya* and not a *qayna*. Ṣirf (a *jāriya mughanniya*): T-S NS 320.5, l. 14. Ṣirf is mentioned in the context of a larger legal dispute, though the fragmentary nature of the document makes it difficult to understand how she figured into it. See Zinger, "Women, Gender, and Law," 232n88. ʿAbīr, an

enslaved singer (*mughanniya*) and professional wailer (*al-nā'iḥa*) who sold for 40 and 1/24 dinars: RNL Yevr.-Arab I 1700.15v. Goitein, *MS*, 1:139. Thank you to Oded Zinger for sharing his draft transcription and Hebrew translation of this scribal notebook.

13. Professional lamenters (wailing women) were also paid: Halevi, "Wailing for the Dead," 14, 27. Some modern ethnographic studies of wailing women in Middle Eastern contexts include Abu-Lughod, "Islam and the Gendered Discourses of Death"; Gamliel, "Performed Weeping"; and idem, "Tears and Ideas." Thanks to Sally Abed for bringing this scholarship to my attention.

14. The Black woman Sa'āda is called a *dāda*: ENA NS 48.6. Her history is discussed in chap. 6. The enslaved (*jāriya*) Nubian woman Sha'ath is not called a *dāda* in the deed of quittance that mentions her. Her childcare duties are described, however. See T-S 16.134, ll. 16–18. Goitein, *MS*, 1:135.

15. T-S 12.432, ll. 11–14. A man named Joseph approached the owner (fem.), or handler, of the enslaved wet nurse (*Sitt [al-]jār[iya] al-murḍi'a*). The letter writer states that she is only worth half of the proposed price, which is not specified. Thanks to Alan Elbaum for bringing this document to my attention. The more common term for wet nurse in *geniza* documents is *dāya*, but these women are not generally described as enslaved when they are mentioned. On enslaved wet nurses in medieval Iberia, see Winer, "Enslaved Wet Nurse"; idem, "Conscripting the Breast."

16. Jinān: F 1908.44SS. Gottheil and Worrell, eds., *Fragments*, no. XLIV. See the more recent edition of this record and its discussion in Frenkel, "Slave Trade," 156–57.

17. *MT*, *Hilkhot Ishut* (Laws of Marriage), 21:1–6. See also *MT*, *Hilkhot Ishut*, 21:14. Maimonides's list mostly repeats the kinds of work found in a list from the 2nd century CE in *M.Ketubbot* 5:5. This list is also discussed in the *Tosefta* and the *Talmuds*. For a critical reading of the Mishnaic list and an assessment of how it has been (mis)used in modern scholarship, see Gopalakrishnan, "Wives' Work." In his rendition, Maimonides adds the task of feeding the husband's riding beast to the list found in the earlier Mishnah.

18. *MT*, *Hilkhot Ishut*, 21:5–7. No matter how many enslaved people a husband and/or wife owned, the wife was required to spin thread following the presumption that "idleness leads to lewdness." *MT*, *Hilkhot Ishut*, 21:3. The practical and symbolic value of enslaved labor for slave-owning Jewish women is discussed at length in chap. 6.

19. *MT*, *Hilkhot Ishut*, 21:1. *ha-kol ke-minhag ha-medina*.

20. Commonly referenced simply as Sherira Gaon. On the dates for the geonim of Iraq and Palestine, see Brody, *Geonim*, 341–45, and Rustow, *Heresy*, 363.

21. Lewin, *Oṣar ha-Geonim*, *Ketubbot* 59, no. 429, vol. 8, pp. 170–71. Maimonides seems to understand that "grinding" entailed working a mill, or monitoring the work of the miller, and not necessarily grinding grain by hand. *MT*, *Hilkhot Ishut*, 21:5. On the technologies of grinding and milling, and their historical evolutions, see Gopalakrishnan, "Wives' Work," 432–34.

22. Marriage documents from the *geniza* used these idealized lists of labors to emphasize the duty and subordination of women to their husbands. See a postnuptial agreement in which the bride is compelled to agree to "never sit idle," but to bake, cook, and produce linen and wool textiles: PER H 82, ll. 9, 14–16. Goitein, *MS*, 3:214–15.

23. Enslaved women preferred for "domestic" labor: Goitein, *MS*, 1:134, 137. The most common "type" of enslaved male found in *geniza* records is the *ghulām*, who was usually bound to

merchants and communal officials. *Ghulāms*, compared to *waṣīfs*, were probably less likely to do labor within the household. I plan a more comprehensive study of the scopes of their activities in future publications. Eunuchs are omitted from these numbers because there is no record of their ownership in the *geniza* documents. The *geniza* does furnish evidence of their trafficking to Egypt in chap. 1, and sparse additional evidence of their activities in their service of the caliphs, sultans, and their retinues. Eunuchs in Fatimid Egypt: Tolino, "Eunuchs"; El-Azhari, *Queens, Eunuchs and Concubines*. See also Hogendorn, "The Hideous Trade"; El-Cheikh, "Servants at the Gate"; Marmon, *Eunuchs and Sacred Boundaries*; Trabelsi, "Eunuchs, Power, and Slavery."

24. See chap. 1. Two exceptions: Khulla bt. Shabbāt owned a *ghulām*; a woman sold a *Rūmī mamlūk*. See, respectively, TS 10J7.10c and chap. 6, 8n. I have not found evidence that discusses free women being alone with enslaved men. There are ample discussions of free men residing alone with enslaved females, and such references are generally meant to indicate that a Jewish man is using the woman as a sex slave. See chap. 5.

25. The history of sexual slavery among Egyptian Jews animates much of chap. 5, see also the discussion in chap. 1.

26. *MT*, *Hilkhot Ishut*, 21:3–8. Wives are instructed not to do this work during *nidda* (a state of ritual impurity due to menstruation).

27. On Maimonides's attitudes toward menstruation, ritual purity, and married household life, see Krakowski, "Maimonides' Menstrual Reform." Discussed in chap. 6.

28. Frenkel, "Slavery in Medieval Jewish Society," 257.

29. Harrison, "Fusṭāṭ Reconsidered." See the discussion and illustrations of Harrison's reconstructions in Krakowski, *Coming of Age*, 277–79. See also Goitein, *MS*, 4:1–105, 226–61; idem, "A Mansion in Fusṭāṭ," esp. the diagram on p. 22.

30. Lewicka, *Food and Foodways*. A *geniza* document lists payments for materials and workers involved in the construction and repair of a wind catcher and sewage gutter: ENA 2808.63. Published in Gil, *Documents*, no. 18, pp. 187–88.

31. Narkiss, "Jewish Bread or Cheese Stamp." Delivery of baked bread: see the discussion in chap. 6 and the sources there in 12n. The design of the bread stamp in figure 4.2 is not a specifically Jewish design, but it may be associated with the biblical king Solomon, who it was believed controlled spirits (*jinn*) and magic. Thus the symbol could have an apotropaic (protection from evil) function. See the Quran 27:17. Thanks to Stephennie Mulder for consulting with me about this bread stamp design in a private communication and for recommending the essay al-Saleh, "Amulets and Talismans." Note the latter's extensive bibliography.

32. See the discussions in chaps. 3 and 6.

33. Dowries of slave-owning women: T-S J1.29; MS Heb. d 66/48 + 66/47. See the editions and translations in Goitein, "Three Trousseaux." Enslaved and freed people also wore simple versions of the clothing that brides received in their dowries. See chap. 8.

34. Nāṣir-i Khusraw, *Book of Travels*, 69.

35. Nāṣir-i Khusraw, *Book of Travels*, 69.

36. Nāṣir-i Khusraw, *Book of Travels*, 66–72.

37. Enslaved women (*jāriyas*) sent to deliver items: MS Heb. d 66/59b, l. 19; T-S AS 147.18, l. 1; JRL Series B 6116, ll.7–8. The *jāriya* as mobile factotum: Balafrej, "Instrumental Jawārī," 117.

38. *MT*, *Hilkhot mechira*, 18:1–4. My translation differs slightly from Touger's. *Qeliot*: "roasted seeds," or "roasted grain."

39. Women and girls of course did productive labor that contributed to personal and household wealth, mainly through different kinds of textile work, and unpaid work in the home. Krawkowski, *Coming of Age*, esp. 160–65. Slave-owning women are not, however, identified with professional titles as men are and I have thus excluded them from this analysis. The connection between free and enslaved women's labor is also discussed in chap. 6.

40. Sometimes professional titles are given after the name of the slave owner's father. Such is the case for [A]bū al-ʿIzz son [of] Abū ʿImrān the potion maker (*al-sharābī*). Who is the potion maker? Is it Abū al-ʿIzz or his father Abū ʿImrān? Did Abū al-ʿIzz follow in his father's professional footsteps? Further, men often did a succession of different kinds of work over the course of their lives and could occupy multiple roles simultaneously. I use the aggregate data for gender and occupation to think broadly about the connections between slavery, gender, labor, and the social status of slave owners.

41. Even though Ibn Buṭlān regarded sex as a common and expected form of enslaved labor, sex was not considered part of *khidma*.

42. Seʿadya b. Abraham and ʿAbīr: T-S 8J8.4. The perfumer Abū ʿAlī sells the woman Misk: T-S 13J37.12r. Additional examples of slave-owning medical workers are in the appendix. Goitein, *MS*, 1:133; 2:263.

43. An account list of a charitable trust does list "the hired worker of Ḥasan the perfumer (*al-ʿaṭṭār*)." Mention of such hired workers in the *geniza* are uncommon, however. See T-S NS J342v, published in Gil, *Documents*, no. 43, 242–44.

44. For a work of speculative fiction set in a premodern Cairene apothecary run by a Jewish pharmacist, see Chakraborty, *City of Brass*, esp. 8–13.

45. Chipman and Lev, "Syrups from the Apothecary's Shop."

46. Chipman and Lev, "Syrups from the Apothecary's Shop," 144–45.

47. Chipman and Lev, "Syrups from the Apothecary's Shop."

48. No arsenic in the courtyard: T-S 10J28.13, l. 12. Published in Gil, *Documents*, no. 98, 372–74.

49. Popper, *History of Egypt*, 103–4. See also "The Slave Woman of al-Manṣūr Ḥājjī," Teaching Medieval Slavery and Captivity, www.medievalslavery.org/middle-east-and-north-africa/source-the-slave-women-of-al-man%e1%b9%a3ur-hajji/.

50. Schiel, "Mord von zarter Hand."

51. Barker, *That Most Precious Merchandise*.

52. As an analogy, consider that the author of one medieval Syrian cookbook credits a recipe for pickled citrus fruit to "the slave girls (*jawār[ī]*) of the caliphal palace." Perry, ed., *Scents and Flavors*, recipe no. 8.52.

53. Another of Moses Maimonides's writings is a dietary manual that he wrote for an unknown Ayyubid official so that he could more potently use his many enslaved women for procreation and his own pleasure. See Bos, *Maimonides* On Coitus, ix, 7, 26 and chap. 5, 78n.

54. Goitein, *MS*, 1:79, 101–4 passim. See also Shatzmiller, *Labour*, 121. The silk weaver Abū al-Faraj's slave owning is a subject in chap. 5.

55. Candle maker and seller: Araḥ al-Shammāʿ, T-S 8J4.21. Goldsmith: Abū Yaʿqūb Joseph b. Samuel b. Naḥūm: T-S 8J5.1a. He is not called *al-ṣāʾigh* in this document, but the amount and types of gold in the inventory of his estate indicate that he was a goldsmith.

56. T-S AS 147.18, JRL Series B 6116.

57. In the business accounts he kept in India, the Jewish merchant and slave owner Abraham b. Yijū records payments that were made for the maintenance of other people's slaves (*al-'abīd*) and "the smelter's boy" (*ṣabī al-sabbāk*). See T-S 20.137v, (B)1, l. 8; (B)2, l. 2; and (D), l. 2. Translation in Goitein and Friedman, *India Traders*, 635–43, where they suggest "workmen" for *ṣibyān* in 639n19 and "son or servant" for *ṣabī* at 640n30.

58. Yefet b. Shemarya sells the woman Rahaj: ENA 4011.63. Gil identifies the parnas Abū 'Alī al-Ne'emān as this Yefet b. Shemarya in T-S 16.222, published in *Documents*, no. 50, 262–64. The "*jāriya* of the parnas": T-S Misc. 28.184. It was a Qaraite courtier, Abū Sa'd Ibrāhīm al-Tustarī, whose former enslaved woman, Raṣad, became the concubine mother of the Fatimid caliph al-Mustanṣir. See chaps. 1 and 2.

59. Ḥanūn b. 'Allūn: T-S Ar. 42.174. Published by both Khan *ALAD*, no. 56, 262–63, and 'Aodeh, "Eleventh Century Letters," no. 5, 219–20. Note that Khan and 'Aodeh read this document differently with regard to certain details. Another Christian scribe, 'Abd al-Masīḥ b. Maqāra b. Harūn, and a business associate of the trader and communal leader Nahray b. Nissim, purchased the Nubian woman Na'īm from Nahray's widow, Sitt al-Munā, in 1115. T-S 18J1.17v. 'Aodeh, "Eleventh Century Letters," no. 68, 417–18, and Perry, *6th/12th Century Supplementary Deed of Sale*. While Jewish scribes wrote bills of sale for enslaved people, and were almost certainly involved in connecting would-be sellers and buyers, no direct evidence of them as individual slave owners has been preserved.

60. See appendix 3 for Moses b. Samuel; Zakkār b. 'Ammār; Joshua b. Dosā; Evyatar ha-Kohen; *al-rayyis*; and Zakkay *ha-dayyan*.

61. Taqarrub once belonged to another enslaved woman, a Coptic *umm walad* of the Fatimid caliph al-'Azīz. On account of her owner's station, this *umm walad* is known as *al-sayyida* al-'Azīziyya, or al-'Azīza (d. 995). The caliph al-'Azīz freed al-'Azīza and married her. The princess Sitt al-Mulk was their free-born daughter. See Cortese and Calderini, *Women and the Fatimids*, 117–18; Rustow, "Petition to a Woman," 12; Lev, *Administration of Justice*, 143.

62. Sitt al-Mulk is a compelling figure, both to medieval and modern historians. As Cortese and Calderini put it: "Court maverick, daddy's girl, a fratricide to some, to many the brain behind some high-profile murders, Sitt al-Mulk stands out as one of those few women who are extensively written about in medieval Islamic sources." Her notoriety is one reason why we learn some details about a few of the reportedly four thousand enslaved women that she controlled. Cortese and Calderini, *Women and the Fatimids*, 117–18.

63. Ibn Buṭlān, *Risāla*, 356. The translation is a revised version of the one in Swain, *Economy, Family, and Society*, 272. Cf. Lewis, *Islam*, 2:244. See the discussion of enslaved people's use of acquired knowledge in chap.7.

64. Enslaved men were also sometimes literate. See the discussion of the *ghulām* and freedman Faraj in chap. 8.

65. See chap. 6.

66. T-S 12.582. On this incident, see esp. the introduction and chap. 5.

67. Ghosh, *Antique Land*; idem, "The Slave of MS. H.6"; Goitein and Friedman, *India Traders*, 52–89 passim; Goitein and Friedman, eds., *Abraham ben Yijū*; Lambourn, *Abraham's Luggage*, see esp. 37–66 for an overview of Ben Yijū's life in India. Some of Ben Yijū's letters and accounts are published in Goitein, *Letters of Medieval Jewish Traders*; Goitein and Friedman, *India Traders*; idem, *Abraham ben Yijū*; and Lambourn, *Abraham's Luggage*.

68. IOM D 55.10. Goitein and Friedman, eds., *India Traders*, 54–57 passim, and idem, *Abraham ben Yijū*, 162–66, passim.

69. The scholar Ophira Gamliel argues that Ashū was not an enslaved woman but a free woman and member of the Nāyar caste of landowners. See Gamliel, "Aśu the Convert." In her reading, Abraham b. Yijū created a deed of manumission for Ashū as a legal stratagem to protect the Jewish status of the children that he apparently had with her. The implication is that Abraham lied about Ashū's legal status because it was his best option in Jewish law to convince Jews back in Yemen, Egypt, and beyond that his children were "proper Jews" for the purpose of their future marriages. The Jewish legal texts discussed in chaps. 1 and 6 show that jurists did suspect some men of lying about the status of enslaved women, and the timing of their manumission. Thus, it is at least plausible to suspect Ibn Yijū of creating a fictional history for Ashū. For present purposes, I stress that merchants like Ben Yijū, of which there were many, commonly bought and sold women for sex across the Mediterranean and Indian Ocean worlds. More research is needed about the social history of slavery in medieval Kerala between 1000–1250. Could, for example, historical contingencies lead to the enslavement of a higher-class women like a Nāyar (the class to which Ashū seems to have belonged)? A recent publication on slavery in medieval South India is Orr, "Slavery and Dependency."

70. Ibn Baṭṭūṭa's date of death: A. Miquel, "Ibn Baṭṭūṭa." On Ibn Baṭṭūṭa as a slave owner: Tolmacheva, "Concubines."

71. Tolmacheva, "Concubines," 171–72. He divorced his Indian wives and left them there.

72. See the discussions in chaps. 1, 5, and the conclusion.

73. Evidence suggests that prostitutes were free women and not enslaved. Cortese and Calderini, *Women and the Fatimids*, 203.

74. Friedman, "Polygyny in Jewish Tradition"; idem, "*Halacha* as Evidence"; idem, "Women and the India Trade." On sex with minor girls, see Krakowski, *Coming of Age*, 119, 129–40. Free women sometimes had sexual relations, both in and out of marriage, but we know little about their sexual activities. Women's sexuality is even more rarely discussed than men's liaisons due to the confluence of legal sanctions, social pressure, and cultural taboo that surrounded it. One case, rare in its documentation, in which a woman committed adultery and became pregnant, is discussed in Friedman, "Women and the India Trade," 173–75.

75. Goldberg, *Trade and Institutions*, 12–13, 48–49, 78–84.

76. T-S 10J16.1. Published in Goitein, "Portrait." See also Friedman, "Women and the India Trade," 173. ʿArūs is the purple-dye merchant (*al-arjawānī*, poss. *al-urjuwānī*) who purchased a *jāriya* from a Christian scribe. See 59n in this chapter.

77. Goitein surmises that the lacuna be completed "who ser[ves them drinks]." Note Friedman's corrections to Goitein's edition: Friedman, "Women and the India Trade," 173n52.

78. T-S 13J13.24. Goitein, *MS*, 2:279–80; Constable, *Housing the Stranger*, 101, 105; Frenkel, "*The Compassionate and Benevolent*" (2006 Hebrew edition), 495–97; idem, "Medieval Alexandria," 29.

79. ENA 3901.5. Edited by Naïm Vanthieghem and translated by Marina Rustow. Published in PGP: https://geniza.princeton.edu/documents/32717/.

80. Probably sought intervention: Only the first part of the petition is preserved, which contains the description of the problem. The section of the petition that would normally contain the request (the *qiṣṣā*) is lost. See Rustow, "Fatimid Petition," 368.

81. ENA 3901.5. Translation by Rustow. The petitioner does not state that the man and woman had sex. I argue that descriptions of situations in which men and women are described as being alone together are meant to imply that they are having sex. See my analysis of such sources in chap. 6.

82. T-S NS J286. Goitein, *Letters of Medieval Jewish Traders,* 339. Thanks to Brendan Goldman for bringing this document and ENA 3901.5 to my attention.

83. Goitein, *MS,* 3:147; Friedman, "Monogamy Clause"; idem, "Pre-Nuptial Agreements"; idem, *Jewish Polygyny.*

84. Friedman, "Monogamy Clause"; idem, "Pre-Nuptial Agreements"; idem, *Jewish Marriage*; idem, *Jewish Polygyny.*

85. Ashur, "India Trade." See also idem, "Engagement and Betrothal Documents"; idem, "Protecting the Wife's Rights."

86. Such a case is discussed in chap. 7.

Chapter 5. Slavery and Masculinity

1. DK 232.1 and T-S 10J17.22, the latter of which was written after the former. DK 232.1 is transcribed in Steiner, *Három arab kézirat,* iv–vi, no. 2. See also Goitein, *MS,* 3:24nn54–55; Friedman, *Jewish Polygyny,* 33n104. Zinger, *Living with the Law,* 131–33; Yagur, "Religious Identity," 84. Samuel b. Ḥananya's son Moses is mentioned as a slave owner in chap. 4 and in appendix 3.

2. On the meaning of *qazzāz,* see chap. 4, 54n. Abū al-Faraj's wife identifies herself only as *'abdatuhu* (his slave) in the address on the verso of DK 232.1. "His slave," or "your slave," is a common expression used by supplicants in petitions to their would-be patrons as a sign of deference and respect. See Khan, ed., *ALAD,* 306–10; Rustow, "Petition to a Woman"; and idem, *Lost Archive,* 96.

3. See the explanation of the delayed marriage gift and "ransom-divorce" in Zinger, *Living with the Law,* ix. See also Friedman, "Ransom-Divorce."

4. T-S 10J17.22, ll. 20–22. A similar claim is made in DK 232.1v, l. 3–4. We also read that Samuel had ordered Abū al-Faraj to send the *jāriya ilā al-ḥujra,* which he refused to do. It seems that *ḥujra* was a term used in the Mamluk era to denote a holding room for enslaved people. Here it may refer to such a place at a slave market, which would make it a rare reference in the *geniza* corpus to a standing (permanent) slave market in Fustat-Cairo. DK 232.1, ll. 20–21. Hagedorn, *Domestic Slavery in Syria and Egypt,* 40. See the discussion of the local slave trade in chap. 3.

5. T-S 10J17.22, ll. 20–22. *Annahu lam yukhrijhā al-dilāla.* On broker's fees (*dilāla*), see Goitein, *MS,* 1:160–61, 185; Rāġib, *Actes de vente,* 2:50; Goitein and Friedman, *India Traders,* 577n3; and see the discussion in chap. 3.

6. Goitein, *MS,* 1:130–47; Friedman, *Jewish Polygyny,* 32–34, 290–339; Frenkel, "Slavery in Medieval Jewish Society"; Yagur, "Religious Identity," chap. 2 and especially pp. 101–15. For the Fatimid period more specifically, see Cortese and Calderini, *Women and the Fatimids,* 45–46, 70–83. See also chap. 1 and the sources cited there.

7. Friedman, "Monogamy Clause"; idem, "Master and Slave Girl"; idem, "Pre-Nuptial Agreements"; idem, *Jewish Polygyny.* On this ambiguity and liminality, see Yagur, "Religious Identity," chap. 2; idem, *Crossing the Line.*

8. Friedman, *Jewish Polygyny*, 34. On Islamic and Jewish laws of sexual slavery, see chap. 1.

9. Frenkel, "Slavery in Medieval Jewish Society."

10. ENA 3765.10, verso. The author of the letter is unknown, but the circumstances surrounding this missive and its contents are well documented. Mark R. Cohen found a continuation of ENA 3765.10 in T-S 18J4.16. See Mark R. Cohen, "New Light." Cohen and Gil date the letter to 1039. Jacob b. ʿAmram was alive as late as 1060. See Goitein, *MS*, 2:24–25; Gil, *Palestine*, 2:332–34. Death date according to Gil, *History of Palestine, 634–1099*, 858.

11. ENA 3765.10v, ll. 22–23. See the translation in Cohen, "New Light," 12, 21–22, 25.

12. Cf. Gamliel, "Aśu the Convert" and chap. 4, 69n.

13. Maimonides, *Responsa*, 2:373–75, no. 211.

14. Maimonides, *Responsa*, 2:373–75, no. 211. Emphasis mine. See the partial translation in Yagur, "Community's Borders," 61.

15. Frenkel argues that these rulings reflect that Maimonides and his contemporaries yielded to "a widespread social phenomenon." See Frenkel, "Slavery in Medieval Jewish Society," 256; Yagur, "Religious Identity," 105–15. See also El-Leithy's analysis of sexual slavery among the Coptic clergy in chap. 1 and Weitz, *Between Christ and Caliph*; idem, "Slavery and the Historiography of Non-Muslims."

16. Lomba, "Maimonides, Abraham ben Moses," and the sources cited there. Friedman, "Responsa of R. Abraham Maimonides"; and Russ-Fishbane, *Judaism, Sufism, and the Pietists*.

17. Freimann and Goitein, *Abraham Maimuni*, no. 21. It is possible that the continued discussion of the *pilegesh* was in part prompted by Qaraite Jews, who did not accept rabbinic law as authoritative and for whom the biblical text (the Written Torah) was paramount. In one prenuptial agreement, composed according to Qaraite traditions, a groom agrees not to take a *pilegesh*. See Friedman, "Monogamy Clause," 22.

18. Assaf, "From the Treasury of the Geniza"; Goitein, "Geniza Papers," 37 and n6; Goitein, *MS*, 1:134; Friedman, *Jewish Polygyny*, 319–30.

19. Roth, "Asking Questions." Scholars debate whether responsa queries may be trusted as descriptions of actual events and social practices, or whether they are abstracted, hypothetical scenarios tailored to other purposes, rhetorical, jurisprudential, and so forth. Lifshitz, "Legal Status"; Soloveitchik, *Use of Responsa*; Lieberman, "One Question, Two Answers"; idem, "One Jurist, Two Answers"; and Zinger, *Living with the Law*, 23–26 passim.

20. DK 231.2 (alt: XXV). The document is torn away below the second query and, thus, no response is preserved.

21. DK 231.2. I have omitted the lengthy encomium to Abraham Maimonides with which this query writer begins (ll. 1–5). The last line of this translation (l. 12) follows Friedman's transcription in idem, *Jewish Polygyny*, 323. My reading of the original agrees with Friedman's reconstruction.

22. Or. 10652.2 (alt: Gaster 1638.2). This manuscript is also torn at the top and bottom edges, perhaps because its owner wanted to keep this specific query for reference. On the verso, a note reads "Legal responses (Ar. *fatāwā*) addressed to the leader of this period, the one who is relied upon in his generation, the leader of the nation, the Nagid, may his glory be enhanced." Translation from Goitein, "Geniza Papers," 36.

23. T-S 6J2.15 + T-S 10K8.13. Friedman published the larger, bottom part of this responsum (T-S 10K8.13) in Friedman, *Jewish Polygyny*, 319–22. T-S 6J2.15 is unpublished, though its image is available in CUDL (Cambridge University Digital Library), FGP, and PGP.

24. T-S 10K8.13, ll. 2–3.

25. Here an allusion to Judges 17:6, 21:25, and Jeremiah 12:11.

26. T-S 10K8.13.

27. T-S 10K8.13. The litany of questions in this query serves a rhetorical purpose. Yet the narrative details provided by the author are not simply gratuitous. See the sources cited in this chapter at 19n. On responsa queries that contain such "simple and clear-cut" issues, see Goitein, *MS*, 3:339.

28. The flax trade was one mainstay of *geniza* merchants' activity. Gil, "Flax Trade," and Goldberg, *Trade and Institutions*.

29. *Aksāhā kiswa ḥasana mā labisathā zawjatuhu min ʿumrihā*. T-S 10K8.13, ll. 4–5. Friedman, *Jewish Polygyny*, 320.

30. On the *geṭ* (bill of divorce), see Zinger, *Living with the Law*, vii–ix, 1–2, 79–83 passim. See also Friedman, "Ransom-Divorce," and idem, "Divorce upon the Wife's Demand." See also the discussion in this book's conclusion that assesses such behavior in light of Zinger's arguments about the "masculinity of belonging" in the Egyptian Jewish community. Idem, *Living with the Law*, 149–50.

31. It does not seem likely that the writers' references to *qiddushin* and *ketubba* are indirect references to the dormant Jewish legal category of the *pilegesh*. The Jerusalem and Babylonian Talmuds discuss *pilagshut* (concubinage) in the most sparing terms. While the Jerusalem Talmud specifies that the *pilegesh* must be betrothed to her master (with *qiddushin*), the Babylonian Talmud does not require it. Neither tradition requires a master to give a *pilegesh* a *ketubba* that would specify her rights in the arrangement. See chap. 1, 49n, 50n.

32. On the Jewish laws of slavery and conversion, chap. 1.

33. DK 232.1v, ll. 2–4; T-S 10J17.22, ll. 21–22.

34. DK 232.1r, ll. 9 and v, ll. 1–4, 7. See 53n in this chapter.

35. T-S Misc. 27.4.23 + 29. First published in Friedman, "Master and Slave-Girl." An updated edition and Hebrew translation is published in idem, *Jewish Polygyny*, 314–19. See also Yagur, "Religious Identity," 106, 122, 242, 255, 285. See also "A Merchant's Tale" in Cobb, *Race for Paradise*, 169–74. This "tale" describes a merchant who purchases a woman in Crusader-era Acre (Akko) and returns to Egypt with her.

36. Her name is partly obliterated where the document is torn in two. T-S Misc. 27.4.23 + 29, l. 6. Friedman and Yagur read A-K(h)-T(h)-R-Y. The letter *tav* is mostly illegible and the letter *resh* and *dalet* can be hard to distinguish in this scribe's handwriting. Ak[th]arī is a good solution but not the only possible one. Akbarī is another a possibility. There is another freedwoman, named Ibtidāʾ or Aktharā, in Or. 10588.3 (1154). I prefer here as elsewhere to acknowledge this ambiguity and to use a nickname for her based on an aspect of her history that we do know.

37. Yagur, "Religious Identity," 106, and see the sources cited there in n143. MS heb d 66/37, l. 15 in Gil, *Palestine*, 3: 463–464, no. 581, which Gil joined with MS heb d 66/93 in idem, *Ishmael*, 4:318–20, no. 699. ENA 4011.8 mentioned in idem, *Palestine*, 1:164n307.

38. We should not discount the possibility that someone informed on ʿEli to undermine him intentionally as part of some larger dispute. Yagur, "Religious Identity," 99–100. See my

discussion of Moses Maimonides's responsum no. 211 in this chapter and in chap. 7. At the same time, Abraham b. Yijū's case illustrates that men with children by their freed wives took their own initiative to create evidence that would support their children's claims to being born Jewish (from a free Jewish woman). On Abraham's case, see also chap. 4.

39. Karras, *Boys to Men*, 10.

40. Karras, *Boys to Men*, 10–11, 157–59 passim. Andreas Gotzmann has analyzed how Jewish men in early modern Ashkenaz also asserted their masculinity in competition with each other, and against their wives' interests, by deviating from legal and behavioral norms. See Gotzmann, "Respectability Tested." For a thought-provoking study of one "ideal" type of medieval Jewish man in Ashkenazi culture, see Boyarin, *Unheroic Conduct*. On this subject, see also Cullum, "Clergy, Masculinity and Transgression"; Hadley, "Introduction," 12–13; McSheffrey, "Men and Masculinity."

41. Armstrong-Partida, *Defiant Priests*, 17, 19.

42. Armstrong-Partida, *Defiant Priests*, 19.

43. Armstrong-Partida, *Defiant Priests*, 16–28.

44. Connell, *Masculinities*, 37.

45. *MT, Hilkhot Naḥalot*, 4:6. Discussed in chap. 1.

46. *Wa-laysa huwa mimman yahtamm bi-dīn*. DK 231.2, l. 8. Friedman, *Jewish Polygyny*, 322–24.

47. Freimann and Goitein, *Abraham Maimuni*, no. 21. Judges 17:6, 21:25. See also the translation and discussion earlier in this chapter of the fourth responsa query sent to Abraham Maimonides. It alludes to these words from the book of Judges as well as Jeremiah 12:11: "No man pays any heed." T-S 10K8.13, l. 7.

48. T-S 10K8.13. See the discussion of the limits of excommunication as an effective tool in chap. 1 and the sources cited there at 57n.

49. On the efficacy of excommunication, see chap. 1, 57n. On the issue of Jews and state power more broadly, see Rustow, *Lost Archive*, 264–67, and Goldberg, *Trade and Institutions*, 164–84, 244, 292–93. Jewish women also litigated in Muslim legal venues. See Zinger, "'She Aims to Harass Him,'" and the discussion in chaps. 6 and 7.

50. Maimonides, *Responsa*, no. 211. The query refers to the enslaved woman as a "beautiful captive" (*shifḥa yefat to'ar*). See the discussion in chap. 1.

51. Maimonides, *Responsa*, no. 211. The author uses the Hebrew *halshin 'oto* to emphasize the act of one Jew informing on another to non-Jewish authorities.

52. As Krakowski and Zinger note, a woman's access to effective male relatives was crucial for her ability to negotiate a favorable marital match and to negotiate the legal arena. Krakowski, *Coming of Age*, 15, 65–66, 171, 294–98; Zinger, *Living with the Law*, 64 passim.

53. DK 232.1. "I inform your Excellency, our lord, may you rule forever, that I am a desolate woman. I do not have (any option) except recourse to God and you. I have fallen in with a man who is not ashamed by his untoward words. My father does not provide for me from his income and my brother is (too) young and bashful (to help). I have fallen, truthfully, into great distress." Translation by myself and Oded Zinger. Idem, *Living with the Law*, 131–32. On the rhetoric of women's desolation and being "cut off," see Zinger, "Use of Social Isolation."

54. See also the discussion of T-S Misc. 23.8, discussed in chap. 6. A woman sues her brother over her purchase of a "defective" woman named Iftikhār. She went to the *qāḍī* to

appeal her case when her meeting with Jewish mediators failed to produce a satisfactory result for her.

55. "I demand justice" departs from Goitein's more literal translation of *wa-Abū Saʿīd* [Ibn Jamāhir] *yaqūl* [[*la-nā*]] *lā ukhallī ḥaqqī* (I will not relinquish my claim!). See T-S 12.582, l. 10.

56. These are not Ṣāfī's words, but an interpretation of them. His rhetorical strategy speaks to the pervasive patronage culture in which Ṣāfī himself participated as an always potential lower *mawlā* of his owner.

57. Jews in Egypt called migrants from Ifrīqiyya *Maghribīs* (men from the west). See Goldberg, *Trade and Institutions*, 41. Here the specific phrase is *wāḥid min al-tujjār al-mughāriba*. T-S 12.582, l. 12.

58. The word choice of *al-mughāriba* is meant to emphasize that the merchant who tried to intercede on Ṣāfī's behalf was not local and thus did not have a reputation, or associates, who might support him in his bid. He was thus at a major disadvantage vis-à-vis Ibn Jamāhir and his Muslim colleagues. T-S 12.582, l. 13.

59. T-S 12.582, l. 13–14. Goitein reads *wa-naṣa[bū la-hu]*, which he translates as "they threa[tened him]." The beginning of line 14 reads *al-juʿl wa-ghayri-hi*. A plausible reconstruction is *wa-naṣabū ʿalayhi al-juʿl wa-ghayrihi*. "They threatened him with (a) fine and other things." See Blau, *Dictionary*, 698 and Friedman, *Dictionary of Medieval Judeo-Arabic*, 536–37.

60. Following Goitein's translation in idem, *Letters*, 338. Cf. Blau, *Dictionary*, 176.

61. T-S 12.582, l. 14: *bi-khuṣāra*. Goitein translates this as "only after incurring the loss of money." See Goitein, *Letters of Medieval Jewish Traders*, 338.

62. S. D. Goitein, "African Port," 189–91.

63. Ibn Jamāhir was also known by his Hebrew name Ḥalfon b. Shemarya ha-Levi. In some documents, his *nasab* is written as Ibn *JMYHR* or Ibn *JMYYHR*. See Goitein and Friedman, *India Traders*, 526n6. He was active in Fustat, Aden, and Mangalore (India) as a merchant in textiles and pepper. Goitein and Friedman, *India Traders*, 96n29, 149–50, 331n13, and 524–26.

64. On the *wakīl al-tujjār*, see Margariti, *Aden*, 178–94, 210–11. This *wakīl al-tujjār* was Maḍmūn b. Ḥasan b. Bandār. Margariti, *Aden*, 39, 179, 180, 183–184, 187–193. Ibn Jamāhir's surviving family: T-S 13J8.17, ll. 4–5.

65. T-S 13J8.17, ll. 16–18. Translation from Goitein and Friedman, *India Traders*, 524–29. First published in Assaf, "Relations."

66. On the ways that orphans and enslaved girls were sometimes thought of analogously, see chap. 6.

67. Abū al-Ḥasan: T-S Misc. 24.137.4v. Goitein, *MS*, 2:570; 3:38, 435, n19, 443; 4:456, n110; 5:132, 542n23, 543, 629; Yagur, "Religious Identity," 88, 318. Goitein cites this document as the verso, but it appears as the recto in FGP.

68. T-S Misc. 24.137.4v, ll. 12ff. The relevant passage is on the bottom half of the page and is written perpendicular to the text above it. Even though Sitt al-Riʾāsa is described as *al-ṣaghīra*, it is not clear that she was a minor. A wedding trousseau dated to 1156, about four years before this will was drafted, seems to belong to her. RNL Yevr.-Arab. I 1700.25v cited in Goitein, *MS*, as Firkovitch II NS 1700, f.25a. Goitein, *MS*, 4:456.

69. T-S NS 321.54, ll. 7–8. The date is 1091 (l. 1). Goitein, *MS*, 3:358, 507. See also Perry, "Conversion."

70. T-S NS 321.54, l. 7.

71. T-S NS 321.54, l. 10, 13. On the use of *aṣḥābunā* in *geniza* documents, see Goldberg, *Trade and Institutions*, 38–39, and Margariti, "*Aṣḥābunā l-tujjār.*"

72. T-S NS 321.54, ll. 11–15. Sa'd al-Mulk was himself a prominent member of the local Jewish community. Rustow, *Heresy*, 378.

73. Connell, *Masculinities*, 37: "[T]he relationships constructing masculinity are dialectical; they do not correspond to the one-way causation of a socialization model."

74. The place of slavery in communal boundary-making is also a key aspect of Yagur's body of work. In particular idem, "Community's Borders"; idem, *Crossing the Line.*

75. Maimonides, *Responsa*, no. 211. Following Zinger, *Living with the Law*, 204n33.

76. *MT, Hilkhot 'avadim*, 9:8. My translation makes minor changes to Eliyahu Touger's.

77. Compare, for example, Maimonides's appeal to slave owners to the Muslim jurist al-Ghazālī's (d. 1111) instructions. Franz, "Slavery in Islam," 84–86.

78. Bos, ed., *Maimonides* On Coitus, 18, 26 (English), 27 (Arabic).

79. Zinger, "'She Aims to Harass Him,'" 186.

Chapter 6. Slavery and Femininity

1. Emphasis mine. T-S Misc. 25.107, ll. 12–15. The year is 1230. Goitein, *MS*, 1:144. There he cites it as T-S Box 25, f. 107. Partial transcription in Rivlin, *Inheritance and Wills*, 394–96. Sitt al-Dalāl enjoins that Munā shall not be harmed using the Judeo-Arabic *wa-lā tuḍāma*. Goitein and Rivlin read this word differently. See Goitein, *MS*, 1:144; 436n92, and Rivlin, *Inheritance and Wills*, 395–96. The reading *wa-lā tuḍāma* is supported by the scribe's placement of a dot above the Hebrew *tsadi* to denote an Arabic *ḍād*, as he clearly does in the word *tuḍāma* and above the Hebrew *gimmel* in the Judaeo-Arabic *jāriya*.

2. Goitein, "Wills"; idem, "Dispositions." See also T-S 13J24.10 in which a man describes the illness and death of his *jāriya*. As Krakowski notes in PGP, he quotes a condolence formulary from *BT, Berakhot*, 16b. This specific condolence is used to console someone upon the death of their donkey (*ḥamor*), or an enslaved person (*'eved* or *shifḥa*). On condolences for the deaths of enslaved people, see also Goitein, *MS*, 1:143. T-S 28.8 it is an epistolary model for how to write a letter of condolence upon the death of an enslaved woman. Friedman, *Jewish Polygyny*, 352; Yagur, "Religious Identity," 82n48. Such condolences parallel the congratulations that slave owners sent each other upon the successful purchase of enslaved people. Goitein, *MS*, 1:132n7.

3. On wills in the *geniza*, see Rivlin, *Inheritance and Wills*. Rachel Richman is currently writing a doctoral dissertation on women's property and social capital that makes extensive use of this type of document. Jewish men, too, used their deathbed declarations to free their household servants. See chaps. 3 and 5.

4. A key intervention comes in Stuard, "Ancillary Evidence." In the nineteenth-century United States: Jones-Rodgers, *They Were Her Property*.

5. T-S 13J21.18, discussed in chaps. 2 and 3. T-S NS J23, see chap. 2 and esp. chap. 7. See also JRL B 3311.

6. T-S J1.29. See chap. 3.

7. See T-S 18J1.17v and Maimonides, *Responsum*, no. 211. A fragmentary record suggests that Egyptian Jews also transacted with Muslim women. See T-S AS 202.415, first identified

by Alan Elbaum. The brief note mentions a *jāriya* named Shaʿaf, who belonged to the woman Fāṭima bt. [.r . . .].

8. On this subject, see chaps. 1 and 3. Another exception to this general rule: a mother sold her son a *Rūmī mamlūk*. Goitein, *MS*, 3:331, 501.

9. Analogous to kinship: McKee, "Households," 64.

10. Precedents in Jewish law encouraged masters to sell slaves who did not convert to Judaism after a period of time. Wacholder, "Halakhah"; Urbach, *Laws Regarding Slavery*. I have not found evidence in the *geniza* that Jewish owners sold enslaved people because they did not convert to Judaism. On enslaved people's conversion, see chaps. 7 and 8. Yagur, "Captives, Converts, and Concubines"; idem, "Shaving Hair"; idem, *Crossing the Line*.

11. Harkavy, ed., *Zikhron kamma geonim*, 224–25, no. 431. Frenkel, "Slavery in Medieval Jewish Society," 251. A second medieval responsum indicates that not all Jewish women were used to milling grain and that enslaved women were considered necessary for this task. Assaf, ed., *Teshuvot ha-geonim*, 21, no. 2. Gil, *Jews in Islamic Countries*, 610n338.

12. Lewicka, *Food and Foodways*, 102n126, 121, citing al-ʿAbdarī, *Al-Madkhal ilā tanmiyat al-aʿmāl*, 4:170, 172. Public bake-houses were also "liminal spaces" in Venetian Crete. See Lauer, "Jewish Women," 306.

13. Krakowski, *Coming of Age*.

14. Krakowski, *Coming of Age*, 183, 189–205. Krakowski emphasizes that seclusion was a marker of class status.

15. T-S NS J401k. The record states that maintenance will be given *la-hā wa-li-man yakhdimuhā* (to her for someone to serve her). The final sentence of the document is illegible, but may well read *wa-yakūn dhālika jāri[ya . . .* (It is this slav[e girl . . .). Krakowski, *Coming of Age*, 199–200. A second document related to this case is also preserved: T-S NS J401m. Weiss, "Legal Documents," nos. 240, 247. Goitein, *MS*, 3:193, 467.

16. T-S NS J401k, l. 13–14. See also a letter written for a free woman that explains that "the only person among us who comes and goes" is a woman (or girl) named Sutayt. Sutayt's legal status is not stated. She could be an enslaved person or another household dependent. ENA 2808.52, l. 4. Gil, *Malkhut*, 2:883–85; Krakowski, *Coming of Age*, 200n67. This letter mentions Nahray b. Nissim and thus likely dates to the second half of the eleventh century.

17. Krakowski, *Coming of Age*, 192.

18. See chap. 4.

19. *MT*, *Hilkhot Ishut*, 21:1–6. See also *MT*, *Hilkhot Ishut*, 21:14.

20. *MT*, *Hilkhot Ishut*, 21:1–6. Enslaved wet nurses are rare in *geniza* documents. See the discussion in chap. 4. Women's work and slaves' work were also conflated in Roman Palestine. See Hezser, *Jewish Slavery*, 73.

21. "Favorite" concubines have their own enslaved attendants: Marmon, "Domestic Slavery," 9. T-S 10K8.13, a *geniza* responsum discussed in chap. 5, describes an enslaved woman whom a Jewish man treated as "the lady of the house," but this does not mean that she owned her own slave.

22. On the roles of hairdresser (*māshiṭa*) and body-hair remover (*al-ṣāniʿa*), see Cortese and Calderini, *Women and the Fatimids*, 201–3. An enslaved Nubian *māshiṭa* (hairdresser) belonged to a family in the ninth-century Fayyūm. Thanks to Robin Seignobos for this reference from an unpublished conference paper. Enslaved women might have performed midwifery,

though the *geniza* evidence does not indicate that the midwives (sg. *qābila*) Jews used were enslaved.

23. New York: ENA NS 48.6 (formerly JTS *Geniza* Misc., 6). Goitein, *MS*, 1:135. Translated in Goitein, "Side Lights," 85–87. My translation differs in some minor aspects. This document is undated, but Goitein suggests a possible date range for this document based on the mention of a woman with the uncommon name Sitt al-Sirr. She appears in a marriage contract (ENA NS 48.18) written in the scribal hand of Ḥalfon b. Menasse who was active between 1100 and 1138. Goitein speculates that the dying mother was entrusting the education of her daughter to the enslaved woman Sa'āda.

24. This writing is another example of how common words for enslaved women (*waṣīfa* and *jāriya*) are juxtaposed in ways that suggest a division of enslaved labor within a household. Here the *jāriya* Sa'āda is also called a child-nurse (*dāda*), which is not a common term found in the *geniza* corpus.

25. ENA NS 48.6.

26. Ibid., ll.13–16.

27. ENA NS 48.6v, ll. 1–5 and right margin.

28. Krakowski, *Coming of Age*, 62–6; Bourdieu, *Outline*, 33–38. Frenkel also proposes a framework for studying personal connections using the "unofficial" language of "friendship, love, and kindness" as well as social networks organized through "entangled circles." See Frenkel, *"The Compassionate and Benevolent,"* xvi–xvii.

29. Krakowski observes how family marriages documented in the *geniza* could serve "to transform empty 'official kinship ties' into living bonds of 'practical kinship'—rather than to strengthen an already cohesive family unit." Krakowski, *Coming of Age*, 62–63.

30. McKee, "Households," 64.

31. Jewish merchants also used the language of patronage. See Marina Rustow, "Formal and Informal Patronage."

32. Moses Maimonides states in the *Mishneh Torah* that men should provide for orphans instead of for enslaved people. See chap. 3, 138n. On the court as the "father of orphans," see this chapter and 34n.

33. Krakowski, *Coming of Age*, 41–43.

34. Cohen, *Poverty and Charity*, 236–39.

35. Krakowski, *Coming of Age*, 174.

36. T-S 13J8.17, ll. 4–5. Discussed in chap. 5.

37. Evidence shows that this same 'Eli ha-Kohen transferred money to orphaned girls. T-S 8J4.14b, verso.

38. T-S 18J3.2. Krakowski, *Coming of Age*, 171.

39. T-S 12.493, ll. 14–18. Translation based on Krakowski, *Coming of Age*, 202; Goitein, "Side Lights," 88–89, 101. See also evidence for freed women's textile work in Hagedorn, *Domestic Slavery in Syria and Egypt*, 152, 167, 190.

40. T-S 12.493, ll. 7–9. "[S]omeone should come to the house and teach them prayer so that they should not grow up like animals not knowing 'Hear, oh Israel' [a basic prayer]." Translation based on Krakowski, *Coming of Age*, 1.

41. Krakowski, *Coming of Age*, 165–76. In his work on medieval poverty, Mark R. Cohen distinguishes between "structural" and "conjunctural" poverty. Structural refers to "permanent

destitution" (chronic). Conjunctural poverty occurs due to "specific, intermittent circumstances." The working poor could end up in this category due to sudden events or particular circumstances. See idem, *Poverty and Charity*, chap. 1, "A Taxonomy of the Poor." Enslaved and freed people also experienced poverty. See the discussion in chaps. 7 and 8.

42. Sources for this period are silent when it comes to institutions that resemble orphanages. In the Jewish community, Cohen observes that orphans "were cared for by a mixed economy of public and private charity." Idem, *Poverty and Charity*, 236; idem, *Voice of the Poor*.

43. T-S 8J4.14. Goitein, *MS*, 5:212–14. Krakowski, "Female Adolescence," 58n77; Goitein and Friedman, *Maḍmūn*, 331; Krakowski, *Coming of Age*, 163n86.

44. T-S 8J4.14, l. 9.

45. T-S 8J4.14, ll. 15–18.

46. T-S 13J22.2. Editions in Goitein, "Wills and Deathbed Declarations," 111–13, and Gil, *Documents*, 270–74. English translation in Goitein, *MS*, 5:147–49. See also idem, *MS*, 1:135, 138; 2:244, 416; 3:273, 411; 4:353, 358.

47. *Juwārihā* [*sic*]: T-S 13J22.2, l. 19. In l. 20, the scribe uses a dual form (*-humā*) to indicate the two girls.

48. T-S 13J22.2v, ll. 5–7. Gil thinks this must be jewelry and, specifically, a diadem (tiara). Gil, *Documents*, 274n21. Sitt al-Ḥusn's calculations provide an interesting comparison to a man's decision to sell his *waṣīf* to pay for his burial expenses: MS Heb. f 56/12.

49. She was married (after a previous divorce) to Nathan b. Samuel. On Nathan's role as a scribe for documents related to slavery, see chap. 7.

50. *Juwāri* is spelled this way in the document without a long *-ī*. See 47n in this chapter.

51. T-S 13J22.2, ll. 19–20. Judeo-Arabic followed by the Hebrew *me-ha-yom ve-la-aḥer.*

52. T-S 13J22.2, ll. 23–28. *in kānū* [*sic*] *yahūd al-hayba*: more literally, "that they are God-fearing (pious) Jews." My translation differs from Goitein's. In his English translation, Goitein includes the sentence: "Both the gift and the permission to live in the house depended upon this condition." I believe that this was intended to be his own comment upon the text and not a part of his translation of the original text. See Goitein, *MS*, 5:147–49.

53. On piety and manumission in Islam, see chap. 1. For rabbinic Jewish precedents, see *BT*, *Giṭṭin*, 37b, and *MT*, *'Avadim* 9:6.

54. *wahabat lil-qodesh*: T-S 13J22.2, l. 23. For comparison, the Mālikī and Ḥanafī Islamic legal schools provided frameworks for masters to will a charitable endowment (*waqf*) to their freed slaves. Ron Shaham observes that in many such cases the masters who willed a *waqf* to their freed slaves were childless. He argues that this practice reflects the "fictive kin ties" between masters and slaves (also freedmen) and that slaves gained social and economic protections through such ties. See Shaham, "Masters," 162, 178, and Fay, "Women and Waqf." Moshe Gil seems to view Sitt al-Ḥusn's actions as reflecting Islamic patronage practices in which "*mawālī* benefit from the family *waqf*." Gil, *Documents*, 274n16.

55. Goitein, *MS*, 2:99–103. Uses for charitable funds: Gil, "Maintenance"; Gil, *Documents*, 82–118.

56. There are additional textual examples in which freed slaves receive lodging from their owners. In one case, a former owner also asked her freed woman to relinquish part of the property she had been granted. ENA NS 16.11. Goitein, *MS*, 5:134.

57. Compare to the wardrobe of the enslaved woman, Misk, discussed in chap. 8.

58. On the use of "virgin" in *geniza* marriage documents, see Krakowski, *Coming of Age*, 38, 44, 181–206.

59. Goitein, *MS*, 1:135–36; 5:148. Cf. Perry, "Goitein."

60. T-S Misc. 24.137.4.

61. ʿŪd al-Zān: RNL Yevr.-Arab. I 1700.25v cited in Goitein, *MS* as Firkovitch II NS 1700, f.25a.

62. Ṣalaf: T-S 10J28.16. See Goitein, *MS*, 4:456. Ṣalaf and her history are discussed in chap. 7.

63. A related clause, prohibiting a man from taking a second wife, is also found in marriage documents from the twelfth century. Friedman, "Monogamy Clause," 22, 26; Friedman, *Jewish Polygyny*. On the historical development of *geniza* wedding documents, see also Ashur, "Engagement and Betrothal Documents"; idem, "Protecting the Wife's Rights"; idem, "India Trade."

64. BL Or. 5566C16. The wife is the daughter of "the head of the rabbinic academy," whose name is also not legible in this document. Goitein surmised that the father might have been Maṣliaḥ ha-Kohen Gaon, however, the father mentioned here was deceased (l. 3), and Maṣliaḥ was still alive when this deed was written.

65. Or. 5566C.16, l. 2: *ilā khidmat baytihi* (to the service of his house). Writers would sometimes use the word house (*bayt*) in reference to their wives out of a sense of propriety, which is possible here. Though *zawj[atihi]* is also used in l. 9. Ghazāl is called a *jāriya* and a *shifḥa*.

66. Or. 5566C.16, l. 4.

67. "Iron sheep property": Zinger, *Living with the Law*, viii–ix, 158n14. Women could own enslaved people who were not technically iron sheep property but categorized instead as *melog*. *Melog* would include inherited enslaved people, for example, and the husband would have no say in their sale. Ibid., ix.

68. T-S 18J1.17. See Perry, "Aramaic Bill of Sale."

69. T-S 18J1.17r, ll. 31–34. Perry, "Aramaic Bill of Sale," 459–60.

70. Friedman, "Master and Slave Girl." The correct shelf mark for this document is T-S NS 246.28 and not T-S Box K 27, f. 45 verso. Cf. Goitein's notecard no. 11637. For an example of a canceled manumission in Islamic Iberia, see de la Puente, "Islamic Law."

71. Translation based on Friedman, "Master and Slave Girl," 63, with some minor changes.

72. "[We signed it and gave it to him]" is Friedman's reconstruction and is language commonly found in similar legal documents from the *geniza*. See Friedman, "Master and Slave Girl," 63.

73. Zinger, "'She Aims to Harass Him'"; idem, "Jewish Women."

74. T-S Misc. 23.8. The year according to the given Seleucid date is 1438. The Hebrew month was probably Ṭevet; the document is partly obliterated where the month is written in l. 27. The document does not specify that Ḥasana and Solomon are brother and sister, but their relation is virtually certain. They both have a father identified as Menasse ha-Kohen.

75. T-S Misc. 23.8, ll. 4–9.

76. T-S Misc. 23.8, ll. 10–26.

77. Zinger, "'She Aims to Harass Him,'" 183.

78. Zinger, "Women, Gender and Law," esp. 73–129, 317–27; idem, "Use of Social Isolation."

79. Zinger, "'She Aims to Harass Him.'"

80. Zinger, "'She Aims to Harass Him.'"

81. Karras, *Boys to Men*, 157. See the discussion of masculinity in chap. 5 and the conclusion.

82. Zinger, "'She Aims to Harass Him,'" 186.

83. Karras, *Boys to Men*, 8–12, 152–59.

84. Maimonides, *Responsa*, no. 234. Thanks to Eve Krakowski for bringing this responsum to my attention.

85. Krakowski, "Maimonides' Menstrual Reform," 245, 278–80.

86. Krakowski, "Maimonides' Menstrual Reform," 252–56, 277–78.

87. This is a reference to the medical theory that illnesses were caused by an imbalance among the bodily humors. For a concise explanation of humoral pathology, see Dols and Gamal, eds., *Medieval Islamic Medicine*, 10–11. On patients' experiences of illness in *geniza* documents, see Elbaum, "'Fire in My Heart.'"

88. Maimonides, *Responsa*, no. 234. Free women also beat enslaved women. See the discussion of Yaṣe'a's conversion to Islam in chap. 7.

89. Sold to raise capital: see chap. 3.

90. In his response to the query, Maimonides does not acknowledge the *jāriya*'s beating. Maimonides, *Responsa*, no. 234.

Chapter 7. Lives in Slavery

1. F 1908.44SS. Edited in Gottheil and Worrell, *Fragments*, no. XILV; Goitein, *MS*, 1:141. Goitein's observation is correct that the Gottheil-Worrell translation is faulty. See the updated edition and analysis in Frenkel, "Slave Trade," 156–58, which includes an updated edition Jinān (Frenkel reads "Jannān") is called a *muwallada*. Wafā' is called a *ṣabiyya* (young girl).

2. Goitein and Frenkel note that it was illegal to separate mothers from their minor children, and that it was likely then that Jinān remained close by. See Schacht, *Introduction*, 127, 152. The buyer also agreed to pay 2 dinars per month, which would support this conclusion. I suggest in chap. 4 that Jinān may have been purchased as a wet nurse, who could be rented out by her new owner. This would explain the relatively high price of 34 dinars as well as Wafā''s age (two) at the time of sale, when children might be weaned from breastfeeding. On the dates of Nathan b. Samuel's activity (fl. 1128–54), see Goitein, *MS*, 2:513. On wet nurses, see also chap. 3, 122n and chap. 4, 15n.

3. T-S J1.29. See also the discussion in chap. 3. The other *waṣīfa* is Nisā'. The two *jāriyas* are ʿIzz and [Da]lāl. Goitein, "Three Trousseaux," 97.

4. T-S 8J12.3. Goitein, *MS*, 2:514. The welfare official (spelled here as *parnās*) is Zayn b. Abū al-Riḍā. The daughters' names are Nasab, Furs, and Sāda.

5. Rustow, *Heresy*, xx–xxi and 6n.

6. Oded Zinger currently oversees a research project into the networks of this Ḥalfon b. Menasse.

7. T-S 12.140. See Goitein, *MS*, 1:135, 138; 3:255, 483. The multiplicity of slavery-related documents produced by Nathan and Mevorakh suggest a small chance that "the Diadem" mentioned as the recipient of *waṣīfa* trafficked on a ship was this very Nathan b. Samuel. See T-S 8J10.9

and the discussion in chap. 2. There is another enslaved Dhahab mentioned nearly a hundred years later. T-S NS J226v, sec. 2. The date 1244 is found on the recto in two different places. See Goitein, *MS*, 3:262, 485n78.

8. T-S AS 147.23. Goitein notes that the handwriting is Mevorakh b. Nathan's. Goitein, *MS*, 3:289, 491. We know that the document was written between 1140 and 1159, as it invokes the authority of Samuel *ha-nagid*, who is Samuel b. Ḥananya.

9. One scenario that explains the existence of deeds is that Nathan and Mevorakh wanted evidence that Sitt al-Ḥusn was purchasing two people to whom she possessed a clear title.

10. Sumr's sellers in T-S AS 147.23 say that they received 12.5 dinars for her from their uncle, El'azar ha-Levi. This sum is about 7.5 dinars below the average price for a person. The price may reflect that Sumr was a young child.

11. A case in point is Tawfīq. There are three bills of sale for enslaved women named Tawfīq: ENA 4020.11, 25 dinars, undated; T-S NS 320.15, a copy or version of ENA 4020.11; MS Heb. b 12/20, 16.75 dinars, dated to the month of Tammuz, 1100; T-S NS 320.29, a note about the sale of a minor (*dūn al-bulūgh*) named Tawfīq for 18.75 dinars, dateable to the floruit of Ḥalfon b. Menasse (1100–38), in whose hand the note is written. In Heid. Or. 79, a freedwoman named Tawfīq approves a real estate transaction in Spring 1127. These are all conceivably the same Tawfīq. However, these Tawfīqs are not the same as the Nubian woman named Tawfīq who was sold to a Christian (*al-naṣrānī*) in 1230: T-S Ar. 39.245. See also the entries in appendixes 1 and 2.

12. Assemblage is a method and way of thinking that is transdisciplinary. My approach draws most immediately from its use by archaeologists who use assemblage to make sense of a group of objects from a similar period to imagine their shared context and culture. Hamilakis and Jones, "Archaeology and Assemblage."

13. See chap. 2 and further in this chapter.

14. See appendixes 1 and 2. Compare to a trend identified by Hagedorn in a Mamluk-era corpus in idem, *Domestic Slavery in Syria and Egypt*, 130.

15. Laura Culbertson, "Life-Course Approach."

16. On the *muwallads*, see chap. 3. Some scholarship on child slavery: Schneider, *Kinderverkauf und Schuldknechtschaft*; Campbell et al., eds., *Children in Slavery*; Grubbs, "Child Enslavement." One slave who probably does not belong in this group is the *waṣīf* Fayrūz found in the bill of sale MS Heb. b 13/19. Goitein assumed that the *waṣīf al-muwallad* Fayrūz sold in 1175 for 12 dinars was a child based on his price. See Goitein, *MS*, 1:138, 435n50. Yet there are other male and female slaves sold for 12 dinars or less who are also not described in any manner as sons, daughters, or minors. See T-S 13J8.3, T-S 10J9.32, T-S 8J8.4, and ENA 2727.37. Slaves described as *muwallad(a)* are also not necessarily children. The designation refers to the circumstances of the slave's birth and upbringing.

17. On the Islamic law of *umm walad*, see chap. 1. On Ibn Jamāhir's enslaved concubine and their son, see the introduction and chap. 5. On the "Canaanite slave," see chap. 1.

18. The seller is Sitt al-Ḥusn bt. Abraham, wife of Yakhīn. T-S 13J6.7, l. 6. This is not the same Sitt al-Ḥusn who freed Dhahab and Sitt al-Sumr. Her full name is Sitt al-Ḥusn bt. Sa'āda. T-S 13J22.2, ll. 10–11.

19. T-S 13J6.7. The document is torn at the top and bottom where the date and signatures would be. While the date is missing, one of the parties, Abū al-Futūḥ al-Ṣayrafī, is mentioned

in a document dated by Gil to ca. 1165. See T-S Ar. 18(1)155. Edited in Gil, *Documents*, 300–4, no. 67. The fact that both husbands participate in the sale suggests that ʿUshshāq had been part of the seller's "iron sheep property" and would become the same for the buyer. Goitein observes that the name ʿUshshāq is in the plural form and was thus short for Sitt al-ʿUshshāq, which would translate as "Queen of Lovers." Goitein, "Slaves and Slave Girls," 11n2; Goitein, *MS*, 1:141. In appendix 1, I use "Mistress of All Lovers."

20. T-S 13J6.7,ll. 8–10: *wa-annahā qallabathā wa-khabarathā wa-ʿalimat bi-sāʾir ʿuyūbihā, wa-ʿilalihā, wa-amrādihā al-bāṭina fī-hā wal-ẓāhira wa-ʿalimat annahā ḥāmil wa-artaḍat bi-hā.* The buyer's name is Sitt al-Fakhr. In the medieval Middle East, potential buyers routinely inspected slaves to assess their health and disposition. Ibn Buṭlān devotes considerable attention to methods designed to detect early-stage pregnancies. For commentary and a partial translation of this work, see Swain, *Economy, Family, and Society*, 270–79. Ibn Buṭlān's work is discussed in chaps. 2 and 4.

21. T-S 13J6.7. See the discussion of the "slave-girl clause" that some brides included in their wedding documents to protect them against enslaved women whom they found objectionable. Jurists also ruled that Jewish men who had sex with enslaved women should sell them and "distance" themselves from them. See chaps. 1 and 5. Sitt al-Fakhr's husband, Abū al-Futūḥ al-Ṣayrafī (the banker), would also have been in proximity to ʿUshshāq in his household. Enslaved women also had intimate attachments to men outside their household.

22. Another possible explanation for ʿUshshaq's pregnancy would be that she had an encounter or ongoing attachment with another man that she met in her comings and goings in Fustat. See the discussion of the woman Ṣayd, who sought to marry another enslaved man further in this chapter.

23. BL OR 10653.5, l. 10. The two are valued together at 40 dinars. The document is torn vertically and the mother's name is lost along with the right side of the page. Goitein, *MS*, 1:138, 434n54.

24. T-S 20.93b. Goitein speculates that the Ḥidhq sold here may be the same woman sold in the year 1105 in T-S 16.188. The Ḥidhq in 1105 is sold alone. The buyer in 1094 is different than the seller in 1105, though there could have been multiple sales of Ḥidhq in the intervening years. See Goitein, *MS*, 2:137. Another Ḥidhq is sold in T-S 8J5.5 (2v), but she is described as "from the west" (*al-maghribiyya*) and not as a Nubian. When the merchant ʿEli b. Yefet purchased Umm Nūbiyya in Ashkelon, he also bought her daughter. See chap. 5.

25. T-S 16.20, l. 15. See Goitein, *MS*, 1:138, 434n53. The year was 1241. Elʿazar b. Yefet sold the pair to Solomon b. Ṣedaqa for 40 dinars. Another family was sold together: T-S 16.15, ll. 19–20. However, this is a badly damaged, smudged, and faded bill of sale for the *shifḥa* Ẓarf and her son Muwaffaq. See the edition in Assaf, "Slaves and the Slave Trade," 274–75. Ẓarf and Muwaffaq are mentioned in ll. 10–11 in Assaf's transcription. It appears that Assaf's edition was done before conservators reattached the upper lefthand corner of this document. His transcription begins ten lines into the reconstructed original whose photograph is now available in FGP. A third *shifḥa* named R[i]ḍā is also mentioned in this document (l. 23 in Assaf's edition, l. 32 in the document as displayed in FGP). There is no apparent familial connection between R[i]ḍā and the other two slaves. See also Goitein, *MS*, 1:134, 434n54, 64.

26. T-S 13J3.3. See the discussion further in this chapter.

27. On medieval conceptions of *bulūgh*, see Krakowski, *Coming of Age*, 116, 136n80, 158n70, 169n106, 30, and in Hagedorn, *Domestic Slavery in Syria and Egypt*, 56, 86–7, 93, 95, 98 passim.

28. PER H 23, l. 5. The upper-right corner of this bill of sale is lost and thus this *waṣīfa*'s name is not preserved. Tawfīq: T-S NS 320.29, l. 5. Weiss, "Legal Documents," no. 197; Goitein, *MS*, 3:331, 501n81. Thought she was a Christian: chap. 3, 106n, 119n.

29. Muqbil: T-S 13J8.3, l. 10–11. See Goitein, *MS*, 1:138, 434n55.

30. Ibn Buṭlān, *Risāla*, 358; Hagedorn, *Domestic Slavery in Syria and Egypt*, 73.

31. T-S NS J23, l. 11. *Jāriya ʿumruhā* (six) *sanīn*. The Hebrew letter *vav* is used to denote "six." See chaps. 2 and 3 about a woman in Egypt who wrote her uncle in the town of al-Bahnasā for his help purchasing a five- or six-year-old "Black girl." T-S 13J21.18.

32. Return to the *bilād al-hind*: T-S NS J23, l. 5. The city Kollam is also mentioned: Ibid., right margin, l. 15. It does not seem that Kollam was this merchant's most recent point of departure. Rather, he is relating news about markets and merchants there.

33. T-S NS J23, l. 13. Goitein, "New Light"; Sato, "Slave Traders."

34. Many scholars of slavery confront the limits of whose story the "rules" and conventions of history allow to be told. For a few relevant examples, see Ghosh, *Antique Land*; Ghosh, "Slave of MS. H. 6"; Hartman, "Venus in Two Acts"; Montalvo, *Enslaved Archives*.

35. T-S NS J23v, l. 9. Nahrwāra (sometimes Naharwāra in Goitein): Goitein and Friedman, *India Traders*, 172–73, 188, 190n26, 205–207, 211, 220, 237, 239, 561n51 passim. An Indian (*hindī*) *waṣīf* was sold by the perfumer Yefet ha-Levi in Fustat in 1194. Goitein suggests that his name is Patan. I think this is probably incorrect. P-[D-N] is possible. Patan is an appealing solution, as the term is used sometimes to refer to a region of Gujarat. MS Heb. b 12/32, l. 18. Goitein, *MS*, 1:133, 432n14; 2:528n48. Other enslaved people described as Indian (*hindī, hindiyya*) are listed in appendix 1.

36. Perry, "Slavery and the Slave Trade," 137, 140–45.

37. Prasad, "Female Slavery," 269–75; Prasad, *Lekhapaddhati*; Strauch, *Lekhapaddhati-Lekhapañcāśikā*. Note that Strauch suggests corrections to some of Prasad's readings of the surviving manuscript sources. On the language of this manual, Strauch writes that it is "Jaina-, and/or, Gujarātī-Sanskrit." Ibid., 15.

38. Prasad, "Female Slavery," 271–73; Strauch, *Lekhapaddhati-Lekhapañcāśikā*, 188–90 (Sanskrit edition), 402–5 (German translation).

39. Prasad, "Female Slavery," 273–74; Strauch, *Lekhapaddhati-Lekhapañcāśikā*, 190–92, 405–8.

40. This is a geographical designation and not one indicating a genealogy. Prasad, "Female Slavery," 273n17; Strauch, *Lekhapaddhati-Lekhapañcāśikā*, 405.

41. Prasad, "Female Slavery," 273; Strauch, *Lekhapaddhati-Lekhapañcāśikā*, 405–6.

42. Prasad, "Female Slavery," 273; Strauch, *Lekhapaddhati-Lekhapañcāśikā*, 406.

43. Prasad, "Female Slavery," 273; Strauch, *Lekhapaddhati-Lekhapañcāśikā*, 406–407.

44. "Leading men of the city" is based on "pañcamukhanagara," which is left untranslated in Prasad, "Female Slavery," 274, and Strauch, *Lekhapaddhati-Lekhapañcāśikā*, 408. See Sircar, *Indian Epigraphical Dictionary*, 231: "'a city in which there are five leading men'"; Jain, *Trade and Traders*, 188, 232. Thanks to Harshita Kamath and Ellen Gough for consulting with me about this term.

45. See the packing list of Abraham b. Yijū in India (T-S NS 324.114) that animates Elizabeth Lambourn's global microhistory, *Abraham's Luggage*, esp. 1–10, and, by Amir Ashur and Lambourn, in the book's appendix, 252–67.

46. On the *balīj* as a refuge for enslaved women, see Lambourn, *Abraham's Luggage*, 193–95, 265n49.

47. Khalilieh, "Overview," 87, 96.

48. Lambourn, *Abraham's Luggage*, 195. See the sources cited in n15 and the discussion there about other enslaved women being forcibly confined to their *balīj*. Thanks to Brian Ulrich for sharing his research on slavery in the "Wonders of India (*ajā'ib al-hind*)" literature via personal communication and in Ulrich, "Portrayals." See also the tales that describe violence and rape of enslaved women in Freeman-Grenville, ed., *Book of the Wonders of India*.

49. On travel between western India and Egypt, see Tibbetts, *Arab Navigation*; Chaudhuri, *Trade and Civilisation*, 126; Margariti, *Aden*, 38–41; Goitein and Friedman, *India Traders*, 8–11, 157–64; Beresford, *Ancient Sailing Season*, 213–35; Prange, *Monsoon Islam*, 27–48; Lambourn, *Abraham's Luggage*, 45–46, 52. Thanks to Margariti and Anwesha Das for their bibliographic recommendations on Indian Ocean travel.

50. Margariti, *Aden*; Perry, "Slavery and the Slave Trade," and see the sources cited there, esp. 138nn22–23, 150–52.

51. Translation from Smith, ed., *Traveller*, 162. This passage continues to describe the legal stratagems that slave-buying men would use to exploit enslaved women for sex and then try to sue the seller on account of her "defects." On the slave trade to and within Yemen, see Magdalena Moorthy-Kloss, "Slavery in Medieval Arabia." On the figure of the slave trader (*al-nakhkhās*), see chap. 2; Richards, "Fragments," 89–90; al-Shayzarī, *Islamic Market Inspector*, 102–3.

52. Or. 1081 J1. Translated in Goitein, *Letters of Medieval Jewish Traders*, 207–12; Friedman, ed., *Rambam*, 206–23.

53. Margariti is preparing a transhistorical study of Dahlak. See also Margariti, "Thieves or Sultans?"

54. Goitein, *MS*, 1:211–17, 273–352. It took one letter from Fustat fifty days to reach the city of Qūṣ in Upper Egypt. Ibid., 1:290, 298.

55. T-S 13J22.2. See chap. 6.

56. T-S Misc. 24.137.4. See chaps. 5 and 6.

57. Our knowledge of childhood in the Jewish community of medieval Egypt is limited, especially from the perspective of how children experienced everyday life. Krakowski, *Coming of Age*, studies women's transition from childhood to the age of first marriage.

58. Sa'āda is called the elder (*al-kabīra*) only in comparison to 'Afāf, a younger (*al-ṣaghīra*) enslaved woman in the household. ENA NS 48.6. See chap. 6.

59. In chronological order: T-S 12.93; T-S K 15.39; T-S K 15.50; T-S 18J1.17r; T-S 18J1.17v; Halper 342; T-S NS 324.132. This evidence is discussed further in this chapter.

60. See the bill of sale (T-S 16.188) for the Nubian woman Ḥidhq as analyzed in chap. 3.

61. T-S 12.93. Khāliṣa's genealogy is lost where the document is destroyed (l. 7). The handwriting appears to belong to the scribe Hillel b. 'Eli, who composed other bills of sale: T-S 18J1.12; possibly: ENA 4011.48; MS Heb. b 12/20 and T-S NS J368, the latter of which is a fragment that mentions an enslaved woman and her price of 22.5 dinars.

62. T-S 18J1.17r + v. The recto contains the 1108 bill of sale. The 1115 sale is recorded on the verso. The most recent editions are in Perry, "Aramaic Bill of Sale," and idem, "Supplementary Bill of Sale." On Nahray as a "petty" slave trader, see chap. 2 and cf. Frenkel, "Slave Trade."

63. Khan, *ALAD*, 9.

64. There is one Judeo-Arabic *faṣl* that I know of, and it is for the purchase and sale of the woman Misk in 1165. T-S 13J37.12. See Perry, "Supplementary Deed of Sale," 139–42, and the figures 6.2–6.3 there.

65. Halper, 342. This record is dateable to the years 1127 to 1138, which mark the years when Maṣliah ha-Kohen was a head of the Egyptian Jewish community. The scribe appears to be Ḥalfon b. Menasse, who was active during this period. See Weiss, "Legal Documents." Shabbetay b. Joseph sold a slave in October 1143 to Pinḥas b. El'azar. The name of the *jāriya waṣīfa* is not known. T-S NS 320.50c.

66. "Na'īm *jāriya ma'tūqa*: T-S NS 324.132d, l. 6. 'Alam, the *jāriya* of al-Sh-b-r[..]" received 5 dirhams. Ibid., l. 8. Thanks to Moshe Yagur for bringing this reference to my attention. Sarab the freedwoman (*al-ma'tūqa*) received a cloak (*jūkhāniyya*): T-S NS 324.132c, l. 14. On the clothing of freedwomen as one index of their socioeconomic standing after slavery, see the next chapter.

67. Russ-Fishbane, *Aging in Medieval Jewish Culture*, 338–39, 342–43n27.

68. Zinger, Living with the Law, 143.

69. Humphreys, *Islamic History*, 284–305. Other corpora and dossiers have been assembled. E.g., Rāġib, *Actes de vente*, and see additional analysis in Marmon, "Intersections of Gender, Sex, and Slavery," 207; Bruning, "Slave Trade Dynamics."

70. T-S 13J36.11. See chap. 3.

71. *Wa-kull man yaṭlub yasta'riḍhā ta'mal muṣība ḥattā lā yashtarīhā.* In the document, we read *yasta'ḍirhā*. As Oded Zinger suggested to me, this is probably a scribal error.

72. Ibn Buṭlān: Swain, *Economy, Family, and Society*, 271–73. Ibn Buṭlān, *Risāla*, 387–89.

73. A *geniza* letter explains that that one slave buyer had prearranged a *jāriya*'s purchase for 10 dinars. Without providing a further explanation, he reports that her owner suddenly refused to sell her and had her bound with ropes. *Tu'aqqad bil-ḥibāl*: T-S 12.293r, right margin. Thanks to Oded Zinger for bringing this to my attention.

74. Ibn Buṭlān, *Risāla*, 357. Translation slightly modified from Swain, *Economy, Family, and Society*, 273. See also Barker, "Purchasing a Slave," 20n37. This advice implies that some women-inspectors were suspected of not disclosing pregnancies of enslaved women.

75. "Theorists of power": Morgan, "*Partus Sequitur Ventrem*," 16, 15n55; Roberts, *Freedom as Marronage*, 15.

76. "Muslims": the text reads *goyyim*, which in this Muslim-majority context indicates Muslims and not Christians. Freimann and Goitein, *Responsa*, no. 98, p. 152. See English translations in Perry, "Conversion," 144–45, and Frenkel's translation in "Slave Trade," 151–52.

77. Freimann and Goitein, *Responsa*, no. 98, p. 152. On code-switching in *geniza* documents, Wagner and Connolly, "Code-Switching." See also Wagner, *Linguistic Variety*, 110–13, and the sources cited there.

78. *MT*, *Hilkhot Issurei bi'a*, 12:11. The phrase is also used in contemporaneous *geniza* documents. T-S 10J17.16, published in Yagur, "Religious Identity," 337–38, and see 139–40, 193 passim.

79. For a fifteenth-century case in Alexandria in which an enslaved woman is beaten by her mistress and threatens to convert to Islam, see Fabri, *Evagatorium*, 167–68. Translated by Barker as "Felix Fabri's Wanderings in the Holy Land," Teaching Medieval Slavery and Captivity, https://medievalslavery.org/middle-east-and-north-africa/source-felix-fabris-wanderings-in-the-holy-land/.

80. Petry, *Criminal Underworld*, 198–99; idem, "Female Slaves and Transgression," 82.

81. Hurvitz et al., eds., *Conversion*, 11. An enslaved convert takes refuge with a Muslim judge and recites the *shahāda*: Petry, *Criminal Underworld*, 198–99; idem, "Female Slaves and Transgression," 82. In sixteenth-century Damascus, Muslims brought a Jewish boy, accompanied by his family, to the Muslim court and claim that he uttered the *shahāda*. A *shaykh* converted the boy, and a judge issued a written ruling that confirmed it. El-Leithy, "Conversions to Islam," 320.

82. El-Leithy, "Conversions to Islam," 318–19.

83. Blau, ed., *Responsa of Moses Maimonides*, no. 211.

84. More literally, What are you? (*Wa-sa'al[ū]hā ayy shay' hiya?*)

85. *Fa-a'irad 'alayhā al-pesh'ut*. See Blau, *Dictionary*, 504.

86. *Wa-qālat anā yahūdiyya, bint [yahūdiyya] anā.*

87. As we read in chap. 5, he recommended that her owner free her and marry her In this case, it was the lesser of two evils. Blau, ed., *Responsa of Moses Maimonides*, no. 211.

88. Cf. Or. 1080 J30. A woman thought to be a Muslim explains to a Muslim judge that she was in fact Jewish when she was kidnapped at a water well in 'Aydhāb and made a slave. See chap. 2.

89. In Arabic sources, the term *ḥaẓiyya* (favorite) indicates a woman whom a man prefers over others in his possession. He may exempt her from some labor and even provide her with her own servants. See Marmon, "Domestic Slavery," 9–10; Marmon, "Female Sexual Slavery," 201–2. I have not found this term in *geniza* sources. The description of men's behaviors does indicate their favored treatment of some women, however.

90. Sally McKee, "Slavery," 282.

91. Johnson, "On Agency."

92. Evidence and analysis of the mobility of enslaved people is discussed in chap. 4.

93. The House of Exchange (*dār al-ṣarf*): T-S 8J19.27v, address, left side. A letter from a silk merchant to Nahray b. Nissim. Translated in Goitein, *Letters of Medieval Jewish Traders*, 45–49; the coppersmiths' market (*sūq al-naḥḥāsīn*): MS Heb. d 74/44v, l. 2; Gil, *Palestine*, 2: 536–37, no. 299; the Perfumers' Market . . . (*sūq al-'aṭṭārīn*): T-S 10J12.16, margin, ll. 6–8.

94. Ibn Buṭlān, *Risāla*, 356. The translation is a revised version of the one in Swain, *Economy, Family, and Society*, 272. Cf. Lewis, *Islam*, 2:244. Why would he warn against purchasing a *jāriya muwallada* from a merchant or importer? Perhaps this is an allusion to enslaved people as covert agents. This evidence is also discussed in chap. 4.

95. ENA 2727.37b. A bill of sale, or detailed notes for a sale. The Ṣandal mentioned is probably the personal name of the *ghulām*. Maimonides also noted that stealing and running away were among the known "defects" of enslaved people and that buyers could therefore not sue to return a slave on the basis of such defects. See chap. 3, 47n. When Ḥasana sued her brother over *jāriya* Iftikhār's defects, theft and running away are also mentioned. T-S Misc. 23.8. See chap. 6.

96. Halper, 400, l. 15.

97. Halper 400, ll. 15–16. Goitein translates *afsadathā* as "alienated her from me." I suggest "enticed her," because there is no preposition (e.g., *'alā* or *bayn*) or suffix ending to suggest that "from me" was intended. See also Friedman and Ashur, *Dictionary*, 534, s.v. "'alā nafsaha." The address on the verso is to "my son, Abū al-'Izz b. Bishr." Halper 400v, l. 1. One possible explanation for these dynamics is that the sisters co-own Tawfīq.

98. Lane-Poole, *A History of Egypt*, 145–50; Lev, *State and Society*, 43–46; Walker, *Exploring an Islamic Empire*, 62–64; Rustow, *Heresy*, 328. These events also tie in to the seizure of a major diplomatic gift. T-S AS 149.3. See chap. 2, 28n.

99. Or. 1080 J71, ll. 10–11. Goitein, *MS*, 1:143–44; 3:162, 462; 4:369, 439; 5:220–21; Gil, *Kingdom of Ishmael*, 4:48–51, no. 619; Gil, "Institutions and Events," 163. Goitein writes that this letter is from the 1060s. Gil dates the letter to September 26, 1070. See also the description by Alan Elbaum and Yusuf Umrethwala in PGP. "Tunneled," or bore a hole through a wall. See Or. 1080 J71, l. 10; Kazimirski, *Dictionnaire*, 1318, s.v., "naqaba." *Waybatayn* (2 *waybas*): Or. 1081 J71, l. 11. On common weights and measures, see Goitein, *MS*, 1:360–61.

100. Or. 1080 J71, ll. 14–15.

101. This is based on one of Goitein's inferences, with which I agree. In the closing of her letter, the wife tells her husband that "Wala' kisses your hand" (sends greetings). Wala' (Passion) resembles other common slave names. She also lacks a *nasab* or other identifier, which suggests that she is an enslaved woman. Or. 1080 J71, ll. 19–20. Goitein, *MS*, 1:144, 435n83.

102. Another ambiguous circumstance is a *jāriya* who was "lost from the house" (*ḍā'at min baytihā*). T-S 12.585, ll. 6–7. The verb is commonly used by merchants to describe when commercial goods are "lost" in extenuating circumstances. One wonders whether the *jāriya* fled, was kidnapped, or whether she died and the writer here emphasizes that the monetary value she represented was thus "lost."

103. An eleventh-century Islamic (Ḥanafī) legal manual describes how people who captured and returned enslaved people were to be paid. See the "Book of Fugitive Slaves (*Kitāb al-ibāq*)" in al-Qudūrī (d. 1037), *The* Mukhtaṣar *of Imām Abū l-Ḥusayn Aḥmad b. Muḥammad b. Aḥmad b. Ja'far b. Ḥamdān al-Qudūrī al-Baghdādī: A Manual of Islamic Law According to the Ḥanafī School*, ed. Ṭāhir Maḥmood Kiānī (Ta-Ha Publishers, 2010). Partial translation in Lewis, *Islam*, 2:239.

104. Al-Jawbarī, *Book of Charlatans*; Bosworth, *Mediaeval Islamic Underworld*; Petry, *Criminal Underworld*; Richardson, *Roma*. In the Islamic East, it appears that enslaved people who fled their captivity joined such groups. See Richardson, *Roma*, 27, 170n72.

105. Richardson, *Roma*, 63. Moshe Yagur is preparing a study on these very topics for Fustat and Cairo based on *geniza* documents, Arabic writings, and archaeological findings. Schmierer-Lee and Yagur, "Genizah Street View"; Yagur, "Living in the City."

106. Richardson, *Roma*, 35.

107. Petry, *Criminal Underworld*, 225; idem, "Female Slaves and Transgression."

108. Richardson, *Roma*, 63–68. Constable, "Funduq, Fondaco, and Khān"; idem, *Housing the Stranger*.

109. Richardson, *Roma*, 68.

110. Richardson, *Roma*, 63–67.

111. Richardson, *Roma*, 63.

112. Richardson, *Roma*, 66.

113. See P.KhanQasrIbrim inv. 74.1.29/11.3, edited in Khan, *Medieval Nubia*, 245, 471, concerning a report that servants had run away from Aswan toward Nubia.

114. On this term, see Kars, "Maroons and Marronage." As she explains, "'Petit marronage,' or running away, refers to a strategy of resistance in which individuals or small groups, for a variety of reasons, escaped their plantations for a short period of days or weeks and then returned."

115. al-Jawbarī, *Book of Charlatans*, 356–59; Richardson, *Roma*, 64–65.

116. al-Jawbarī, *Book of Charlatans*, 319–20, sec. 21.2–21.3. From Humphrey Davies's translation.

117. L-G Arabic II.129. Goitein, *MS*, 3:275, 475n49; Wagner, "Language of Women"; idem, "Genizah Sociolinguistics," 6–8. Or. 1080 J25v, ll. 4–12. See Goitein, *MS*, 1:433n33, where he identifies Ṣayd as a free woman; this identification was before he read L-G Arabic II.129, in which Ṣayd tells the judge that she is a *mamlūka*. T-S 10J7.6(2v) is a third document, a scribal record for the sale of a *jāriya* named Ṣayd that dates to the mid-twelfth century. Previous scholarship identified Ṣayd as a Muslim. This is incorrect and results from a misinterpretation of the word *musallama* (i.e., not *muslima*), which indicates that payment was made and received. Credit to Oded Zinger for first noting the correct reading in a personal communication.

118. More specifically, distressing to the woman dictating the letter to the person who wrote it. Wagner, "The Language of Women"; idem, "Genizah Sociolinguistics," 6–7.

119. L-G Arabic II.129, ll.; Or. 1080 J25v, ll.

120. L-G Arabic II.129, l. 12; Or. 1080J25v, ll. 6–8.

121. L-G Arabic II.129, ll. 13–14.

122. Patterson, *Slavery and Social Death*; Bodel and Scheidel, eds., *Human Bondage*.

123. See Toledano, "Ottoman Elite Enslavement," 136–50, and the other essays in that volume; Bodel, "Death and Social Death," 81–108; Johnson, *Wicked Flesh*, 3. Orlando Patterson argues that his critics have misread him and that his definition of slavery using these characteristics was not meant to be understood in absolute terms.

In the preface to the 2018 edition of *Slavery and Social Death*, Patterson adds that "the ultimate cruelty of slavery was that [enslaved people's social relations] had no legitimacy outside of what the slaveholder permitted. In light of such fatal uncertainties all relations were precarious, provisional, and tenuous; all community verged on the chaos that could rain down at any time from the *deus ex machina* of the slaveholder's economic calculations or personal whim." Patterson, *Slavery and Social Death*, ix–x.

I find that this formulation does not account overall for the evidence in this book that illustrates how enslaved people could be litigants in courts of law, albeit ones who were structurally disadvantaged vis-à-vis other groups. More generally, my own views accord with scholars who frame their studies in more open-ended terms. See Vlassopoulos, "Does Slavery Have a History?"; Rio, *Slavery After Rome*; Perry et al., "Slavery in the Medieval Millennium," 21–24; Rio, "Slavery in the Carolingian Empire." See also the multiple chapters that engage with Patterson's work in volume 2 of *The Cambridge World History of Slavery*, 585, s.v. "Patterson, Orlando."

Chapter 8. Freed People and the Jewish Community

1. T-S 8J12.2, ll. 4–17. This translation is from Goitein, *MS*, 5:149–50 with my own emendations. The term used for slave is *amti*, or it could have been vocalized as *amtay*, both first-person possessives of the Aramaic term *amta* and spelled here without an *aleph*. Bar-Asher Siegal, *Introduction*, 104. The handwriting is Mevorakh b. Nathan's. Mevorakh wrote other slavery-related documents as discussed in chap. 7.

2. See appendixes 2 and 3. Some caveats attend this approximation. Freed people who appear in *geniza* records were most likely enslaved in Jewish households, because the social ties they forged were factors that induced them to remain in this community. Still, it is possible that a person freed by a Muslim or Christian owner converted to Judaism and entered the Jewish community in this way. Moreover, freed people who were themselves Christians or Muslims could have maintained or created social and economic ties with Jews.

3. For example, "Tawfīq the freedwoman (*meshuḥreret*)" seems to have kept her "slave name." Heid. Or. 79. One case in which a woman's "slave name" and new name as a freed person is given is in the bill of manumission is that of Ashū, who became Berakha. IOM D 55.10.

4. Yagur, *Crossing the Line*, 196–201.

5. Yagur, "Captives, Converts, and Concubines," 93–95.

6. *MT*, *Hilkhot mila* (Laws of Circumcision), 1:3–6; Yagur, "Captives, Converts, and Concubines," 91–93, 95, 101; idem, "Community's Borders," 58, 60, 70. As Yagur notes, there is no documentary evidence in the *geniza* of enslaved boys' and men's circumcision. Rare evidence of ritual immersion is discussed further in this chapter.

7. Yagur, "Community's Borders," 57–58.

8. "Idolater (lit. star worshippers)": *MT*, *Hilkhot Issurei Bi'a*, 12:11. In *BT*, Sanhedrin, 58b, the law refers not to "idolaters" but to non-Jews. Finkelstein, *Conversion*, 108–48; Yagur, "Community's Borders," 57–58. There were other rituals that may have sometimes been used for converts, such as cutting their hair and nails. This is not attested in documentary sources for freed converts, but it is discussed in the responsa that Egyptian Jews copied, read, and deposited in the *geniza*. Yagur, "Captives, Converts, and Concubines"; idem, "Shaving Hair."

9. Yagur, "Community's Borders," 57–58.

10. Yagur, "Community's Borders," 59.

11. Yagur, "Religious Identity," 129–30; idem, "Community's Borders," 60–63; idem, *Crossing the Line*, esp. 100–4. And see the discussions in chaps. 1 and 7.

12. Yagur's work meticulously shows how Jewish family life and communal politics were unsettled when Jews tried to reconcile the realities of daily life (what Jews did in practice) with the ambiguities that were intrinsic to the Jewish laws of slavery, manumission, and conversion. This is the main subject of Yagur, "Religious Identity," 72–131. See also idem, "Community's Borders," 60–63 passim, and idem, "Captives, Converts, and Concubines."

13. Goitein, *MS*, 1:144, 436n95. A medieval *responsum* that preserves this gaonic ruling is found in the *geniza*. MS Heb. c 18/37–38. The query begins on the verso of folio 37, line 3. A partial edition is in Ginzberg, *Geonica*, 2:72–84. See also Perry, "Daily Life of Slaves," 193–94. On Sitt al-Ḥusn's deathbed declaration, see chap. 6. Abū al-Ḥasan freed Gharaḍ and Kashf in a deathbed declaration. See chaps. 3 and 5.

14. *MT*, *Hilkhot 'avadim*, 5:3. Yagur, "Religious Identity," 42–43.

15. In the Islamic context, it is conspicuous that no *geniza* document has yet to be identified in which enslaved people purchased their freedom as a *mukātab(ba)*. A possible exception is T-S NS J152 + T-S NS J110, in which a man frees a woman "after he received her price from her." T-S NS J152, l. 8. The document is fragmentary and it is not clear who the antecedent of "her" is. Did the enslaved woman acquire the funds needed to purchase her freedom? Or did another woman buy her freedom? Weiss, "Ḥalfon," nos. 210, 214.

16. Yagur, "Religious Identity," 68–69, 90, 100, 108–9, 122, 229; Yagur, "Community's Borders," 58.

17. T-S Misc. 24.137.4. See chaps. 5 and 7.

18. See appendix 3. Deeds were also kept because there could later be suspicion about the freed status of a person and their heir, as well as the timing of a person's manumission. I say "at least" because additional *geniza* documents continue to come to light through new research. On the timing of manumission, see the cases of Abraham b. Yijū and 'Eli b Yefet in chap. 5.

19. Yagur, "Community's Borders," 58. The same Arabic term, *mawlā*, can mean both freed slave (client) and refer to the former owner and manumitter (patron). In *geniza* records that I have read, the term is only used in the masculine. Cf. Urban, "Freedwomen and Kinship."

20. Yagur, "Religious Identity," 96–97.

21. Miriam is another freedwoman who married a Jewish man: T-S J1.11.

22. Heid. Or. 79. This is a real estate deed for which Tawfīq made a *qinyan*, which tells us that her husband's sale of real estate required her permission. One explanation for this is that the property was part of her wedding dowry.

23. The freed girls Dhahab and Sitt al-Sumr and the woman Nushuww also possessed a share of some real estate. See chap. 3.

24. MS heb f. 56/53. Her dower (from her husband) was 40 dinars (10 up front and 30 as part of her delayed marriage gift). On dowry (property that the bride brings into the marriage) and dower values, and their roles in first marriages, see Krakowski, *Coming of Age*, 142–53. Zinger, *Living with the Law*, vii–ix.

25. MS heb f. 56/53. The *jūkhāniyya*, which was probably like a caftan. *Dabīqī* linen was named after the Lower Egyptian town where it was produced. Stillman, "Medieval Female Attire," 585.

26. Stillman, "Medieval Female Attire," 584.

27. Recall the merchant from Alexandria who purchased a concubine, abandoned his wife and children in Alexandria, and then put the *jāriya* up in her own residence with "fine clothing the likes of which his wife had never worn in her lifetime." T-S 6J2.15 + T-S 10K8.13. See chap. 5.

28. Or. 1080J142 + T-S Misc. 25.53. Translation from Goitein, *MS*, 4:335–38.

29. As Oded Zinger notes, the *dīwān al-mawārīth* "was notorious for its eagerness to seize the estates of non-Muslims without heirs and was often unscrupulous in its actions." Zinger, "Introduction to the Legal Arena," 115.

30. MS Heb. c 28/54, ll. 10–11. The inheritance dispute: Goitein, *MS*, 2:582n15; Rustow, "Limits of Communal Autonomy," 147. Munā's marriage contract: MS heb f. 56/53. Her husband was Abū al-Faraj al-Tinnīsī Yeshu'a ha-Levi b. Abraham. Munā is identified as the freedwoman of one Ibn Futayḥ. Goitein, *MS*, 1:145. Freed people did buy or otherwise acquire enslaved

people. See Freimann and Goitein, *Abraham Maimuni*, no. 98; Hagedorn, *Domestic Slavery in Syria and Egypt*, 128.

31. T-S AS 145.1. Goitein, *MS*, 3:395; Friedman, *Jewish Polygyny*, 331–32, 379. Her dowry was 4 dinars (150 silver dirhams). Her marriage gifts were worth about 2.25 dinars (90 silver dirhams). This Mubāraka is not the same freedwoman discussed in chapter 5, where a *parnas* recruits a Jewish woman to help her find a marital match a century earlier. T-S NS 321.54.

32. T-S 24.5. The bride's name is lost. Goitein, *MS*, 1:436. The gift of 3 dinars is below the threshold of 5 dinars that Goitein identified as a typical minimum for most marriages. See Goitein, *MS*, 3: 120–21. T-S 10J17.16: Khalaf the freedman marries a Jewish woman in the last quarter of the twelfth century. Yagur, "Religious Identity," 96n109, 337–38.

33. T-S 24.5, l. 8.

34. On the residential trends for married couples, see Krakowski, *Coming of Age*, 47–56.

35. T-S K15.65, see the left side and ll. 2–6. Goitein assumed that this freedman's former owner was this same Abū Saʿīd b. Jamāhir. This connection is not stated in the document. See idem, *Letters of Medieval Jewish Traders*, 335–36. Cf. Friedman and Goitein, *Maḍmūn*, 470n4, and Yagur, "Religious Identity," 93n98. One wonders if the freedman's wife was one of the two orphan girls who lived in Ibn Jamāhir's household. The freedman's name, [.*ā*..] is mostly obliterated. I am tempted to suggest [Ṣ]ā[fī], but that would suggest the possibility of a truth stranger than fiction given the conflict between the *ghulām* of the same name and Ibn Jamāhir in ʿAydhāb. See T-S K15.65, l. 2 and the discussion in chap. 5.

36. Or. 10588.3. Two other divorces involving freed people and their children are in T-S NS J226v (left side). The woman may be named [Dha]hab, but this would not be the same Dhahab whom Sitt al-Ḥusn freed. The date of the divorce is nearly one hundred years after that of Dhahab's manumission. ENA 972.3: the divorcée Sitt al-Dalāl.

37. Or. 10588.3. Edited in David, "Divorce Among the Jews," 1:176–7. Abū al-Murajjā's father Nathan and his brother Mevorakh were well-known scribes whose hands can be found on several documents related to Jewish slave-owning. See chap. 7.

38. Or. 10588.3, ll. 3, 5–6.

39. Cohen, *Poverty and Charity*; idem, *The Voice of the Poor.*

40. T-S 8J5.14, l. 2. The freedwoman known as "the mother of Baqā" receives a *jūkhāniyya*: T-S Ar. 52.247b, column 2, l. 14.

41. T-S K15.13b, l. 11. Goitein, *MS*, 1:147, 424. Edited in Gil, *Pious Foundations*, 357–59. Gil reads her name as "Sirb," in *Pious Foundations*, 359n12.

42. T-S 16.133. Assaf, *Texts and Studies*, 140–42; Goitein, *MS*, 1:146–47, 436; Ben-Sasson, ed., *Jews of Sicily*, 143–45; Simonsohn, *Jews in Sicily*, 17–18. Cf. T-S Ar. 7.13v: The freedman Najīb gave a donation, but it is not clear for what purpose. Goitein surmises that the donations listed were for two musicians who had played at a gathering. Goitein, *MS*, 1:147, 436n111; 2: 505. Yagur, *Crossing the Line*, 65n84.

43. MS Heb. d 66/78. Goitein, *MS*, 1:133, 432n11, where Goitein states erroneously that the *ghulām*'s name is "Ṣāfī." Hebrew edition in Frenkel, *"The Compassionate and Benevolent,"* 252–53; Yagur, "Religious Identities," 77–78n25.

44. IOM D 55.10. Goitein and Friedman, *India Traders*, 55–57, 632–33. The practice of naming converts (and not just freed slave converts) as the son or daughter of Abraham is based on the biblical prooftext from Genesis 17:4, 17:8, that refers to the patriarch as "father of a

multitude of nations." Goitein and Friedman, *India Traders*, 57n18. On Abraham b. Yijū's slave owning, see chap. 4 and 69n.

45. T-S 16.105. Goitein, *MS*, 1:145.

46. MS Heb. f 56/53, l.1.

47. MS Heb. c 28/54, ll. 10–11. This was also the formulation in the legal name of "Tawfīq the freedwoman and wife of Levi," when she was asked to give permission for her husband to sell some real estate. See the discussion earlier in this chapter.

48. T-S 10J23.1. Goitein, *MS*, 1:436; Bareket, "Abiathar ben Elijah ha-Kohen." Abiathar is also written as Evyatar. Possibly connected to T-S 8J15.24, as mentioned in Goitein and Friedman, *Maḍmūn*, 63 and n3.

49. Prenuptial agreement: T-S NS 259.37 + T-S 8J5.3. Friedman, *Jewish Polygyny*, 106–9 (only T-S 8J5.3); Ashur, "Engagement Documents," 86–91. See T-S 10J2.15, a bill of divorce for Sitt al-Bayt the daughter of Muwaffaq the freedman (*ha-meshuḥrar*). Goitein, *MS*, 1:145, 436. See also the works of Yehezkel David.

50. ENA 972.8, l. 6. Friedman, *Jewish Polygyny*, 106. David, "Formulae of the Bill of Divorce," 62, 69.

51. T-S 12.175, ll. 21–29. English translations in Goitein, *MS*, 5; Stillman, "East-West Relations," 249–58. Edition in Gil, *In the Kingdom of Ishmael*, 2:439–43. Bareket, "Ibn ʿAwkal Family," and Rustow, "Tāhertī Family."

52. The letter was sent by Joseph and Nissim b. Berekhya. T-S 12.175v, l. 1. They call Faraj "the freedman of my (late) uncle (*ʿatīq ʿammī*)."

53. T-S 8.12. Translation from Goitein, *Letters of Medieval Jewish Traders*, 82–84. See also Gil, *Ishmael*, 2:485–87, no. 166. Goitein dates this letter to ca. 1020 (Gil to 1015), about five years after Faraj visited Fustat to meet Ibn ʿAwkal. This letter closely resembles another sent by Faraj to the Ibn ʿAwkal family: DK 246.1. See Gil, *Ishmael*, 2:487–90, no. 167. Though they both share details about Faraj's request for pearls, and about the timing of pilgrim traffic, they are separate letters written in different years.

54. Goitein, *Letters of Medieval Jewish Traders*, 82–84.

55. T-S 8.12. In his salutation, Faraj writes: "From their grateful Faraj" and not "[F]rom (your)." He uses the third-person pronoun as a sign of respect. On the language of merchant letters and of patronage, see Goldberg, *Trade and Institutions*; and Marina Rustow, "Formal and Informal Patronage."

56. Faraj was not the only freedman to make a living in trade. Mevasser (formerly Bishāra) was a freedman and mercantile partner to other men and invested his own capital in joint ventures. T-S 8J4.11 + T-S NS J6 + T-S 8J4.12. Ackerman-Lieberman, "Partnership Culture," 172–77. Mevasser also had a daughter, who married and divorced a Jewish man: ENA 972.3.

57. T-S 8J16.4. Shtober, "Queries," 262–68. Goitein, *MS*, 1:146, 436; 2: 48–49 520n2, 607n44, 533nn53–54; 5: 486. Partial English translation in Zinger, "'She Aims to Harass Him,'" 178, 181, and idem, *Living with the Law*, 64. An unpublished edition and draft translation by Goitein is held among his personal notes by the PGP.

58. Zinger, "'She Aims to Harass Him,'" 178n80.

59. T-S 8J16.4, ll. 10–11, 15; verso, ll. 1–2. Zinger's translation. See idem, "'She Aims to Harass Him,'" 178. Failing tax farmers, who were debtors in arrears to the state, could end up in prison. See Bondioli, "Sicilian Tithe Business," 214. For recent scholarship on tax farming in

medieval Egypt, see Wickham, "Power of Property"; Bondioli, "Peasants, Merchants, and Caliphs."

60. T-S 8J16.4v, right and bottom margins. Goitein's translation with my emendations.

61. T-S 8J16.4, l. 9. Zinger, "'She Aims to Harass Him,'" 178n179.

62. See the discussion in chap. 1 and the sources there at 59n.

63. Yagur, "Saʿāda."

64. T-S 12.872. Yagur, "Saʿāda."

65. Yagur, "Saʿāda."

66. Abū al-Maʿālī's b. Khalaf al-Dajājī's name is written "Abū al-Maʿānī" in the memorial list T-S Ar. 6.28. On this discrepancy, see Yagur, "Saʿāda."

67. T-S Ar. 6.28. Goitein, *MS*, 3:31. Published in Friedman, *Jewish Polygyny*, 294–96. Yagur, "Saʿāda."

68. Yagur, "Saʿāda."

Conclusion

1. *MT, Hilkhot ḥameṣ u-maṣa* (Laws of Leavened and Unleavened Bread), 7:2. Emphasis mine. Perry, "Power, Mastery, and Competition," 461.

2. Barker, *That Most Precious Merchandise*, 3, 10, 13, 318, 209; Eltis and Engerman, "Dependence, Servility, and Coerced Labor," 2.

3. Or after conception in some traditions.

4. Here Krakowski writes specifically about "the early female life course." Idem, *Coming of Age*, 4.

5. Krakowski, *Coming of Age*, 4, 20, 301.

6. Krakowski, *Coming of Age*, 302; Zinger, *Living with the Law*, 12, 22, 145 passim.

7. Spaulding, "Medieval Christian Nubia." See also chap. 2 and the sources cited there.

8. In the Mamluk period, private merchants did organize large-scale slave trading, but they were also supported by the sultanate. See chap. 2, 79n. For the earlier Ayyubid period, see also chap. 2, 58n.

9. See chap. 3 and the sources cited there. Indians and other Asian groups were sometimes considered types of Black people. Schine, *Black Knights*, 15. In *geniza* records, Black seems to have been applied mostly to people from northeast Africa.

10. Hagedorn, *Domestic Slavery in Syria and Egypt*, 145, 169. Medieval Arab authors included Abyssinians among the types of Blacks. Hagedorn, *Domestic Slavery in Syria and Egypt*, 86, 122. In scores of fifteenth-century biographies for enslaved Abyssinian women and their children, there is no association made between them and blackness. I have an article in progress on this subject.

11. Heng, *Invention of Race*; Schine, *Black Knights*; and see the sources cited in chap. 3, 97n.

12. Karras, "Desire, Descendants, and Dominance," 17; Frenkel, "Slavery in Medieval Jewish Society," 258.

13. Zinger, *Living with the Law*, 149–50.

14. See also Connell, *Masculinities*, 37.

15. Zinger, "'She Aims to Harass Him,'" 186.

16. See chap. 3, 67n.

17. On marronage, see the discussion in chap. 7 and there in 114n.

18. See appendixes 1 and 2 and the discussion there on this figure in 1n.

19. Yagur, *Crossing the Line*, and see his other publications in the bibliography.

20. Krakowski, *Coming of Age*.

21. This book is not comprehensive in its study of the enslaved men who worked as agents for merchants across the Mediterranean and Indian Ocean. The book's notes and appendix 3 do provide references for most of these individuals.

22. The Nubian heartlands of southern Egypt were flooded due to the construction of the Aswan High Dam. Displaced Nubians dispersed throughout Egypt and clustered in cities like Cairo and Alexandria. Geiser, *Egyptian Nubian*; Carruthers, *Flooded Pasts*.

23. This juxtaposition is made clear in the novel's epigraphs, which contrast the valor of the Nubian archers who repelled an attempted invasion by Muslim forces in the seventh century to the later conquest of Nubia during the Mamluk sultanate and which led to the enslavement of numerous Nubian captives. ʿAlī, *Dongola*, see the second epigraph and 1–2 in the English translation by Theroux. See also Abbas, "Egypt, Arab Nationalism, and Nubian Diasporic Identity"; DiMeo, "Unimaginable Community"; and Gilmore, "'Minor Literature in a Major Voice.'"

24. ʿAlī, *Dongola*, x, y, 39 (Theroux, trans., 16, 17, 26).

25. ʿAlī, *Dongola*, 39 (Theroux, trans., 26).

26. The surviving sources do not permit a precise census of the numbers of enslaved and free persons as a proportion of the overall Egyptian Jewish population. Yet a memorial list (T-S NS 320.7) from the twelfth century shows that enslaved and freed people made up 7 percent of the recorded deaths in the Jewish community of Fustat during the winter and early spring of 1126. Compare this tentative figure to the findings of Yossef Rapaport in his study of the medieval Fayyūm. In the villages of this region, he notes that slavery was virtually "nonexistent" Idem, *Rural Economy and Tribal Society*, 133. In larger towns such as Madinat al-Fayyūm, the tax figures that Rapaport reports suggest that the enslaved population would have been around 1 percent of the total population. See the tax figures at idem, *Rural Economy and Tribal Society*, 132, 134, 136, 138, and note the total population estimate of the town (4,000–5,500) at ibid., 74.

27. On Krakowski's notion of "ordinary culture," see Krakowski, *Coming of Age*, 4, 20, 301. Her analysis is not focused on slave owning as part of ordinary culture. I find the concept helpful to understand how Jewish slave-owning worked in medieval Egypt.

28. Ali, *Slavery and Marriage*, 7–8, 21–22.

29. Stein, "Maidservant and Her Master's Voice"; Labovitz, "The Purchase of His Money"; idem, "More Slave Women, More Lewdness"; idem, "Freedom and Honor"; Kriger, "Sex Rewarded, Sex Punished." Catherine Hezser has recently written extensively about Jews and slavery in antiquity. Among her works are Hezser, *Jewish Slavery in Antiquity*; "What Was Jewish About Jewish Slavery?"; and *Jewish Monotheism and Slavery*.

30. In his final letter to his brother Moses, David Maimonides sends greetings to the family's freedman (*al-ʿatīq*.) Or. 1081 J1v, margin, l. 5. On this letter, see chap. 7, 52n.

31. Weitz, "Slavery and the Historiography of Non-Muslims." Note especially the parallels between the role that sex slavery plays among Syriac elites in the earlier ʿAbbasid era in comparison to the Jewish merchants of Fatimid and Ayyubid Egypt.

32. On Coptic slave-owning in medieval Egypt, see chap. 1, 62n.

33. Goldenberg, "'It Is Permitted to Marry a Kushite.'

34. A Kushite *jāriya* is part of a Jewish woman's dowry: Halper 341 + Halper 348. The land of Kush: Benjamin of Tudela, *Itinerary*, 68 (English), 62 (Hebrew). Goldenberg, *Curse of Ham*, 17–75; idem, *Black and Slave*, 7–11 passim. Goldenberg rightly emphasizes the ambiguity of the terms Kush and Kushite. The historical context for the Egyptian sources (ca. 10th–13th c.) suggest that it was used in the wedding dowry (Halper 341 + Halper 348) to mean a type of "dark-skinned" person who was recognized as lawfully enslaveable according to Islamic and Jewish law. Statistically this *jāriya* was most likely to be Nubian but could have had a different origin.

Appendixes

1. For the rate of manumission: The number of enslaved people in appendix 1 (175) was added to the number of freed people in appendix 2 (56). There are 11 individuals marked with an asterisk who appear in appendixes 1 and 2, but they are only counted once each for the number of enslaved people. The total number of enslaved and formerly enslaved people is 220 (175 + 45). The proportion of freed to enslaved people is 56 to 220, which I simplify in the book as around one-quarter.

2. See the discussion in chap. 7.

3. On the term *ʿajamiyya*, see chap. 3, 114n.

4. See chap. 4, 69n.

5. I am not certain about the best English translation here. See Lane, *Dictionary*, 2462.

6. Goitein noted that this Ghazāl was also called by the name Bidʿa. This is possible but not certain given the fragmentary preservation of the document.

7. Possibly Jaḥū[n].

8. An Abū al-Faḍl is the recipient of the letter T-S 13J33.10. An Abū al-Faḍl is mentioned as Nadd's seller in RNL Yevr.-Arab I 1700.15v and RNL Yevr.-Arab I 1700.22v.

9. See the discussion of Naʿīm's history in chap. 7.

10. See Lane, *Lexicon*, 1169.

11. Dating based on the appearance of *ha-Sar* Nathanel in Or. 10653.5, who appears in documents written in the hand of Ḥalfon b. Menasse: T-S 16.119 and ENA NS 18.9.

12. See previous note.

13. I am uncertain about this reading. It could be a reference to this Tawfīq's *jins* as of the Nubian town of Faras or the Persian province of Fars. Another possibility is that the scribe, Ḥalfon b. Menasse, misheard or misspelled *Tarsāwiyya*. Cf. Tawfīq 1 and MS Heb. b 12/20.

14. This is a name I use for a woman whose slave name is not fully legible. See the discussion in chap. 5, 36n.

15. Based on the names of the buyer and seller, it seems that T-S NS J449, Mosseri VII, 58.1 (which names Abnūsa), and T-S 8J8.16 are probably related (copies or different versions of documents) to the same transaction.

16. See the discussion in chap. 4 and there at 69n.

17. T-S NS J6 + T-S 8J4.12 + T-S 8J4.11. Edition in Ackerman-Lieberman, "Partnership Culture," 2: 172–74. ENA 972.3: in 1128, Bishāra the *meshuḥrar* is mentioned as the father of a

divorcée. She is called "Sitt al-Dalāl bt. Mevasser, the one called Bishāra the freedman (ha-meshuḥrar)."

18. Edition in Yagur, "Religious Identity," 313–14.

19. Edition in Rivlin, *Inheritance and Wills*, 395–96, no. 10.

20. Edition in Yagur, "Religious Identity," 319.

21. There is a small chance that this is the same person as in appendix 1. See the discussion in chap. 7.

22. On *Rūmī* as Roman, see chap. 3, 41n.

23. Yagur, "Religious Identity," 284; L. Blau, *Jüdische Ehescheidung*, 102–3.

24. Edition in Yagur, "Religious Identity," 329–31.

25. For "iron sheep property," see chap. 6, 67n, and the sources cited there.

26. See chap. 4.

27. On the ambiguities of professional identifications see chap. 4.

28. His identification is by Frenkel, "*The Compassionate and Benevolent*," 292.

29. On the use of Hebrew in Joseph's *kunya* and how to read his name, see Friedman, "India Trader's Partnership," 78, and the sources cited there in 4–5n.

30. Thanks to Oded Zinger for pointing out that ʿAbīr's seller, Abū al-Barakāt, could be the same as Fayrūz's buyer.

31. See appendix 2, 23n.

32. Schwab, *Catalog*.

33. See 32n.

34. A Nathan b. Joseph is also involved in slave sale in Mosseri VII, 69.2.

35. Edition in Yagur, "Religious Identity," 313–14.

BIBLIOGRAPHY

Abbas, Fatin. "Egypt, Arab Nationalism, and Nubian Diasporic Identity in Idris Ali's *Dongola: A Novel of Nubia*." *Research in African Literatures* 45 (2014): 147–66.

Abbott, Nabia. "Women and the State in Early Islam." *Journal of Near Eastern Studies* 1 (1942): 341–68.

al-ʿAbdarī, Abū ʿAbd Allāh b. Muḥammad Ibn al-Ḥājj. *Al-Madkhal ilā tanmiyat al-aʿmāl bi-taḥsīn al-niyya*. 4 vols. Cairo: Al-Maṭbaʿa al-Miṣriyya bil-Azhar, 1929.

Abulafia, David. "The Servitude of Jews and Muslims in the Medieval Mediterranean: Origins and Diffusion." *Mélanges de l'École Française de Rome: Moyen Âge* 112 (2000): 687–714.

Abu-Lughod, Lila. "Islam and the Gendered Discourses of Death." *International Journal of Middle East Studies* 25, no. 2 (1993): 187–205.

Ackerman-Lieberman, Phillip. (See also Liberman, Phillip.) *The Business of Identity: Jews, Muslims, and Economic Life in Medieval Egypt*. Stanford University Press, 2014.

———. "Contractual Partnerships in the Geniza and the Relationship Between Islamic Law and Practice." *Journal of the Economic and Social History of the Orient* 54 (2011): 646–76.

———. "Legal Writing in Medieval Cairo: 'Copy' or 'Likeness' in Jewish Documentary Formulae." In *From a Sacred Source: Genizah Studies in Honor of Professor Stefan C. Reif*, edited by Ben Outhwaite and Siam Bhayro, 1–24. Brill, 2011.

———. "Nahray Ben Nissim." In *EJIW*.

———. "A Partnership Culture: Jewish Economic and Social Life Seen Through the Legal Documents of the Cairo Geniza." 2 vols. PhD diss., Princeton University, 2007.

Ackermann-Lieberman, Phillip, and Onur Yildirim. "Slavery, Slave Trade." In *EJIW*.

Adams, William Y. "Baqṯ Treaty." In *Coptic Encyclopedia*, 2:343b–44b, 1991.

Adler, Marcus N., ed. *The Itinerary of Benjamin of Tudela: Critical Text, Translation and Commentary*. London: Henry Frowde, 1907.

Aḥmad b. ʿAbd Allāh (attributed). *Rasāʾil ikhwān al-ṣafāʾ wa-khullān al-wafāʾ*. Edited by Khayr al-Dīn al-Zirkilī. 4 vols. Al-Maṭbaʿa al-ʿArabiyya bi-Miṣr, 1928.

Albin, Andrew, Mary C. Erler, Thomas O'Donnell, Nicholas L. Paul, and Nina Rowe, eds. *Whose Middle Ages?: Teachable Moments for an Ill-Used Past*. Fordham University Press, 2019.

Alexander, J. "Islam, Archaeology and Slavery in Africa." *World Archaeology* 33 (2001): 44–60.

Ali, Adam. "Zanj Revolt in the Abbasid Caliphate (Iraq)." In *Oxford Research Encyclopedia of African History*, 2022. https://doi.org/10.1093/acrefore/9780190277734.013.933.

ʿAlī, Idrīs. *Dongola: A Novel of Nubia*. Translated by Peter Theroux. University of Arkansas Press, 1998.

ʿAlī, Idrīs. *Dunqulā*. 2014 ed. Al-Karma lil-Nashr wal-Tawzīʿ, 1993.

Ali, Kecia. "Concubinage and Consent." *International Journal of Middle East Studies* 49 (2017): 148–52.

———. *Marriage and Slavery in Early Islam*. Harvard University Press, 2010.

Alibhai, Ali Asgar Hussamuddin. "Through the Eyes of Jūdhar: Reconstructing the Tenth-Century World of a Fatimid Chamberlain 2018." PhD diss., Harvard University, 2018.

Alston, Richard, J. A. Baird, and April Pudsey. "Introduction: Between Words and Walls: Material and Textual Approaches to Housing in the Graeco-Roman World." In *Housing in the Ancient Mediterranean World: Material and Textual Approaches*, edited by April Pudsey and J. A. Baird, 1–26. Cambridge University Press, 2022.

Amitai, Reuven. "The Mamlūk Institution, or One Thousand Years of Military Slavery in the Islamic World." In *Arming Slaves: From Classical Times to the Modern Age*, edited by Christopher Leslie Brown and Philip D. Morgan, 40–78. Yale University Press, 2006.

Anooshahr, Ali. "Military Slavery in Medieval North India." In *The Cambridge World History of Slavery: Volume 2, AD 500–AD 1420*, edited by Craig Perry, David Eltis, Stanley Engerman, and David Richardson, 362–82. Cambridge University Press, 2021.

ʿAodeh, Ṣabiḥ. "Eleventh Century Letters of Jewish Merchants from the Cairo Geniza" (Hebrew). PhD diss., University of Tel-Aviv, 1992.

———. "Sitt Al-Munā, the Desired Woman—a Bill of Sale for a Slave Woman from the Year 1115 CE Found in the Geniza" (Hebrew). In *ʿAle ʿAsor: Proceedings of the Tenth Conference of the Society for Judaeo-Arabic Studies*, edited by Daniel Lasker and Haggai Ben-Shammai, 195–202. Ben Gurion University, 2008.

Antrim, Zayde. *Routes and Realms: The Power of Place in the Early Islamic World*. Oxford University Press, 2012.

Arad, Dotan. "The Community as an Economic Body: The Property of the Cairo Mustaʿrib Community in Light of Genizah Documents" (Hebrew). *Ginzei Qedem* 7 (2011): 25–69.

Armstrong-Partida, Michelle. *Defiant Priests: Domestic Unions, Violence, and Clerical Masculinity in Fourteenth-Century Catalunya*. Cornell University Press, 2017.

———. "Race, Skin Colour, Enslavement and Sexuality in the Late Medieval Mediterranean." *Journal of Medieval History* 50 (2024): 477–99.

Ashur, Amir. "Engagement and Betrothal Documents from the Cairo Geniza" (Hebrew). PhD diss., Tel Aviv University, 2006.

———. "The India Trade and the Emergence of the Engagement Contract: A Cairo Geniza Study." *Medieval Globe* 3 (2017): 27–46.

———. "Protecting the Wife's Rights in Marriage as Reflected in Pre-Nuptials and Marriage Contracts from the Cairo Genizah and Parallel Arabic Sources." *Religion Compass* 6/8 (2012): 381–89.

Assaf, Simḥa. *Be-ohole Yaʿaḳov: peraḳim me-ḥaye ha-tarbut shel ha-Yehudim bi-yeme ha-benayim*. Mossad ha-Rav Kook, 1965.

———. "Book of Formularies of Rav Hai Son of Sherira Gaon" (Hebrew). *Tarbiṣ* 1 (1930): 5–72.

———. "From the Treasury of the Geniza" (Hebrew). *Sinai* 14 (1946): 1–8.

———. "The Relations Between the Jews of Egypt and Aden in the Twelfth Century" (Hebrew). *Bulletin of the Jewish Palestine Exploration Society* 12 (1948): 116–19.

———. "Slaves and the Slave Trade Among the Jews in the Middle Ages: According to Hebrew Sources" (Hebrew). *Zion* 4 (1939): 91–125.

———. "Slaves and the Slave Trade in the Middle Ages" (Hebrew). *Zion* 5 (1940): 271–80.

———. *Texts and Studies in Jewish History* (Hebrew). Jerusalem: Mossad ha-Rav Kook, 1946.

Assaf, Simḥa, ed. *Teshuvot ha-geonim: ve-liqqutei sefer ha-din le-Yehudah Barṣiloni.* Jerusalem: ha-Madpis, 1927.

Assis, Yom Tov. "Sexual Behaviour in Mediavel Hispano-Jewish Society." In *Jewish History: Essays in Honour of Chimen Abramsky*, edited by Steven J. Zipperstein, Chimen Abramsky, and Ada Rapoport-Albert, 25–59. P. Halban, 1988.

Astren, Fred. "*Dhimma.*" In *EJIW.*

ʿAthamina, Khalil. "How Did Islam Contribute to Change the Legal Status of Women: The Case of the Jawārī, or the Female Slaves." *Al-Qanṭara: Revista de Estudios Árabes* 28 (2007): 383–408.

Austen, Ralph A. "The Mediterranean Islamic Slave Trade Out of Africa: A Tentative Census." *Slavery & Abolition* 13 (1992): 214–48.

Aykan, Yavuz. "On Freedom, Kinship, and the Market: Rethinking Property and Law in the Ottoman Slave System." *Quaderni Storici* 154 (2017): 3–29.

Baadj, Amar. "The Political Context of the Egyptian Gold Crisis During the Reign of Saladin." *International Journal of African Historical Studies* 47 (2014): 121–38.

Bacharach, Jere L. "African Military Slaves in the Medieval Middle East: The Cases of Iraq (869–955) and Egypt (868–1171)." *International Journal of Middle East Studies* 13 (1981): 471–95.

al-Baghdādī, Muwaffaq al-Dīn ʿAbd al-Laṭīf. *A Physician on the Nile: A Description of Egypt and Journal of the Famine Years.* Translated by Tim Mackintosh-Smith. New York University Press, 2021.

Bagnall, Roger S., Jane L. Rowlandson, and Dorothy J. Thompson, eds. *Slavery and Dependence in Ancient Egypt: Sources in Translation.* Cambridge University Press, 2024.

Baird, J. A., and April Pudsey, eds. *Housing in the Ancient Mediterranean World: Material and Textual Approaches.* Cambridge University Press, 2022.

Baker, Colin F. "A Note on an Arabic Fragment of Ibn Buṭlān's The Physicians' Dinner Party from the Cairo Genizah." *Journal of the Royal Asiatic Society* 3 (1993): 207–13.

Balafrej, Lamia. "Automated Slaves, Ambivalent Images, and Noneffective Machines in al-Jazari's Compendium of the Mechanical Arts, 1206." *21: Inquiries into Art, History, and the Visual* 3 (2022): 737–74.

———. "Domestic Slavery, Skin Colour, and Image Dialectic in Thirteenth-Century Arabic Manuscripts." *Art History* 44 (2021): 1012–36.

———. "Instrumental Jawārī: On Gender, Slavery, and Technology in Medieval Arabic Sources." *Al-ʿUṣūr al-Wusṭā* 31 (2023): 96–126.

Balbaʿ, Aḥmad Fuad. *The Baqṭ Treaty Between the Governor of Egypt and the Elite of Nubia from the Perspective of Slavery During the First Seven Islamic Centuries* (Arabic). al-ʿArabī lil-Nashar, 2008.

Ballan, Mohamed. "Borderland Anxieties: Lisān al-Dīn Ibn al-Khaṭīb (d. 1374) and the Politics of Genealogy in Late Medieval Granada." *Speculum* 98 (2023): 448–95.

Bano, Shadab. "Slave Markets in Medieval India." *Proceedings of the Indian History Congress* 61 (2000): 365–73.

Bar-Asher Siegal, Elitzur A. *Introduction to the Grammar of Jewish Babylonian Aramaic*. Ugarit-Verlag, 2013.

Barber, Mathew. "Reappraising the Arabic Accounts for the Conflict of 446/1054–5: An Egyptian Perspective on Constantine IX and His Immediate Successors." In *Transmitting and Circulating the Late Antique and Byzantine Worlds*, edited by Hugh Jeffery and Mirela Ivanova, 170–98. Brill, 2019.

Bareket, Elinoar. "Abiathar Ben Elijah Ha-Kohen." In *EJIW*.

———. "Ibn ʿAwkal Family." In *EJIW*.

———. *The Jewish Leadership in Fustat in the First Half of the Eleventh Century* (Hebrew). Diaspora Research Institute, 1995.

Barker, Hannah. "Purchasing a Slave in Fourteenth-Century Cairo: Ibn al-Akfānī's *Book of Observation and Inspection in the Examination of Slaves*." *Mamlūk Studies Review* 19 (2016): 1–23.

———. "Reconnecting with the Homeland: Black Sea Slaves in Mamluk Biographical Dictionaries." *Medieval Prosopography* 30 (2015): 87–104.

———. "The Risk of Birth: Life Insurance for Enslaved Pregnant Women in Fifteenth-Century Genoa." *Journal of Global Slavery* 6 (2021): 187–217.

———. *That Most Precious Merchandise: The Mediterranean Trade in Black Sea Slaves, 1260–1500*. University of Pennsylvania Press, 2019.

———. "What Caused the 14th-Century Tatar–Circassian Shift?" In *Slavery in the Black Sea Region, c.900–1900*, edited by Felicia Roşu, 339–63. Brill, 2021.

Barnes, Ruth. "Indian Cotton for Cairo: The Royal Ontario Museum's Gujarati Textiles and the Early Western Indian Ocean Trade." *Textile History* 48 (2017): 15–30.

Baron, Salo W. "Ghetto and Emancipation." In *The Menorah Treasury: Harvest of a Half Century*, edited by Leo Schwarz, 50–63. Jewish Publication Society of America, 1973.

Barrett, Caitlín E., and Jennifer Carrington, eds. *Households in Context: Dwelling in Ptolemaic and Roman Egypt*. Cornell University Press, 2023.

Bauer, Thomas. *Warum es kein islamisches Mittelalter gab: Das Erbe der Antike und der Orient*. Verlag C. H. Beck, 2018.

Becker, C. H. "ʿAbd Allāh b. Saʿd." In *EI2*.

Beech, George, and James Powell. "Prosopography." In *Medieval Studies: An Introduction*, 2nd ed., 185–226. Syracuse University Press, 1992.

Bellefonds, Y. Linant de. "Hiba." In *EI2*.

Ben-Naeh, Yaron. "Blond, Tall, with Honey-Colored Eyes: Jewish Ownership of Slaves in the Ottoman Empire." *Jewish History* 20 (2006): 315–32.

Ben-Sasson, Menahem, ed. *The Jews of Sicily, 825–1068: Documents and Sources* (Hebrew). Ben Zvi Institute, 1991.

Ben-Shammai, Haggai. "Medieval History and Religious Thought." In *The Cambridge Genizah Collections: Their Contents and Significance*, edited by Stefan Reif and Shulamit Reif, 136–49. Cambridge University Press, 2002.

Ben-Ur, Aviva. *Jewish Autonomy in a Slave Society: Suriname in the Atlantic World, 1651–1825*. University of Pennsylvania Press, 2020.

Bensch, Stephen. "From Prizes of War to Domestic Merchandise: The Changing Face of Slavery in Catalonia and Aragon, 1000–1300." *Viator* 25 (1994): 63–93.

Beresford, James. *The Ancient Sailing Season*. Brill, 2013.

Beshir, Beshir Ibrahim. "New Light on Nubian Fāṭimid Relations." *Arabica* 22 (1975): 15–24.

Bessard, Fanny. *Caliphs and Merchants: Cities and Economies of Power in the Near East (700–950)*. Oxford University Press, 2020.

Biale, David. *Power and Powerlessness in Jewish History: The Jewish Tradition and the Myth of Passivity*. Schocken Books, 1986.

Biermann, Felix, and Marek Jankowiak, eds. *The Archaeology of Slavery in Early Medieval Northern Europe: The Invisible Commodity*. Springer International Publishing, 2021.

Biran, Michal. "Forced Migrations and Slavery in the Mongol Empire (1206–1368)." In *The Cambridge World History of Slavery: Volume 2, AD 500–AD 1420*, edited by Craig Perry, David Eltis, Stanley Engerman, and David Richardson, 79–99. Cambridge University Press, 2021.

Blau, Joshua, ed. *A Dictionary of Mediaeval Judaeo-Arabic Texts* (Hebrew). The Academy of the Hebrew Language, 2006.

Blau, Ludwig. *Die jüdische Ehescheidung und der jüdische Scheidebrief: Eine historische Untersuchung*. Vol. 2. Verlag von Karl J. Trübner, 1912.

Blumenthal, David R. "Images of Women in the Hebrew Bible." In *Marriage, Sex, and Family in Judaism*, edited by Michael J. Broyde and Michael Ausubel, 15–60. Rowman & Littlefield Publishers, 2005.

Blumenthal, Debra. *Enemies and Familiars: Slavery and Mastery in Fifteenth-Century Valencia*. Cornell University Press, 2009.

Bodel, John. "Death and Social Death." In *On Human Bondage: After Slavery and Social Death*, edited by John Bodel and Walter Scheidel, 81–108. John Wiley & Sons, 2016.

Bodel, John, and Walter Scheidel, eds. *On Human Bondage: After Slavery and Social Death*. John Wiley & Sons, 2016.

Bondioli, Lorenzo M. "Peasants, Merchants, and Caliphs: Capital and Empire in Fatimid Egypt." Ph. D. diss., Princeton University, 2021.

———. "The Sicilian Tithe Business: State and Merchants in the Eleventh-Century Islamic Mediterranean." *Medieval Worlds* 14 (2021): 208–28.

Bos, Gerrit. "Maimonides' *On Coitus*: A New Parallel Arabic-English Edition and Translation." Brill, 2018.

Bosworth, Clifford Edmund. *The Mediaeval Islamic Underworld*. 2 vols. Brill, 1976.

———. "'Ajam." *Encyclopaedia Iranica*.

Bourdieu, Pierre. *Outline of a Theory of Practice*. Cambridge University Press, 1977.

Boussac, Marie-Françoise, Jean-François Salles, and Jean-Baptiste Yon, eds. *Ports of the Ancient Indian Ocean*. Primus Books, 2016.

Bowen, Donna Lee. "Muslim Juridical Opinions Concerning the Status of Women as Demonstrated by the Case of 'Azl." *Journal of Near Eastern Studies* 40 (1981): 323–28.

Boyarin, Daniel. *Unheroic Conduct: The Rise of Heterosexuality and the Invention of the Jewish Man*. University of California Press, 1997.

Bramoullé, David. *Les Fatimides et la mer (909–1171)*. Brill, 2020.

———. "Les ports du pays beja à l'époque fatimide." In *Networked Spaces: The Spatiality of Networks in the Red Sea and Western Indian Ocean*, edited by Caroline Durand, Julie Marchand, Bérangère Redon, and Pierre Schneider, 285–304. MOM Éditions, 2022.

———. "The Fatimids and the Red Sea (969–1171)." In *Navigated Spaces, Connected Places: Proceedings of Red Sea Project V Held at the University of Exeter*, 16–19 September 2010, edited by Dionysus A. Agius, John P. Cooper, Athena Trakadas, and Chiara Zazzaro, 127–35. Archaeopress, 2012.

———. "Trade Relations Between Sicily, Ifrīqiya, and Egypt Under the Fatimids and Zirids of Ifrīqiya (Tenth–Eleventh Centuries)." In *Mapping Pre-Modern Sicily: Maritime Violence, Cultural Exchange, and Imagination in the Mediterranean, 800–1700*, edited by Emily Sohmer Tai and Kathryn L. Reyerson, 93–109. Mediterranean Perspectives. Springer International Publishing, 2022.

Brett, Michael. "Ifrīqiya as a Market for Saharan Trade from the Tenth to the Twelfth Century A.D." *Journal of African History* 10 (1969): 347–64.

Brockopp, Jonathan E. *Early Mālikī Law: Ibn ʿAbd al-Ḥakam and His Major Compendium of Jurisprudence*. Brill, 2000.

———. "Slaves and Slavery." In *Encyclopaedia of the Qurʾān*. Vol. 5. Edited by Jane Dammen McAuliffe. Brill, 2005.

Brody, Robert. *The Geonim of Babylonia and the Shaping of Medieval Jewish Culture*. Yale University Press, 1998.

Brody, Robert, ed. *A Hand-List of Rabbinic Manuscripts in the Cambridge Geniza Collections: Taylor-Schechter New Series*. Vol. 1. Cambridge University Press, 1998.

———. *Teshuvot Rav Natronai bar Hilai Ga'on*. 2 vols. Ofeq Institute, 1994.

Brown, Jonathan A. C. *Slavery & Islam*. Oneworld Academic, 2019.

Browne, Gerald M. *Old Nubian Texts from Qaṣr Ibrim III*. Egypt Exploration Society, 1991.

Bruning, Jelle. "Slave Trade Dynamics in Abbasid Egypt: The Papyrological Evidence." *Journal of the Economic and Social History of the Orient* 63 (2020): 682–742.

———. "Islamic Tombstones for Slaves from Abbasid-Era Egypt." *Slavery & Abolition* 44 (2023): 616–37.

———. "Voluntary Enslavement in an Abbasid-Era Papyrus Letter." *Journal of the Royal Asiatic Society* 33 (July 2023): 643–59.

Brunschvig, R. "ʿAbd." In *EI2*.

Burnard, Trevor. *Mastery, Tyranny, & Desire: Thomas Thistlewood and His Slaves in the Anglo-Jamaican World*. University of North Carolina Press, 2004.

Burstein, S. M. "The Hellenistic Fringe: The Case of Meroë." In *Hellenistic History and Culture*, edited by Peter Green, 38–66. University of California Press, 1993.

Calderini, Simonetta. "Sayyida Raṣad: A Royal Woman as 'Gateway' to Power During the Fatimid Era." In *Egypt and Syria in the Fatimid, Ayyubid and Mamluk Eras V: Proceedings of the 11th, 12th and 13th International Colloquium Organized at the Katholieke Universiteit Leuven in May 2001, 2002 and 2003*, edited by U. Vermeulen and K. D'hulster, 27–36. Peeters, 2007.

Cameron, Averil, ed. *Fifty Years of Prosopography: The Later Roman Empire, Byzantium and Beyond*. Oxford University Press, 2003.

Campbell, Gwyn. "East Africa in the Early Indian Ocean World Slave Trade: The Zanj Revolt Reconsidered." In *Early Exchange Between Africa and the Wider Indian Ocean World*, 275–303. Palgrave Macmillan, 2016.

———. "Introduction: Slavery and Other Forms of Unfree Labour in the Indian Ocean World." *Slavery & Abolition* 24 (2003): ix–xxxii.

Campbell, Gwyn, Suzanne Miers, and Joseph Calder Miller, eds. *Children in Slavery Through the Ages*. Ohio University Press, 2009.

Caswell, Fuad Matthew. *The Slave Girls of Baghdad: The Qiyān in the Early Abbasid Era*. I. B. Tauris, 2011.

Chakraborty, S. A. *The City of Brass*. Harper Voyager, 2017.

Chaudhuri, K. N. *Trade and Civilisation in the Indian Ocean: An Economic History from the Rise of Islam to 1750*. Cambridge University Press, 1985.

Chehata, Chafik. "*Dhimma*." In *EI2*.

Chipman, Leigh. "How to Read a Medical Prescription." *Jewish History* 32 (2019): 487–96.

Chipman, Leigh, and Efraim Lev. "Syrups from the Apothecary's Shop: A Genizah Fragment Containing One of the Earliest Manuscripts of *Minhāj al-Dukkān*." *Journal of Semitic Studies* 51 (2006): 137–68.

Choueka, Yaacov. "Computerizing the Cairo Genizah: Aims, Methodologies and Achievements." *Ginzei Qedem* 8 (2012): 9–30.

Chwat, Ezra. "Al-Fāsī, Isaac Ben Jacob." In *EJIW*.

Cobb, Paul M. *The Race for Paradise: An Islamic History of the Crusades*. Oxford University Press, 2014.

Cobin, David M. "A Brief Look at the Jewish Law of Manumission." *Chicago-Kent Law Review* 70 (1995): 1339–48.

Cohen, Mark R. "Feeding the Poor and Clothing the Naked: The Cairo Geniza." *Journal of Interdisciplinary History* 35 (2005): 407–21.

———. "Geniza for Islamists, Islamic Geniza, and the 'New Cairo Geniza.'" *Harvard Middle Eastern and Islamic Review* 7 (2006): 129–45.

———. "Islamic Policy Toward the Jews from the Prophet Muhammad to the Pact of 'Umar." In *A History of Jewish-Muslim Relations: From the Origins to the Present Day*, edited by Abdelwahab Meddeb and Benjamin Stora, translated by Jane Marie Todd and Michael B. Smith, 58–73. Princeton University Press, 2013.

———. *Maimonides and the Merchants: Jewish Law and Society in the Medieval Islamic World*. University of Pennsylvania Press, 2017.

———. "New Light on the Conflict over the Palestinian Gaonate, 1038–1042, and on Daniel b. 'Azarya: A Pair of Letters to the Nagid of Qayrawan." *Association of Jewish Studies Review* 1 (1976): 1–39.

———. *Poverty and Charity in the Jewish Community of Medieval Egypt*. Princeton University Press, 2005.

———. *Under Crescent and Cross: The Jews in the Middle Ages*. 2008 reissue. Princeton University Press, 1994.

———. *The Voice of the Poor in the Middle Ages: An Anthology of Documents from the Cairo Geniza*. Princeton University Press, 2005.

Cohen, Shaye J. D. *From the Maccabees to the Mishnah*. Westminster John Knox Press, 2014.

Collins, Robert O. "Slavery in the Sudan in History." *Slavery & Abolition* 20 (1999): 69–95.

Connell, R. W. *Masculinities.* 2nd ed. University of California Press, 2005.

Conrad, Lawrence. "Ibn Buṭlān in *Bilad Al-Shām*: The Career of a Travelling Christian Physician." In *Syrian Christians Under Islam: The First Thousand Years*, edited by David Thomas, 131–57. Brill, 2001.

Constable, Anthony R., and William Facey, eds. *The Principles of Arab Navigation.* Arabian Publishing, 2013.

Constable, Olivia Remie. "Funduq, Fondaco, and Khān in the Wake of Christian Commerce and Crusade." In *The Crusades from the Perspective of Byzantium and the Muslim World*, edited by Angeliki E. Laiou and Roy P. Mottahedeh, 145–56. Washington, DC: Dumbarton Oaks Research Library and Collection, 2001.

———. *Housing the Stranger in the Mediterranean World: Lodging, Trade, and Travel in Late Antiquity and the Middle Ages.* Cambridge University Press, 2003.

Cortese, Delia, and Simonetta Calderini. *Women and the Fatimids in the World of Islam.* Edinburgh University Press, 2006.

Crone, Patricia. *Slaves on Horses: The Evolution of the Islamic Polity.* Cambridge University Press, 1980.

Crone, Patricia, and A. J. Wensinck. "Mawlā." In *EI2*.

Culbertson, Laura. "A Life-Course Approach to Household Slaves in the Late Third Millennium B.C." In *Slaves and Households in the Near East*, edited by Laura Culbertson, 33–48. The Oriental Institute of the University of Chicago, 2011.

———. "Slaves and Households in the Near East." In *Slaves and Households in the Near East*, edited by Laura Culbertson. The Oriental Institute of the University of Chicago, 2011.

Cullum, P. H. "Clergy, Masculinity and Transgression in Late Medieval England." In *Masculinity in Medieval Europe*, edited by D. M. Hadley, 178–96. Longman, 1999.

Curness, Adele. "'Slavery' Outside the Slave Trade: The Movement and Status of Captives Between Byzantine Calabria and the Islamic World." In *Transmitting and Circulating the Late Antique and Byzantine Worlds*, 102–22. Brill, 2019.

Dann, Michael. "Between History and Hagiography: The Mothers of the Imams in Imami Historical Memory." In *Concubines and Courtesans: Women and Slavery in Islamic History*, edited by Matthew S. Gordon and Kathryn A. Hain, 244–65. Oxford University Press, 2017.

David, Abraham. "Benjamin Ben Jonah of Tudela." In *EJIW*.

David, Yeḥezkel. "Formulae of the Bill of Divorce as Reflected in the Geniza Documents and Other Sources" (Hebrew). Master's thesis, University of Tel Aviv, 1991.

———. "Divorce Among the Jews According to Cairo Geniza Documents and Other Sources" (Hebrew). PhD diss., 2 vols, Tel Aviv University, 2000.

Davis, David Brion. *Inhuman Bondage: The Rise and Fall of Slavery in the New World.* Oxford University Press, 2006.

De Troia, Nicoletta. "The Oases of Egypt's Western Desert from Byzantine to Islamic Rule: Problems and New Perspectives." *Journal of Late Antiquity* 15 (2022): 277–303.

Decker, Sarah Ifft. *The Fruit of Her Hands: Jewish and Christian Women's Work in Medieval Catalan Cities.* Penn State University Press, 2022.

Delvaux, Matthew C. "Transregional Slave Networks of the Northern Arc, 700–900 C.E." PhD diss., Boston College, 2019.

Despret, Vinciane. "From Secret Agents to Interagency." *History and Theory* 52 (2013): 29–44.

DiMeo, David. "Unimaginable Community: The Failure of Nubian Nationalism in Idris Ali's *Dongola*." *Research in African Literatures* 46 (2015): 72–89.

Dirbas, Hekmat. "Naming of Slave-Girls in Arabic: A Survey of Medieval and Modern Sources." *Zeitschrift für Arabische Linguistik* 69 (2019): 26–38.

Dollinger, Marc. *Black Power, Jewish Politics: Reinventing the Alliance in the 1960s*. Revised edition. New York University Press, 2024.

Edwards, David N. "Islamic Archaeology in Nubia." In *Handbook of Ancient Nubia*, edited by Dietrich Raue, 965–84. De Gruyter, 2019.

———. "Slavery and Slaving in the Medieval and Post-Medieval Kingdoms of the Middle Nile." In *Slavery in Africa: Archaeology and Memory*, edited by Paul Lane and Kevin C. MacDonald, 79–108. Oxford University Press, 2011.

El-Azhari, Taef. *Queens, Eunuchs and Concubines in Islamic History, 661–1257*. Edinburgh University Press, 2019.

Elbaum, Alan. "'The Fire in My Heart and the Pain in My Eyes': Interdependence and Outburst in the Illness Letters of the Cairo Geniza." *Speculum* 98 (2023): 122–63.

El-Cheikh, Nadia Maria. "Servants at the Gate: Eunuchs at the Court of Al-Muqtadir." *Journal of the Economic and Social History of the Orient* 48 (2005): 234–52.

El-Leithy, Tamer. "Conversions to Islam in a Late Medieval Chronicle from Damascus." In *Conversion to Islam in the Premodern Age: A Sourcebook*, edited by Nimrod Hurvitz, Christian C. Sahner, Uriel Simonsohn, and Luke Yarbrough, 317–22. University of California Press, 2020.

———. "Coptic Culture and Conversion in Medieval Cairo, 1293–1524 A.D." Ph.D. diss., Princeton University, 2005.

Elon, Menachem. *Jewish Law: History, Sources, Principles*. Vol. 4. Jewish Publication Society, 1994.

Eltis, David. *Atlantic Cataclysm: Rethinking the Atlantic Slave Trades*. Cambridge University Press, 2024.

Eltis, David, and Stanley L. Engerman. "Dependence, Servility, and Coerced Labor in Time and Space." In *The Cambridge World History of Slavery: Volume 3, AD 1420–AD 1804*, edited by David Eltis and Stanley L. Engerman, 1–22. Cambridge University Press, 2011.

Eltis, David, and Stanley L. Engerman, eds. *The Cambridge World History of Slavery: Volume 3, AD 1420–AD 1804*. Cambridge University Press, 2011.

Emrani, Haleh. "'Who Would Be Mine for the Day!': Irano-Judaic Marriage Customs in Late Antiquity." *Iranian Studies* 49 (March 3, 2016): 217–31.

Endelman, Todd M. "In Defense of Jewish Social History." *Jewish Social Studies* 7 (2001): 52–67.

Engel, David. "A Colleague Not a Sacred Authority—Reflections on Salo Baron's Scholarly Opus." *Association of Jewish Studies Review* 38 (2014): 441–45.

Epstein, Steven. *Speaking of Slavery: Color, Ethnicity, & Human Bondage in Italy*. Cornell University Press, 2001.

———. "Attitudes Toward Blackness." In *The Cambridge World History of Slavery: Volume 2, AD 500–AD 1420*, edited by Craig Perry, David Eltis, Stanley Engerman, and David Richardson, 214–39. Cambridge University Press, 2021.

Erlich, Haggai. "Jabarti." In *EI3*.

Ettinghausen, Richard. "Early Realism in Islamic Art." In *Islamic Art and Archaeology: Collected Papers*, edited by Myriam Rosen-Ayalon, 158–81. Gebr. Mann Verlag, 1984.

Faber, Eli. *Jews, Slaves, and the Slave Trade: Setting the Record Straight*. New York University Press, 1998.

Fabri, Felix. *Evagatorium in Terrae Sanctae, Arabiae et Egypti peregrinationem*. Edited by Conrad Hassler. Stuttgart: Societatis Literariae Stuttgardiensis, 1843.

Fage, J. D., ed. *The Cambridge History of Africa: Volume 2: From c.500 BC to AD 1050*. Cambridge University Press, 1979.

Fancy, Hussein. "Captivity, Ransom, and Manumission, 500–1420." In *The Cambridge World History of Slavery: Volume 2, AD 500–AD 1420*, edited by Craig Perry, David Eltis, Stanley Engerman, and David Richardson, 53–75. Cambridge University Press, 2021.

———. *The Mercenary Mediterranean: Sovereignty, Religion, and Violence in the Medieval Crown of Aragon*. University of Chicago Press, 2016.

Farias, Paulo Fernando de Moraes. "Models of the World and Categorial Models: The 'Enslavable Barbarian' as a Mobile Classificatory Label." *Slavery and Abolition* 1 (1980): 115–31.

Fauvelle-Aymar, François-Xavier. "Desperately Seeking the Jewish Kingdom of Ethiopia: Benjamin of Tudela and the Horn of Africa (Twelfth Century)." *Speculum* 88 (2013): 383–404.

———. *The Golden Rhinoceros: Histories of the African Middle Ages*. Princeton University Press, 2018.

Fay, Mary Ann. "Women and Waqf: Toward a Reconsideration of Women's Place in the Mamluk Household." *International Journal of Middle East Studies* 29 (1997): 33–51.

Feldman, David Michael. *Birth Control in Jewish Law: Marital Relations, Contraception, and Abortion as Set Forth in the Classic Texts of Jewish Law*. Jason Aronson, 1998.

Finkelstein, Menachem. *Conversion: Halakhah and Practice*. Translated by Edward Levin. Bar-Ilan University Press, 2006.

———. *Ha-Giyur: halakha u-ma'aseh*. Bar Ilan University Press, 1994.

Fontaine, Janel M. "Early Medieval Slave-Trading in the Archaeological Record: Comparative Methodologies." *Early Medieval Europe* 25 (2017): 466–88.

Foreman, Gabrielle P. et al. "Writing About Slavery/Teaching About Slavery: This Might Help." Google Doc. Accessed January 2, 2025. https://docs.google.com/document/d/1A4TEdDgYslX-hlKezLodMIM71My3KTNozxRvoIQTOQs/edit?tab=t.0.

Foucault, Michel. "The Subject and Power." In *Michel Foucault: Beyond Structuralism and Hermeneutics*, edited by Hubert L. Dreyfus and Paul Rabinow, 2nd ed., 208–26. University of Chicago Press, 1983.

Franklin, Arnold. "Ibn Sarjado, Aaron (Khalaf) Ben Joseph Ha-Kohen." In *EJIW*.

———. *This Noble House: Jewish Descendants of King David in the Medieval Islamic East*. University of Pennsylvania Press, 2013.

Franz, Kurt. "Slavery in Islam: Legal Norms and Social Practice." In *Slavery and the Slave Trade in the Eastern Mediterranean (c. 1000–1500 CE)*, edited by Reuven Amitai and Christoph Cluse, 51–141. Brepols, 2017.

Freamon, Bernard K. *Possessed by the Right Hand: The Problem of Slavery in Islamic Law and Muslim Cultures*. Brill, 2019.

Freeman-Grenville, G.S.P., ed. *The Book of the Wonders of India: Mainland, Sea and Islands.* East-West Publications, 1981.

Freimann, A. H., and S. D. Goitein, eds. *Abraham Maimuni: Responsa* (Hebrew). Jerusalem: Mekize Nirdamim, 1937.

Frenkel, Miriam. *"The Compassionate and Benevolent": Jewish Ruling Elites in the Medieval Islamicate World: Alexandria as a Case Study.* Translated by Tzemah Yoreh. Revised edition. De Gruyter and the Ben Tzvi Institute, 2021.

———. *"The Compassionate and Benevolent": The Leading Elite in the Jewish Community of Alexandria in the Middle Ages* (Hebrew). Ben Zvi Institute, 2006.

———. "The Jewish Community of Aleppo During the Genizah Period" (Hebrew). Master's thesis, Hebrew University, 1990.

———. "Medieval Alexandria—Life in a Port City." *Al-Masāq* 26 (2014): 5–35.

———. "'Proclaim Liberty to Captives and Freedom to Prisoners': The Ransoming of Captives by Medieval Jewish Communities in Islamic Countries." In *Gefangenenloskauf im Mittelmeerraum: Ein interreligioser Vergleich. Akten der Tagung vom 19. bis 21. September 2013 an der Universität Paderborn*, 83–97. Georg Olms Verlag, 2015.

———. "The Slave Trade in Geniza Society." In *Slavery and the Slave Trade in the Eastern Mediterranean (c. 1000–1500 CE)*, edited by Reuven Amitai and Christoph Cluse, 143–61. Brepols, 2017.

———. "Slavery in Medieval Jewish Society Under Islam: A Gendered Perspective." In *Männlich und weiblich schuf Er sie: Studien zur Genderkonstruktion und zur Eherecht in der Mittelmeerreligionen*, edited by Matthias Morgenstern, Christian Boudignon, and Christiane Tietz, 249–59. Vandenhoeck and Ruprecht, 2011.

Frenkel, Yehoshua. "Slavery in 17th-Century Ottoman Jerusalem in Light of Several Sharia Court Records." In *Slaves and Slave Agency in the Ottoman Empire*, edited by Gül Şen and Stephan Conermann, 237–82. Vandenhoeck and Ruprecht Verlage, 2020.

Friedman, Mordechai A. "Divorce upon the Wife's Demand as Reflected in Manuscripts from the Cairo Geniza." *Jewish Law Annual* 4 (1981): 103–26.

———. "The Ethics of Medieval Jewish Marriage." In *Religions in a Religious Age*, edited by S. D. Goitein, 103–38. Association for Jewish Studies, 1974.

———. "*Halacha* as Evidence for the Study of Sexual Mores Among Jews in Medieval Islamic Countries: Face Coverings and *Mut'a* Marriages" (Hebrew). In *A View into the Lives of Women in Jewish Societies: Collected Essays*, edited by Yael Azmon, 143–59. Zalman Shazar Center for Jewish History, 1995.

———. "An India Trader's Partnership in Almería (1139)." *Sefarad* 76 (2016): 75–96.

———. *Jewish Marriage in Palestine: A Cairo Genizah Study.* 2 vols. Tel Aviv University and Jewish Theological Seminary of America, 1980.

———. *Jewish Polygyny in the Middle Ages: New Documents from the Cairo Geniza* (Hebrew). The Bialik Institute, 1986.

———. "Maimonides, Zuta, and the *Muqaddams*: A Story of Three Bans" (Hebrew). *Zion* 70 (2005): 473–528.

———. "Master and Slave Girl: Two Geniza Documents." *Gratz College Annual of Jewish Studies* 1 (1972): 56–63.

———. "The Minimum Mohar Payment as Reflected in the Geniza Documents: Marriage Gift or Endowment Pledge?" *Proceedings of the American Academy for Jewish Research* 43 (1976): 15–47

———. "The Monogamy Clause in Jewish Marriage Contracts." *Perspectives in Jewish Learning* 4 (1972): 20–40.

———. "Polygyny in Jewish Tradition and Practice New Sources from the Cairo Geniza." *Proceedings of the American Academy for Jewish Research* 49 (1982): 33–68.

———. "Pre-Nuptial Agreements with Grooms of Questionable Character: A Geniza Study." *Dine Israel* VI (1975): 105–22.

———. "The Ransom-Divorce: Divorce Proceedings Initiated by the Wife in Mediaeval Jewish Practice.". *Israel Oriental Studies* 6 (1976): 288–307.

———. "Responsa of R. Abraham Maimonides from the Cairo Geniza: a Preliminary Review." *Proceedings of the American Academy for Jewish Research* 56 (1990): 29–49.

———. "Women and the India Trade" (Hebrew). In *From Sages to Savants: Studies Presented to Avraham Grossman*, edited by Yosef Kaplan, B. Z. Kedar, and Yosef Haker, 157–85. Merkaz Zalman Shazar le-Toldot Yisrael, 2010.

Friedman, Mordechai A., ed. *A Dictionary of Medieval Judeo-Arabic: In the India Book Letters from the Geniza and in Other Texts* (Hebrew). Ben Zvi Institute, 2016.

———. *The Rambam and the Cairo Geniza* (Hebrew). Israel Academy of Arts and Sciences, 2023.

Friedman, Saul S. *Jews and the American Slave Trade*. Transaction Books, 1998.

Friedman, Yvonne. "Charity Begins at Home? Ransoming Captives in Jewish, Christian and Muslim Tradition." *Studia Hebraica* 6 (2006): 55–67.

———. *Encounter Between Enemies: Captivity and Ransom in the Latin Kingdom of Jerusalem*. Brill, 2002.

Fynn-Paul, Jeffrey. "Empire, Monotheism and Slavery in the Greater Mediterranean Region from Antiquity to the Early Modern Era." *Past and Present* 205 (2009): 3–40.

———. "Introduction. Slaving Zones in Global History: The Evolution of a Concept." In *Slaving Zones: Cultural Identities, Ideologies, and Institutions in the Evolution of Global Slavery*, edited by Damian Pargas and Jeff Fynn-Paul, 1–22. Brill, 2018.

Gadamer, Hans-Georg. *Truth and Method*. Translated by Joel Weinsheimer and Donald G. Marshall. 2nd revised edition. Continuum, 1993.

Gamal, Adil S., ed. *Medieval Islamic Medicine: Ibn Riḍwān's Treatise "On the Prevention of Bodily Ills in Egypt."* Translated by Michael W. Dols. University of California Press, 2023.

Gamliel, Ophira. "Aśu the Convert: A Slave Girl or a Nāyar Land Owner?" *Entangled Religions* 6 (2018): 201–46.

Gamliel, Tova. "Performed Weeping: Drama and Emotional Management in Women's Wailing." *TDR (1988-)* 54 (2010): 70–90.

———. "Tears and Ideas: Therapeutic Aspects of 'Traditional' Wailing Performance." *Journal of Ritual Studies* 28 (2014): 45–63.

Garcin, Jean-Claude. *Un Centre Musulman de la Haute-Égypte Médiévale: Qūṣ*. 2nd ed. Institut français d'archéologie orientale, 2005.

Garnsey, Peter. *Ideas of Slavery from Aristotle to Augustine*. Cambridge University Press, 1996.

Geiser, Peter. *The Egyptian Nubian: A Study in Social Symbiosis*. American University in Cairo Press, 1986.

Gelder, Geert Jan van. "Slave-Girl Lost and Regained: Transformations of a Story." *Marvels & Tales* 18 (2004): 201–17.

Geus, Klaus. "Claudius Ptolemy on Egypt and East Africa." In *The Ptolemies, the Sea and the Nile: Studies in Waterborne Power*, edited by Dorothy J. Thompson, Kostas Buraselis, and Mary Stefanou, 218–31. Cambridge University Press, 2013.

Ghosh, Amitav. *In an Antique Land: History in the Guise of a Traveler's Tale*. Penguin Books, 1992.

———. "The Slave of MS. H.6." In *Subaltern Studies VII*, edited by Partha Chatterjee and Gyanendra Pandey, 159–220. Oxford University Press, 1992.

Ghosh, Suchandra. "Anahilapura: Understanding Its Expansive Network During the Time of the Chaulukyas." *Asian Review of World Histories* 6 (2018): 236–45.

Gil, Moshe. *Documents of the Jewish Pious Foundations from the Cairo Geniza*. Brill, 1976.

———. "The Flax Trade in the Mediterranean in the Eleventh Century A.D. as Seen in the Merchants' Letters from the Cairo Geniza." *Journal of Near Eastern Studies* 63, no. 2 (2004): 81–96.

———. *A History of Palestine, 634–1099*. Translated by Ethel Broido. Cambridge University Press, 1992.

———. *In the Kingdom of Ishmael* (Hebrew). 4 vols. Tel Aviv University, 1997.

———. "Institutions and Events of the Eleventh Century Mirrored in Geniza Letters (Part I)." *Bulletin of the School of Oriental and African Studies* 67 (2004): 151–67.

———. "The Jewish Merchants in the Light of Eleventh-Century Geniza Documents." *Journal of the Economic and Social History of the Orient* 46 (2003): 273–319.

———. *Jews in Islamic Countries in the Middle Ages*. Translated by David Strassler. Brill, 2004.

———. "Maintenance, Building Operations, and Repairs in the Houses of the Qodesh in Fustat: A Geniza Study." *Journal of the Economic and Social History of the Orient* 14 (1971): 136–95.

———. *Palestine During the First Muslim Period (634–1099)* (Hebrew). 3 vols. Tel Aviv University, 1983.

Giladi, Avner. *Muslim Midwives: The Craft of Birthing in the Premodern Middle East*. Cambridge University Press, 2015.

Gilli-Elewy, Hend. "On the Provenance of Slaves in Mecca During the Time of the Prophet Muhammad." *International Journal of Middle East Studies* 49 (2017): 164–68.

Gilmore, Christine. "'A Minor Literature in a Major Voice': Narrating Nubian Identity in Contemporary Egypt." *Alif: Journal of Comparative Poetics* (2015): 52–74.

Ginzberg, Louis. *Geonica*. Vol. 2. Jewish Theological Seminary, 1909.

Ginzburg, Carlo. *History, Rhetoric, and Proof*. The Menahem Stern Jerusalem Lectures. University Press of New England, 1999.

Glancy, Jennifer A. *Slavery in Early Christianity*. Oxford University Press, 2002.

Glymph, Thavolia. "Paper Tracings in the Spectacularly Boisterous Archive of Slavery." Presidential Address presented at the Annual Meeting of the American Historical Association, New York, January 4, 2025.

Goitein, S. D. "Cairo: An Islamic City in the Light of the Geniza Documents." In *Middle Eastern Cities: Ancient, Islamic, and Contemporary Middle Eastern Urbanism, A Symposium*, edited by Ira M. Lapidus, 80–96. University of California Press, 1969.

———. "Dispositions in Contemplation of Death: A Geniza Study." *Proceedings of the American Academy for Jewish Research* 46/47 (1979): 155–78.

———. "A Document from the African Port of ʿAydhāb from the Time of the Head of the Rabbinic Academy Joshua b. Dosā" (Hebrew). *Tarbiṣ* 21 (1950): 185–91.

———. "The Exchange Rate of Gold and Silver Money in Fatimid and Ayyubid Times: A Preliminary Study of the Relevant Geniza Material." *Journal of the Economic and Social History of the Orient* 8 (1965): 1–46.

———. "Geniza Papers of a Documentary Character in the Gaster Collection of the British Museum." *Jewish Quarterly Review* 51 (1960): 34–46.

———. "Human Rights in Jewish Thought and Life in the Middle Ages." In *Essays on Human Rights: Contemporary Issues and Jewish Perspectives*, edited by David Sidorsky, 247–64. The Jewish Publication Society of America, 1979.

———. "The Interplay of Jewish and Islamic Law." In *Jewish Law in Legal History and the Modern World*, edited by Bernard S. Jackson, 61–77. Brill, 1980.

———. *Letters of Medieval Jewish Traders*. Princeton University Press, 1974.

———. "A Mansion in Fusṭāṭ: A Twelfth-Century Description of a Domestic Compound in the Ancient Capital of Egypt." In *Patterns of Everyday Life*, edited by David Waines, 19–34. Routledge, 2017.

———. *A Mediterranean Society: The Jewish Communities of the Arab World as Portrayed in the Documents of the Cairo Geniza*. 6 vols. University of California Press, 1967–93.

———. "New Light on the Beginnings of the Kārim Merchants." *Journal of the Economic and Social History of the Orient* 1 (1958): 175–84.

———. *Palestinian Jewry in Early Islamic and Crusader Times: In the Light of the Geniza Documents* (Hebrew). Edited by Joseph Hacker. Yad Izhak Ben Zvi Publications, 1980.

———. "Portrait of a Medieval India Trader: Three Letters from the Cairo Geniza." *Bulletin of the School of Oriental and African Studies* 50 (1987): 449–64.

———. "Side Lights on Jewish Education from the Cairo Geniza." In *Gratz College Anniversary Volume*, edited by Isidore David Passow and Samuel Tobias Lachs, 83–110. Gratz College, 1971.

———. "Slaves and Slave Girls in the Cairo Geniza Records." *Arabica* 9 (1962): 1–20.

———. "Three Trousseaux of Jewish Brides from the Fatimid Period." *Association of Jewish Studies Review* 2 (1977): 77–110.

———. "Urban Housing in Fatimid and Ayyubid Times (As Illustrated by the Cairo Geniza Documents)." *Studia Islamica* 47 (1978): 5–23.

———. "Wills and Deathbed Declarations from the Cairo Geniza" (Hebrew). *Sefunot* 8 (1964).

Goitein, S. D., and Mordechai A. Friedman. "Abraham Ben Yijū, a Jewish Trader in India" (Hebrew). *Teʿuda* 15 (1999): 259–92.

———. *Abraham Ben Yijū: India Trader and Manufacturer (India Book 3)* (Hebrew). Ben Zvi Institute, 2010.

———. *India Traders of the Middle Ages: Documents from the Cairo Geniza*. Brill, 2008.

———. *Joseph Lebdī: Prominent India Trader (India Book 1)* (Hebrew). Ben Zvi Institute, 2009.

———. *Maḍmūn Nagid of Yemen and the India Trade (India Book 2)* (Hebrew). Ben Zvi Institute, 2010.

Goitein, S. D., Mordechai A. Friedman, and Amir Ashur. *Ḥalfon and Judah Ha-Levi: The Lives of a Traveling Scholar and Poet Laureate According to Geniza Documents (India Book 4)* (Hebrew). 2 vols. Ben Zvi Institute, 2013.

Golb, Norman. "The Topography of the Jews of Medieval Egypt, VI: Places of Settlement of the Jews of Medieval Egypt." *Journal of Near Eastern Studies* 33 (1974): 116–49.

Goldberg, Jessica L. "On Reading Goitein's A Mediterranean Society: A View from Economic History." *Mediterranean Historical Review* 26 (2011): 171–86.

———. *Trade and Institutions in the Medieval Mediterranean: The Geniza Merchants and Their Business World.* Cambridge University Press, 2012.

———. "The Use and Abuse of Commercial Letters from the Cairo Geniza." *Journal of Medieval History* 38 (2012): 127–54.

Goldenberg, David M. *Black and Slave: The Origins and History of the Curse of Ham.* De Gruyter, 2017.

———. *The Curse of Ham: Race and Slavery in Early Judaism, Christianity, and Islam.* Princeton University Press, 2003.

———. "'It Is Permitted to Marry a Kushite.'" *Association of Jewish Studies Review* 37 (2013): 29–49.

Goldman, Brendan. "Arabic-Speaking Jews in Crusader Syria: Conquest, Continuity and Adaptation in the Medieval Mediterranean." PhD diss., Johns Hopkins University, 2018.

———. "Mediterranean Notables and the Politics of Survival in Islamic and Latin Syria: Two Geniza Documents on the Frankish Siege of Tripoli." *Crusades* 16 (2017): 1–19.

Goldstein, Eric L. *The Price of Whiteness: Jews, Race, and American Identity.* Princeton University Press, 2006.

Gomez, Michael A. *African Dominion: A New History of Empire in Early and Medieval West Africa.* Princeton University Press, 2018.

González-Ruibal, Alfredo, Jorge de Torres, Manuel Antonio Franco Fernández, Candela Martínez Barrio, and Pablo Gutiérrez de León Juberías. "Asia in the Horn. The Indian Ocean Trade in Somaliland." *Archaeological Research in Asia* 27 (2021): 1–28.

Goody, Jack. "Slavery in Time and Space." In *Asian and African Systems of Slavery*, edited by James L. Watson, 16–42. University of California Press, 1980.

Gopalakrishnan, Pratima. "Wives' Work: Gender and Status in a List from the Mishnah." *Journal of Law and Religion*, 2023, 1–13.

Gordon, Matthew S. "'Arib Al-Ma'muniya: A Third/Ninth-Century 'Abbasid Courtesan." In *Views from the Edge: Essays in Honor of Richard W. Bulliet*, 86–100. Columbia University Press, 2004.

———. *The Breaking of a Thousand Swords: A History of the Turkish Military of Samarra (A.H. 200-275/815-889 C.E.).* SUNY Press, 2001.

———. "Introduction: Producing Songs and Sons." In *Concubines and Courtesans: Women and Slavery in Islamic History*, edited by Matthew S. Gordon and Kathryn A. Hain, 1–10. Oxford University Press, 2017.

———. "The Place of Competition: The Careers of 'Arīb al-Ma'mūnīya and 'Ulayya Bint al-Mahdī, Sisters in Song." In *'Abbasid Studies: Occasional Papers of the School of 'Abbasid Studies, Cambridge, 6–10 July 2002*, 61–81. Peeters, 2004.

———. "Preliminary Remarks on Slaves and Slave Labor in the Third/Ninth-Century 'Abbāsid Empire." In *Slaves and Households in the Near East*, edited by Laura Culbertson, 71–84. The Oriental Institute of the University of Chicago, 2011.

———. "The Samarra Mutiny of 256/869." *Slavery & Abolition* 44 (2023): 658–81.

———. "Slavery in the Islamic Middle East (c. 600–1000)." In *The Cambridge World History of Slavery: Volume 2, AD 500–AD 1420*, edited by Craig Perry, David Eltis, Stanley Engerman, and David Richardson, 337–61. Cambridge University Press, 2021.

Gordon, Matthew S., and Kathryn A. Hain, eds. *Concubines and Courtesans: Women and Slavery in Islamic History*. Oxford University Press, 2017.

Gottheil, Richard J. H., and William H. Worrell, eds. *Fragments from the Cairo Genizah in the Freer Collection*. Macmillan, 1927.

Gotzmann, Andreas. "Respectability Tested: Male Ideals, Sexuality, and Honor in Early Modern Ashkenazi Jewry." In *Jewish Masculinities*, edited by Paul Lerner, Benjamin Maria Baader, and Sharon Gillerman, 23–49. Indiana University Press, 2012.

Grant, Philip. "Entangled Symbols: Silk and the Material Semiosis of the Zanj Rebellion (869–83)." *Al-'Uṣūr al-Wusṭā: The Journal of Middle East Medievalists* 30 (2022): 573–602.

Green, Monica, and Lori Jones. "The Evolution and Spread of Major Human Diseases in the Indian Ocean World." In *Disease Dispersion and Impact in the Indian Ocean World*, edited by Gwyn Campbell and Eva-Maria Knoll, 25–57. Palgrave Macmillan, 2020.

Greene, Molly. *Catholic Pirates and Greek Merchants: A Maritime History of the Mediterranean*. Princeton University Press, 2010.

Greif, Avner. "Reputation and Coalitions in Medieval Trade: Evidence of the Maghribi Traders." *Journal of Economic History* 49 (1989): 857–82.

Grubbs, Judith Evans. "Child Enslavement in Late Antiquity and the Middle Ages." In *The Cambridge World History of Slavery: Volume 2, AD 500–AD 1420*, edited by Craig Perry, David Eltis, Stanley Engerman, and David Richardson, 155–84. Cambridge University Press, 2021.

Gruszczyński, Jacek, Marek Jankowiak, and Jonathan Shepard, eds. *Viking-Age Trade: Silver, Slaves and Gotland*. Routledge, 2020.

Guo, Li. *Commerce, Culture, and Community in a Red Sea Port in the Thirteenth Century: The Arabic Documents from Quseir*. Brill, 2004.

Hadley, D. M., ed. "Introduction: Medieval Masculinities." In *Masculinity in Medieval Europe*, 1–18. Longman, 1999.

Hagedorn, Jan Hinrich. *Domestic Slavery in Syria and Egypt, 1200–1500*. V & R unipress, 2020.

Halevi, Leor. "Wailing for the Dead: The Role of Women in Early Islamic Funerals." *Past & Present* 183 (2004): 3–39.

Halm, H. "Der Nubische Baqṭ." In *Egypt and Syria in the Fatimid, Ayyubid and Mamluk Eras. II. Proceedings of the 4th and 5th International Colloquium, Katholieke Universiteit Leuven, 1995–1996*, edited by U. Vermeulen and D. De Smet, 63–103. Peeters, 1998.

Hamilakis, Yannis, and Andrew Meirion Jones. "Archaeology and Assemblage." *Cambridge Archaeological Journal* 27 (2017): 77–84.

al-Ḥarīrī. *Impostures: Fifty Rogue's Tales Translated Fifty Ways*. Translated by Michael Cooperson. New York University Press, 2020.

———. *Maqāmāt Abī Zayd al-Sarūjī*. Edited by Michael Cooperson. New York University, 2020.

Harkavy, A. E., ed. *Zikhron kamma geonim u-ve-yeḥud rav Sherira ve-rav Hai beno ve-ha-rav rabbi Yiṣḥaq al-Fāsī*. Berlin: H. Itzkowski, 1887.

Harper, Kyle. *Slavery in the Late Roman World, AD 275–425*. Cambridge University Press, 2011.

Harrison, Matthew James. "Fusṭāṭ Reconsidered: Urban Housing and Domestic Life in a Medieval Islamic City." PhD diss., University of Southampton, 2016.

Hartman, Saidiya. "Venus in Two Acts." *Small Axe: A Caribbean Journal of Criticism* 12, no. 2 (2008): 1–14.

Hary, Benjamin, and Marina Rustow. "Karaites at the Rabbinical Court: A Legal Deed from Mahdiyya Dated 1073 (T-S 20.187)." *Ginzei Qedem* 2 (2006): 9–36.

Hava, J. G. *Al-Farā'id al-durrīyah: Arabic-English Dictionary*. Beirut: Catholic Press, 1951.

Hayton. "Flos Historiarum Terre Orientis." In *Recueil des Historiens des Croisades, Documents arméniens*, 2: 113–254. Paris: Impremiere nationale, 1906.

Heffening, W. "Mutʿa." In *EI2*.

Heffening, W., and G. Endress. "Tadbīr." In *EI2*.

Heng, Geraldine. *The Invention of Race in the European Middle Ages*. Cambridge University Press, 2018.

Hershenzon, Daniel. *The Captive Sea: Slavery, Communication, and Commerce in Early Modern Spain and the Mediterranean*. University of Pennsylvania Press, 2018.

Herzig, Tamar. "Slavery and Interethnic Sexual Violence: A Multiple Perpetrator Rape in Seventeenth-Century Livorno." *American Historical Review* 127 (2022): 194–222.

Hezser, Catherine. *Jewish Monotheism and Slavery*. Cambridge University Press, 2024.

———. *Jewish Slavery in Antiquity*. Oxford University Press, 2005.

———. "Slavery and the Jews." In *Cambridge World History of Slavery: Volume 1, the Ancient Mediterranean World*, edited by Keith Bradley and Paul Cartledge, 438–55. Cambridge University Press, 2011.

———. "What Was Jewish About Jewish Slavery in Late Antiquity?" In *Slavery in the Late Antique World, 150–700 CE*, edited by Chris L. de Wet, Maijastina Kahlos, and Ville Vuolanto, 129–48. Cambridge University Press, 2022.

Hinds, Martin, and Hamdi Sakkout. "A Letter from the Governor of Egypt Concerning Egyptian-Nubian Relations in 141/758." In *Studies in Early Islamic History*, edited by Jere L. Bacharach, Lawrence I. Conrad, and Patricia Crone, 160–87. Darwin Press, 1996.

Hirschberg, H. Z. "The Almohad Persecutions and the India Trade: A Letter from the Year 1148" (Hebrew). In *Yitzhak F. Baer Jubilee Volume: On the Occasion of His Seventieth Birthday*, edited by S. W. Baron, B. Dinur, S. Ettinger, and I. Halpern, 134–53. Historical Society of Israel, 1960.

Hoffman, Adina, and Peter Cole. *Sacred Trash: The Lost and Found World of the Cairo Geniza*. Schocken Books, 2010.

Hogendorn, Jan. "The Hideous Trade. Economic Aspects of the 'Manufacture' and Sale of Eunuchs." *Paideuma: Mitteilungen zur Kulturkunde* 45 (1999): 137–60.

Holmes, Catherine. "Treaties Between Byzantium and the Islamic World." In *War and Peace in Ancient and Medieval History*, edited by John France and Philip de Souza, 141–57. Cambridge University Press, 2008.

Hoyland, Robert G. *In God's Path: The Arab Conquests and the Creation of an Islamic Empire*. Oxford University Press, 2015.

Hsy, Jonathan, and Julie Orlemanski. "Race and Medieval Studies: A Partial Bibliography." *Postmedieval* 8 (2017): 500–31.

Humphreys, R. Stephen. *Islamic History: A Framework for Inquiry*. Revised edition. Princeton University Press, 1991.

Hunwick, John O. "Aḥmad Bābā on Slavery." *Sudanic Africa* 11 (2000): 131–39.

———. "Black Slaves in the Mediterranean World: Introduction to a Neglected Aspect of the African Diaspora." In *The Human Commodity: Perspectives on the Trans-Saharan Slave Trade*, edited by Elizabeth Savage, 5–38. Frank Cass, 1992.

———. "A Region of the Mind: Medieval Arab Views of African Geography and Ethnography and Their Legacy." *Sudanic Africa* 16 (2005): 103–36.

Hunwick, John O., and Eve Troutt Powell, eds. *The African Diaspora in the Mediterranean Lands of Islam*. Markus Wiener Publishers, 2002.

Hurvitz, Nimrod, Christian C. Sahner, Uriel Simonsohn, and Luke Yarbrough, eds. *Conversion to Islam in the Premodern Age: A Sourcebook*. University of California Press, 2020.

Ibn Buṭlān. "Risāla jāmiʿat al-funūn al-nāfiʿa fī shirāʾ al-raqīq wa-taqlīb al-ʿabīd." In *Nawādir al-makhṭūṭāt*, edited by ʿAbd al-Salām Hārūn. Second edition. Muṣṭafā al-Bābī al-Ḥalabī, 1972.

Ibn al-Faqīh al-Hamadhānī. *Mukhtaṣar kitāb al-buldān (The Abridged Book of Countries)*. Edited by M. J. de Goeje. Brill, 2014.

Ibn al-Saʿī. *Consorts of the Caliphs: Women and the Court of Baghdad*. Edited by Shawkat M. Toorawa. Translated by the Editors of the Library of Arabic Literature. New York University Press, 2015.

Ibn ʿIdhārī al-Marrākushī. *Al-Bayān al-mughrib fī akhbār al-Andalus wal-Maghrib (The History of North Africa and Islamic Spain since the Conquest until the 11th Century)*. Edited by E. Levi-Provençal and G. S. Colin. 4 vols. Beirut: Dār al-Kutub al-ʿIlmiyyah, 2009.

Insoll, Timothy. "Archaeological Perspectives on Contacts Between Cairo and Eastern Ethiopia in the 12th to 15th Centuries." *Journal of the Economic and Social History of the Orient* 66 (2023): 154–205.

Ivanova, Mirela, and Hugh Jeffery. *Transmitting and Circulating the Late Antique and Byzantine Worlds*. Brill, 2019.

Jackson, Peter. "Turkish Slaves on Islam's Indian Frontier." In *Slavery & South Asian History*, edited by Indrani Chatterjee and Richard Maxwell Eaton, 63–82. Indiana University Press, 2006.

Jain, V. K. *Trade and Traders in Western India (AD 1000–AD 1300)*. Munshiram Manoharlal Publishers Pvt. Ltd., 1990.

Jankowiak, Marek. "What Does the Slave Trade in the Saqaliba Tell Us About Early Islamic Slavery?" *International Journal of Middle East Studies* 49 (2017): 169–72.

Jastrow, Marcus, ed. *Dictionary of the Targumim, the Talmud Babli and Yerushalmi, and the Midrashic Literature*. Hendrickson Publishers, 2003.

al-Jawbarī, Jamāl al-Dīn ʿAbd al-Raḥīm. *The Book of Charlatans*. Edited by Manuela Dengler. Translated by Humphrey Davies. New York University Press, 2020.

Jefferson, Rebecca J. W. *The Cairo Genizah and the Age of Discovery in Egypt: The History and Provenance of a Jewish Archive*. I. B. Tauris, 2021.

Johnson, Jessica Marie. "Markup Bodies: Black [Life] Studies and Slavery [Death] Studies at the Digital Crossroads." *Social Text* 36 (2018): 57–79.

———. *Wicked Flesh: Black Women, Intimacy, and Freedom in the Atlantic World.* University of Pennsylvania Press, 2020.

Johnson, Walter. "On Agency." *Journal of Social History* 37 (2003): 113–24.

Jones-Rodgers, Stephanie E. *They Were Her Property: White Women as Slave Owners in the American South.* Yale University Press, 2019.

Kanarfogel, Ephraim. "Rabbinic Attitudes Toward Nonobservance in the Medieval Period." In *Jewish Tradition and the Nontraditional Jew*, edited by Jacob J. Schacter, 3–35. J. Aronson, 1992.

Kapitaikin, Lev. "David's Dancers in Palermo: Islamic Dance Imagery and Its Christian Recontextualization in the Ceilings of the Cappella Palatina." *Early Music* 47 (2019): 3–23.

Karras, Ruth Mazo. "Desire, Descendants, and Dominance: Slavery, the Exchange of Women, and Masculine Power." In *The Work of Work: Servitude, Slavery, and Labor in Medieval England*, edited by Allen J. Frantzen and Douglas Moffat, 16–29. Cruithne Press, 1994.

———. *From Boys to Men: Formations of Masculinity in Late Medieval Europe.* University of Pennsylvania Press, 2003.

Kars, Marjoleine. "Maroons and Marronage." In *Oxford Bibliographies Online: Atlantic World*, edited by Trevor Burnard. Oxford University Press, 2016.

Katz, Marion Holmes. "Concubinage, in Islamic Law." In *EI3*.

. "Gender and Law." In *EI3*.

———. *Wives and Work: Islamic Law and Ethics Before Modernity.* Columbia University Press, 2022.

Kazimirski, Albert. *Dictionnaire Arabe-Français.* 2 vols. Maisonneuve, 1860.

Keats-Rohan, K.S.B. *Prosopography Approaches and Applications: A Handbook.* Unit for Prosopographical Research, 2007.

Kelly, Samantha. "Before the Solomonids: Crisis, Renaissance and the Emergence of the Zagwe Dynasty (Seventh–Thirteenth Centuries)." In *A Companion to Medieval Ethiopia and Eritrea*, 31–56. Brill, 2020.

Kennedy, Hugh. *The Armies of the Caliphs: Military and Society in the Early Islamic State.* Routledge, 2001.

al-Khalidi, Fatima Kassab. "The Baqt Treaty Under Islamic Law." *Journal of Sharia and Law* 2018 (2021): 35–42.

Khalilieh, Hassan S. *Admiralty and Maritime Laws in the Mediterranean Sea (ca. 800–1050): The Kitāb Akriyat al-Sufun vis-à-vis the Nomos Rhodion Nautikos.* Brill, 2006.

———. "Human Jettison, Contribution for Lives, and Life Salvage in Byzantine and Early Islamic Maritime Laws in the Mediterranean." *Byzantion* 75 (2005): 225–35.

———. "An Overview of the Slaves' Juridical Status at Sea in Romano-Byzantine, and Islamic Laws." In *Histories of the Middle East: Studies in Middle Eastern Society, Economy and Law in Honor of A.L. Udovitch*, edited by Roxani Eleni Margariti, Adam Sabra, Petra Sijpesteijn, and Abraham L. Udovitch, 73–100. Brill, 2011.

Khan, Geoffrey. *Arabic Documents from Early Islamic Khurasan.* Nour Foundation in association with Azimouth Editions, 2007.

———. *Arabic Documents from Medieval Nubia.* Open Book Publishers, 2024.

———. *Arabic Legal and Administrative Documents in the Cambridge Genizah Collections.* Cambridge University Press, 1993.

Kheir, El-Hag H. M. "A Contribution to a Textual Problem: 'Ibn Sulaym al-Aswānī's *Kitāb Akhbār al-Nūba wa-l-Maqurra wa-l-Beja wa-l-Nīl*.'" *Arabica* 36 (1989): 36–80.

Khusraw, Nāṣir-i. *Nasir-i Khusraw's Book of Travels: Safarnāma*. Translated by W. M. Thackston. Mazda Publishers, 2001.

Kim, Dorothy. "Introduction to Literature Compass Special Cluster: Critical Race and the Middle Ages." *Literature Compass* 16 (2019): e12549.

Krakowski, Eve. *Coming of Age in Medieval Egypt: Female Adolescence, Jewish Law, and Ordinary Culture*. Princeton University Press, 2018.

———. "Female Adolescence in the Cairo Geniza Documents." PhD diss., University of Chicago, 2012.

———. "Maimonides' Menstrual Reform in Egypt." *Jewish Quarterly Review* 110 (2020): 245–89.

Krakowski, Eve, and Marina Rustow. "Formula as Content: Medieval Jewish Institutions, the Cairo Geniza, and the New Diplomatics." *Jewish Social Studies: History, Culture, Society* 20 (2014): 111–46.

Kriger, Diane. *Sex Rewarded, Sex Punished: A Study of the Status "Female Slave" in Early Jewish Law*. Academic Studies Press, 2008.

La Vaissière, Étienne de. *Samarcande et Samarra: élites d'Asie centrale dans l'empire Abbasside*. Association pour l'Avancement des Études Iraniennes, 2007.

Labovitz, Gail. *Marriage and Metaphor: Constructions of Gender in Rabbinic Literature*. Rowman & Littlefield, 2009.

———. "More Slave Women, More Lewdness: Freedom and Honor in Rabbinic Constructions of Female Sexuality." *Journal of Feminist Studies in Religion* 28, no. 2 (2012): 69–87.

———. "The Purchase of His Money: Slavery and the Ethics of Jewish Marriage." In *Beyond Slavery: Overcoming Its Religious and Sexual Legacies*, edited by Bernadette J. Brooten and Jacqueline L. Hazelton, 91–105. Palgrave Macmillan, 2010.

Lambourn, Elizabeth A. *Abraham's Luggage: A Social History of Things in the Medieval Indian Ocean World*. Cambridge University Press, 2019.

Lane, Edward William. *Arabic-English Lexicon*. Fungar Publication Co., 1955.

Lane, Paul J. "Slavery in Africa c. 500–1500: Archaeological and Historical Perspectives." In *The Cambridge World History of Slavery: Volume 2, AD 500–AD 1420*, edited by Craig Perry, David Eltis, Stanley Engerman, and David Richardson, 531–52. Cambridge University Press, 2021.

Lane-Poole, Stanley. *A History of Egypt in the Middle Ages*. 4th edition. 2008 reprint. Routledge, 1925.

Langermann, Y. Tzvi, and Yosef Stern, eds. *Adaptations and Innovations: Studies on the Interaction Between Jewish and Islamic Thought and Literature from the Early Middle Ages to the Late Twentieth Century, Dedicated to Professor Joel L. Kraemer*. Peeters, 2007.

Lankila, Tommi Petteri. "Saracen Maritime Raids in the Early Medieval Central Mediterranean and Their Impact in the South Italian Terraferma (650–1050)." PhD diss., Princeton University, 2017.

Lauer, Rena N. *Colonial Justice and the Jews of Venetian Crete*. University of Pennsylvania Press, 2019.

———. "Jewish Women in Venetian Candia: Negotiating Intercommunal Contact in a Premodern Colonial City, 1300–1500." In *Religious Cohabitation in European Towns (10th–15th Centuries)*, edited by John Tolan and Stéphane Boissellier, 293–309. Turnhout, 2015.

Lecker, Michael. "Research Report: The Prosopography of Early Islamic Administration." *Jerusalem Studies in Arabic and Islam* 34 (2008): 529–33.

Ledbetter, Holley. "Aestheticizing Enslavement. Representations of *Jawārī* in Fatimid Visual Culture." *Convivium* 11 (2024): 116–28.

Leibman, Laura Arnold. *Once We Were Slaves: The Extraordinary Journey of a Multiracial Jewish Family.* Oxford University Press, 2021.

Lemche, N. P. "The Manumission of Slaves: The Fallow Year, the Sabbatical Year, the Jobel Year." *Vetus Testamentum* 26 (1976): 38–59.

Lenski, Noel, and Catherine M. Cameron, eds. *What Is a Slave Society? The Practice of Slavery in Global Perspective.* Cambridge University Press, 2018.

Lerner, Judith A. "The Seal of a Eunuch in the Sasanian Court." *Journal of Inner Asian Art and Archaeology* 1 (2006): 113–18.

Lev, Yaacov. *The Administration of Justice in Medieval Egypt: From the Seventh to the Twelfth Century.* Edinburgh University Press, 2020.

———. "Army, Regime and Society in Fatimid Egypt, 358-487/968-1094." *International Journal of Middle East Studies* 19 (1987): 337–65.

———. "Aspects of the Egyptian Society in the Fatimid Period: Wise Fools and Critics of the Powerful." In *Egypt and Syria in the Fatimid, Ayyubid and Mamluk Eras III*, edited by U. Vermeulen and J. van Steenbergen, 1–31. Uitgeverij Peeters, 2001.

———. "David Ayalon (1914–1998) and the History of Black Military Slavery in Medieval Islam." *Der Islam* 90 (2013): 21–43.

———. "The Perception of the Others: Rūm and Franks (Tenth–Twelfth Centuries)." In Dār al-Islām/Dār al-Ḥarb: *Territories, Peoples, Identities*, edited by Giovanna Calasso and Giuliano Lancioni, 63–73. Brill, 2017.

———. *State and Society in Fatimid Egypt.* Brill, 1991.

Levi, Scott C., and Ron Sela, eds. *Islamic Central Asia: An Anthology of Historical Sources.* Indiana University Press, 2010.

Levtzion, Nehemia, and J.F.P. Hopkins, eds. *Corpus of Early Arabic Sources for West African History.* Cambridge University Press, 1981.

Levy-Rubin, Milka. *Non-Muslims in the Early Islamic Empire: From Surrender to Coexistence.* Cambridge University Press, 2011.

———. "*Shurūṭ ʿUmar*: From Early Harbingers to Systematic Enforcement." In *Beyond Religious Borders: Interaction and Intellectual Exchange in the Medieval Islamic World*, edited by David M. Freidenreich and Miriam Goldstein, 30–43. University of Pennsylvania Press, 2012.

Lewicka, Paulina. *Food and Foodways of Medieval Cairenes: Aspects of Life in an Islamic Metropolis of the Eastern Mediterranean.* Brill, 2011.

Lewin, B. M., ed. *Oṣar ha-geonim (Thesaurus of the Gaonic Responsa and Commentaries, Following the Order of the Talmudic Tractates).* Central Press, 1928.

Lewis, Bernard. *Race and Slavery in the Middle East.* Oxford University Press, 1990.

Lewis, Bernard, ed. *Islam: From the Prophet Muhammad to the Capture of Constantinople.* 3 vols. Oxford University Press, 1987.

Lewis, I. M. "Berberā." In *EI2*.

Lieberman, Phillip. (See also Ackerman-Lieberman, Phillip.) "Methodological Essay on Commercial Contracts." *Jewish History* 32 (2019): 429–39.

———. "One Jurist, Two Answers: Law, Advocacy, and Social Reality in the Jewish Community of the Medieval Islamicate World." *Jewish Quarterly Review* 111 (2021): 211–35.

———. "One Question, Two Answers: Rabbinic Responsa as Legal Advocacy in the Medieval Islamic World." *Jewish History* 31 (2017): 47–65.

Lifshitz, Berachyahu. "The Legal Status of the Responsa Literature." In *Authority, Process and Method: Studies in Jewish Law*, edited by Hanina Ben-Menahem and Neil S. Hecht, 59–100. Harwood Academic Publishers, 1998.

Lindsay, James E. *Daily Life in the Medieval Islamic World.* Hackett, 2005.

Little, Donald P. "Six Fourteenth Century Purchase Deeds for Slaves from al-Ḥaram al-Sharīf." *Zeitschrift der Deutschen Morgenländischen Gesellschaft* 131 (1981): 297–337.

———. "Two Fourteenth-Century Court Records from Jerusalem Concerning the Disposition of Slaves by Minors." *Arabica* 29 (1982): 16–49.

Loiseau, Julien. "Abyssinia at al-Azhar: Muslim Students from the Horn of Africa in Late Medieval Cairo." *Northeast African Studies* 19 (2019): 61–84.

———. "L'histoire désurbanisée: À propos de Qûs et des travaux de Jean-Claude Garcin." *Histoire* 5 (2006): 137–46.

Løkkegaard, F. "Baḳṭ." In *EI2*.

Lomba, Joaquín. "Maimonides, Abraham Ben Moses." In *EJIW*.

Maceachern, Scott. "State Formation and Enslavement in the Southern Lake Chad Basin." In *West Africa During the Atlantic Slave Trade: Archaeological Perspectives*, edited by Christopher R. DeCorse, 131–51. Leicester University Press, 2001.

Magdalino, Paul. "Paphlagonians in Byzantine High Society." In *Byzantine Asia Minor (6th–12th Cent.)*, edited by Stelios Lampakis. The National Hellenic Research Foundation, 1998.

Maimonides, Moses. *Mishneh Torah, Sefer Kinyan*. Edited by Eliyahu Touger. Moznaim Publishing Corporation, 1997.

———. *Responsa of Maimonides* (in Hebrew). Edited by Joshua Blau. 4 vols. Rubin Mass Ltd. Publishers, 1986.

Makki, Fouad. "The Spatial Ecology of Power: Long-Distance Trade and State Formation in Northeast Africa." *Journal of Historical Sociology* 24 (2011): 155–85.

Mann, Jacob. "The Responsa of the Babylonian Geonim as a Source of Jewish History, Part II: The Political Status of the Jews." *Jewish Quarterly Review* 10 (1919): 121–51.

al-Maqrīzī, Aḥmad b. ʿAlī. *Al-Sulūk li-maʿrifat duwal al-mulūk (The Path to Knowledge about the Reigns of Kings)*. 8 vols. Beirut: Dār al-Kutub al-ʿIlmīyah, 1997.

———. *Ittiʿāẓ al-ḥunafāʾ bi-akhbār al-aʾimmā al-fāṭimiyyīn al-khulafāʾ (The Exhortation of Believers: On the History of the Fatimid Caliph-Imāms)*. Edited by Jamāl al-Dīn al-Shayyāl. 3 vols. Cairo: al-Majlis al-Aʿlā li-l-Shuʾūn al-Islāmiyya, 1967.

———. *Kitāb al-mawāʿiẓ waʾl-iʿtibār fī dhikr al-khiṭaṭ waʾl-āthār (The Book of Exhortations and Reflections Concerning the Remembrance of the Districts and Monuments of Egypt)*. Edited by Madīḥah al-Sharqāwī and Muḥammad Zaynhum. 3 vols. Cairo: Maktabah Madbulī, 1998.

Margariti, Roxani. *Aden and the Indian Ocean Trade: 150 Years in the Life of a Medieval Arabian Port.* University of North Carolina Press, 2007.

———. "*Aṣḥābunā l-tujjār*—Our Associates, the Merchants: Non-Jewish Business Partners of the Cairo Geniza's India Traders." In *Jews, Christians and Muslims in Medieval and Early*

Modern Times: A Festschrift in Honor of Mark R. Cohen, edited by Arnold Franklin, Roxani Eleni Margariti, Marina Rustow, and Uriel Simonsohn, 40–58. Brill, 2014.

———. "Thieves or Sultans? Dahlak and the Rulers and Merchants of Indian Ocean Port Cities, 11th–13th Centuries." In *Red Sea IV: Connected Hinterlands: The Fourth International Conference on the Peoples of the Red Sea Region*, edited by Lucy Blue, John Cooper, Ross Thomas, and Julian Whitewright, 155–63. Archaeopress, 2010.

———. "Wrecks and Texts: A Judeo-Arabic Case Study." In *Maritime Studies in the Wake of the Byzantine Shipwreck at Yassıada, Turkey*, edited by Deborah N. Carlson, Justin Leidwanger, and Sarah M. Kampbell, 189–201. Texas A&M University Press, 2015.

Margariti, Roxani, Adam Sabra, Petra Sijpesteijn, and Abraham L. Udovitch, eds. *Histories of the Middle East: Studies in Middle Eastern Society, Economy and Law in Honor of A. L. Udovitch*. Brill, 2011.

Margoliouth, George. "Some British Museum Genizah Texts." *Jewish Quarterly Review* 14 (1902): 303–20.

Marienberg, Evyatar. "'Canaanites' in Medieval Jewish Households." In *The Gift of the Land and the Fate of the Canaanites in Jewish Thought*, edited by Katell Berthelot, Joseph E. David, and Marc Hirshman, 285–96. Oxford University Press, 2014.

Marmon, Shaun. "Domestic Slavery in the Mamluk Empire: A Preliminary Sketch." In *Slavery in the Islamic Middle East*, edited by Shaun Marmon, 1–23. Markus Wiener Publishers, 1999.

———. *Eunuchs and Sacred Boundaries in Islamic Society*. Oxford University Press, 1995.

———. "Intersections of Gender, Sex, and Slavery: Female Sexual Slavery." In *The Cambridge World History of Slavery: Volume 2, AD 500–AD 1420*, edited by Craig Perry, David Eltis, Stanley Engerman, and David Richardson, 185–213. Cambridge University Press, 2021.

Marmon, Shaun, ed. *Slavery in the Islamic Middle East*. Markus Wiener Publishers, 1999.

al-Masʿūdī, Abū al-Ḥasan ʿAlī. *Murūj al-dhahab (Meadows of Gold)*. 7 vols. Lebanese University, 1966–79.

Mattingly, David J., Martin J. Sterry, and David N. Edwards. "The Origins and Development of Zuwīla, Libyan Sahara: An Archaeological and Historical Overview of an Ancient Oasis Town and Caravan Centre." *Azania: Archaeological Research in Africa* 50 (2015): 27–75.

Mauder, Christian. "Thomas Bauer, Warum es kein islamisches Mittelalter gab: Das Erbe der Antike und der Orient." *Al-ʿUṣūr al-Wusṭā* 28 (2020): 465–70.

Mayerson, Philip. "The Role of Flax in Roman and Fatimid Egypt." *Journal of Near Eastern Studies* 56 (1997): 201–7.

McCormick, Michael. "New Light on the 'Dark Ages': How the Slave Trade Fueled the Carolingian Economy." *Past & Present* 177 (2002): 17–54.

———. *Origins of the European Economy: Communications and Commerce, A.D. 300–900*. Cambridge University Press, 2002.

McKee, Sally. "Domestic Slavery in Renaissance Italy." *Slavery & Abolition* 29 (2008): 305–26.

———. "Households in Fourteenth-Century Venetian Crete." *Speculum* 70 (1995): 27–67.

———. "Slavery." In *The Oxford Handbook of Women and Gender in Medieval Europe*, edited by Judith M. Bennett and Ruth Mazo Karras, 281–94. Oxford University Press, 2013.

McSheffrey, Shannon. "Men and Masculinity in Late Medieval London Civic Culture: Governance, Patriarchy and Reputation." In *Conflicted Identities and Multiple Masculinities: Men in the Medieval West*, edited by Jacqueline Murray, 243–78. Garland Publishing, Inc., 1999.

Mez, Adam. *The Renaissance of Islam*. Translated by Salahuddin Khuda Bukhsh. 1st ed. AMS Press, 1937.

Miller, Joseph C. *The Problem of Slavery as History: A Global Approach*. Yale University Press, 2012.

Miquel, A. "Ibn Baṭṭūṭa." In *EI2*.

Mirza, Younus Y. "Remembering the Umm Al-Walad: Ibn Kathir's Treatise on the Sale of the Concubine." In *Concubines and Courtesans: Women and Slavery in Islamic History*, edited by Matthew S. Gordon and Kathryn A. Hain, 297–323. Oxford University Press, 2017.

Moda'i, Nissim b. Ḥayyim. *Teshuvot ha-geonim: Sha'arei ṣedeq*. Jerusalem: Kelal u-ferat̲, 1966.

Monés, Hussain. "Djawhar Al-Ṣiḳillī." In *EI2*.

Montalvo, Maria R. *Enslaved Archives: Slavery, Law, and the Production of the Past*. Johns Hopkins University Press, 2024.

Montpetit, Mathilde. "Eunuchs and the Practice of Power in the Early Songhay Empire." *Journal of West African History* 9 (2023): 21–40.

Moorthy Kloss, Magdalena. "Slavery in Medieval Arabia." In *The Palgrave Handbook of Global Slavery throughout History*, edited by Damien A. Pargas and Juliane Schiel, 139–58. Palgrave Macmillan, 2023.

———. "Slaves at the Najahid and Rasulid Courts of Yemen (412–553 AH/1021–1158 CE and 626–858 AH/1229-1454 CE)." D. Phil. thesis, University of Vienna, 2019.

———. *Unfree Lives: Slaves at the Najahid and Rasulid Courts of Yemen*. Brill, 2024.

Morgan, Jennifer L. "*Partus Sequitur Ventrem*: Law, Race, and Reproduction in Colonial Slavery." *Small Axe: A Caribbean Journal of Criticism* 22, no. 1 (2018): 1–17.

Mottahedeh, Roy P. *Loyalty and Leadership in an Early Islamic Society*. 2001 reprint. I. B. Tauris, 1980.

Mummey, Kevin, and Kathryn Reyerson. "Whose City Is This? Hucksters, Domestic Servants, Wet-Nurses, Prostitutes, and Slaves in Late Medieval Western Mediterranean Urban Society." *History Compass* 9 (2011): 910–22.

Munro-Hay, S. C. "Kings and Kingdoms of Ancient Nubia." *Rassegna di Studi Etiopici* 29 (1982): 87–137.

Murray, Alan V. "Prosopography." In *Palgrave Advances in the Crusades*, edited by Helen J. Nicholson, 109–29. Palgrave Macmillan, 2005.

al-Musabbiḥī. *Al-Juz' al-arba'ūn min akhbār Miṣr (The fortieth chapter of the History of Egypt)*. Edited by Ayman Fu'ād Sayyid and Thierry Bianquis. Cairo: Institut français d'archéologie orientale, 1978.

Myers, Ella. "Beyond the Psychological Wage: Du Bois on White Dominion." *Political Theory* 47 (February 1, 2019): 6–31.

Myrne, Pernilla. *Female Sexuality in the Early Medieval Islamic World: Gender and Sex in Arabic Literature*. I. B. Tauris, 2020.

al-Nābulusī, 'Uṯmān ibn Ibrāhīm. *The* Villages of the Fayyum*: A Thirteenth-Century Register of Rural, Islamic Egypt*. Edited by Yossef Rapoport and Ido Shahar. Brepols, 2018.

Najmabadi, Afsaneh. "Genus of Sex or the Sexing of *Jins*." *International Journal of Middle East Studies* 45 (2013): 211–31.

Narkiss, M. "A Jewish Bread or Cheese Stamp of the Fatimid Period" (Hebrew). *Bulletin of the Jewish Palestine Exploration Society* 12 (1945): 72–74.

Neusner, Jacob, and Tamara Sonn, eds. *Comparing Religions Through Law: Judaism and Islam.* Routledge, 1999.

Nielson, Lisa. "Gender and the Politics of Music in the Early Islamic Courts." *Early Music History* 31 (2012): 235–61.

———. *Music and Musicians in the Medieval Islamicate World: A Social History.* I. B. Tauris, 2021.

Nirenberg, David. *Anti-Judaism: The Western Tradition.* W. W. Norton & Company, 2013.

al-Nuwayrī, Shihāb al-Dīn. *Nihāyat al-arab fī funūn al-adab (The Ultimate Ambition in the Branches of Erudition).* 31 vols. Cairo: Dār al-Kutub wal-wathāiq al-qūmīyah, 2010.

Oliver, Roland, ed. *The Cambridge History of Africa: Volume 3: From c.1050 to c.1600.* Cambridge University Press, 1977.

Olsson, J. T. "The World in Arab Eyes: A Reassessment of the Climes in Medieval Islamic Scholarship." *Bulletin of the School of Oriental and African Studies* 77 (2014): 487–508.

Olszowy-Schlanger, Judith. *Karaite Marriage Documents from the Cairo Geniza: Legal Tradition and Community Life in Mediaeval Egypt and Palestine.* Brill, 1998.

Orr, Leslie C. "Slavery and Dependency in Medieval South India." In *The Cambridge World History of Slavery: Volume 2, AD 500–AD 1420*, edited by Craig Perry, David Eltis, Stanley L. Engerman, and David Richardson, 313–34. Cambridge: Cambridge University Press, 2021.

Osswald, Ranier. *Das islamiche Sklavenrecht.* Ergon, 2017.

Outhwaite, Ben, M. Schmierer-Lee, and C. Burgess. *Discarded History: The Genizah of Medieval Cairo.* Apollo–University of Cambridge Repository, 2018. https://doi.org/10.17863/CAM.13917.

Pargas, Damian A., and Juliane Schiel, eds. *The Palgrave Handbook of Global Slavery throughout History.* Palgrave Macmillan, 2023.

Patterson, Orlando. *Slavery and Social Death: A Comparative Study.* 2018 edition, with a new preface. Harvard University Press, 1982.

Peacock, David, and Andrew Peacock. "The Enigma of 'Aydhab: A Medieval Islamic Fort on the Red Sea Coast." *International Journal of Nautical Archaeology* 37 (2008): 32–48.

Pearce, S. J. "The Inquisitor and the Moseret: The Invention of Race in the European Middle Ages and the New English Colonialism in Jewish Historiography." *Medieval Encounters* 26 (2020): 145–90.

Pearson, Robin, and David Richardson. "Insuring the Transatlantic Slave Trade." *Journal of Economic History* 79 (2019): 417–46.

Pellat, Charles. "Al-Rādhāniyya." In *EI2.*

Perry, Charles, ed. *Scents and Flavors: A Syrian Cookbook.* New York University Press, 2017.

Perry, Craig. "A 6th/12th-Century Supplementary Deed of Sale for the Nubian Slave Woman Na'īm (Gen. T-S 18 J 1.17v)." In *From Qom to Barcelona: Aramaic, South Arabian, Coptic, Arabic, and Judeo-Arabic Documents*, edited by Andreas Kaplony and Daniel Potthast, 127–51. Brill, 2021.

———. "An Aramaic Bill of Sale for the Enslaved Nubian Woman Na'īm." *Jewish History* 32 (2019): 441–49.

———. "Conversion as an Aspect of Master-Slave Relationships in the Medieval Jewish Community." In *Contesting Inter-Religious Conversion in the Medieval World*, edited by Yaniv Fox and Yosi Yisraeli, 135–59. Routledge, 2017.

———. "The Daily Life of Slaves and the Global Reach of Slavery." PhD diss., Emory University, 2014.

———. "Goitein and the Study of Slavery in the Medieval Islamic World." *Jewish History* 32 (2019): 535–39.

———. "Historicizing Slavery in the Medieval Islamic World." *International Journal of Middle East Studies* 49 (2017): 133–38.

———. "Power, Mastery, and Competition: Jewish Slave Owners in Medieval Egypt." In *Israel in Egypt: The Land of Egypt as Concept and Reality for Jews in Antiquity and the Early Medieval Period*, 461–88. Brill, 2020.

———. "Slavery and Agency in the Middle Ages." In *The Cambridge World History of Slavery: Volume 2, AD 500–AD 1420*, edited by Craig Perry, David Eltis, Stanley Engerman, and David Richardson, 240–67. Cambridge University Press, 2021.

———. "Slavery and the Slave Trade in the Western Indian Ocean World." In *The Cambridge World History of Slavery: Volume 2, AD 500–AD 1420*, edited by Craig Perry, David Eltis, Stanley Engerman, and David Richardson, 123–52. Cambridge University Press, 2021.

Perry, Craig, David Eltis, Stanley Engerman, and David Richardson. "Slavery in the Medieval Millenium." In *The Cambridge World History of Slavery: Volume 2, AD 500–AD 1420*, edited by Craig Perry, David Eltis, Stanley Engerman, and David Richardson, 1–24. Cambridge University Press, 2021.

Perry, Craig, David Eltis, Stanley Engerman, and David Richardson, eds. *The Cambridge World History of Slavery: Volume 2, AD 500–AD 1420*. Cambridge University Press, 2021.

Petry, Carl F. *The Criminal Underworld in a Medieval Islamic Society*. Middle East Documentation Center, 2012.

———. "Female Slaves and Transgression in Medieval Cairo and Damascus: Gendered Aspects of Bondage and Criminality in the Mamluk Period (648/1250–922/1517)." *Orient* 54 (2019): 75–84.

Pierce, Richard Holton. "Nubian Toponyms in Medieval Nubian Sources." *Dotawo: A Journal of Nubian Studies* 4 (2017): 35–56.

Pinto, Karen C. "Capturing Imagination: The Buja and Medieval Islamic Mappa Mundi." In *Views from the Edge: Essays in Honor of Richard W. Bulliet*, edited by Lawrence G. Potter, Jean-Marc Ran Oppenheim, and Neguin Yavari, 154–83. Columbia University Press, 2004.

———. *Medieval Islamic Maps: An Exploration*. University of Chicago Press, 2016.

Pipes, Daniel. *Slave Soldiers and Islam: The Genesis of a Military System*. Yale University Press, 1981.

Popović, Alexandre. *La Révolte des esclaves en Iraq au IIIe, IXe siècle*. P. Geuthner, 1976.

———. *The Revolt of African Slaves in Iraq in the 3rd/9th Century*. Translated by Leon King. Markus Wiener Publishers, 1999.

Popper, William, ed. *History of Egypt, 1382–1469 A.D. Translated from the Arabic Annals of Abu l-Maḥasin Ibn Taghrî Birdî*. University of California Press, 1954.

Pouwels, Randall L. "Eastern Africa and the Indian Ocean to 1800: Reviewing Relations in Historical Perspective." *International Journal of African Historical Studies* 35 (2002): 385–425.

Powell, Eve Troutt. *Tell This in My Memory: Stories of Enslavement from Egypt, Sudan, and the Ottoman Empire*. Stanford University Press, 2012.

Power, Timothy. *The Red Sea from Byzantium to the Caliphate AD 500–1000*. American University in Cairo Press, 2012.

Powers, David S. "Kadijustiz or *Qāḍī*-Justice? A Paternity Dispute from Fourteenth-Century Morocco." *Islamic Law and Society* 1 (1994): 332–66.

Prange, Sebastian. *Monsoon Islam: Trade and Faith on the Medieval Malabar Coast*. Cambridge University Press, 2018.

Prasad, Pushpa. "The Economy of Gujarat in the Thirteenth Century." In *Economic History of Medieval India, 1200–1500*, edited by Irfan Habib, 8:12–32. Longman, 2011.

———. "Female Slavery in Thirteenth-Century Gujarat: Documents in the *Lekhapaddhati*." *Indian Historical Review* 15 (1991): 269–75.

———. *Lekhapaddhati: Documents of State and Everyday Life from Ancient and Early Medieval Gujarat, 9th to 15th Centuries*. Oxford University Press, 2007.

Puente, Cristina de la. "Islamic Law, Slavery, and Feelings: A Fourth/Tenth-Century Andalusi Notarial Model on the Manumission of an Unruly and Bad-Tempered Female Slave." *Hawwa* 19 (2021): 294–313.

al-Qaddūmī, Ghādah al-Ḥijjāwī, ed. *Book of Gifts and Rarities (Kitab al-Hadāyā wa al-Tuḥaf): Selections Compiled in the Fifteenth Century from an Eleventh-Century Manuscript on Gifts and Treasures*. Harvard University Press, 1996.

al-Qudūrī. *The* Mukhtaṣar *of Imām Abū l-Ḥusayn Aḥmad b. Muḥammad b. Aḥmad b. Ja'far b. Ḥamdān al-Qudūrī al-Baghdādī: A Manual of Islamic Law According to the Ḥanafī School*. Edited by Ṭāhir Maḥmood Kiānī. Ta-Ha Publishers, 2010.

Qutbuddin, Tahera. "Idrīs 'Imād al-Dīn." *EI3*.

Raffield, Ben. "The Slave Markets of the Viking World: Comparative Perspectives on an 'Invisible Archaeology.'" *Slavery & Abolition* 40 (2019): 682–705.

Rāġib, Yūsuf. *Actes de vente d'esclaves et d'animaux d'Égypte médiévale*. 2 vols. Cairo: Institut français d'archéologie orientale, 2002.

Rapoport, Yossef. "Women and Gender in Mamluk Society: An Overview." *Mamluk Studies Review* 11 (2007): 1–45.

———. *Rural Economy and Tribal Society in Islamic Egypt: A Study of al-Nābulusī's* Villages of the Fayyum. Brepols, 2018.

Ray, Jonathan. *The Sephardic Frontier: The Reconquista and the Jewish Community in Medieval Iberia*. Cornell University Press, 2006.

Raymond, André. *Cairo*. Translated by Willard Wood. Harvard University Press, 2000.

ar-Raziq, Ahmed Abd. "Un document concernant le mariage des esclaves au temps des Mamlūks." *Journal of the Economic and Social History of the Orient* 13 (1970): 309–14.

Reilly, Benjamin. *Slavery, Agriculture, and Malaria in the Arabian Peninsula*. Ohio University Press, 2015.

Rey, M. I. "Reexamination of the Foreign Female Captive: Deuteronomy 21:10–14 as a Case of Genocidal Rape." *Journal of Feminist Studies in Religion* 32 (2016): 37–53.

Richards, D. S. "Fragments of a Slave Dealer's Day-Book from Fusṭāṭ." In *Documents de l'Islam médiéval: nouvelles perspectives de recherche*, edited by Yūsuf Rāġib, 89–96. Cairo: Institut français d'archéologie orientale, 1991.

Richardson, Kristina. "The Boundaries and Geographies of Medieval Blackness." In *Islam on the Margins: Studies in Memory of Michael Bonner*, edited by Robert Haug and Steven Judd, 220–34. Brill, 2022.

———. *Roma in the Medieval Islamic World: Literacy, Culture, and Migration*. I. B. Tauris, 2022.

———. "Singing Slave Girls (*Qiyan*) of the ʿAbbasid Court in the Ninth and Tenth Centuries." In *Children in Slavery Through the Ages*, edited by Gwyn Campbell, Joseph C. Miller, and Suzanne Miers, 105–18. Ohio University Press, 2009.

Rinehart, Nicholas. "Reparative Semantics: On Slavery and the Language of History." *Commonplace: The Journal of Early American Life*. January 2022. https://commonplace.online/article/reparative-semantics/.

Rio, Alice. *Slavery After Rome, 500–1100*. Oxford University Press, 2017.

———. "Slavery in the Carolingian Empire." In *The Cambridge World History of Slavery: Volume 2, AD 500–AD 1420*, edited by Craig Perry, David Eltis, Stanley Engerman, and David Richardson, 431–52. Cambridge University Press, 2021.

———. *Slaving and the Funding of Elite Status in Early Medieval Europe (ca. 800–1000 AD)*. Joseph C. Miller Memorial Lecture Series. EB-Verlag, 2024.

Rivlin, Yosef. *Inheritance and Wills in Jewish Law* (Hebrew). Bar Ilan University Press, 1999.

Roach, Andrew. "The People Trafficking Princes: Slaves, Silver and State Formation in Poland." *Slavonica* 25 (2020): 132–56.

Roberts, Neil. *Freedom as Marronage*. University of Chicago Press, 2015.

Robinson, Chase. "Slavery in the Conquest Period." *International Journal of Middle East Studies* 49 (2017): 158–63.

Robinson, Majied. "Statistical Approaches to the Rise of Concubinage in Islam." In *Concubines and Courtesans: Women and Slavery in Islamic History*, edited by Matthew S. Gordon and Kathryn A. Hain, 11–26. Oxford University Press, 2017.

Rødland, Henriette, Stephanie Wynne-Jones, Marilee Wood, and Jeffrey Fleisher. "No Such Thing as Invisible People: Toward an Archaeology of Slavery at the Fifteenth-Century Swahili Site of Songo Mnara." *Azania: Archaeological Research in Africa* 55 (2020): 439–57.

Rosenthal, F., C. E. Bosworth, J. Wansbrough, G. S. Colin, H. Busse, and B. Spuler. "Hiba." *EI2*.

Rosman, Moshe. *How Jewish Is Jewish History?* The Littman Library of Jewish Civilization, 2007.

Roth, Pinchas. "Asking Questions: Rabbis and Philosophers in Medieval Provence." *Journal of Jewish Studies* 67 (2016): 1–14.

Rotman, Youval. *Byzantine Slavery and the Mediterranean World*. Harvard University Press, 2009.

———. "Enslavement for Manumission: The Creation of Byzantine 'Private Subjects.'" *Slavery & Abolition* 44 (2023): 638–57.

Rowson, Everett K. "The Traffic in Boys: Slavery and Homoerotic Liaisons in Elite ʿAbbāsid Society." *Middle Eastern Literatures* 11 (2008): 193–204.

Ruffini, Giovanni. "Documentary Evidence and the Production of Power in Medieval Nubia." *Afriques. Débats, méthodes et terrains d'histoire* 7 (2016). https://doi.org/10.4000/afriques.1871.

———. "The History of Medieval Nubia." In *The Oxford Handbook of Ancient Nubia*, edited by Geoff Emberling and Bruce Beyer Williams, 759–71. Oxford University Press, 2021.

Ruffini, Giovanni, ed. *The Bishop, the Eparch and the King: Old Nubian Texts from Qasr Ibrim (P. QI IV)*. Journal of Juristic Papyrology Supplements, XXII. University of Warsaw, 2014.

Ruggles, D. Fairchild. "Mothers of a Hybrid Dynasty: Race, Genealogy, and Acculturation in al-Andalus." *Journal of Medieval and Early Modern Studies* 34 (2004): 65–94.

Russ-Fishbane, Elisha. *Ageing in Medieval Jewish Culture*. Littman Library of Jewish Civilization, 2022.

———. *Judaism, Sufism, and the Pietists of Medieval Egypt: A Study of Abraham Maimonides and His Times*. Oxford University Press, 2015.

Rustow, Marina. "The Diplomatics of Leadership: Administrative Documents in Hebrew Script from the Geniza." In *Jews, Christians and Muslims in Medieval and Early Modern Times: A Festschrift in Honor of Mark R. Cohen*, edited by Arnold Franklin, Roxani Eleni Margariti, Marina Rustow, and Uriel Simonsohn, 306–51. Brill, 2014.

———. "The Fatimid Petition." *Jewish History* 32 (2019): 351–72.

———. "Formal and Informal Patronage Among Jews in the Islamic East: Evidence from the Cairo Geniza." *Al-Qanṭara: Revista de estudios árabes* 29 (2008): 341–82.

———. "The Genizah and Jewish Communal History." In *From a Sacred Source: Genizah Studies in Honor of Professor Stefan C. Reif*, edited by Ben Outhwaite and Siam Bhayro, 289–318. Brill, 2011.

———. *Heresy and the Politics of Community: The Jews of the Fatimid Caliphate*. Cornell University Press, 2008.

———. "Kalah in the Lands of Java: T-S Ar. 30.42." Cambridge University Library, November 1, 2021. https://www.lib.cam.ac.uk/collections/departments/taylor-schechter-genizah-research-unit/fragment-month/fotm-2021/fragment-9.

———. "At the Limits of Communal Autonomy: Jewish Bids for Intervention from the Mamluk State." *Mamlūk Studies Review* 13 (2009): 134–59.

———. *The Lost Archive: Traces of a Caliphate in a Cairo Synagogue*. Princeton University Press, 2020.

———. "A Petition to a Woman at the Fatimid Court (413–414 A. H./1022–23 C. E.)." *Bulletin of the School of Oriental and African Studies* 73 (2010): 1–27.

———. "Sahlān Ben Abraham." In *EJIW*.

———. "Tāhertī Family." In *EJIW*.

———. "Tustarī Family." In *EJIW*.

Saar, Ortal-Paz. "Geniza Magical Documents." *Jewish History* 32 (2019): 477–86.

al-Sakhāwī, Muḥammad ibn ʿAbd al-Raḥmān. *Al-Ḍaw' al-lāmiʿ li-āhl al-qarn al-tāsiʿ (The Shining Light upon the People of the Ninth Century)*. 12 vols. Dār Maktabat al-Ḥayāt, 1966.

Salaymeh, Lena, and Zvi Septimus. "Temporalities of Marriage: Jewish and Islamic Legal Debates." In *Talmudic Transgressions: Engaging the Work of Daniel Boyarin*, edited by Charlotte Elisheva Fonrobert, Ishay Rosen-Zvi, Aharon Shemesh, and Moulie Vidas, 201–39. Brill, 2017.

al-Saleh, Yasmine. "Amulets and Talismans from the Islamic World." Metropolitan Museum of Art. November 1, 2010. https://www.metmuseum.org/essays/amulets-and-talismans-from-the-islamic-world.

Sanders, Paula. "The Fāṭimid State, 969–1171." In *The Cambridge History of Egypt: Islamic Egypt, 640–1517*, edited by M. W. Daly and Carl F. Petry, 1:121–74. Cambridge University Press, 1998.

———. *Ritual, Politics, and the City in Fatimid Cairo*. SUNY Press, 1994.

Sato, Tsugitaka. "Slave Traders and Kārimī Merchants During the Mamluk Period: A Comparative Study." *Mamlūk Studies Review* 10 (2006): 141–55.

Savage, Elizabeth. "Berbers and Blacks: Ibāḍī Slave Traffic in Eighth-Century North Africa." *Journal of African History* 33 (1992): 351–68.

Sayyid, Ayman Fu'ād, ed. *The Fatimids and Their Successors in Yaman: The History of an Islamic Community*. Arabic edition and English summary of Idrīs 'Imād al-Dīn's *'Uyūn al-Akhbār*, vol. 7. I. B. Tauris, 2002.

Schacht, Joseph. "Ibn Buṭlān." *EI2*.

———. "Umm al-Walad." In *EI2*.

———. *An Introduction to Islamic Law*. Clarendon Press, 1964.

Schechter, Solomon. "Saadyana." *Jewish Quarterly Review* 14 (1902): 197–249.

Schiel, Juliane. "Mord von zarter Hand: Der Giftmordvorwurf im Venedig des 15. Jahrhunderts." In *Mediterranean Slavery Revisited (500-1800)/Neue Perspektiven auf Mediterrane Sklaverei (500-1800)*, edited by Stefan Hanß and Juliane Schiel, 201–28. Chronos Verlag, 2014.

Schiel, Juliane, and Stefan Hanß. "Semantics, Practices and Transcultural Perspectives." In *Mediterranean Slavery Revisited (500-1800)/Neue Perspektiven auf Mediterrane Sklaverei (500-1800)*, edited by Stefan Hanß and Juliane Schiel, 11–24. Chronos Verlag, 2014.

Schiel, Juliane, Isabelle Schürch, and Aline Steinbrecher. "On Slaves, Horses, and Dogs: Trialogue on the Benefits of Debates about Agency for Social History" (German). In *Neue Beitrage zur Sozialgeschichte*, 17–48. Chronos Verlag, 2017.

Schimmel, Annemarie. *Islamic Names*. Edinburgh University Press, 1989.

Schine, Rachel. *Black Knights: Arabic Epic and the Making of Medieval Race*. University Of Chicago Press, 2024.

———. "Conceiving the Pre-Modern Black-Arab Hero: On the Gendered Production of Racial Difference in *Sīrat al-amīrah dhāt al-himmah*." *Journal of Arabic Literature* 48 (2017): 1–29.

———. "Race and Blackness in Premodern Arabic Literature." *Oxford Research Encyclopedias, Literature*, 2021. https://doi.org/10.1093/acrefore/9780190201098.013.1298.

———. "Translating Race in the Islamic Studies Classroom." *Al-'Uṣūr al-Wusṭā* 30 (2022): 320–83.

Schneider, Irene. "Freedom and Slavery in Early Islamic Time (1st/7th and 2nd/8th Centuries)." *Al-Qanṭara: Revista de estudios árabes* 28 (2007): 353–82.

———. *Kinderverkauf und Schuldknechtschaft: Untersuchungen zur frühen Phase des islamischen Rechts*. Deutsche Morgenländische Gesellschaft: Kommissionsverlag F. Steiner, 1999.

Schorsch, Jonathan. *Jews and Blacks in the Early Modern World*. Cambridge University Press, 2004.

———. "Revisiting Blackness, Slavery, and Jewishness in the Early Modern Atlantic." In *Religious Changes and Cultural Transformations in the Early Modern Western Sephardic Communities*, edited by Yosef Kaplan, 512–40. Brill, 2019.

Schwab, M. "Les manuscrits du Consistoire Israélite de Paris provenant de la Gueniza du Caire." *Revue des études juives* 62–64 (1912/1911): 62: 107–19, 267–77; 63: 100–20, 276–96; 64: 181–41.

Scott-Patterson, Carolyn I. "Compendium Pilegesh(ium): Bilhah, Legitimacy, and the Pilegesh Question." Master's thesis, Claremont Graduate University, 2015.

Shaham, Ron. "Masters, Their Freed Slaves, and the Waqf in Egypt (Eighteenth–Twentieth Centuries)." *Journal of the Economic and Social History of the Orient* 43 (2000): 162–88.

Shāhīn, Nissim b. Jacob Ibn. *An Elegant Composition Concerning Relief After Adversity.* Translated by William M. Brinner. Yale University Press, 1977.

Shatzmiller, Maya. "Aspects of Women's Participation in the Economic Life of Later Medieval Islam: Occupations and Mentalities." *Arabica* 35 (1988): 36–58.

———. *Labour in the Medieval Islamic World.* Brill, 1994.

———. "Women and Wage Labour in the Medieval Islamic West: Legal Issues in an Economic Context." *Journal of the Economic and Social History of the Orient* 40 (1997): 174–206.

Al-Shayzarī, ʿAbd al-Raḥmān b. Naṣr. *The Book of the Islamic Market Inspector: Nihāyat al-rutba fī ṭalab al-ḥisba (The Utmost Authority in the Pursuit of Ḥisba).* Translated by R. P. Buckley. Journal of Semitic Studies Supplement 9. Oxford University Press, 1999.

Shenoda, Maryann M. "Displacing *Dhimmī*, Maintaining Hope: Unthinkable Coptic Representations of Fatimid Egypt." *International Journal of Middle East Studies* 39 (2007): 587–606.

Shinnie, P. L. "Christian Nubia." In *The Cambridge History of Africa*, edited by J. D. Fage, 556–88. Cambridge University Press, 1979.

———. "The Nilotic Sudan and Ethiopia, c. 660 BC to c. AD 600." In *The Cambridge History of Africa*, 2:210–71. Cambridge University Press, 1979.

Shtober, S. "Queries Attributed to Rabbi Abraham Maimonides: New Material from the Geniza" (Hebrew). *Shenaton ha-mishpat ha-ʿIvri* 14–15 (1987–88): 245–81.

Shweka, Roni. "Bustanay (Ḥaninay) Ben Kafnay." *EJIW.*

Sijpesteijn, Petra M. "Baqṭ." *EI3.*

Silverstein, Adam J. "From Markets to Marvels: Jews on the Maritime Route to China ca. 850–ca. 950 CE." *Journal of Jewish Studies* 58 (2007): 91–104.

Simmons, Adam. "A Note Towards Quantifying the Medieval Nubian Diaspora." *Dotawo: A Journal of Nubian Studies* 6 (2019): 23–39.

———. *Nubia, Ethiopia, and the Crusading World, 1095–1402.* Routledge, 2022.

Simonsohn, Shlomo, ed. *The Jews in Sicily: Volume 1 (383–1300).* Brill, 1997.

Sircar, D. C., ed. *Indian Epigraphical Glossary.* Motilal Banarsidass, 1966.

Skinner, Patricia. "Confronting the 'Medieval' in Medieval History: The Jewish Example." *Past & Present* 181 (2003): 219–47.

Skoda, Hannah. "Slave Voices and Experiences in the Later Medieval Europe." *History Compass* 21 (2023): e12784.

Smith, G. R., ed. "Ṣulayḥids." In *EI2.*

———. *A Traveller in Thirteenth-Century Arabia: Ibn al-Mujāwir's* Tārīkh al-mustabṣir. The Hakluyt Society, 2008.

Smith, Romney David. "The Business of Human Trafficking: Slaves and Money Between Western Italy and the House of Islam Before the Crusades (c.900–c.1100)." *Journal of Medieval History* 45 (2019): 523–52.

Sokoloff, Michael. *A Dictionary of Jewish Babylonian Aramaic of the Talmudic and Geonic Periods.* Bar Ilan University Press, 2002.

Soloveitchik, Haym. *The Use of Responsa as a Historical Source* (Hebrew). Zalman Shazar Center for Jewish History, 1990.

Spaulding, Jay. "Medieval Christian Nubia and the Islamic World: A Reconsideration of the Baqt Treaty." *International Journal of African Historical Studies* 28 (1995): 577–94.

Stein, Dina. "A Maidservant and Her Master's Voice: Discourse, Identity, and Eros in Rabbinic Texts." *Journal of the History of Sexuality* 10 (2001): 375–97.

Steiner, Vilmos. *Három arab kézirat az ó-kairói genizából* (Three Arabic Manuscripts from the Cairo Geniza). Budapest: Márkus Samu, 1909.

Stillman, Norman. "East-West Relations in the Islamic Mediterranean in the Early Eleventh Century: A Study in the Geniza Correspondence of the House of Ibn 'Awkal." PhD diss., University of Pennsylvania, 1970.

———. "The Eleventh-Century Merchant House of Ibn 'Awkal (A Geniza Study)." *Journal of the Economic and Social History of the Orient* 16 (1973): 15–88.

Stillman, Yedida K. "The Importance of the Cairo Geniza Manuscripts for the History of Medieval Female Attire." *International Journal of Middle East Studies* 7 (1976): 579–89.

Stone, Ken. "Marriage and Sexual Relations in the World of the Hebrew Bible." In *The Oxford Handbook of Theology, Sexuality, and Gender*, edited by Adrian Thatcher, 173–88. Oxford University Press, 2014.

Strauch, Ingo. *Die Lekhapaddhati-Lekhapañcāśikā: Briefe und Urkunden im mittelalterlichen Gujarat.* Dietrich Reimer Verlag, 2002.

Stroumsa, Sarah. *Maimonides in His World: Portrait of a Mediterranean Thinker*. Princeton University Press, 2009.

Stuard, Susan Mosher. "Ancillary Evidence for the Decline of Medieval Slavery." *Past & Present* (1995): 3–28.

Subrahmanyam, Sanjay. "Connected Histories: Notes Towards a Reconfiguration of Early Modern Eurasia." *Modern Asian Studies* 31 (1997): 735–62.

Sutherland, Samuel S. "The Study of Slavery in the Early and Central Middle Ages: Old Problems and New Approaches." *History Compass* 18 (2020): e12633.

Swain, Simon. *Economy, Family, and Society from Rome to Islam: A Critical Edition, English Translation, and Study of Bryson's Management of the Estate.* Cambridge University Press, 2013.

Talbi, Mohamed. "Law and Economy in Ifrīqiya (Tunisia) in the Third Islamic Century: Agriculture and the Role of Slaves in the Country's Economy." In *The Islamic Middle East, 700–1900 : Studies in Economic and Social History*, edited by A. L. Udovitch, 209–49. The Darwin Press, 1981.

Talhami, Ghada Hashem. "The Zanj Rebellion Reconsidered." *International Journal of African Historical Studies* 10 (1977): 443–61.

Targarona, Judit. "Ibn Naghrella, Samuel (Abū Ibrāhim Ismāʿīl) Ben Joseph Ha-Nagid." In *EJIW*.

Teaching Medieval Slavery and Captivity. "Source: The Slave Woman of al-Manṣūr Ḥājjī." Accessed July 25, 2021. https://medievalslavery.org/middle-east-and-north-africa/source-the-slave-women-of-al-man%e1%b9%a3ur-hajji/.

Teller, Adam. *Rescue the Surviving Souls: The Great Jewish Refugee Crisis of the Seventeenth Century.* Princeton University Press, 2020.

Tibbetts, G. R. *Arab Navigation in the Indian Ocean Before the Coming of the Portuguese: Being a Translation of Kitāb al-Fawāʾid fī uṣūl al-baḥr waʾl-qawāʿid of Aḥmad b. Mājid al-Najdī.* Royal Asiatic Society, 1971.

Tillier, Mathieu. "The Mazalim in Historiography." In *The Oxford Handbook of Islamic Law*, edited by Anver M. Emon and Rumee Ahmed, 357–80. Oxford University Press, 2018.

Toch, Michael. "Was There a Jewish Slave Trade (or Commercial Monopoly) in the Early Middle Ages?" In *Mediterranean Slavery Revisited (500-1800)/Neue Perspektiven auf Mediterrane Sklaverei (500-1800)*, edited by Stefan Hanß and Juliane Schiel, 421–44. Chronos Verlag, 2014.

Toledano, Ehud R. "Ottoman Elite Enslavement and 'Social Death.'" In *On Human Bondage*, edited by John Bodel and Walter Scheidel, 136–50. Wiley-Blackwell, 2016.

Toledano, Jacob Moses. "Manuscript Sources" (Hebrew). *Hebrew Union College Annual* 4 (1927): 449–66.

Tolino, Serena. "Eunuchs in the Fatimid Empire: Ambiguities, Gender and Sacredness." In *Celibate and Childless Men in Power: Ruling Eunuchs and Bishops in the Pre-Modern World*, edited by Serena Tolino, Almut Höfert, and Matthew M. Mesley, 246–67. Routledge, 2017.

Tolmacheva, Marina. "Concubines on the Road: Ibn Battuta's Slave Women." In *Concubines and Courtesans: Women and Slavery in Islamic History*, edited by Matthew S. Gordon and Kathryn A. Hain, 163–89. Oxford University Press, 2017.

———. "Toward a Definition of the Term Zanj." *Azania: Archaeological Research in Africa* 21 (1986): 105–13.

Tor, D. G. "*Mamlūk* Loyalty: Evidence from the Late Seljuq Period." *Asiatische Studien/Études Asiatiques* 65 (2011): 767–96.

———. "The Mamluks in the Military of the Pre-Seljuq Persianate Dynasties." *Iran* 46 (2008): 213–25.

Tougher, Shaun. *The Eunuch in Byzantine History and Society*. Routledge, 2009.

———. "In or Out? Origins of Court Eunuchs." In *Eunuchs in Antiquity and Beyond*, edited by Shaun Tougher, 143–59. The Classical Press of Wales, 2002.

Trabelsi, Salah. "Eunuchs, Power, and Slavery in the Early Islamic World." In *Sex, Power and Slavery*, edited by Gwyn Campbell and Elizabeth Elbourne, 541–57. Ohio University Press, 2014.

Traboulsi, Samer. "The Queen Was Actually a Man: Arwā Bint Aḥmad and the Politics of Religion." *Arabica* 50 (2003): 96–108.

Treptow, Tanya and Tasha Vorderstrasse, eds. *A Cosmopolitan City: Muslims, Christians, and Jews in Old Cairo*. Oriental Institute Museum Publications 38. The Oriental Institute of the University of Chicago, 2015.

Trouillot, Michel-Rolph. *Silencing the Past: Power and the Production of History*. Beacon Press, 1995.

Twersky, Isadore. *Introduction to the Code of Maimonides (Mishneh Torah)*. Yale University Press, 1980.

———. "Some Non-Halakic Aspects of the Mishneh Torah." In *Jewish Medieval and Renaissance Studies*, edited by Alexander Altmann, 95–118. Harvard University Press, 1967.

Udovitch, A. L. *Partnership and Profit in Medieval Islam*. Princeton University Press, 1970.

Ulrich, Brian. "Portrayals of the Slave Trade in the Book of the Wonders of India." Annual Meeting of the Middle Eastern Studies Association. Montreal, 2023.

Urbach, E. E. *The Laws Regarding Slavery: As a Source for Social History of the Period of the Second Temple, Mishnah and Talmud*. Arno Press, 1979.

Urban, Elizabeth. *Conquered Populations in Early Islam: Non-Arabs, Slaves, and the Sons of Slave Mothers*. Edinburgh University Press, 2020.

———. "Race, Gender and Slavery in Early Islamicate History." *History Compass* 20 (2022): e12727.

Vanthieghem, Naïm. "Quelques contrats de vente d'esclaves de la collection Aziz Atiyya." *Journal of Juristic Papyrology* 44 (2014): 163–87.

Vantini, Giovanni. *Oriental Sources Concerning Nubia*. Heidelberger Akademie der Wissenschaften, 1975.

Vlassopoulos, Kostas. "Does Slavery Have a History? The Consequences of a Global Approach." *Journal of Global Slavery* 1 (2016): 5–27.

Wacholder, B. Z. "The Halakhah and the Proselyting of Slaves During the Gaonic Era." *Historia Judaica* 18 (1956): 89–106.

Wagner, Esther-Miriam. "Genizah Sociolinguistics: The Language of Women." In *Language, Gender and Law in the Judaeo-Islamic Milieu*, edited by Zvi Stampfer and Amir Ashur, 1–13. Brill, 2020.

———. *Linguistic Variety of Judaeo-Arabic in Letters from the Cairo Genizah*. Brill, 2010.

Wagner, Esther-Miriam, and Magdalen Connolly. "Code-Switching in Judaeo-Arabic Documents from the Cairo Geniza." *Multilingua* 37 (2018): 1–23.

Wagner, Veruschka. "Slave Voices in Ottoman Court Records—A Narrative Analysis of the Istanbul Registers from the Sixteenth and Seventeenth Centuries." In *Narratives of Dependency: Textual Representations of Slavery, Captivity, and Other Forms of Strong Asymmetrical Dependencies*, edited by Elke Brüggen and Marion Gymnich, 141–60. De Gruyter, 2024.

Wakin, Jeanette, ed. *The Function of Documents in Islamic Law: The Chapters on Sales from Ṭaḥāwī's* Kitāb al-shurūṭ al-kabīr. SUNY Press, 1972.

Walker, Paul E. *Caliph of Cairo: al-Hakim bi-Amr Allah, 996–1021*. American University in Cairo Press, 2009.

———. *Exploring an Islamic Empire: Fatimid History and Its Sources*. I. B. Tauris, 2002.

———. "The Ismaili Daʿwa in the Reign of the Fatimid Caliph al-Ḥākim." *Journal of the American Research Center in Egypt* 30 (1993): 161–82.

Ward, Eric K. "Skin in the Game: How Antisemitism Animates White Nationalism." *Public Eye Quarterly*, June 29, 2017.

Wasserstein, David J. "Samuel Ibn Naghrīla ha-Nagid and Islamic Historiography in al-Andalus." *Al-Qanṭara: Revista de etudios árabes* 14 (1993): 109–25.

Weiss, Gershon. "Formularies (Sheṭārot) Reconstructed from the Geniza." *Gratz College Annual of Jewish Studies* 2 (1973): 29–42.

———. "Formularies (*Sheṭārot*) Reconstructed from the Geniza (Part II)." *Gratz College Annual of Jewish Studies* 3 (1974): 63–76.

———. "Legal Documents Written by the Court Clerk Halfon b. Manasse (Dated 1100–1138): A Study in the Diplomatics of the Cairo Geniza." PhD diss., University of Pennsylvania, 1970.

Weitz, Lev. *Between Christ and Caliph: Law, Marriage, and Christian Community in Early Islam*. University of Pennsylvania Press, 2018.

———. "Slavery and the Historiography of Non-Muslims in the Medieval Middle East." *International Journal of Middle East Studies* 49 (2017): 139–42.

Weschenfelder, Petra. "The Integration of the Eastern Desert into the Islamic World: Beja Groups in Medieval Islamic Geography and Archaeological Records." In *Navigated Spaces, Connected Places: Proceedings of Red Sea Project V Held at the University of Exeter, 16-19 September 2010*, edited by Dionysus A. Agius, John P. Cooper, Athena Trakadas, and Chiara Zazzaro, 221–28. Archaeopress, 2012.

Whitaker, Cord J. *Black Metaphors: How Modern Racism Emerged from Medieval Race-Thinking*. University of Pennsylvania Press, 2019.

Wickham, Chris. *The Donkey and the Boat: Reinterpreting the Mediterranean Economy, 950–1180*. Oxford University Press, 2023.

———. "The Power of Property: Land Tenure in Fāṭimid Egypt." *Journal of the Economic and Social History of the Orient* 62 (2019): 67–107.

Winer, Rebecca Lynn. "Conscripting the Breast: Lactation, Slavery and Salvation in the Realms of Aragon and Kingdom of Majorca, c. 1250–1300." *Journal of Medieval History* 34 (2008): 164–84.

———. "The Enslaved Wet Nurse as Nanny: The Transition from Free to Slave Labor in Childcare in Barcelona After the Black Death (1348)." *Slavery & Abolition* 38 (2017): 303–19.

———. *Women, Wealth, and Community in Perpignan, c. 1250–1300*. Ashgate, 2006.

Wolf, Lior, Rotem Littman, Naama Mayer, Tanya German, Nachum Dershowitz, Roni Shweka, and Yaacov Choueka. "Identifying Join Candidates in the Cairo Genizah." *International Journal of Computer Vision* 94 (2011): 118–35.

Wood, Kirsten E. "Gender and Slavery." In *The Oxford Handbook of Slavery in the Americas*, edited by Mark M. Smith and Robert L. Paquette, 513–34. Oxford University Press, 2010.

Wyatt, David. "Slavery in Northern Europe (Scandinavia and Iceland) and the British Isles, 500–1420." In *The Cambridge World History of Slavery: Volume 2, AD 500–AD 1420*, edited by Craig Perry, David Eltis, Stanley Engerman, and David Richardson, 482–507. Cambridge University Press, 2021.

Yagur, Moshe. "Captives, Converts, and Concubines: Gendered Aspects of Conversion to Judaism in the Medieval Near East." In *Language, Gender and Law in the Judaeo-Islamic-Milieu*, edited by Zvi Stampfer and Amir Ashur, 88–109. Brill, 2020.

———. "The Cautious Beginnings of Sephardi Self-Identification: A View from the Cairo Geniza (Tenth-Thirteenth Centuries)." *Journal of Medieval Iberian Studies* 15 (2023): 1–23.

———. "The Community's Borders; Converts and Renegades." In *The Jews in Medieval Egypt*, edited by Miriam Frenkel, 47–71. Academic Studies Press, 2021.

———. *Crossing the Line: Jewish Identity in Medieval Egypt* (Hebrew). Shazar Center for Jewish History, 2025.

———. "The Donor and the Gravedigger: Converts to Judaism in the Cairo Geniza Documents." In *Contesting Inter-Religious Conversion in the Medieval World*, edited by Yaniv Fox and Yosi Yisraeli, 115–34. Routledge, 2019.

———. "Living in the City: Jews and Their Residences in Medieval Fusṭāṭ." *Medieval History Journal* 27 (2024): 411–40.

———. "Religious Identity and Communal Boundaries in Geniza Society (10th–13th Centuries): Proselytes, Slaves, Apostates" (Hebrew). PhD diss., Hebrew University, 2017.

———. "Religiously Mixed Families in the Mediterranean Society of the Cairo Geniza." *Mediterranean Historical Review* 35 (2020): 27–42.

———. "Saʿāda the Enslaved Woman: Immersion and Oblivion, T-S 12.872." Taylor-Schechter Genizah Research Unit. Fragment of the Month, 2019. https://www.repository.cam.ac.uk/handle/1810/302189.

———. "Shaving Hair and Paring Nails: The Origins and Transmutations of a Unique Rite of Passage in Medieval Judaism." (Hebrew.) *Tarbiṣ* 88 (2021): 109–32.

Yarbrough, Luke B. *Friends of the Emir: Non-Muslim State Officials in Premodern Islamic Thought.* Cambridge University Press, 2019.

Yerushalmi, Yosef Hayim. "Servants of Kings and Not Servants of Servants: Some Aspects of the Political History of the Jews." In *The Faith of Fallen Jews: Yosef Hayim Yerushalmi and the Writing of Jewish History*, edited by David N. Myers and Alexander Kaye, 245–76. Brandeis University Press, 2014.

Zeitlin, Solomon. "Slavery During the Second Commonwealth and the Tannaitic Period." *Jewish Quarterly Review* 53 (1963): 185–218.

Zhang, Zekun. "State and Slavery in the Tang Empire." PhD diss., Yale University, 2024.

Zilfi, Madeline. *Women and Slavery in the Late Ottoman Empire: The Design of Difference.* Cambridge University Press, 2010.

Zinger, Oded. "Finding a Fragment in a Pile of Geniza: A Practical Guide to Collections, Editions, and Resources." *Jewish History* 32 (2019): 279–309.

———. "Introduction to the Legal Arena." In *The Jews in Medieval Egypt*, edited by Miriam Frenkel, 86–123. Academic Studies Press, 2021.

———. "Jewish Women in Muslim Legal Venues: Seven Legal Documents from the Cairo Genizah." In *Language, Gender and Law in the Judaeo-Islamic Milieu*, edited by Zvi Stampfer and Amir Ashur, 38–87. Brill, 2020.

———. *Living with the Law: Gender and Community Among the Jews of Medieval Egypt.* University of Pennsylvania Press, 2023.

———. "'She Aims to Harass Him': Jewish Women in Muslim Legal Venues in Medieval Egypt." *Association of Jewish Studies Review* 42 (2018): 159–92.

———. "Social Embeddedness in the Legal Arena According to Geniza Letters." In *From Qom to Barcelona: Aramaic, South Arabian, Coptic, Arabic and Judeo-Arabic Documents*, edited by Andreas Kaplony and Daniel Potthast, 152–82. Brill, 2021.

———. "The Use of Social Isolation (*Inqiṭāʿ*) by Jewish Women in Medieval Egypt." *Journal of the Economic and Social History of the Orient* 63 (2020): 820–52.

———. "Women, Gender and Law: Marital Disputes According to Documents from the Cairo Geniza." PhD diss., Princeton University, 2014.

Zouache, Abbès. "Remarks on the Blacks in the Fatimid Army, Tenth–Twelfth Century CE." *Northeast African Studies* 19 (2019): 23–60.

INDEX OF MANUSCRIPTS AND JEWISH TEXTS CITED

Geniza Documents

Geniza documents are organized by city, collection, and shelf mark. References for published *geniza* documents are given in the notes. For most shelf marks, further information and bibliography can be found in PGP, FGP, and, increasingly, through the International Collection of Digitized Hebrew Manuscripts (Ktiv) of the National Library of Israel (https://www.nli.org.il/en/discover/manuscripts/hebrew-manuscripts).

Budapest: Hungarian Academy of Sciences

DAVID KAUFMAN COLLECTION

DK 228.3, 193, 203
DK 230.4, 193
DK 231.2, 193, 244n117, 254nn20–21, 256n46
DK 232.1, 195, 203, 216, 253nn1–2, 4, 255nn 33–34, 256n53
DK 238.3, 194
DK 246.1, 196, 275n53
DK 370, 231–32n62

Cambridge: Cambridge University Library

JACQUES MOSSERI COLLECTION

Mosseri VII 58.1, 188, 193, 204, 210, 244n118, 278n15
Mosseri VII 69.2, 188, 279n34
Mosseri VII 129.2, 242n96
Mosseri VII 160.1, 199

LEWIS-GIBSON COLLECTION

L-G Arabic II.129, 192, 194, 209, 216, 271nn117, 119–21

ORIENTAL COLLECTION

Or. 1080 J25, 192, 194, 216, 271nn117, 119–20
Or. 1080 J30, 234n104, 240–41n74, 269n88
Or. 1080 J71, 193, 209, 216, 270nn99–101
Or. 1080 J142 + T-S Misc. 25.53, 204, 213, 242n96, 273n28
Or. 1080 J258, 191
Or. 1080 J273, 189, 209, 211, 238n29
Or. 1080 J281, 194
Or. 1081 J1, 267n52, 277n30
Or. 1081 J24, 194, 200

TAYLOR-SCHECHTER GENIZAH COLLECTION

T-S 8.12, 189, 196, 201, 275nn53, 55
T-S 8.18, 201
T-S 12.8 + T-S 10J4.9, 197, 206, 207
T-S 12.93, *146*, 190, 211, 212, 267nn59, 61
T-S 12.140, 189, 207, 217, 263n7
T-S 12.175, 189, 196, 212, 275nn51, 52
T-S 12.254, 202, 232nn63, 65, 247n3
T-S 12.285, 202, 241n84
T-S 12.293, 268n73
T-S 12.327, 240n72, 241nn78–79

Published Arabic and Old Nubian Documents Cited

References for published editions and translations of these shelf marks are provided in the notes. Further information about Arabic documents may be found in the Checklist of Arabic Documents (https://www.naher-osten.uni-muenchen.de/isap/isap_checklist/index.html) and the Arabic Papyrological Database (https://www.apd.gwi.uni-muenchen.de/apd/show_new.jsp). Information about Old Nubian documents may be found at the MedNub site (https://www.medievalnubia.info/dev/index.php/Main_Page).

Index of Jewish Texts Cited

GENERAL INDEX

Names in the appendixes are indexed only if they appear in the main text or notes.

234n106; gang labor, 4–5; pre-Fatimid military slavery, 43; relations with Nubia, 54–55; state-sponsored slave trade, 42–46; use of enslaved people, 13. *See also* slave trade to Egypt
El'azar (husband of Ḥasana bt. Menasse ha-Kohen), 130, 131
El'azar ha-Levi, 264n10
El'azar b. Yefet, 208, 211, 265n25
'Eli ha-Kohen, 116, 125, 260n37
'Eli b. Nathanel, 233n82
'Eli b. Yefet b. al-Wāsitī, 109–10, 165, 201, 255n38, 265n24
enslaved people: condolences for deaths of, 258n2; criminals, 237n19; documentation by gender and type, *68*; as dowries, inheritances, and gifts, 74–76, 119, 128, 137–38, 140, 241n85, 263n3, 265n23; female genital mutilation of, 56; lies about origins of, 77, 243n106; literacy of, 96, 251n64; marriage between, 25, 224n9; *muwallads*, 62, *68*, 77, 139–40, 236n8, 244n112; names for, 49, 162, 272n3; numbers of, 183, 277n26; and power, 19; protections and rights of, 24–25; religious identity recorded, 50; resistance to sales transactions, 72, 240n69; with same name in documents, 138, 264n11; terms for, 260n24. *See also* child slavery; "defects" (Ar. *'ayb*, pl. *'uyūb*); enslaved people, lives of; manumission; *individual names*
enslaved people, lives of: enslaved people as "theorists of power," 150–54; Na'īm (enslaved Nubian woman), 145–50, *146*, *148–49*; networks, knowledge, and attachments, 154–56, 270n99, 270nn101–102; overview, 137–39, 158–59, 180–81, 271n123; urban *marronage*, 156–58. *See also* child slavery; "defects" (Ar. *'ayb*, pl. *'uyūb*); enslaved people; manumission; *individual names*
enslavement: and famine, 56–58, 142–43, 235n125, 235nn127–128; gendered patterns of, 89–90, 249n26; methods of, 51–56, 79, 234n96
ethnicity (*jins*, pl. *ajnās*). See *jins* (pl. *ajnās*) (type)
eunuchs, 5, 24, 36, 248–49n23
European women as slaves, 244n117
Evyatar ha-Kohen (gaon), 96, 205
exchange rates, 72, 240n70
excommunication (*ḥerem*), 107, 112–13, 227n57
Ezra (merchant associate of Nahray b. Nissim), 48

Fakhr (daughter of Abū al-Murajjā b. Nathan), 166
famine and enslavement, 56–58, 142–43, 235n125, 235nn127–128
Faraḥ b. Samuel al-Qābisī, 74, 208, 213
Faraj (freedman of Barhūn al-Tāhirtī), 168–69, 196, 201, 212, 275nn52–53, 275nn55–56
al-Fāsī, Isaac b. Jacob ("the Rif"), 29, 226n38
Fatimid caliphate, 36–38, 41, 43. *See also* slave trade to Egypt; *individual caliphs*
Fayrūz (enslaved boy), 65, 203, 204
al-Fayyūm, *xxiii*, 108, 277n26
female genital mutilation, 56
feminine honor, 121–22
femininity. *See* slavery and femininity
flax trade, 108, 255n28
Frankish (*Ifranjiyya*), *68*, 77
Franz, Kurt, 23–24, 247n1
Freamon, Bernard, 4, 224n2
free women: male relatives as protectors, 113, 256nn52–53; professional titles, 250n39; and religious commandments, 26, 225n20; rights and prerogatives defended, 128–32; sex outside of marriage, 98–99; sexuality, 252n74; as slave owners, 18, 89, 249n24; transactions in local slave markets, 119, 258n7. *See also* dowries; slavery and femininity

freed people and the Jewish community: becoming a freed person, 163–64, 272n6, 272n8; integration in community, 170–71; marriage, divorce, and risk of poverty, 165–67; naming, genealogy, and clientage, 167–70, 272n3; overview, 19, 160–63, *161*, 171–72, 181–82, 272n3. *See also* manumission
Frenkel, Miriam, 10, 104–5, 254n15, 260n28
Friedberg Genizah Project (FGP), 7
Friedman, Mordechai, 10, 99, 105, 106, 109, 128–29, 129–30
Fūq (enslaved woman), 140, 242n92
Furs bt. Zayn b. Abū al-Riḍā, 213, 263n4

gang labor, 4–5
gender: and enslavement, 89–90, 249n26; kinship and patronage culture, 124–28, 260nn28–29, 260n31; protections of enslaved people, 24–25. *See also* slavery and femininity; slavery and masculinity
geniza documents: slave markets mentioned in, 46–47, 231–32n62; as source, 137–38
geonim (sg. gaon) (heads of rabbinic academies), 28–30
geopolitical relations and slave trade, 16–17. *See also* diplomatic gifts (*hadiyya*s); diplomatic slave trade; political economy and slave trade
Gharaḍ (enslaved woman; freed), 116, 196, 206
Ghazāl 1 (enslaved woman), 129, 189, 207, 215, 262n65
Ghazāl 3 (enslaved woman), 96, 189, 278n6
ghilmān (sg. *ghulām*), as a term, 25, 248–49n23
Ghosh, Amitav, 10
Gil, Moshe, 226n40, 261n48, 261n54
Goa, 13
Goitein, S. D., 9–10, 66, 70, 105, 270n101
Goldberg, Jessica, 8, 10, 73
Goldenberg, David, 80, 246n137, 246n138
Gotzmann, Andreas, 256n40
Greek: meanings of, 234n98; *Rūmī* as translation for, 238–39n38
Gujarat, 141–42

Ḥadāriba (Beja sub-group), 55, 56. *See also* Beja
*hadiyya*s (diplomatic gifts). *See* diplomatic gifts (*hadiyya*s)
Hai (Hayya) b. Sherira (gaon), 33, 238n37, 243n111
hairdressers (*māshiṭa*s), 122, 259n22
al-Ḥākim, caliph: diplomatic gifts to, 36; and Ibn Mukārim's father, 230n25; sale of slaves to *dhimmī*, 12, 231–32n62; subordination of *dhimmī*, 34; use of African troops, 44
Ḥalfon ha-Levi b. Nethaniel, 49, 201
Ḥalfon b. Menasse, 70–71, *72*, 78, 137, 244n117, 244n119, 260n23, 268n65
Ḥalfon b. Shemarya ha-Levi. *See* Abū Saʿīd b. Maḥfuẓ (Ibn Jamāhir)
Ḥam (son of Noah), curse of, 80, 246nn137–138
Ḥanūn b. ʿAllūn, 95, 205, 244n117, 251n59
ḥaqq al-sulṭān (government tax), 70, 71, 240n59
ḥaqq al-sūq (market tax), 70, 71, 240n59
Harper, Kyle, 247n1
Harrison, Matthew, 91
Ḥasan of *dār al-raqīq*, 231–32n62
Ḥasan the perfumer, 250n43
Ḥasana bt. Menasse ha-Kohen, 130–32, 200, 213, 262n74, 269n95
ḥaẓiyya (favorite concubine), as a term, 153, 269n89
Hebrew slave (*ʿeved ʿivri*), 27, 225n25, 225n27
*hiba*s (gifts), as a term, 230n35. *See also* diplomatic gifts (*hadiyya*s)
Ḥidhq 1 (enslaved Nubian woman), 140, 189, 209, 211, 238n31, 265n24
Ḥidhq 1's daughter, 140, 189, 209, 211, 238n31
Ḥidhq 2 (enslaved Nubian woman), 63–65, *64*, 67, 68–69, 206, 207, 215